D0930410

WRITING PORTFOLIOS IN THE CLASSROOM

Policy and Practice, Promise and Peril

WRITING PORTFOLIOS IN THE CLASSROOM

Policy and Practice, Promise and Peril

Edited by

Robert C. Calfee
Stanford University

Pamela Perfumo
University of California, Berkeley

LAWRENCE ERLBAUM ASSOCIATES, PUBLISHERS
1996   Mahwah, New Jersey

Lawrence Erlbaum Associates, Inc., Publishers
10 Industrial Avenue
Mahwah, New Jersey 07430

Cover design by Gail Silverman

Library of Congress Cataloging-in-Publication Data

Writing portfolios in the classroom : policy and practice, promise and
  peril / edited by Robert C. Calfee, Pamela Perfumo.
      p.   cm.
  Includes bibliographical references and indexes.
  ISBN 0-8058-1835-9 (cloth : alk. paper). — ISBN 0-8058-1836-7
(pbk. : alk. paper)
    1. Portfolios in education—United States. 2. English language—
Composition and exercises—Study and teaching (Elementary)—United
States. 3. Grading and marking (Students)—United States.
I. Calfee, Robert C. II. Perfumo, Pamela.
LB1029.P67N75 1996
371.2'72—dc20   96-22692
                                                              CIP

Printed in the United States of America
10 9 8 7 6 5 4 3 2 1

Contents

Preface

This volume presents chapters by researchers, practitioners, and policy makers who study the impact of classroom portfolios in the assessment of writing achievement by elementary and middle-grade students. The impetus for the volume is a project supported by a contract from the Office of Educational Research and Improvement (OERI) to the Center for the Study of Writing and Literacy at the University of California, Berkeley. Under the auspices of this project, we conducted a national survey of exemplary projects, arranged for a series of "video visits," and held several working conferences. This volume reports the results of the project activities, along with a wide array of contributions by other authors to a Portfolio Conference held at Stanford University in April 1994. The conference was cosponsored by several other OERI centers and labs: UCLA/CRESST, FWREL, NRRC, CSL.

The two chapters in Part I, the "Authentic Assessment of Classroom Writing," serve to set the stage for the remainder of the volume. In chapter 1, Calfee and Freedman present a historical perspective, and then develop the conceptual framework that serves as a background for many of the other activities described in later sections. This chapter concludes by highlighting several tensions ("messy matters") that afflict a broad range of innovative assessment methods, including writing portfolios.

In chapter 2, Herman and her CRESST colleagues (Maryl Gearhart and Pamela Aschbacher) follow with a discussion of the numerous practical issues that confront today's researchers and practitioners. This chapter reflects the experience and skill that UCLA's CRESST team has acquired over the past decade in moving from promising ideas to the pragmatics of design and implementation. It complements the earlier chapter by showing how several of the tensions can be addressed through more careful consideration of design and implementation issues. The chapter offers concrete suggestions for connecting classical issues like reliability and validity with innovative topics like reflectivity and learning opportunities.

The six chapters in Part II, "Guideposts From Research," view the phenomenon of writing portfolios through a variety of broadview lenses, each of which highlights one or more tensions in the field. Calfee and Perfumo (chap. 3) report the empirical findings from a national survey of nominated writing portfolio programs. Quantitative and qualitative analyses turned up three themes of importance to the portfolio "movement": teacher enthusiasm, weak technical foundations, and a distaste for grading and evaluation. The authors propose the *Teacher Logbook* as a link between the student portfolio and other audiences.

In chapter 4, Yancey focuses on a unique feature of contemporary views of portfolio assessment—the opportunity for student reflection. Neither multiple-choice tests nor on-demand writing samples offer any opportunities for students to think (and write) about their achievements; portfolio "reflections" are often little more than a brief "letter to the reader." Yancey explores the possibilities for portfolio reflections to transcend these limits.

The tension between internal and external forces in assessment of student achievement is the theme of chapter 5 by Murphy and Camp. On the one hand, portfolios provide the opportunity for documenting classroom performance that is richly contextualized, that offers a picture of the best that a student can do. On the other hand, advocates of hard-headed (or tough-minded) accountability want to be sure that the data reflect the achievements of individual students working on their own under standardized conditions. This chapter offers a rich array of concrete examples of how this tension plays out in practice across a variety of settings.

Myers, in chapter 6, hearkens back to a notion first introduced by Bird—the portfolio as metaphor. Myers focuses on the implications of portfolio assessment for the "national standards" movement, drawing on Bruno Latour's account of the influence of sailing ships as "portfolios" during the golden age of geographic explorations between 1300 and 1800. In a tour de force, Myers links this episode with the distinction between formative and summative evaluation.

The case studies reported by Jordan and Purves (chap. 7) continue the theme of the portfolio as metaphor. This chapter explores teachers' metaphors in understanding how they think about portfolio assessment. The authors note the substantial dissimilarities in the operational definitions—the metaphors—among the teachers, leading them to wonder about the feasibility of portfolios for large-scale assessment. If portfolios look so different from one teacher to the next, how can they be used for any common accountability? They suggest computer hypertext as a metaphor for addressing this issue.

Finally, Wile and Tierney (chap. 8) raise some fundamental concerns about locus of control in the case of portfolios. Given that portfolios are rich and personal collections of student writing, is it proper for these collections to be subjected to public scrutiny—to assessment. They emphasize the constructivist possibilities of portfolios, and the opportunities for negotiation between students and other interested parties.

The title for Part III, "The View From the Field," is a misnomer in some respects. The previous chapters address numerous practical issues, and the chapters in this section convey important conceptual issues. Nonetheless, the balance in these chapters is toward pragmatics. In chapter 9, Perfumo describes the video-visit technique developed as part of the Center for the Study of Writing (CSW) project to enrich the survey results reported in chapter 3. Although created in response to a research problem, the video visit has important implications for professional development in portfolio assessment and elsewhere—if the time can be found for such activities.

Klimenkov and LaPick (chap. 10), two teachers from an elementary school in the San Francisco Bay area, present a compelling account of the impact of classroom portfolios on the relations among students, teachers, and parents when students have responsibility for gauging their progress. This chapter takes the reader directly into the classroom.

An Arizona public school serving Navajo children provides the context for chapter 11 by Koelsch and Trumbull. The Chinle Schools employ portfolios to bridge the Navajo culture and the culture of schooling. Native Americans have traditionally been poorly served by conventional educational practices, and this chapter suggests ways in which portfolios may dis-alienate students from the strangeness of schooling.

The California Learning Record, modeled after the Primary Learning Record in Great Britain, has become a powerful force for teacher-based assessment in California. Barr and Hallam (chap. 12) describe the development of this system and its linkage with large-scale assessment needs. Of particular importance in their account is a description of the role of moderation in assuring consistency in teacher judgments.

In chapter 13, Biggam and Teitelbaum take the reader across the country to Vermont, where a ground-breaking statewide portfolio assessment program has been built on the efforts of individual classroom teachers. In addition to providing an account of the Vermont program, these authors present a developmental rubric that spans the transition from preliteracy to early fluency. Most rubric systems are based on accomplishment rather than development, and this chapter offers a view of assessment that may be more appropriate for the early years of schooling.

In her report on restructuring student assessment in the Bay Village, Ohio, schools, McCabe (chap. 14) describes the challenges to district administrators in supporting a major paradigm shift in how the entire community viewed the task of measuring achievement. The shift meant changes in curriculum, instruction, and in people. McCabe recounts the achievements and frustrations during this process.

In the final section, "The Potential of Writing Portfolios," Patricia Belanoff offers insights that are, as she notes, from afar. The working conference, the basis for Belanoff's remarks in chapter 15, center around elementary and middle school settings. Belanoff brings to this chapter a distinguished career in college writing, from which she speaks from the perspective of scholar, researcher, and teacher. But because her experiences are all at the college level, she has been able to bring to these contributions a fresh and provocative perspective. We considered writing a postscript, but we think that Belanoff has said what needs to be said.

Robert C. Calfee
Pamela Perfumo

PART ONE

AUTHENTIC ASSESSMENT OF CLASSROOM WRITING

CHAPTER ONE

Classroom Writing Portfolios: Old, New, Borrowed, Blue

Robert C. Calfee
Stanford University

Sarah Warshauer Freedman
University of California, Berkeley

Catchy labels are attention-grabbers. Whoever first expressed the idea of portfolios of student work might have conjured up images of capable professionals opening impressive binders filled with polished displays of art, a far more appealing vision than dreary worksheets and multiple-choice tests.[1] Writing instruction seems especially suited to portfolio assessment and programs have sprung up around the country based on the metaphor. Like most metaphors, this one must be handled with care. Students are not professionals, and placing assignments into a manila folder does not guarantee a basis for assessment.

The chapters in this volume explore the current status of the portfolio concept—theory, research, and practice. The focus throughout the volume is on the tension between classroom assessment and externally mandated testing. This chapter places the writing portfolio in historical context (old), examines the mesh between portfolios and recent developments in cognition and learning (new), looks at the linkage between portfolios and other innovative ideas (borrowed), and then reminds the reader of the especially tumultuous state of today's American public schools (blue). We conclude the chapter by proposing a conceptual framework for the role of portfolios

---

[1]Sweet (1976) is the first reference to "writing portfolios" we have discovered in ERIC. In his research, the experience portfolio is a one-page checklist where students can indicate their interest in various writing topics. Times have certainly changed.

in the assessment of student writing, our effort to provide a coherent linkage among the chapters in this volume.

THE OLD

They say that WYTIWYG—"what you test is what you get." For more than 50 years, testing has come to mean the standardized, group-administered, multiple-choice test. Critics have argued that we have gotten low-level outcomes, rote memorization, and mindless practice. Originally designed for cheap and efficient selection of soldiers during the World Wars, the multiple-choice technology came to play an increasingly important role in public education from the 1950s onward. The concurrent emphasis on efficient management was well-served by standardized testing; it satisfied accountability requirements, allowed placement of students with special needs, and provided data to evaluate competing programs. Standardized tests meshed with the concept of behavioral outcomes, and textbook publishers began to align their materials with objectives-based scope-and-sequence charts. Alignment came into its own with the evolution of criterion-referenced tests explicitly designed to determine curriculum goals (Bloom, Hastings, & Madaus, 1971; a counterargument was made by Glaser, 1981). Textbook publishers incorporated worksheets and end-of-unit-tests into their materials, linking external tests to the daily routines of classroom instruction.

Writing instruction was not easily assessed by the multiple-choice technology, and so writing fell by the wayside. Literacy became identified with reading, more specifically with an image of reading as the acquisition of basic skills. As for writing, what should be taught? Many of the answers took a negative slant. Studies appeared to show that teaching grammar was not only boring but ineffective. How should writing be taught? Paraphrasing model paragraphs and copying summaries from book covers was not very inspiring. How should writing be assessed? The obvious answer was that teachers should grade student compositions. Although standardized reading tests could boast reliabilities in the .9 range (high levels of item consistency), research showed that teachers disagreed on writing performance, with reliabilities around .5 (low inter-rater consistency). Surveying the situation in America's schools during the 1970s, Applebee (1980) found that relatively little time was spent on writing instruction, most student compositions were a few sentences or perhaps a paragraph, and the first draft was generally the only draft.

THE NEW

The founding of the Bay Area Writing Project in 1972 and the National Writing Project in 1974 began to dramatically alter this state of affairs. The Project brought together classroom teachers who were interested in the teaching of writing to a summer institute where they could share their knowledge, practice their own writing, and talk about how to revitalize the field of composition instruction. From the outset, the project, drawing on the experience of successful teachers and the research of the time (Britton, Martin, McLeod, & Rosen, 1975; Calkins, 1986; Emig, 1971; Graves, 1983; Perl, 1979; Sommers, 1980) emphasized the concept of *writing as a process*, the notion that students need to be taught to think through their ideas as well as revise their writing, and that teachers needed to provide space and time for the thinking and reworking of ideas that meaningful writing requires. The Writing Project also pushed for the assessment of whole pieces of writing rather than piecemeal multiple-choice snippets, and led the way in popularizing holistic scoring for state, district, and school-level assessment programs (Myers, 1980).

Following the summer institutes, participants served as teacher-consultants in local school districts, passing on their knowledge to other teachers through formal projects and informal interactions. At Writing Project sites, the yearly cycle just described quickly created a network of teachers committed to the importance of writing, confident in their professional status, and convinced of the importance of teacher-based assessment. These teachers depended on neither textbooks nor tests, and were rather distrustful of external mandates.

The Writing Project is now active in more than 150 sites in every state and several foreign countries. During its growth over the past 20 years, the model has sustained the centrality of the classroom teacher, and the stimulation generated by professional exchanges. It has offered teachers a unified voice for speaking to the importance of writing in the literacy curriculum.

In the late 1970s, policymakers hurried to the front of the parade. Legislators throughout the nation mandated writing tests as part of state assessments. To be sure, these on-demand tests bore little resemblance to the practices being promulgated by Writing Project teachers. Process writing emphasized student-initiated topics, whereas mandated tests employed predetermined prompts. In process writing, student work was scaffolded by instruction, whereas mandated tests were standardized with no support allowed by the teacher. Process writing allowed students adequate time to plan, compose, and revise, whereas on-demand tests were restricted to a single session and a prescribed amount of time. Process writing was a social event, whereas state testing placed the individual on his or her own. In process writing, evaluation was a collaboration between student and teacher, whereas mandated tests were scored by external judges using predetermined rubrics. Nonetheless, the introduction of mandated writing tests meant that many more teachers began to pay attention to writing—especially teachers at the "test" grades (usually fourth and eighth grades, along with high school juniors or seniors).

The most recent episode in the history of writing assessment in this country emerged in the 1980s under a variety of labels—authentic assessment, performance-based testing, portfolios. The initiating goal in this movement was the urge to link assessment policies with what many teachers saw as a more authentic curriculum—in both reading and writing. What should be taught as reading? From the perspective of a 1960s objective-based curriculum, the answer was basic skill in decoding and answering questions. The Whole Language movement of the 1980s (Goodman, Goodman, & Hood, 1989) emphasized instead the reader's engagement in a story. Remembering the facts about *The Diary of Anne Frank* was part of the process, but reliving the experience was the more critical outcome. What should be taught as writing? An objectives-based answer emphasized the surface features of performance; grammar and spelling could be quickly and reliably judged from a fill-in-the-blank exercise. Writing Project teachers talked instead about purpose, audience, voice, development, and coherence.

The language of this movement had a novel ring to it, but it also incorporated classical elements. Reading instruction began to emphasize critical analysis. The Greek *kritikos* was a person chosen to judge merits and faults, to get to the root of the matter. Attention switched from decoding to comprehension. Speed and accuracy in oral reading are no guarantee of genuine understanding from this perspective. *Comprehend* comes from the same root as *prehensile*, with the sense of grasping, struggling, wrestling, "getting it" by rebuilding a passage. The focus turned to the student's reactions, reflections, and personalization of a piece of literature, a classical concept.

Writing instruction also employed elements of the classical rhetoric. Planning and development were important elements in writing, as important for the teacher as it was for the final product. Students once more had to explain what they were doing and why. Ideas like thematic development and persuasive argumentation returned to the curriculum. The ancient Greeks would recognize the concepts.

The emphasis on comprehension and rhetorical coherence was supported by an emerging line of innovative research on situated, social, and strategic cognition as the foundation for powerful learning. A mouthful, to be sure. The behavioral learning of the 1940s and 1950s was concrete and observable, attractive both scientifically and administratively. Functional relations between stimulus and response sufficed for this model, which provided powerful techniques for behavior control. The cognitive revolution of the 1960s and 1970s moved inside the mind, the computer as metaphor, to explore intellectual capabilities and thought processes. Information from the sensory channels entered short-term memory, where it was translated for storage in long-term memory. Problem solving, linguistic competence, semantic networks—these concepts reopened the study of the mind (Berliner & Calfee, in press).

By the 1980s, the strengths and limits of the computer metaphor had become apparent, and a new revolution emerged in our understanding of thought and learning. Human beings are not machines. We are social, we communicate, we are adaptive, and we can plan. Computers, in contrast, do not perform any of these activities unless a human being has programmed them to do so. They do not communicate unless they are connected by cables. They work the same no matter where they are plugged in. We now have a rich understanding of social cognition, of group thinking, and of the effect of context on these processes. But despite more than a decade of research studies spanning a variety of disciplines to explore these concepts, these ideas have yet to take root in today's classrooms.

What might it mean for curriculum, instruction, and assessment to be situated, social, and strategic? It certainly means more than simply exposing students to textbook content and then testing whether the content has been stored in memory. Situated learning happens when learning is connected with prior experiences and beliefs. If learning is not situated, it is less likely to have any genuine impact on students' perceptions and understandings. Most graduates know that the earth turns relative to the sun, causing sunrise and sunset; they have studied this topic in textbooks and tests from fourth grade on. Nonetheless, students see the sun set in the west in the evening, and cannot imagine standing on a globe that is actually rotating away from the sun. They study literary works that convey messages of enormous thematic import—*The Grapes of Wrath*, *To Kill a Mockingbird*, and *Freedom Road*—but appear to leave these studies affected little by the thematic values. They memorize textbook accounts about the hazards of poor diet, inadequate exercise, and drugs like tobacco and alcohol, but statistics and anecdotes suggest that these learnings are not thereby connected to daily reality for many people. School is one thing, the real world is another. It is easy to administer a multiple-choice test to assess content coverage, but judging the degree of situated learning is more difficult.

Social learning means working together toward genuinely shared ends. More is needed instructionally than occasional cooperative learning sessions. Learning in groups can be more effective and more satisfying than working alone. We sometimes must work as individuals, and too many cooks can indeed spoil a soup. But the democratic principle of e pluribus unum is more than an ideal; today's world has moved beyond the assembly-line era to a time when our lives as citizens and workers require teamwork. Yesterday's norms depend on examinations in which an individual's accomplishments are judged by how well he or she can work in isolation in competition with others. In fact, the student's ability to get along with thirty other individuals is critical if the classroom is to promote learning, and this capability is equally important in the world beyond school. Report cards sometimes address these issues by including a behavior category, but this is typically used to identify troublemakers rather than peacemakers. There are no formal tests of getting along together.

Finally, cognitively strategic learning emphasizes the importance of transfer to new situations. The only constant for tomorrow is change, and today's schooling is worthwhile only as it prepares graduates for circumstances that cannot be predicted, that builds on content, but that goes on to explore broader meanings and deeper extensions. Strategic learning encompasses three distinctive principles: it is *active*, it is *reflective*, and it is *expansive*. Students can learn by rote practice, but they are unlikely to learn about learning unless they are invested in a purposeful endeavor. A youngster may take a test or even write a passable essay about the causes of the Civil War, then wipe the slate clean a day later. Being able to explain yourself is the essence of reflectiveness; "Why?" is largely neglected in classroom discourse. Authentic assessment asks the student to "show your work." Learning is expansive when it moves beyond the immediate context for application in new and unpredictable situations. In life outside of schools, the answers can seldom be found at the back of the book. For instance, how does analysis of the Civil War help understand the several other civil wars going on around the world today? The daily newspapers suggest that policymakers do not have clearcut answers about either causes or remedies in this matter, and so the question is a real one. Judging students' responses to the question is not easily relegated to a Scantron machine.

Only recently have the innovative concepts of cognitive learning begun to influence assessment, and even now only indirectly. Some of the groups hard at work on authentic assessment build on cognitive foundations (e.g., Resnick, 1987). At the level of classroom practice, however, teachers are predominately oriented toward activities more than concepts, toward demonstrating mastery of learned tasks more than transfer to new situations. Performance is more important than thinking, doing more than explaining.

THE BORROWED

Central to all of the movements just mentioned—whole language, process writing, authentic assessment—has been the establishment of professional communities, the borrowing of ideas among teachers. The conceptual foundations sketched provide a starting point for a common language, in the sense that they seem to share a common ideology, partly grounded in Deweyian philosophy, partly based on cognitive psychology. Unfortunately, the various movements use different words, so that connections are not easily established.

The problem is that education is a practical enterprise, and as such requires a blending of ideas, engineering, and art. Scientists and scholars can contribute to the ideas, but it is in the field of practice that the engineering and art must be worked out. In an earlier time, the technology was simple and did not require professional judgment. Most schools in the U.S. could follow a factory model, each laborer at his or her individual workbench, teachers isolated within their individual classrooms. No need for the continuing dialogue that is the hallmark of other professions. Education that guarantees a high level of intellectual and social development for all students cannot be prepackaged, but calls for professional decision making, which in turn requires a professional language as the foundation for interaction.

And so it is understandable that where programs like whole language, process writing, and authentic assessment are having substantial impact, teachers have managed to network with one another. Sometimes the linkages are school-wide, more often they take shape as mentor or "buddy" systems. The school seems the natural unit for establishing these connections, but cross-school alliances have a unique potential as seen in the National Writing Project and other professional networks.

Several observers have commented on the value of local ownership, the idea that teachers must develop their own understanding of the concepts and practices. This strategy carries the risk of reinventing wheels, but we think that it makes sense for several reasons. First, if today's teaching rested on a more clearly established professional foundation, then teachers would encounter preservice experiences in thinking through comprehending and adapting new ideas at a conceptual level during their college careers and induction into the vocation. In fact, teaching during the past 50 years has been "managed," in the sense that teachers are generally told what to do. Now, when suddenly expected to make significant decisions on their own initiative, teachers are understandably taken aback and reluctant. It is only through collegial opportunities that support this process from beginning to end that genuine professionalism can develop. These experiences require sustained support and feedback over a matter of years; it is not enough to attend a summer institute and then return to the isolation of the individual classroom.

Unfortunately, opportunities for collegial interaction remain rare in today's schools. Unlike Japanese teachers, for whom as much as half the day is spent in collegial activities, American teachers spend most of the working day with children. Faculty meetings, after-school workshops, and committee sessions provide scant time for serious discussion, and are in any event typically occupied with mundane matters disconnected from serious discussion of instructional practice. If meetings were really substantive, they could be quite worthwhile. Freedman (1994) in her comparative study of U.S. and British schools found that British teachers routinely participated in department meetings where they discussed and debated curriculum orientations and theories about student learning, and where they analyzed the needs of particular students. Their most important exchanges came from opportunities to discuss details of practice against their specific contexts, to design and experiment together toward genuine instructional projects. Despite the barriers to collaboration, a repeated theme from innovative programs in the U.S. is the revitalization that comes from interaction with other teachers around matters of genuine importance to education (Lieberman, 1992; Darling-Hammond, 1994). The event may be as apparently mundane as a two-week summer session spent scoring portfolios; nonetheless, it is a chance to share ideas about student learning, and teachers value the experience. In fact, teachers involved in writing portfolio assessment, even when the assessment task is externally mandated and controlled, routinely praise the opportunity for collegial interaction around student accomplishments—the opportunity to borrow.

THE BLUE

The blue reflects the sad reality that the innovations sketched here come at a time when support for education is ebbing throughout many parts of the U.S. The federal role has focused increasingly on national standards and tests. To be sure, the Office of Education has adopted a policy that supports school-wide programs under some conditions. This policy offers possibilities for teachers to interact, and even the promise of funds for professional development. But the encouragement for school-wide programs is encumbered in regulations, the funding is threatened with cutbacks, and administrators are understandably skeptical about a program that offers greater freedom and responsibility, but also offers the risk of less control. At the state level, policies and practices for school reform vary widely, and schools no longer top the priority list in many places; crime, prisons, the economy, health care, and welfare have displaced attention from educational issues, even though effective education offers the only long-term remedy to the former problems.

We are not saying that concerns about schools have declined; politicians and the media continue to decry declines in public education (a claim not supported by the evidence; cf. Berliner & Biddle, 1996; Calfee & Patrick, 1995), and the importance to our country's future of providing higher quality education (a claim that is clearly on the mark). The federal and state policy initiatives to provide leadership and establish control are forward-looking; challenging curriculum frameworks, teachers capable of centering instruction around student needs, and authentic assessment are all found in the rhetoric. Although standardized multiple-choice tests remain the primary technology for gauging achievement, several state and national programs have explored the feasibility of alternative methods, including performance tasks and portfolios (e.g., Gentile, Martin-Rehrman, & Kennedy, 1995). The daunting challenge is to link these mandated efforts at reform to the realities of schools and classrooms scattered around the many ecological niches throughout our nation. We confront the dilemma of shaping a common vision in a situation where one size does not fit all. Moreover, as we place these words on paper, several states that had taken leadership in assessment innovations have precipitously terminated the programs and returned to conventional multiple-choice tests (e.g., Arizona, California, North Carolina).

THE CLASSROOM WRITING PORTFOLIO

This volume explores the efforts of elementary and middle school teachers to employ portfolios as a way to promote student writing. It springs from a project of the National Center for the Study of Writing and Literacy (NCSW) that investigated current practices in portfolio assessment of writing in the elementary and middle grades. The goal of the project was to understand the ways in which portfolios serve the classroom teacher for instructional decisions. A secondary purpose was to examine the value of classroom portfolios for other accountability purposes, including grades, parent reports, and evaluation of school programs. The focus was on locally determined portfolio practices, and the project did not explore portfolios that resulted from state or federal mandates.

We proposed four tasks in the project: (a) development of a conceptual framework for analyzing student portfolios, (b) analysis of current classroom practice through surveys, interviews and focus groups, intensive case studies, and review of various publications, (c) examination of evaluation techniques and standard-setting, and (d) investigation of aggregation strategies. Three project activities are covered elsewhere in this volume: an innovative survey strategy based on techniques familiar to teachers operating from a whole language perspective (chapter 3), a technique that we dubbed the "video visit" for acquiring contextually grounded information about portfolio methods (chapter 9), and a working conference that brought together researchers and practitioners around the topic of writing portfolios (the remaining chapters in the volume).

Several discernible themes run throughout this complex array of data: (a) commitment to student portfolios has an energizing effect on teachers and students, (b) portfolios in practice encompass a wide variety of methods and purposes, (c) standard-setting, grading, and aggregation receive little systematic consideration when teachers initiate portfolios, and (d) portfolios mean a lot of work for teachers (and presumably for students). It also appears that, whatever this "portfolio thing" is, it seems to have arrived on the scene, at least for the time being. As one of the practices that fall under the broader category of authentic assessment, portfolios are important in the part of the reform movement that emphasizes teacher autonomy and more genuine instructional experiences. Exactly what is a portfolio within this context? A metaphor, for one thing (Bird, 1990). Our mind's eye easily envisions an architect, artist, or model striding down Madison Avenue with an enormous binder under his or her arm—an aspiring and competent individual on the way to success! Portfolios are clearly positive, whatever they may be.

Metaphors offer models and allegories, but they are not the real thing. Students are not accomplished professionals. They are not competing for top spots. We are talking about kids in the elementary and middle grades learning about their interests and their potential. A portfolio—*port*: to carry; *folio*: paper—has a clear meaning on New York's Madison Avenue, but what about Sacramento's Mack Elementary School? From one perspective, student portfolios have a long history in this country—binders with notes, folders with assignments, backpacks with scribblings. But a portfolio seems clearly more than a collection of papers; after all, a wastebasket could fulfill this definition. And today's activities require more than transferring student assignments from a three-ring binder to a manila folder with an accompanying name change.

"Real" Portfolios

Looking more closely at the metaphor may be helpful. What about professional portfolios? These collections differ from notebooks (or wastebaskets) in several respects. They are prepared with a particular *purpose* in mind. An artist's portfolio aims to send a thematic message. An architect's portfolio is designed to convince a client. An investment portfolio should promise a profit, the more the better. A poet's portfolio is a collection of efforts, both published and unpublished, with quality more important than quantity. The academic's curriculum vita and the professional's "bio" highlight job accomplishments over a life span.

The portfolios of experts are *selective*. An architect may include a progression of drawings in a folder, demonstrating how she approaches a problem, but the final drawing is presented as the best work. Pianists spend enormous amounts of time practicing scales, but these are not included in their recordings. Scientists conduct numerous experiments that may be well-intended but on reflection not very thoughtful, and these excursions do not show up in their curriculum vita. Learning, even when it goes relatively smoothly, entails trial and error. Portfolios seldom contain any "outtakes."

Professional portfolios call for *judgments*. They are designed to withstand the rigors of evaluation by informed judges. In this sense, the gymnast's acrobatics and the skater's performance are portfolios-in-action. Performer and judge are on the same page, in the sense that both share a common perspective on contents and criteria for assessment. Both understand that the primary purpose of a portfolio is for evaluation. Professional portfolios are graded, both absolutely and relatively. In Olympic competitions, the panel of judges lifts its cards to display the ratings of a diving performance; television commentators explain why this splash merits a 9.2 whereas a previous one received a 9.8. The panel's assessment is subjective, but it must justify its ratings against a set of criteria. The ratings are also relative; one performance is of greater merit than another.

Finally, these portfolios are *transportable*. They are designed to be of similar value no matter where they are go. The demands on an architect may be different in San Diego and Duluth, but certain fundamental elements transfer from one location to another. An equestrian who triumphs in Long Island is likely to be respected in Long Beach. This facet of portfolios is arguably the least defensible, because context is always a factor. The New York fashion model may be welcomed in San Francisco but not in Los Angeles, and the weather in Duluth poses different architectural challenges than the balm of San Diego. But the basic idea is to establish consistency within certain boundary conditions.

Student Portfolios

Learners are not professionals; novices are not experts. How does the metaphor connect with classrooms and learning? What else should students "collect" other than the massive accumulations that they already aggregate? When and how should evaluation proceed? In what ways does portfolio assessment supplement or replace prevailing practices? How does it connect with standardized tests, grades, retention, or assignment to special programs? These and related questions are not to be found in the metaphor. The contexts are very dissimilar, so the analogies quickly fail. New answers must be devised for what are genuinely new questions.

Nonetheless, the metaphor does offer a plan for approaching these matters through the four categories introduced previously. The most sensible *purpose* for portfolios in the elementary and middle grades, it seems to us, is the documentation of student learning and growth. We are talking not about experts but about novices moving toward expertise. The emphasis should therefore be on progress rather than accomplishment.

Student portfolios should thus be *selective*, but now the choices should reflect student development from the beginning of the school year toward definable curriculum goals at year's end. Because this activity is taking place in classrooms, the record should clearly document opportunity to learn, and the teacher's comments about instructional scaffolding. Objectives-based testing often alludes to skill mastery; third-graders are unlikely to demonstrate mastery in any significant domains, but they can reasonably be expected to display progress on the continuum from novice to expert. It therefore makes sense to *select* work samples that show movement along this continuum.

If student portfolios are to serve for assessment, then they must include *judgments*, whether in the form of grades, narrative comments, or measures. Several studies have revealed that today's teachers are uneasy about rendering judgment when the evidence is complex. They often speak of portfolios as an opportunity for dialogue with students; grades are based on tests. This discomfort springs from several sources. One is the lack of professional preparation for evaluating student work (Stiggins, 1994). Another is the difficulty of the task (Wiggins, 1993). But this unease also reflects a classical tension: Should school grades reflect progress, effort, or accomplishment? Rubrics for mandated portfolio assessment, which serve as models for class-room portfolios, frequently portray olympian qualities rather than describing either progress or effort. These rubrics lay out a fixed standard of expertise and accomplishment rather than a developmental scale showing movement from beginner to expert. None of the rubrics with which we are familiar incorporates mention of students' attitudes and motivations. Most call for a holistic score, which is poorly suited for either documenting growth or for identifying strengths and areas where help is needed. In a word, teachers are probably correct in their uneasiness about the role of portfolios in formal assessment. At certain points in schooling it makes sense to make summative assessments; when students leave elementary school for middle or junior high school and when they move on to high school, the faculty should be able to gauge students' level of accomplishment. But the main job throughout most of these formative years is formative evaluation, for which portfolios may be ideally suited. But evaluation is needed in any event.

Which brings us to the issue of *transportability*—what elements in the student portfolio need to be carried across grades, schools, and subject matters? Some educators see the portfolio as a steady accumulation from kindergarten through—life? Asked about the practicality of such advice, some rely on technological remedies; scan everything onto a CD-ROM! Although this strategy may be possible, it begs the question: What is important to preserve for assessment purposes? Neither students nor teachers have time or interest to review everything that a student does. The problem becomes more challenging if the portfolio also incorporates instructional information. We suggest that transportability is actually a curriculum issue. Suppose the aim is to document the significant developmental mileposts marking a writer's progress from kindergarten novice to eighth-grade expert. Eighth graders have learned a lot, and individuals differ significantly in style and interest. Where are commonalities to be found? We think that the answer lies in constructing a genuine alignment of assessment with curriculum—a coherent description of the course of study.

Portfolio assessment brings all of the issues sketched earlier into bold relief. In particular, portfolios closely complement the emerging concepts of cognitive learning. If the aim is to document students' progress in learning that is situated, social, and strategic, then the assessment record must include contextual information that informs each of these dimensions. The record of curriculum opportunities and instructional support is certainly a significant part of this context. The portfolio, from this perspective, is not an accumulation of writing samples, but a reflective account of a student's development as supported by his or her teachers. By studying such a folder, teachers and parents should be able to see evidence of growth, but also the conditions that supported learning, the interaction with classmates (and others, including parents), and the blueprint that makes sense of the activity. Portfolios meeting this criterion may vary considerably on the surface, but require a coherent design if they are to transcend anarchy. A major goal of the NCSW project was to construct a framework for such a design, and we turn next to that matter.

A CONCEPTUAL FRAMEWORK
FOR PORTFOLIO ASSESSMENT

We approached the conceptualization of classroom writing assessment portfolios with four practical questions in mind: (a) what purposes and audiences are served by portfolios; (b) what do portfolios look like; (c) how does a teacher "do" a portfolio, and (d) how are portfolios used for evaluation? These four questions provide relatively independent categories for thinking about portfolio design, for classifying different strategies and designs, and for reviewing the tensions mentioned earlier.

Purposes and Audiences

Although the question of why and for whom might seem obvious, the answers are frequently tacit at the classroom level. A teacher attends a reading-writing conference and returns excited about the concept. The leader of a process-writing or whole-language workshop shows how portfolios link with these movements. A principal or district administrator, eager to be on the leading edge, recommends portfolios, perhaps even mandating their use.

None of these questions directly addresses the why question. Enthusiasm, connections with other popular programs, administrative dictate—none of these are genuinely purposeful. Too often the answer is often "because it is there." For teachers searching for innovation and independence, portfolio techniques are attractive: they are flexible, they are student-centered, they are *not* standardized, and they highlight the teacher's professional role. At one level, "why" is legitimately answered with "Because I like them and they are mine!" The exclamation mark is intentional, because teachers can be passionate in their response. Over the long haul, however, purpose requires more than passion.

What other answers are possible? One might suggest that portfolios are more appropriate for gauging higher-level learning outcomes, for connecting instruction with assessment, for giving students more responsibility for assessment, for more adequately informing parents and authorities. These suggestions appear on occasion, but are relatively rare in surveys. Mandates are straightforward: "I'm doing portfolios because the district told us to." Although this answer is honest and not uncommon, it lacks any commitment to genuine purpose.

What about audience—for whom are portfolios constructed and displayed? Some of the most heartfelt answers to this question point to the student as the focal audience. The practical literature in this field offers numerous romantic anecdotes about student involvement in and celebration of their portfolio productions. At one level this idea makes sense; William Zinsser (1990) was convincing when he argued that the most important reader of any composition is the writer; you should write for yourself. But this idea is circumvented when students are mandated to compile portfolios, and when they have no say in the purpose and design of the folders. Some students may find pride in their accomplishments, and portfolios offer many possibilities not to be found in multiple-choice tests. But other students are likely to be just as happy if they can conceal their shortcomings behind the anonymity of random marks with a #2 pencil.

Teachers are clearly an important audience for portfolios, whether or not assessment is an explicit outcome. But the teacher's role as audience can vary markedly: interested browser, harried commentator, engaged dialoguer, formal evaluator. To further complicate matters, the same portfolio may attempt to serve all of these functions, so that one moment the teacher is a supportive and engaging partner, only then to become an unforgiving judge. The teacher also plays a central role in linking portfolios to other audiences: parents, principal, district and state accountants. A unique feature of writing portfolios, unlike on-demand writing samples, is the enormous range of roles that the teacher can play in connecting the student through the portfolio to more remote audiences. We have seen situations in which students were left to their own devices, others in which teachers virtually prepared the portfolio, and some in which teachers set the stage for students to present themselves effectively but genuinely to other audiences. If portfolio assessment is to support the concept of learning that is situated, social, and strategic, then the challenge is to guide students in dealing with the concept of audience, providing instructional support to undergird this essential but demanding task.

Substance and Form

What is a portfolio? What does it look like? What is in it? How is it organized? Detailed answers to these questions depend partly on audience and purpose, but some cross-cutting issues can be identified, and within any given situation a variety of choices offer themselves. As a practical enterprise, the literacy portfolio usually comprises a folder with situated samples of student reading and writing performance (Calfee & Hiebert, 1991; Harp, 1991; Tierney, Carter, & Desani, 1991; Valencia & Calfee, 1991). Practitioners frequently talk about three categories of writing samples: showcase (examples of accomplishment), documentation (records of progress), and evaluation (assignments submitted for grading). These models overlap considerably, but they identify distinctive characteristics and technical demands.

From a curriculum perspective, portfolio contents are driven by a different set of issues. What genre should be included? Personal narratives, in their simplest form, are an easier task for the young writer than technical expositions. Poetry can pique the student's imagination with relatively few constraints (assuming that free verse is permitted), but evaluation is a challenge. What elements of the writing process should be included? Early drafts with technical deficiencies and unrefined development? Final but unpolished drafts? Personal journals with random reflections? Answers to these questions require curriculum guidance; what are the instructional outcomes of the exercise?

A second set of substantive issues centers around the reading-writing connection. These issues are important in portfolio design for several reasons. First, the value that comes from integration of reading and writing has been cogently argued by others (e.g., Moffett & Wagner, 1992). Nonetheless, a long history of separation continues to thwart efforts to blend these two domains both conceptually (the disciplinary handbooks have failed completely to join reading and writing) and practically (basal readers now offer snippets of writing exercises but not a coherent curriculum; writing programs say little about text comprehension or the reading-writing connection; Clifford-Jonich, 1987). The instructional languages are different in the two domains. Portfolio contents often sustain the division; the reading section has a book log, while the writing section has compositions (Flower, 1994; Spivey & King, 1989).

Thirdly, it is becoming increasingly clear that portfolios are markedly enhanced by the inclusion of reflective comments by students and teachers, and even parents. Current techniques may ask the student to complete a cover sheet for each writing sample in which they comment on the strengths and limitations of the piece. Teachers sometimes write notes or "captions" on student work. Reflection is a difficult task, and responses often tend toward the mundane. Students are understandably pleased when they finish an assignment—it is finally done! Reflection is just one more piece of busy-work. When asked about ways to improve a piece, students naturally follow the model of their teacher's remarks—write more, fix the grammar, and correct the spelling. One can imagine more substantial dimensions for critiquing a work: organization, development of ideas, personal voice, thematic integrity. These dimensions reach beneath the surface toward the wellsprings that make writing a personally meaningful part of the curriculum in the elementary and middle grades. The reflective element of the portfolio opens the way to develop these facets of literacy acquisition, but realizing this potential is a substantial and largely unmet challenge.

We have placed the substantive issues at the forefront of this section to emphasize their importance, because we think that function precedes form. Nonetheless, we recognize the need to organize a portfolio, to establish its form, shape and style. In practice, no single format is likely to serve all purposes, so that different portfolios require different structures at different times. A progressive format makes sense for a working portfolio, organization by genre is appropriate for evaluation, and a project-based arrangement offers opportunities for constructing a showpiece. The preceding references offer numerous examples of organizational patterns, and we do not develop the matter further. Our main caution is to warn against developing the portfolio as random accumulation. The circular file approach to portfolios serves neither instruction nor assessment, neither students nor teachers.

Process

The conceptual question under this heading is how to do portfolios. The issues here revolve partly around the student's activities in assembling the various collections described earlier. But they also entail the work of the teacher in constructing a portfolio environment within the classroom, and the efforts of the entire school in supporting the classroom environment.

Several features of portfolio assessment are significant practical guides in shaping these activities:

- Production is more important than recognition; students must demonstrate that they can actually do something, rather than simply picking the right answer.

- Projects are more important than items; the emphasis should be on depth over breadth, on validity over reliability.

- Informed judgment is more important than mechanized scoring; the teacher replaces the Scantron as the central character in the assessment process.

For the student, the process of building a portfolio is ideally directed by a coherent combination of curriculum goals, strategic understandings, and personal interests. Many have written about student-centered learning; portfolios offer a technology for helping this slogan to become a reality. But this goal requires that the portfolio process begin in the early years of schooling with substantial support by the teacher, evolving in the later grades toward increased student responsibility.

For the teacher, assessment becomes a task of applied research: planning, collecting the data, and interpreting the evidence (Calfee & Hiebert, 1991). This perspective differs markedly from the activity-driven approach to daily instruction. Portfolios can easily become little more than a decorative addition to business as usual, but they have the potential to become a lever for strategic and reflective teaching. A paradigm shift of this order of magnitude is likely to require that teachers spend time in consultation and development, that policymakers recognize that genuine reforms will be measured in years rather than months, and that transformations in mindset be valued more than changes in behavior.

Evaluation

Portfolios do not have to be submitted to formal judgment. Professional portfolios usually serve this purpose, but some collections are for the fun of it, for sustaining personal memories, for tradition. The family photo album is a kind of portfolio, but we would not ordinarily think about subjecting it to a formal evaluation ("Aunt Martha seems to have gained some weight and Uncle Fred lost some hair" is not the same as a formal assessment). Indeed, some educators have proposed that portfolios provide a unique opportunity for genuine interaction between student and teacher, or for a unique student experience—efforts to evaluate these artifacts will only undercut the foundational benefits, and intrude on the intrinsic merit of the experience.

Evaluation can be tough. Teachers often report on how difficult it is to assign grades. Wiggins (1993) noted the inherent tension between support and criticism, between buddy and judge. This tension is especially high during the early years of schooling. Kindergarten teachers often object to the turmoil of formal assessments, and many educators question the validity of formalized testing for first graders. The critical question, still lacking a clearcut answer, is how to achieve a reasonable balance between the role of the elementary teacher as advocate versus authority at different grades and in different situations.

But assuming that student evaluation is required and that portfolios are to be part of this process, several questions come to the fore. What parts of the collection should serve for assessment? Who should serve as the judges? When should evaluations be conducted? What standards should be applied? Based on our previous analysis, we offer the following recommendations. First, the classroom teacher is the person in the best position to gauge student achievements in the elementary and middle grades, although it is probably important for these judgments to be moderated by other colleagues inside and outside the school. Second, where assessment of learning—growth, progress, change—is the focus, then continuous formative assessment makes most sense, and is quite feasible when evaluation is local. Occasional summative judgments can then build on this base.

The third issue—standards—merits special attention. The touchstone is the assumption made in the previous paragraph—that the aim of portfolio assessment in the elementary grades is to measure learning. We argued earlier in the chapter that absolute standards of achievement make sense at some points in the school experience. When a student leaves elementary school for junior high or middle school, that is a reasonable time to assess the student's accomplishment of curriculum goals against a set of benchmarks or rubrics. The form of these standards of accomplishment is something of a mystery, in our judgment. They are not really all that clear in the curriculum standards being prepared by various professional organizations. These latter seldom specify with adequate clarity what comprises marginal, adequate, and excellent performance at a given grade level. The general approach is to lay out a qualitative dimension ranging from poor to good to better, to exhort students toward higher achievements.

Lacking in these specifications are substantive criteria for defining the dimensions or for describing the boundaries between one level and another. Scales developed by the National Assessment of Educational Progress (NAEP) for authentic assessment illustrate the current procedures for establishing standards. Level 300 in the reading scale is described as "finds, understands, summarizes, and explains relatively complicated information," whereas level 350 requires the reader to "synthesize and learn from specialized reading materials." In the recent redesign of reading assessment, NAEP (Langer, Campbell, Neuman, Mullis, Persky, & Donahue, 1995) describes levels of extended response to a passage (an important task, because it calls for students to respond in writing to a passage that they have just read). On this scale, *Unsatisfactory* reflects "little or no understanding, repeated, disjointed, or isolated bits from the passage," *Partial* "demonstrates some understanding, but is incomplete, fragmented, and unsupported by appropriate argument or evidence," and *extensive* "includes enough detail and complexity to indicate that the student has developed at least generally appropriate understandings of the passage and the question." A final level, *essential*, continues the pattern of a scale that moves steadily upward, but with features that are diffuse and shifting. Here are two samples (slightly edited to eliminate mechanical differences) from the NAEP report; the question is "If she were alive today, what question would you like to ask Mandy about her career? Explain why the answer to your question would be important to know."

I would like to ask Mandy about how did she feel to usually not be able to participate in sports like baseball so I would know how Mandy felt.
I would ask her how did it feel back there. Because I would want to know how it felt back there at that time.
Why did you like being umpire? It would be important because we wouldn't know why she liked being umpire, when girls weren't supposed to play sports. Unless someone asked her that question, we would never find out.
Did you really like basketball? Did you have any friends or fans? Were you ever at any basketball games? The reason I would ask these questions is because I like basketball too. Were you ever a cheerleader? What color is your hair? Because if you ever get lost people would have to know what color your hair is.

Two of these compositions received a rating of Unsatisfactory, one a rating of Partial, and one of Extensive. The point here is not whether you are able to match these assigned ratings (although that is by no means unimportant), but the way in which you would justify your judgments. And notice, we are taking for granted in this example that it makes sense to judge the performance of fourth graders against a criterion of accomplishment rather than progress—how well could each of these four students write the year before this assignment?

To the degree that standard setting seems unclear for constrained assessments designed by national experts with substantial funding, we find reason for concern about the prospects for locally developed portfolios that are more open-ended and that must rely on limited resources and expertise. Establishing absolute standards of accomplishment probably demands the best that can be achieved by the combined efforts of professionals, practitioners, and academics. It probably calls for a combination of situated assessments like portfolios and on-demand examinations like the California Learning Assessment System (CLAS), now unfortunately defunct. It certainly requires that we continue to struggle with the challenge of establishing more effective procedures for ensuring judgments that are consistent, generalizable, and valid.

The current enamorment with national standards may be a matter of looking for lost keys under the nearest lamppost. Evaluation is often associated with control, and it is tempting for those in power to resort to centralization and standardization, which offers the promise of consistent rubrics and procedures. We agree with Wiggins (1993) on the overriding importance of validity, which leads us to the conclusion that the locals are in a far stronger position to decide how to assess learning and to gauge student progress toward established standards. Our rationale here springs from the goal of ensuring that instruction allows all students fulfill their potential (Howe, 1994). If the assessment aim is selection, then it may make sense to establish summative standards at the outset of schooling, thereby eliminating clients without obvious promise as early as possible. Test children on entry to kindergarten and decide whether it is worth trying to educate them. Adaptive, formative standards make more sense when the goal is to optimize progress for every individual. The challenge in this position is to ensure that these local instructional activities, idiosyncratic on the surface, can be certified as valid efforts toward common summative achievements. Portfolios offer opportunities for both formative and summative assessment; they can offer evidence about learning and instructional support for learning, while establishing the degree to which the student has met summative performance criteria. For formative evaluation, standards gauge learning and instruction conjointly; for summative evaluation, standards gauge the level of accomplishment. Although these two sets of standards need to mesh, they are very different in character.

SOME MESSY MATTERS

Conceptual frameworks like the one just described have a neat academic appearance. The real world is considerably more cluttered. The editors of this volume suggested that the authors keep the framework in mind as they prepared their chapters, but their works also reflect their own perspectives as well as the snarly realities with which they have chosen to wrestle.

There is chaos in order, and vice versa. In this final section we highlight several tensions that reappear throughout these chapters as well as the broader literature in the field of portfolio assessment. The first of these tensions centers around the contrast between internally based and externally mandated assessments. What best serves the classroom teacher does not mesh nicely with the needs of administrators and policymakers. Some scholars think that this gap is unbridgeable (e.g., Cole, 1988). We are inclined to think otherwise, and see in portfolios the possibility for spanning this chasm (Freedman, 1993). The proof will eventually come from the pudding, but we think that the incorporation of teacher judgments within public accountability is not only possible but also critically important.

A related tension relates to efforts to standardize the contexts and conditions of assessment. To what degree can or should portfolios and portfolio assessment be kept constant across different contexts, and what are the costs and benefits for students and teachers from such constancy? Bureaucrats are generally more comfortable when things go by the book; even if reality is otherwise, they are reassured through standard operating procedures. Teachers on the front lines often call for flexibility in adapting instruction and assessment to local conditions and diverse student needs. As just indicated, we think it is possible to develop a common standard design that allows—indeed, demands—flexibility.

The third tension arises from the commitment to educational equity (Astin, 1990; Darling-Hammond, 1994; Nettles & Nettles, 1995). When assessment must conform to fixed methods and when developing students must meet fixed levels of performance, both equity and quality can be undermined. Again, some policymakers have emphasized the virtue of high standards for all. We agree on the merits of this policy at certain points in the process of education, but question the imposition of high standards of accomplishment during the early stages of learning, given that students vary considerably in their academic preparation for school. An analogy to the early preparation of athletes makes our point. One approach is to decide to begin by asking a group of 6-year-olds to attempt the high hurdles, and provide further tutelage to those who do not fall down. They probably have natural ability, and someone has probably helped them develop whatever talent they possess. But athletic prowess takes a variety of different forms, and varies with the child's age. A swimming pool may be more appropriate than hurdles for 6-year-olds. Moreover, it probably makes more sense with young children to focus on quality performance with lowered bars than to set the bars at a level where half of the racers trip on their first attempt.

A fourth tension appears when we consider the differential affects of new assessment methods on both students and teachers. These changes are coming at a time of increased demands on teachers because of deteriorating family demographics and declining support for public education. State testing policies, for reasons of efficiency, typically focus on one or two grade levels per school. "Portfolios—I think they do them in fourth grade" is an understandable response of by a harried third-grade teacher. As we noted earlier, the full potential of portfolio assessment is likely to depend on linking this technique to a developmental curriculum, and to procedures and expectations that cut across all grades. This means a schoolwide effort. In England, teachers have a tradition of professional responsibility for educational matters. They have steadfastly resisted efforts to federalize curriculum and assessment at the elementary and middle school levels. Although respectful (and knowledgeable) of national reports and recommendations, they view decisions about *exactly* what to teach and how to assess the learning of young children as local responsibilities. Each school faculty makes time to discuss methods and standards for assessment. Educational advisors, moderators, circuit-riding mentor teachers, ensure a degree of commonality across schools. Their role is not to direct or dictate, but to connect the insights and problems in one school with the work of other faculties.

This list does not exhaust the tensions by any means, nor do we attempt to provide resolutions. The chapters that follow raise other issues and suggest possible accommodations. What seems clear is that portfolio assessment, which arose as a largely grassroots movement, has become a cutting-edge instrument for fundamental reforms in U.S. education. Portfolios are unlikely to achieve this end, however, unless substantively linked to other reform elements. We see in teacher-based classroom assessment—for which portfolios are one source of information about learning outcomes—the potential for genuinely systemic reform, in which all parts of the educational endeavor are conjoined. But in this version of systemic reform, the impetus comes not from policymakers at the top of the hierarchy, but from professional communities at the local school level.

PERSPECTIVES ON THEORY AND PRACTICE

Someone—it may have been Kurt Lewin—said that nothing is so practical as a good theory. The gaps between theory and practice, academics and practitioners, and ideas and activities remain substantial in the field of education. The situation seems quite different in other professions, for whatever reasons, but in education the linkages are much more tenuous. One of the primary aims of this volume is to help bridge the gap. This goal is appropriate for an assessment volume, given the tension between internal and external mandates in the testing domain. We surely do not claim to have achieved success, but the project has managed to bring together individuals representing a variety of perspectives. We have organized the volume to reflect the connections and contrasts between theory and practice. We lead off with chapters that are more conceptual and research-like, moving then toward contributions that are more practical and teacher-like.

To frame these segments, the chapters by Herman, Gearhart, and Aschbacher and Belanoff provide conceptual "bookends." Herman, Gearhart, and Aschbacher anchor new developments in the field with serious questions about the technical foundations for classroom-based assessment and Belanoff reflects on the common themes from the chapters. Herman's background has put her face-to-face with the practicalities of elementary and middle school classrooms, whereas Belanoff shifts us to a very different perspective—equally practical, but focused on the bottom line for the high school graduate entering college.

Achieving coherence in an edited volume is always a challenge. We have approached this task in three ways. First, we have offered the preceding conceptual framework as a road map for readers. Second, literacy—reading and writing—is the focus for all the authors. Finally, one focal question can be posed for each of the chapters: How can classroom reading-writing portfolios enhance curriculum, instruction, and assessment for both local and external accountability? This question is likely to be of increasing importance in years to come. The roadway for educational reform is still murky in parts, but new and improved assessments will almost certainly part of any successful design.

REFERENCES

Applebee, A. N. (1980). *A study of writing in the secondary school.* Urbana, IL: National Council of Teachers of English.

Astin, A. W. (1990). Educational assessment and educational equity. *American Journal of Education, 98,* 458–478.

Berliner, D. A., & Biddle, B. J. (1996). *The manufactured crisis.* Reading, MA: Addison-Wesley.

Berliner, D. A., & Calfee, R. C. (Eds.). (in press). *Handbook of educational psychology.* New York: Macmillan.

Bird, T. (1990). The schoolteacher's portfolio: An essay on possibilities. In J. Millman & L. Darling-Hammond (Eds.), *The new handbook of teacher evaluation* (pp. 241–256). Newbury Park, CA: Sage.

Bloom, B. S., Hastings, J. T., & Madaus, G. F. (1971). *Handbook of formative and summative evaluation.* New York: McGraw-Hill.

Britton, J., Martin, N., McLeod, A., & Rosen, H. (1975). *The development of writing abilities.* London: Macmillan.

Calfee, R. C., & Hiebert, E. H. (1991). Classroom assessment of reading. In R. Barr, M. Kamil, P. Mosenthal, & P. D. Pearson (Eds.), *Handbook of research on reading* (2nd ed., pp. 281–309). New York: Longman Publishers.

Calfee, R. C., & Patrick, C. (1995). *Teach our children well.* Stanford, CA: Portable Stanford.

Calkins, L. M. (1986). *The art of teaching writing.* Portsmouth, NH: Heinemann.

Clifford-Jonich, G. J. (1987). *A Sisyphean task: Historical perspectives on the relationship between writing and reading instruction.* Berkeley, CA: Center for the Study of Writing, University of California

Cole, N. S. (1987). A realist's appraisal of the prospects for unifying instruction and assessment. In C. V. Bunderson (Ed.), *Assessment in the service of learning* (pp. 103–117). Princeton, NJ: Educational Testing Service.

Darling-Hammond, L. (1994). Performance-based assessment and educational equity. *Harvard Educational Review, 64,* 5–30.

Emig, J. (1971). *The composing processes of twelfth graders.* Urbana, IL: National Council of Teachers of English.

Flower, L. (Ed.). (1994). *Making thinking visible: Writing, collaborative planning, and classroom inquiry.* Urbana, IL: National Council of Teachers of English.

Freedman, S. W. (1993). Linking large-scale testing and classroom portfolio assessments of student writing. *Educational Assessment, 1,* 27–52.

Freedman, S. W. (1994). *Exchanging writing, Exchanging cultures: Lessons in school reform from the United States and the United Kingdom.* Cambridge, MA: Harvard University Press.

Gentile, C. A., Martin-Rehrman, J., & Kennedy, J. H. (1995). *Windows into the classroom: NAEP's 1992 Writing portfolio study.* Princeton, NJ: Educational Testing Service.

Glaser, R. (1981). The future of testing: A research agenda for cognitive psychology and psychometrics. *American Psychologist, 36,* 923–936.

Goodman, K. S., Goodman, Y. M., & Hood, W. J. (1989). *The whole language evaluation handbook.* Portsmouth, NH: Heinemann.

Graves, D. H. (1983). *Writing: Teachers and children at work.* Portsmouth, NH: Heinemann.

Harp, B. (1991). *Assessment and evaluation in whole language programs.* Norwood, MA: Christopher-Gordon Publishers.

Hiebert, E. H., & Calfee, R. C. (1992). Assessment of literacy: From standardized tests to performances and portfolios. In A. E. Farstrup & S. J. Samuels (Eds.), *What research says about reading instruction* (pp. 70–100). Newark, DE: International Reading Association.

Howe, K. R. (1994). Standards, assessment, and equality of educational opportunity. *Educational Researcher, 23,* 27–33.

Langer, L. A., Campbell, J. R., Neuman, S. B., Mullis, I. V. S., Persky, C., & Donahue, P. L. (1995). *Reading assessment redesigned*. Princeton, NJ: Educational Testing Service.

Lieberman, A. (1992). *The changing contexts of teaching*. Chicago, IL: National Society for the Study of Education.

Moffett, J., & Wagner, B. J. (1992). *Student-centered language arts* (4th ed.). Portsmouth, NH: Boynton/Cook.

Myers, M. (1980). *A procedure for writing assessment and holistic scoring*. Urbana, IL: National Council of Teachers of English.

Nettles, M. T., & Nettles, A. L. (1995). *Equity and excellence in educational testing and assessment*. Boston: Kluwer.

Perl, S. (1979). The composing processes of unskilled college writers. *Research in the Teaching of English, 13*, 317–333.

Resnick, L. B. (1987). *Education and learning to think*. Washington, DC: National Academy Press.

Sommers, N. (1980). Revision strategies of student writers and experienced writers. *College Composition and Communication, 31*, 378–388.

Spivey, N. N., & King, J. R. (1989). Readers as writers composing from sources. *Reading Research Quarterly, 24*, 7–26.

Stiggins, R. J. (1994) *Student-centered classroom assessment*. New York: Merrill.

Sweet, J. (1976). The experience portfolio: An approach to student writing. *English Journal, 65*, 50.

Tierney, R. J., Carter, M. A., & Desani, L. (1991). *Portfolio assessment in the reading-writing classroom*. Norwood, MA: Christopher Gordon.

Valencia, S. W., & Calfee, R. C. (1991). The development and use of literacy portfolios for students, classes, and teachers. *Applied Measurement in Education, 4*, 333–346.

Wiggins, G. P. (1993). *Assessing student performance: Exploring the purpose and limits of testing*. San Francisco, CA: Jossey-Bass.

Winfield, L. F., & Woodward, M. D. (1994). Assessment, equity, and diversity in reforming America's schools. *Educational Policy, 8*, 3–27.

Zinsser, W. K. (1990). *On writing well* (4th ed.). New York: Harper.

CHAPTER TWO

Portfolios for Classroom Assessment: Design and Implementation Issues

Joan L. Herman
Maryl Gearhart
Pamela R. Aschbacher
Center for Research on Evaluation, Standards,
and Student Testing (CRESST)
UCLA Graduate School of Education and Information Studies

Portfolio assessment has made a dramatic entry into the 1990s assessment scene offering great promise: Assessments that will right the wrongs of traditional measurement practice; assessments that will help, not hurt or subvert, the instructional process; assessments that will provide bridges, not barriers, to student accomplishment. The appeal and potential benefits of portfolios are many, particularly when compared to traditional standardized testing. Because portfolios contain the products of classroom instruction, by definition, they should be integrated with it, not an intrusive add-on. In contrast to the focus of traditional testing on discrete skills, well-designed portfolios contain student work reflecting students' accomplishments toward significant curriculum goals, particularly those that require complex thinking and the use of multiple resources. Because the assessment of student performance on these tasks can provide evidence of students' accomplishments and thereby serve as a tool to support the instructional process, portfolio assessment can bolster the efficacy of teachers, encouraging them to consider deeply how students are progressing. Portfolios, in addition, invite students to reflect on and take responsibility for their own progress, the assessment process, and, ultimately, their own learning. Finally, portfolios provide parents and the wider community with credible evidence of student achievement, and inform policy and practice at every level of the educational system, from individual students to the nation as a whole (Freedman, 1993).

The promises of portfolios are enticing, yet claims alone do not assure their realization. In this chapter, we consider issues in moving beyond the banner of rhetoric to the difficult work of designing and building a sound foundation for portfolio assessments. We explore one set of design parameters for accomplishing these purposes and, based on working knowledge and available research, compare existing practice with these design requirements. We end with implications for future policy and practice. Our findings are based principally on research conducted at the National Center for Research on Evaluation, Standards, and Student Testing (CRESST), including studies of the implementation and effects of portfolio projects for elementary students' writing, for an interdisciplinary high school humanities project, for an inner-city model technology project, and for a statewide system to assess mathematics and writing. Reports of each of these projects are available separately (Aschbacher, 1993, 1994; Calfee & Perfumo, 1992, 1993a, 1993b; Gearhart, Wolf, Burkey, & Whittaker, 1994; Herman & Winters, 1994; Koretz, 1992, 1993; Koretz, McCaffrey, Klein, Bell, & Stecher, 1993; Koretz, Stecher, Klein, McCaffrey, & Deibert, 1993).

PORTFOLIO DESIGN ISSUES

What's a Portfolio Assessment?

When a portfolio is simply a collection of work, it does not constitute an assessment. The assessment in portfolios exists when there is in place a "process of collecting, synthesizing and interpreting information to aid in decision-making" (Airasian, 1991, p. 5). In the arena of student assessment, information relevant to decision making usually involves what students have accomplished, how well they have progressed, or whether they are prepared and qualified for the next challenge in their lives.

Many current models of a portfolio are not well-designed to serve a clearly specified assessment purpose. Teachers may ask, for example, "Should it be a showcase portfolio (i.e., contain best pieces only), or should it be a working portfolio (i.e., contain all work)? Should my students include their writing from all of their courses or just my language arts class? Should they write a letter of introduction to their portfolio? Should the portfolio contain only final versions of work, or should it contain notes, drafts, and other evidence of the processes students used when composing the work?" Good questions indeed, but we argue that asking any question about the contents of a portfolio before establishing its measurement purpose is putting the cart before the horse.

Collecting work, in short, differs from assessing it; a portfolio becomes an assessment when someone weighs its contents against criteria in order to reach judgments about the value or quality of performance, and, more specifically, to aid decisions about individual students, programs, schools, or other entities. Reaching valid judgments, in turn, requires having available pertinent work on which to base them as well as a relevant judgment scheme. Thus good portfolio assessment requires advance design as well as continuous reflection on a number of questions:[1]

1. What is the assessment purpose(s)?
2. What tasks should be included in the portfolio collection?
3. What standards and criteria will be applied?
4. How will consistency in scoring or judgment be assured?
5. Are the results valid for the intended purpose?
6. How are results used?

We take each of these design questions in turn, raising issues involved in addressing each.

Identifying Priority Purposes

Many Possibilities. According to its advocates, portfolio assessment fulfills many traditional testing purposes as well as some new ones; among these are:

- accountability; evaluating program or curriculum effectiveness.
- evaluating individual student progress; grading; certifying student accomplishment.
- diagnosing students' needs; informing classroom instructional planning; improving instructional effectiveness.
- encouraging teacher efficacy; encouraging reflective practice at the school and classroom levels; supporting teachers' professional development.
- encouraging student efficacy; promoting student self-assessment; motivating student performance.
- communicating with parents.

In the abstract, all of these purposes can be mutually complementary, and collectively they represent strategies for advancing instructional and school reform. For example, if portfolio collections include work exemplifying key curriculum goals from a state or district framework, then such portfolios might be used for purposes of program accountability as well as local evaluation of student achievement. If teachers are utilizing portfolios for diagnosing stu-

---

[1]These design issues are adapted from Herman, Aschbacher, and Winters (1992).

dents' learning needs and instructional planning, then the portfolios might also be used productively to foster students' understandings of the assessment framework and their engagement with self-assessment. Portfolio assessment can support teachers' professional development in contexts where teachers had not routinely assigned or assessed complex work. Indeed, the experience of using rubrics based on disciplinary standards of quality to judge students' portfolio work can acquaint teachers and students with what constitutes good performance in arenas of performance never before considered.

Complementary or Conflicting? Although the hypothetical connections among purposes are almost limitless, the reality of practice unfortunately introduces some conflicts, particularly between the purposes of classroom practice and high stakes assessment. An illustration: One state introduced statewide portfolios to serve accountability, instructional reform, and teacher professional development purposes (Koretz, Stecher, Klein, McCaffrey, 1995). In order to support their instructional reform and teacher professional development aims, the state included as many teachers as possible in the portfolio development and scoring process and left teachers as much latitude as possible regarding what should be included in students' portfolios. This strategy apparently encouraged teacher ownership and support for the portfolio assessment program, and results indicated that the assessment program contributed to instructional change and professional development (Koretz et al., 1995). At the same time, however, the inclusionary, grassroots approach led to some problems with the technical quality of the assessment results, at least in the first years of the program. Portfolio contents were so variable that they were sometimes difficult to score or were unscoreable. Including all teachers in the scoring process also apparently introduced some serious rater agreement problems, lowering the reliability of the assessment to unacceptable levels for accountability purposes.

Because the purposes of portfolio assessment can come into conflict, and trying to serve all may result in compromises that do not serve anyone well, it is critical to set priorities. What are the most important aims of the assessment—the purposes that absolutely need to be achieved? Which are of secondary importance, those that would be nice to include but are not absolutely essential and may be phased in after critical priorities (such as rater agreement) have been met?

Specifying Portfolio Contents: What Tasks Should Be Included?

Portfolio contents need to be structured to reflect priority goals for students' learning and the purposes of the portfolio assessment. Often, of course, the two are highly intertwined. Consider for example, Ms. Juarez, a language arts teacher who includes among her priority goals: that her students can analyze particular kinds of narrative and write their own narratives built on what they have learned from professional authors; that her students can write persuasive pieces, like letters to the editor, that they read and interpret; that her students understand and can utilize key strategies for planning, composing, and revising any piece of work; that her students acquire a sense of efficacy for their learning and an investment in improvement. For Ms. Juarez, portfolios are structured to include written responses to literature, narratives, and persuasive letters, and, for many of these written assignments, documentation of the ways the student utilized the writing process. To serve efficacy and self-assessment goals, Ms. Juarez asks students to select best pieces and to reflect on how these pieces demonstrate learning. Thus by their teacher's design, the students' portfolios contain items that reflect students' learning and accomplished progress toward objectives specifically set by Ms. Juarez. We focus this section on strategies for specifying portfolio contents, and return later to Ms. Juarez's classroom to consider strategies for assessment of those contents by teachers, students, and outside raters.

Determining Priority Goals for Student Performance. Portfolios focus classroom attention on and communicate about what students should be learning and what curriculum outcomes are most valued. What are these priority outcomes? For many teachers, deciding on the handful of desired student outcomes that reasonably encompass their expectations for student learning is a challenge indeed. What *should* students know and be able to do? There are no single right answers. Identifying priority outcomes requires serious, extended reflection and deliberation, and if the assessment is to be for a school or district, coming to consensus requires significant discussion and dialogue with all stakeholders in the school community. The national standards for student performance being developed by various subject matter groups and state curriculum frameworks offer important starting points for such deliberation, although most frameworks leave plenty of room for flexibility and interpretation. The goals for student performance to consider will be those that:

- reflect priority student outcomes.
- use core disciplinary content.
- build deep understanding and require complex thinking and problem solving.
- are meaningful to students.
- are developmentally appropriate.

Building goals on these principles will ensure that the tasks ultimately designed to help students meet those goals are good instructional tasks.

Table 2.1 contains illustrative possibilities for priority goals in three areas. What are the important principles and concepts students should understand and be able to apply? What social and affective dispositions? What meta-cognitive skills?

Winnowing down the list of possibilities to a manageable number of powerful outcomes takes tremendous focus and discipline. Among the questions to consider in the winnowing process: How does the outcome relate to school improvement goals?—focus on those that are highly related to school goals so that classroom decisions are integrated with those of colleagues within and across grade levels. Does the outcome integrate a number of component understandings and skills?—focus on those that do. Is the outcome intrinsically important and critical to students' future success?—focus on such essential goals, not on trivial or superficial ones. Are the outcomes teachable?—focus on outcomes that you can help your students to achieve.

What Tasks Reflect These Outcomes? Having identified outcomes, decisions must be made regarding the kinds of assignments or tasks that should comprise the contents of the portfolio. The question for teachers is

TABLE 2.1
Illustrative Outcomes

---

1.   What concepts and principles central to a working knowledge of this discipline do I want my students to understand and be able to apply?

   - Understand how several narrative genres are structures (utilizing the components of theme, character, setting, plot, and language use), and the ways that they have been adapted playfully by current authors; compose engaging narratives informed by the genres studied.
   - Analyze current events from historical, political, geographic, and multicultural perspectives, and integrate these understandings in persuasive and narrative writing.
   - Understand cause and effect relationships in history and in everyday life, and integrate arguments based on cause and effect when writing persuasive pieces.
   - Communicate effectively orally as well as in print.
   - Use different media effectively to express what they know.

2.   What are the important dispositions and social skills that I want my students to develop?

   - Work independently.
   - Develop a spirit of teamwork and process skills that facilitate group work.
   - Appreciate their individual strengths, have confidence in their abilities.
   - Be persistent in the face of challenges.
   - Take pride in their work.
   - Enjoy and value learning.
   - Have a healthy skepticism about arguments and claims.

3.   What reflective and analytic strategies do I want my students to develop?

   - Discuss ways they can improve their plans and strategies used in creating projects.
   - Reflect on the writing process they use, evaluating its effectiveness and deriving their own plans for how it can be improved in the future.
   - Formulate efficient plans for completing their independent projects and monitoring their progress toward completion.

---

essentially, "What can I have my students do to show how well they have achieved a particular outcome or goal?" Luckily, the statements of outcomes themselves often suggest appropriate tasks. For example, if a desired outcome is that students write effective, persuasive essays or that students analyze period literature with regard to theme, plot, and character, general features of possible tasks have already been decided.

But there are usually many specific tasks or assignments that have the desired features. For example, students could be asked to write a persuasive essay about an endless number of subjects to any number of audiences—the principal, city council members, state legislators, congressional representatives, potential employers. Students could utilize different lengths and formats. Good tasks for including in portfolios are good instructional tasks. They invite and require students to grapple with *significant content*—dominant themes, principles, and concepts of the discipline—and ask that students construct their own meaning and apply their knowledge to complex problems of interest. Such tasks are worth the time and attention given to them.

In fact, there are many more worthwhile tasks and curriculum areas to cover than there is time to complete them. A major challenge then, is to design a feasible number of tasks that artfully incorporate a number of valued outcomes. One possible solution builds on the current push for assignments that cross disciplines and that incorporate interdisciplinary goals. If a goal, for example, is assessment of students' growing competencies with writing, writing may now be found across the curriculum. A writing portfolio could reasonably include samples of writing from science, history, or mathematics; similarly writing samples could explore themes—diversity, change, conflict—that encourage interdisciplinary connections.

A second challenge in the design or selection of portfolio tasks is the relationship of core tasks—such as the narratives and persuasive letters in Ms. Juarez's classroom—to supplementary evidence regarding students' competencies with those tasks—such as a reflective self-assessment about "what I have learned about writing persuasive letters." Students' self-assessments could be considered tasks both in and of themselves as well as evidence of the ways that students understand features of the core assignments, such as persuasive letters. Recognizing the value of reflective analysis, we caution that careful consideration must be given to the assessment uses of students' reflective writings: Should these be assessed, and, if so, how? How can they supplement judgments based just on the competency of the core writing assignments?

Designing a Model That Fits Priority Purposes.   The model for the content and structure of a portfolio must fit priority outcomes and assessment purposes. Let us consider some of the current features of portfolios and the ways that these features may—or may not—address important outcomes.

• Who should decide what goes in the portfolio? The student, the teacher, or the student in consultation with the teacher or peers? If one of the purposes of the portfolio is to support students' investment in learning, then students will need a role in the assessment process. Students might be asked, for example, to select their best pieces, either alone or in consultation with others, and to explain in writing how their selections demonstrate progress. If, on the other hand, a priority purpose is program accountability, and outside scorers will judge students' progress toward state or district standards, then perhaps the teacher should choose work, because he or she may well be more likely than the student to understand the assessment framework.

• Should it be a showcase portfolio (i.e., contain best pieces only), a progress portfolio (i.e., contain evidence of growth over time), or a working portfolio (i.e., contain all work), or should there be provisions for all? This is a question that should be dictated by purpose. If an assessment purports to examine progress within the year, then students and teachers need to be able to look over many pieces of work that show the learning journey. If the purpose of the portfolio is to show the best of what a student is capable, then a showcase portfolio is the appropriate choice. If the portfolio is meant to reflect the experienced curriculum for the year in order to evaluate a program, then a working portfolio that accurately samples what was taught over the year is appropriate.

• Should the portfolio contain only final versions of work, or should it contain notes, drafts, and other evidence of the process students engaged in to produce the work? If the purpose of the assessment is to provide specific information on how students approached their work and how they might improve their process, then drafts and other process data are essential documentation.

• Should the portfolio entries represent samples of work written at different times of the year? Yes, if the purpose of the portfolio is to assess progress, if best work happens at different times, or if the portfolio needs to reflect the full year's curriculum.

• Should the portfolio contain supplementary documentation to make the portfolio more understandable to potential evaluators? A portfolio might include a table of contents, an overview of the purpose of the portfolio, or background information about the student. However, as we have discussed, inclusion of artifacts like these should be motivated by a clear framework for their role in portfolio assessment.

• Should students include reflective self-assessments of their learning? If so, what should students be asked to reflect about? Their progress? Their strengths? What they've learned? What they want or need to learn next? Should the reflection be about individual pieces or about the portfolio as a whole? The answers to these questions depend on priority goals for learning (what kinds of reflection do students need to learn how to do?) and the ways that reflections will be interpreted to provide evidence of learning.

• Should there be a place for parent reflection and feedback? If so, what's the best way to involve them in the assessment process? How and about what should they share their views? These decisions should be shaped by classroom and school goals. For example, is parent reflection being used to help motivate student learning, to inform parents about the curriculum or what their children are achieving, or motivate parents to become more involved in their children's learning?

Each decision made about the structure of portfolios needs to be made with both instruction and assessment purposes in mind so as to avoid designing an assessment tool that fails to meet basic needs. Reviewing the planned contents of a portfolio with an eye to balance of priorities will help reassure the teacher or other portfolio developers that the planned portfolio can capture meaningful evidence of the most valued learning goals.

Specifying Scoring Criteria: Getting at the Quality of Students' Work

Scoring criteria are essential to the process of assessment; without them, a portfolio is just a collection of student work. Criteria should also make public what is expected of students so that teachers, students, and parents can share a common understanding and fulfill their roles in improving student achievement.

What do "good" criteria look like? Herman, Aschbacher, and Winters (1992) suggested that criteria should have the following characteristics:

- sensitive to instruction and assessment purposes.
- keyed to important, developmentally appropriate student outcomes that reflect current conceptions of excellence.
- meaningful and credible to teachers, students, and parents.
- clearly communicated.
- fair and unbiased.

This list of desired characteristics can be used to guide the many decisions that need to be made when developing criteria for judging classroom portfolios. These decisions start at the macro level (what is our focus?) and proceed through micro level issues (such as, how many scale points there should be).

What Is the Focus? This question was posed earlier when considering what contents the portfolio should contain, and it needs to be revisited when developing plans to score the work. The structure and content of scoring need to reflect the purpose of the portfolio assessment, and criteria need to be focused on aspects of student performance which are consonant with those purposes. Such focus starts with the answers to two broad questions: What kind of performance are we trying to measure and what domains of students' knowledge and skill are to be assessed?

First, in terms of kind of performance, although assessments generally focus on how well students are doing on a particular body of work or on a specific assignment, criteria may stress the level or quality of students' accomplishment, students' progress, or both. Although accomplishment is almost always an issue, at times for certain students or subjects, teachers may be more interested in assessing progress than in absolute level of achievement. The important point is that where progress is a focus, criteria need to direct the teacher or other scorers to look for specific aspects of change, growth, or improvement in students' performance. Ideally, these aspects reflect critical features of quality performance (and of judgments of accomplishment) and are key foci of classroom instruction.

The second focus question asks: What domains of performance count? In addition to specific disciplines or subject areas that may be targeted in the assessment, many portfolios are meant to address important affective and metacognitive goals for student performance. Scoring criteria need to reflect the full range of outcomes designated for a portfolio assessment.

For example, if a writing portfolio is designed to include samples of writing across the disciplines or samples of interdisciplinary work, then criteria must be developed to apply to that range of content. To what extent will disciplinary understanding count in making judgments about students' writing? To what extent will interdisciplinary connections count in judgments about students' performance—these are questions of criteria focus. Such questions also force us to consider whether or how to tease apart subject matter domain knowledge from writing ability—or if we cannot separate them, to recognize how they are intertwined when we make inferences about student performance. For example, if students have little understanding of historical concepts, they will have difficulty in writing convincingly about them and will be limited in their ability to demonstrate their writing talents. Our judgments of their writing ability, based on a history topic, thus may underestimate their writing capability. Their content knowledge (in history in this case) affects their writing performance.

But at the same time, when writing portfolios contain work in other disciplines, teachers can make the choice to get double mileage out of students' work, where appropriate. If Ms. Juarez's students' portfolios contain letters to the city council about strategies for stopping pollution, students' work could be assessed on how well it shows application of scientific content and use of scientific problem solving, as well as how persuasive and effective is the rhetoric. Indeed, one might argue that an analysis of persuasive writing regarding a scientific (mathematical, historical) issue could not possibly omit an analysis of the content. Students' written explanations of their math problem solutions could likewise be assessed on both the quality of their mathematical thinking and problem solving as well as on the quality of their written communication.

Including such assessments, of course, requires substantial knowledge of the areas that are to be assessed and may have implications as well for who needs to do the scoring. If mathematical thinking counts, for example, scoring needs to be done by those who have expertise in the mathematical concepts being assessed, and to get full mileage out of the pollution example just mentioned, it would be useful to have scorers who not only understand the science concepts and principles involved but can recognize the misconceptions students are likely to possess. Teachers and scorers must either work in interdisciplinary teams or acquire the full range of expertise necessary to judge the work.

Beyond concerns for disciplinary understandings, many portfolio projects also give attention to affective and metacognitive aspects of student performance. The Pittsburgh Arts PROPEL Project (Gitomer, 1993; Howard, 1990; LeMahieu & Eresh, in press; Wolf, 1989, 1993; Wolf, Bixby, Glenn, & Gardner, 1991; Wolf, LeMahieu, & Eresh, 1992), for instance, scores students' degree of engagement in the writing process in addition to their use of the writing process and a range of resources. Other projects have looked at the quality or growth of students' reflection or self-assessment skills, their willingness to go beyond basic requirements, their involvement in school or community service, and similar objectives.

The development of criteria should be guided by our focus, what we are most trying to measure and improve through the portfolio process.

What Is Our Conception of Excellence in the Target Domains?

Having decided on the major domains to be assessed, we must still determine what aspects of performance will be used to define quality in those domains. For example, what is excellent writing? Should mechanics always count? Should creativity? The criteria selected are what students will eventually internalize, so the decision has far-reaching importance.

Let us return for a moment to Ms. Juarez and her students. She has decided that understanding of narrative genre or competency with persuasive letters are what will count, but she must still consider what constitutes good understanding of narrative or good persuasive writing. Scoring criteria need to contain operational definitions of such learning outcomes. Where will she find help in defining quality? As with the identification of portfolio tasks, there are a number of sources of help and usually no need to start from scratch: the research literature of the discipline; the advice of subject matter experts; curriculum theory in the discipline; the models provided by other states, districts, schools, and teachers who have worked on portfolio projects in the subjects of interest; and the consensus of colleagues. Ms. Juarez may draw upon the National English Language Arts Standards, the California Language Arts Framework, her colleagues in the California Writing Project, or a recent article in Language Arts on narrative. There is no single best definition of quality; instead, credible, well-grounded, non-arbitrary definitions should be the goal.

Definitions of excellent work also need to be fair and unbiased. Criteria should be sensitive to instruction rather than to variables over which educators have no control, such as students' socioeconomic background, culture, or gender. For example, although teachers may legitimately craft criteria so as to reward students who put care into their work, they will want to be careful not to be unfairly swayed by slickness of presentation or other variables that may reflect students' affluence and their access to computers, art supplies, and other resources.

Should the Scoring Be Holistic or Analytic? A holistic scoring rubric requires teachers or other raters to give a single overall score to students' performance, whereas an analytic rubric asks for separate ratings on different aspects of performance. Many rubrics and scoring procedures entail some hybrid of holistic and analytic judgments. The Writing What You Read rubric for narrative portfolios, for example, contains one holistic scale for overall narrative effectiveness and five analytic subscales for the ways that the writer has handled theme, character, setting, plot, and communication (uses of language) in the narrative (Gearhart, Herman, Novak, Wolf, & Abedi, 1994; Wolf & Gearhart, 1993).

Kentucky has developed a holistic approach for the scoring of writing portfolios supplemented with special commendations and recommendations framed in reference to the specific criteria that are encompassed within the holistic judgments: Raters note distinctive qualities of writing such as the sense of purpose, idea development, organization, sentence structure, wording, and grammar errors, but the central judgment is a holistic placement of the students' portfolio writing at the novice, apprentice, proficient, or distinguished levels (Reidy, 1992; Saylor & Overton, 1993).

The purpose of a portfolio assessment as well as practical needs and constraints surrounding its use will shape decisions about what type of scoring rubric to use. Classroom teachers in middle and high schools, for example, may have limited time in which to review and conference with or grade portfolios for their 150 or more students, making holistic or at least simple diagnostic schemes attractive. Holistic schemes do take less time to apply than analytic schemes, and they may be favored where large numbers of portfolios need to be scored and where small differences in time per portfolio can translate into sizable financial savings, particularly with district or state level portfolio assessment systems.

For classroom use of portfolios, however, providing feedback to improve learning is usually the priority, so the results of an analytic scoring may be more useful than a holistic score. Analytic scores directly and explicitly communicate to teachers, parents, and students the salient aspects of desired performance, even though technical studies of many analytic schemes have indicated that students' performance does not generally vary substantially across dimensions (Gearhart, Herman, Baker, & Whittaker, 1992; Wolf & Gearhart, 1994). For example, in several CRESST studies (Gearhart et al., 1992; Gearhart & Wolf, 1994; Wolf & Gearhart, 1993) that utilized the same holistic/analytic rubric for elementary level narrative writing, scores for focus/organization, style, and mechanics were all highly correlated with a holistic general competence judgment; writing that was judged to be competent was generally judged to be well-organized, engaging in style, and mechanically sound. We have argued, however, that statistical results like these may not be relevant if the goal of the assessment is to enhance teachers' and students' understandings of quality performance.

How Can We Define and Communicate Different Levels of Performance? Whether a scoring rubric is based on a single holistic scale or a set of analytic scales, each scale needs to delineate some sort of continuum of quality, and to define markers along that continuum. Rubrics are typically built on views about the best ways to conceptualize and to track students' progress toward quality performance. Although many rubrics view progress in terms of developmental levels (such as Kentucky's ratings of "novice," "apprentice," "proficient," and "expert"), other rubrics, such as those in Vermont's portfolio project, ask raters to note the frequency of desirable features of performance (Abruscato, 1993; Hewitt, 1991, 1993; Mills, 1989; Mills & Brewer, 1988; Stecher & Hamilton, 1994; Vermont Department of Education, 1990, 1991a, 1991b, 1991c, 1991d). CRESST's rubric for scoring students' explanation of content area understanding includes a count of the principles and concepts the students use in their explanations (Baker, Aschbacher, Niemi, & Sato, 1992). This scale was based on empirical evidence that experts in a content area differ from novices in the number of principles and concepts they understand and can integrate into a written explanation. The rubrics piloted by the New Standards Project represent another alternative, a rubric designed to capture the student's need for additional instruction (Learning Research and Development Center, 1991, 1992).

The points along a continuum or scale may be represented by qualitative descriptions and/or numbers or grades. The choice between descriptive or numerical scale is largely one of style and of belief about what implicit messages numbers versus descriptive adjectives send to students, parents, and teachers.

Numerical data, for example, encourages us to deal quantitatively with the data, using descriptive statistics such as average scores to summarize results, compare groups, or compare scores across scales. This is simple and convenient, but it may lead to inappropriate inferences because scale points typically represent ordinal categories of response rather than true integer values. For example, it may be clear that a 4 is better than a 2, but it is probably not literally twice as good; also, depending on how the scales were developed, a 3 on one scale (such as "organization") may not represent performance of equal achievement or progress to a 3 on a different scale (such as "understanding of narrative"). Thus, it is important to be careful how numerical scores are defined and manipulated and what inferences are drawn.

Beyond this concern, some people worry that using numbers distorts the message we want to send back to students, parents, and the community: that complex performance cannot be captured by simple numbers, and that the results of an assessment need to communicate the meaning of those results and provide guideposts for how to improve. It is this last point that is essential. Regardless of whether scale values are numerical, descriptive, or both, it is important to make sure that scales help parents, students, teachers, administrators, and policymakers understand the meaning of the performance in the same way. This common understanding helps assure reliable and fair judgment and sound use of results.

To reach a common understanding, each value on the continuum should be operationally defined in terms of student performance. What are the characteristics of a portfolio that is scored as "developing" as opposed to "exemplary"? What are the attributes of a portfolio that should be assigned a score of 4 on a 6-point scale as opposed to a 3? In addition to defining relevant characteristics and attributes of responses at each scale value, benchmark examples of students' work corresponding to each level help to reinforce the meaning of scores. Teachers, students, and parents may all benefit from reviewing selected portfolios from past classes to get a better sense of the many paths of learning and many ways to show evidence of achievement and growth.

Providing benchmark work for portfolio assessment at the district or state level can be a very complex task. Are the criteria to be applied to the individual pieces or the body of work as a whole? In the Vermont state assessment system, the portfolio rubrics are the basis for scoring each piece, and therefore the scoring manuals can illustrate the criteria with separate pieces of work. Manuals should also explain the ways that the resulting piece scores are aggregated for a total portfolio score. Methods of aggregation may be controversial: Is each piece equally weighted or are some pieces more important than others? In Vermont, this question has been answered differently by outsider evaluators (Koretz, McCaffrey, Klein, Bell, & Stecher, 1993; Koretz, Stecher, Klein, McCaffrey, & Deibert, 1993; Koretz et al., 1995) and by the state (Vermont Department of Education, 1990, 1991a, 1991b, 1991c, 1991d). But if the rubric is for judging the entire portfolio collection as a body, guidelines should provide potential users of the criteria with benchmark portfolios. Although the selection and discussion of sample portfolios that illustrate the criteria is routine practice in large-scale assessment, examples are not typically provided in teachers' guides. Inclusion of sample portfolios in guidebooks to be widely disseminated may seem costly, but may be quite helpful.

How Many Scale Points Should There Be? Whether markers are descriptive or numerical, there tends to be an inverse relationship between ease of achieving consistent scoring and level of differentiation in students' portfolios. For example, it is usually easier for scorers to agree when there are only four points on a scale than when there are six or eight points, because it is easier to agree on the difference between "good" and "excellent" than between "good," "very good," and "excellent." On the other hand, classifying students into only three or four categories may fail to reveal important differences between levels of student work or progress over time. Furthermore, a small number of scale values may preclude the rubric's inclusion of a level that specifies very high standards—a "beyond expectations" category that can inspire the highest possible accomplishment.

What About Grading? Classroom teachers often find it useful to tie their portfolio scoring directly to the course grades they must assign. In this case, they may want to use a scale or set of scales that translate easily to the range of grades used in their local system. For many, this means a 5-point A–F scale; for others, it may mean a 3- or 4-point "needs improvement" to "excellent" scale. The weight of a portfolio in assigning end-of-term or course grades will vary considerably from classroom to classroom as well, depending on what portion of the course goals the portfolio is expected to represent. In some high school English courses the portfolio represents 100% of the course grade; in many other classrooms it contributes considerably less to the final grade. Some teachers do not weigh portfolio grades heavily during the first year because they are learning to use them in their classrooms and do not want to be unfair to students. On the other hand, portfolios that do not contribute at all to a course grade may not be taken seriously by students. To enhance self-reflection and efficacy goals, many teachers have students grade their own portfolios in addition to receiving a grade from the teacher.

Who Should Design the Criteria? Who should be involved in the development, review, and application of criteria? Teachers need to play a significant role in designing or adapting rubrics because it is they who need to be able to implement the rubrics and use the results to guide instructional and grading decisions. They are often glad for models or help from others with greater assessment expertise and resources at nearby universities or local or state education agencies. As mentioned earlier, it is important that those who design criteria collectively have adequate expertise in each of the areas being assessed to do a judicious job.

Whether the portfolio assessment is for classroom or large-scale purposes, involving students in developing or refining the criteria can help the students establish standards for themselves, bolster their efficacy and their evaluation skills, and enable them to understand deeply the meaning of quality performance. Teachers at the same elementary grade, secondary teachers within a department, or teachers within an interdisciplinary team may want to collaborate to design contents and criteria for their classroom portfolios.

If the portfolio assessment is being used for large-scale assessment, such as the district or state level, it is very important that parents and the public also view the criteria as credible and meaningful. Their input may be obtained through focus groups or committees. Even for classroom portfolios, teachers may want to consider typical parent concerns when designing and interpreting criteria and linking them to grading practices.

When Are the Criteria Ready for Use? The process of criteria development is highly iterative. Well-formulated criteria rarely spring easily to form; instead, developing them is a matter of starting with good ideas about what quality in a discipline means, collecting models from others who have developed portfolio rubrics for similar purposes, and then seeing how these ideas apply to actual examples of student and expert work. Which of the models and characteristics can best differentiate different levels of quality in students' work? An initial set of descriptors is then written to reflect salient and meaningful characteristics of performance, and these are tried out with additional samples of students' portfolios until scores appear to capture important levels in the quality of students' portfolio work. Many teachers continue to develop and hone their classroom rubrics over a number of years.

Applying Criteria Consistently:
Fairly Assessing Students' Work

Although assessing portfolios necessarily involves human judgment, the assessment should not be subjective in the sense of conditioned by personal mental characteristics or states and certainly not capricious in the sense that the judgment is likely to vary depending on who is doing the judging, when the judgment is being done, or in what order it is being done. Portfolio assessment needs to minimize such variation. Instead, two teachers or scorers looking at the same portfolio should come to similar judgments about the quality of a student's performance, and that judgment should be similar whether a given student's portfolio is scored at the beginning, middle, or end of a scoring session, or even, for large-scale assessment purposes where the scoring scheme is the same from one year to next, whether that portfolio is scored by this year's raters or scored again by next year's. Fairness and validity demand consistency: A student's score should reflect performance, not scoring irregularities or idiosyncrasies. These issues are particularly important for large scale assessment purposes where large numbers of raters and high stakes may be involved, but even for classroom assessment, teachers will want to assure that they are using a consistent standard to assess students' performance and that their assessments are not based on the vagaries of time or mood. Sound scoring procedures help to assure such consistency.

Clear Criteria. Being clear on criteria is an indispensable first step, not only to being consistent and fair in scoring or grading but in assuring that everyone understands what is expected. In large-scale assessment, a thorough scoring guide that defines the meaning of each score point and provides samples of work exemplifying each value benefits classroom practice and is crucial for training raters to achieve consistency. Training on the meaning of the criteria and how to apply them is a process that requires extensive opportunities to practice and receive feedback on the use of the criteria.

Checks for Consistency Along the Way. In addition to building consensus among scorers about the meaning of criteria and how they are to be applied, a sound scoring process also includes a system for monitoring consistency of scoring. In the large scale context, evidence is collected regarding whether two or more scorers judge the same portfolio in the same way; a single scorer scores the same portfolio similarly, regardless of whether that portfolio is scored earlier or later in the scoring period; the same judge rates a portfolio similarly on different occasions; and a portfolio scored on two separate occasions by two different groups of scorers receives similar scores on both occasions. Although portfolios for classroom purposes do not demand evidence on all these facets, classroom teachers may well want to check their consistency by asking a colleague to score a sample of portfolios, or rerating some portfolios scored early in the scoring process to assure that standards have not shifted.

Assuring Validity: Is the Portfolio Assessment Serving Intended Purposes?

Validity is the term the measurement community uses to describe the quality of an assessment. A valid assessment is one that contributes to good decisions by providing accurate information for specific decision purposes. A valid assessment measures what it is intended to measure, permits accurate and fair conclusions about students' performance, and therefore is a sound basis for particular decision purposes—that is, if it is intended to measure a student's writing capability, the results of the assessment accurately characterize the student's writing ability.

Elementary statistics texts are quick to point out that reliability is a prerequisite to validity. And of course this is the case: An assessment that does not retain its meaning and yield consistent results in the face of superficial changes in the assessment situation cannot provide accurate information for decision making. If, for example, our assessment of a student's writing ability differs wildly between Monday and Tuesday, neither measure alone can be used to accurately characterize students' performance. If results are not consistent or stable, they cannot be valid, because they depend on something other than the underlying capability, which is the target of the assessment. This is one reason we worry so much about assuring consistency of scoring across scorers, time, and occasion, as described earlier.

But reliability is only a small first step toward validation. And validation is a continuing process of gathering evidence about the accuracy of information provided by an assessment and the appropriateness of the use of the information. The higher the stakes—the more important the consequences that ride on a student's performance on an assessment—the greater the need to gather and document evidence of validity formally. In contrast to large-scale assessment, portfolios in classroom assessment are usually one of a number of sources of information teachers have about students' performance, and only one of a number of indicators they use for grading and instructional planning. Thus, although classroom teachers should consider the following issues as they design and use portfolio assessment since they cannot undertake systematic documentation of validity, the following validity issues are treated in abbreviated form.

Do the Scores Adequately Represent What Students Have Learned?

The results of any assessment should tell us something about what students know and can do vis-à-vis the instructional goals we hold for them. What have students learned? Are they building intended capabilities and dispositions? Validity for the purposes of assessing student capabilities needs to be addressed from several different perspectives. First there is opportunity to learn: From a fairness perspective, whether for classroom assessment or program evaluation purposes, students should not be assessed on things they have not been taught. How can they do well on composing an Elizabethan sonnet if they have not had any experience with sonnets of this genre? Similarly, how can the quality of a school be judged on the basis of topics that were absent or given little emphasis? To make inferences about what students have learned relative to curriculum priorities, in short, the assessment must reflect those priorities. Thus, this first issue is basically one of match—do the portfolio and the portfolio assessment rubric reflect any of the important curriculum goals?

How fully the assessment represents the depth and breadth of curriculum priorities is a second arena of concern. How adequately have the domains of curriculum priorities been sampled? If Ms. Juarez asks her students to include only their narrative writing, her goals to foster growth in students' competence with persuasive writing would not be reflected in the portfolios. In this case, portfolio assessment does not reflect all of the important curriculum priorities. Although it is never possible to assess everything fully, coverage is an important issue in content validity. In examining whether there is an adequate match, consider questions such as the following:

- Does the content of the portfolio assessment represent your classroom priorities for curriculum and instruction, including an adequate range of content?
- Do the scoring criteria reflect your curriculum priorities and current understandings of the pathways students typically take in attaining these goals?
- Have students had an opportunity to learn the things that are assessed in the portfolio?

When you answer questions such as these in the affirmative, you have some evidence that your portfolio assessment will lead to accurate conclusions about how well your students have achieved your instructional goals and how effective your classroom instruction has been.

Are the Scores Valid for Making Generalizations About Students' Performance?   For most assessments, we are interested not so much in a student's specific performance as in what we think that performance represents. When we use writing portfolios for assessment purposes, for example, we want to (and too often take for granted that we can) generalize from the specific performance on the portfolio to some important writing capability. We want our assessments to represent enduring knowledge and skills, not transient performance that does not generalize to other situations.

This appears to be a problem area in alternative assessment, where student performance tends to vary from one assessment task to the next cross genres. More specifically, students who write good persuasive essays do not necessarily write good stories or literary critiques. Further, even within a genre, students' performance may vary substantially depending on the topic of the prompts.

How do we know whether the results from a student's assessment represent some larger, meaningful domain of performance? We gather evidence of generalizability by looking at the consistency of students' performance across tasks that are intended to assess the same knowledge, skills, and dispositions.

In the classroom, we can improve the validity of our inferences about students by using as many observations or work samples as possible before making general statements or drawing conclusions about a student's performance capability. Thus a portfolio could contain not just one or two examples of persuasive writing but several.

In the large-scale context where we have ratings of many portfolios by many raters, we can perform statistical analyses, calculating such things as generalizability coefficients to determine with what confidence we can generalize from a few pieces of work to how well a student can perform in a whole domain. Although the technical details of such analyses are well beyond the scope of this book, be aware that in high stakes settings involving mandated tests or portfolios, you would want to look for and demand such evidence.

Are the Scores Unbiased? Do They Fairly Represent the Learning and Accomplishments of All Students? Fairness and bias are critically important issues in any assessment. Students need adequate background knowledge to accomplish the tasks that are assessed in a portfolio. In the context of writing, for example, it is impossible to craft a good essay if you do not know anything relevant to the topic or if you have never written an expository essay. But students from diverse socioeconomic, cultural, and linguistic backgrounds may possess different kinds of prior knowledge and experience, and thus different assignments may favor the prior knowledge and experience of some students more than others. Do students have sufficient background knowledge to engage successfully in their portfolio tasks? Does the content or context of assignments unfairly advantage or disadvantage children from different cultural or language groups? Are assignments reasonably meaningful and motivating for all students? Do assignments contain culturally insensitive material or stereotyping? Answers to questions such as these provide evidence on the bias or fairness of portfolio assessments.

A variety of statistical analyses can be conducted to examine potential bias and are often used in large-scale assessment programs. Although such analyses are beyond the technical scope of this chapter and unnecessary for classroom portfolios, teachers and others need to be vigilant about the underlying issue: Does the assessment enable all students to demonstrate their ability, or does it unfairly advantage or disadvantage particular subgroups within the class? Problems of differences in background knowledge can be minimized if we are sure that all students have had ample opportunity in school to acquire the required knowledge and skills. Teachers must take care to assure that what is being measured has been taught and that their students have had the opportunity to learn relevant content and/or apply desired processes.

Is There Corroborating Evidence That the Portfolio Assessment Supports Accurate Decision Making? Demonstrating that a portfolio assessment is valid for a purpose requires data. For example, if the results of a statewide writing portfolio assessment will be used to identify strengths and weaknesses in a school's writing program, then the state testing program will need to gather evidence that the portfolio scores lead to the same decisions supported by other respected data, such as teachers', administrators', or an outside evaluator's opinions. Or, if we claim that a senior portfolio demonstrates a student's critical thinking and expressive abilities as well as mastery of certain content, we need independent, corroborating evidence (such as test scores, grades, or teacher opinions) that students who do well based on the portfolio have the assessed skills. Similarly, if we use the results of a portfolio assessment to determine who gets into Honors English, we need independent evidence of the relationship between the content of the portfolio assessment, course content, and subsequent course performance. Alternatively, we could see whether students admitted to Honors English based on their portfolio scores, in fact, did well in the course. Did students with higher portfolio scores tend to do better in the class than those with lower portfolio scores?

What About Consequences? Does the Portfolio Assessment Contribute to Meaningful Teaching and Learning? History teaches us that good intentions are not sufficient to assure beneficial results. We want to make sure that our new assessments help rather than hurt schools and the people within them. For mandated testing programs with high stakes, this means continuous attention to the actual effects of those programs and formal studies to evaluate the effects on curriculum, teaching, and student learning. For a teacher in the classroom, it means attention to the local effects of portfolios—to the ways that the portfolios call for complex, rich, and challenging uses of students' minds and to the values implied by the portfolio assessment, such as thoughtfulness, authorship, multiple perspectives, and respect for diversity.

WHAT IS THE STATUS OF CURRENT PRACTICE?

We have outlined a set of issues that need to be considered systematically in the design and use of sound portfolio assessments. We now turn to the question: to what extent does current practice mirror this ideal? In two words, the answer is not well. Current practice too often relies on borrowed ideas and models marked by uneven understanding of essential concepts of good assessment. That current portfolio assessment practice is in this state should come as no surprise. Measurement and assessment concepts are given little sustained attention in most teacher education programs, and professional development efforts rarely address critical issues in assessment development, interpretation, and use (Herman, 1994). Instead, staff development is likely to focus on how to administer, bundle, and handle the logistics of mandated testing and on the curriculum implications of results from mandated tests. In the absence of basic opportunities to learn, it is no wonder that educators frequently lack assessment literacy (Stiggins, 1991; Stiggins et al., 1992).

Focus on Activities, Not Learning

In the vision of assessment offered here is a clear focus on aims for students' learning: Whether those aims are more process- or more outcomes-oriented (e.g., engage in a thoughtful writing process vs. write convincingly; become independent learners vs. write an effective research report), teachers in our model are clear about what they want their students to be able to do. Yet in typical practice, research indicates that teachers may plan their curriculum around classroom activities and have difficulty articulating desired student learning goals (or outcomes) (Cohen, 1990; Cohen et al., 1990; Prawat, 1992). They are concerned with what they and students will do rather than what their students will know and be able to do. Aschbacher (1994), for example, described a case in which teachers participating in a portfolio development project perseverated on what interesting activities might be documented in their students' portfolios rather than what student learning or outcomes would be assessed. When pushed, these teachers could articulate goals in general categories, such as effort or use of important concepts and principles, but they reported feeling out of their depth when asked to define these learning goals more concretely to specify what students should know and be able to do.

The Challenge of Defining and Reaching Consensus on Outcomes

Whether among experts or practitioners, consensus on outcomes is not easy to achieve. There is a current debate in the language arts community, for example, concerning a "romantic" versus a "classical" approach to writing instruction: In the *romantic* view, students must write from their own questions and emotions in order to make their own meaning in the world; in the *classical* view, students are taught to analyze many kinds of writing as a grounding for their efforts to extend their range and flexibility as writers (Gearhart & Wolf, in press). These debates among experts have very different implications for the content of portfolio assessment.

Among practitioners, consensus on the "what" of an assessment requires subject area expertise and sophisticated understanding of content, and teachers do not often have the opportunity to develop such expertise (Aschbacher,

1994; Gearhart, Herman, Novak, Wolf, & Abedi, 1994). In one writing port-folio development project, for example, Gearhart, Herman, and Novak (in press) found that elementary school teachers had little understanding of genre, of the qualities of good writing, or the attributes of good writing instruction. Only with extensive capacity building focused just on the genres of narrative were they able to reach consensus on goals for students' narrative writing and methods for assessing students' progress toward these goals.

Apparent consensus in any context may break down when the dialogue moves from abstract, glittering generalities to the specifics of what students should know and be able to do. Everyone would agree that students need to be literate, but what does literacy really mean, and how would we use portfolio assessment to assess literacy? Aschbacher (1992) used portfolios to assess the implementation of a humanities program that stressed an inter-disciplinary, thematic approach to instruction. Her analysis found very dis-crepant views among teachers as to the meaning of interdisciplinary. A corollary to this observation was that classroom assignments frequently did not require students to employ the complex knowledge and skills which portfolio assessment is supposed to capture.

Difficulties Specifying Criteria
for Judging Student Work

If specifying student outcomes is difficult for practitioners, specifying criteria for judging students' work appears even more so. Aschbacher (1994) re-ported that at almost all of her study sites, educators appeared distinctly uncomfortable and reluctant to develop criteria and standards for assessing student progress and achievement. They simply had not had much experi-ence in doing this type of analytic thinking about fundamental student goals and the developmental sequence(s) by which those goals may be achieved by students. Nor are teachers uniformly up-to-date on the current concep-tions of excellence in the disciplines they teach, conceptions that should be central to criteria. Teachers in the Gearhart study mentioned earlier, for example, were at a loss in defining features of good writing beyond grammar, spelling, and sometimes imagination/creativity. Aschbacher (1994) recounted that even the rare teachers who were intensely reflective about complex student outcomes found it difficult to articulate formally their criteria for judging student portfolios and other work.

Compounding difficulties in articulating substantive criteria for students' performance are the conflicts teachers feel in grading their students. Teachers struggle to balance achievement, effort, talent, student background, and context, and seem hesitant to make their criteria explicit and public for fear of losing the ability to individualize their grading practices. However, in their struggles to be fair to individual students and to use grades for motivational purposes, teachers may not realize that they are not holding all students to the same standards.

Consistency of Scoring Is Difficult

Concerns about consistency of scoring have received the most empirical attention in large scale portfolio assessment programs rather than in classroom assessments. Results thus far have been uneven, as we illustrate with studies of three portfolio assessment programs.

• Results from Vermont's statewide portfolio assessment program, perhaps the most visible example in the country, have been less than stellar. Based on the second year of full implementation, Koretz, McCaffrey, Klein, Bell, and Stecher (1993) reported inter-rater reliabilities for writing portfolios of .56 and .63, at Grades 4 and 8, respectively, a trivial increase from the first year's scoring and insufficient to permit reporting many of the aggregate statistics the state had planned to use: Vermont could not accurately report the proportion of students in the state who achieved each point on the scoring dimensions, and they could not provide accurate data on the comparative performance of districts.

• On the other hand, Pittsburgh Public Schools' writing portfolio assessment program obtained high inter-rater agreement (LeMahieu, Gitomer, & Eresh, in press). Collected over a year following Arts PROPEL program and subsequent PUSD staff development, Pittsburgh portfolios required students to compose, revise, and reflect on their writing, and to select evidence of these processes for their portfolios. Portfolios contained at least six pieces selected to meet such general categories as a satisfying piece, an unsatisfying piece, an important piece, a free pick. Raters were asked to rate the portfolios on each of three dimensions: (a) accomplishment in writing; (b) use of process and resources; (c) and growth and engagement. Despite the amount of latitude raters had in selecting pieces to rate and the broad scope of the scoring criteria, inter-rater agreement correlations ranged from .60–.70, and the generalizability estimate of inter-rater agreement when two raters reviewed each piece was in the .80 range.

• In a third example, raters of elementary-level writing portfolios scored with high levels of inter-rater agreement (Novak, Herman, & Gearhart, in press; Herman, Gearhart, & Baker, 1993). Student portfolios contained final drafts of writing—mainly narrative with some expository writing (mostly summaries and descriptive pieces), poetry, and letters. Raters were recruited from a district that has a long and strong history in analytic writing assessment. Using a rubric constructed from the same dimensions used in their district's writing assessment, raters gave each portfolio a holistic quality score. Average correlations between scores given by pairs of raters was .82, and percentage of absolute agreements for all pairs of raters averaged .98.

Although only illustrative, these three examples do demonstrate both the challenge and possibility of achieving high inter-rater reliability for scoring portfolios. The results suggest that reliability is probably easiest to achieve when one or more of the following are in place: the contents of portfolios are relatively uniform, there is a small number of highly trained raters, experienced scorers use well-honed rubrics, criteria are clearly articulated and illustrated with samples of student work, and the community of practitioners and scorers share experience and values that have evolved over time through close collaboration.

Validity and Meaning of Scores Are Perplexing

The validity of portfolio assessments has been little studied, and the scant evidence that does exist raises more questions than answers. In Vermont, for example, Koretz, Stecher, Klein, McCaffrey, and Deibert (1993) looked at the relationships between portfolio assessments and standard, on-demand assessments in language arts and mathematics, expecting to find at least moderate relationships between portfolio and on-demand assessments within each subject area and little or no relationship between scores across subjects. Although the correlations between writing portfolios and the writing uniform test seemed reasonable, the correlations between subjects were not: After taking differences in reliability into account, mathematics portfolio scores showed about the same relationship to the uniform test in writing as to the uniform test in mathematics. Similarly, Herman, Gearhart, and Baker (1993) found virtually no relationship between scores for writing portfolios and for standard writing assessments: Two thirds of the students who would have been classified as competent based on the portfolio assessment score would not have been so classified on the basis of the standard assessment. Thus it was not the case that a student classified as a capable writer on the basis of the portfolio would necessarily do well when given a standard writing prompt. Furthermore, students classified as capable on the basis of an overall quality score were not always so classified when each piece in the portfolio was scored separately. Thus, which assessment best represents students' skills? Does one context overestimate or another underestimate students' skills? These questions are open to debate.

A Dilemma of Validity and Fairness: Whose Work Is It?

One reason for thinking that portfolios may overestimate individual performance for some students comes from portfolios' very strengths: They are integrated with instruction, and, in good classroom instruction, students often get support in planning, drafting, and revising their writing. Consider what is regarded as exemplary instructional practice. Central to the National Writing Project, for example, is a core instructional model that features multiple stages—prewriting, precomposing, writing, sharing, revising, editing, and evaluation. Each of these stages stands for instructional activities that engage a student with resources and with others—related readings, classroom discussions, field trips, idea webs, small group collaboration, outlining, peer review, review, and feedback. The socially contexted character of student writing is seen both as a scaffold for students' writing process and as a replication of what real writing entails, in that writing is often a very social endeavor. Consider as well what is regarded as exemplary portfolio assessment practice. A "portfolio culture" is viewed as "replacing . . . the entire envelope of assessment . . . with extended, iterative processes, agreeing that we are interested in what students produce when they are given access to models, criticism, and the option to revise" (Wolf, 1993, p. 221). Assessment opportunities are available at multiple classroom moments—in the course of the work that may be added to a portfolio, in the construction of the portfolio, and in a presentation of the portfolio. Thus collaboration, assessment, and revision are continual processes within the classroom.

These visions of an engaged community of learners and reviewers have implications for the validity of classroom portfolios for large-scale assessment purposes. The more developed the community, the more engaged others will be in the work tagged with an individual student's name. Although the locus of authorship may shift outward from the individual student to the community of writers, the shift is unlikely to be systematic. Others' contributions to students' work are likely to vary across assignments, students, and classrooms. An irony emerges that when the student's work is more his or her own, that work may index practices and curriculum that lack certain key features of current reforms.

How is a teacher—or even worse, a rater unfamiliar with a student or the classroom context—to assign an individual student a score for a portfolio collection that includes assisted or collaborative work? Let us consider three related dilemmas posed by the assessment of writing composed with varying, uncertain, and often undocumented contributions from others.

First, does support from teachers, peers, parents, or others make an individual student's work appear better when it is assessed? If our goal is to assess what individual students know and can do, what does portfolio work produced with unknown assistance really tell us? This question may be somewhat less of an issue when portfolios are used for classroom purposes. Teachers, after all, have many indicators of student capability and are intimately aware of the conditions under which work is produced at school. They are less certain of what help may be provided at home by parents or siblings. In large-scale assessment settings, the problem of whose work becomes even more important.

Second, if some students get more help and support than others with their work, are some students then unfairly advantaged and some unfairly disadvantaged by the assessment? There is an important fairness issue here. In a study by Gearhart, Herman, Baker, and Whittaker (1993), elementary teachers reported providing their students different amounts of support; there were variations within classrooms as well as differences across the classrooms participating in the study. Inequities may also emerge when classwork merges with homework. Although the student writer may benefit from efforts to widen his community of readers, the amount and kind of help he can get from parents, other family members, and friends will vary from home to home in ways that become an additional threat to comparisons of the student's writing competence to others.

Third, there are some writings in a portfolio that may be explicitly collaborative. How is a rater to judge a student's competence on the basis of collaborative work? Webb (1993) found substantial differences in students' performance when judged on the basis of cooperative group work compared to that done individually. Not too surprisingly, low-ability students had higher scores on the basis of group work than individual work, and indeed an important rationale for group work is that groups may be able to come up with better solutions than individuals working alone, providing more students with better and more equitable opportunities to learn. But group learning opportunities may not translate well into assessment opportunities: A group product may not help us assess the capabilities of individual members.

Does Portfolio Assessment Impact Teaching?

Despite the obvious challenges of portfolio design and use in the classroom, early implementation results show that the enterprise does have value in instructional reform. Aschbacher's (1994) action research, for instance, showed that teachers' involvement in the development and implementation of alternative assessments had diverse, positive influences on teaching practices, at least when combined with training and follow-up technical support:

- Two thirds of the teachers reported substantial change in the ways they thought about their own teaching. As two teachers explain,

  "I have begun to look at teaching from a different vantage point. I can see more possibilities" (p. 20).

  "The portfolios seem to mirror not only the students' work but the teacher's as well. As a result, I have found the need to rework, reorganize, and reassess my teaching strategies" (p. 22).

- Two thirds reported at least some increase in their expectations for students—more thinking and problem solving and/or higher levels of performance from students.

- For the majority, the experience of working with alternative assessments reinforced the importance of purpose or goals.

These findings mirror those in portfolio projects in California and Vermont. Sheingold, Heller, and Paulukonis (in press), for example, provide evidence that teachers' pilot participation in the California Learning Assessment System portfolio assessment program impacted classroom practice in five ways. Based on self-report data, teachers appeared to be seeking new sources of evidence for assessment, sharing greater responsibility with students for learning and assessment, changing the goals of instruction to mesh with the California state frameworks, using new ways of evaluating evidence, and reconceptualizing their views of the relationships between assessment and instruction.

Benefits Carry Costs

Although the literature is promising with regard to the potential positive effects of portfolios on curriculum and instruction, it also indicates the substantial time and challenges portfolio implementation entails. For example, a majority of principals interviewed in Vermont believed that portfolio assessment generally had salutary effects on their schools in terms of curriculum, instruction, and/or effects on student learning and attitudes, but almost 90% of these same principals characterized the program as burdensome, particularly from the perspective of its demands on teachers (Koretz, Stecher, Klein, McCaffrey, & Deibert, 1993). Nearly every project, in fact, reports the intense and pervasive demands on teachers' time (Aschbacher, 1993; Koretz, Stecher, Klein, McCaffrey, & Deibert, 1993; Wolf et al., 1993, 1994): time for teachers to learn new assessment practices, to understand what should be included in portfolios and how to help students compile them, to develop portfolio tasks, to discern and apply criteria for assessing students' work, to reflect on and fine-tune their instructional and assessment practices, and to work out and manage the logistics. The Vermont study, for example, asking about only some of these demands, found that teachers devoted 17 hours a month to finding portfolio tasks, preparing portfolio lessons, and evaluating the contents of portfolios; and 60% of the teachers surveyed who taught fourth and eighth grades indicated they often lacked sufficient time to develop portfolio lessons (Koretz, Stecher, Klein, McCaffrey, & Deibert, 1993).

IMPLICATIONS FOR POLICY AND PRACTICE

Good portfolio assessment goes hand in hand with sound curriculum and sensitive instruction. Assessment needs to be coordinated with learning; the same conceptions of quality and the same expectations need to permeate both. But existing research suggests that at this point the match is imperfect in most settings. That the teachers of Vermont, for example, need to spend so much time finding or devising portfolio tasks indicates that the understandings and skills that Vermont portfolios are supposed to assess are new to the curriculum and instruction of many teachers. Thus the challenge of portfolio assessment is not simply to collect and assess classroom work according to a sensible design; the challenge is to transform all aspects of classroom work, so that students have the opportunities to develop and demonstrate deep understanding of content knowledge and complex problem-solving and communicative skills.

What is required is a paradigmatic shift not only in assessment but in teaching. We earlier noted the lack of attention to measurement and assessment issues in teachers' professional development. Teachers' knowledge gap in this area is apparent, and steps must be taken and investments made at pre-service and in-service levels to remedy the situation. However, assessment expertise is only part of the challenge, and a small part at that. Teachers are being asked to engage students in new kinds of work, calling for deeper levels of cognitive involvement, rich content, and thorough disciplinary understandings. Teachers also are being asked to employ different instructional strategies—such as cooperative group work, extended assignments, discussion of portfolios, student self-reflection—and to engage in different instructional roles—monitoring, coaching, and facilitating students' performances. We have to understand how hard this is.

Reflecting on the Arts PROPEL experience, Roberta Camp (1993) noted:

> The portfolio is far more than a procedure for gathering samples of student writing. Portfolio reflection has changed the climate of the classroom and the nature of teacher–student interactions. Reflection has become part of an approach to learning in which instruction and assessment are thoroughly integrated. Assessment is no longer an enterprise that takes place outside the classroom; it is one in which teachers and students are actively engaged on a recurring basis as they articulate and apply criteria to their own and one another's writing. (p. 205)

To engage students in such sophisticated assessment practices, teachers themselves need sophisticated and deep understanding of the content, principles, and ways of knowing in their discipline(s). Yet, even in the area of writing, which has the longest history of reform effort, many teachers lack the required base of understanding about the nature of high-quality writing and how best to facilitate it. The implications for pre-service and in-service education as well as for undergraduate education in the disciplines are clear.

Yes, there are substantial challenges ahead if portfolio assessment is to validate the claims made for it and to achieve its many promises. Required are substantial investments in professional development—at the in-service level for the existing cadre and at the pre-service level. Teachers need opportunities to build their assessment knowledge, enrich their content knowledge, and refine and hone their pedagogical skills. They need the opportunity to learn, to have guided practice, and to receive thoughtful follow-up. Educators need to feel ownership of these new assessments and to have available sustained technical assistance. Required also are a school climate and leadership that invite and support risk-taking, change; and time to plan, engage in, and reflect on new practices. Although the effort and costs are considerable, the potential benefits of portfolio assessment for both teaching and learning, according to available evidence, are substantial.

REFERENCES

Abruscato, J. (1993). Early results and tentative implications from the Vermont Portfolio Project. *Phi Delta Kappan, 74*(6), 474–477.

Airasian, P. (1991). *Classroom assessment.* New York: McGraw-Hill.

Aschbacher, P. R. (1992). *Humanitas: A synthesis of four years of evaluation findings, final report.* Los Angeles: University of California, Center for the Study of Evaluation.

Aschbacher, P. R. (1993). *Issues in innovative assessment for classroom practice: Barriers and facilitators* (Tech. Rep. No. 359). Los Angeles: University of California, Center for Research on Evaluation, Standards, and Student Testing (CRESST).

Aschbacher, P. R. (1994, June). Helping educators to develop and use alternative assessments: Barriers and facilitators. *Educational Policy, 8*(2), 202–223.

Baker, E. L., Aschbacher, P. R., Niemi, D., & Sato, E. (1992). *CRESST performance assessment models: Assessing content area explanations.* Los Angeles: University of California, Center for Research on Evaluation, Standards, and Student Testing (CRESST).

Calfee, R. C., & Perfumo, P. A. (1992). *A survey of portfolio practices.* Berkeley: University of California, Center for the Study of Writing.

Calfee, R. C., & Perfumo, P. (1993a). *Student portfolios and teacher logs: Blueprint for a revolution in assessment* (CSW Tech. Rep. TR-65). Berkeley, CA: University of California, Center for the Study of Writing.

Calfee, R. C., & Perfumo, P. (1993b). Student portfolios: Opportunities for a revolution in assessment. *Journal of Reading, 36,* 532–537.

Camp, R. (1993). The place of portfolios in our changing views of writing assessment. In R. E. Bennett & W. C. Ward (Eds.), *Construction versus choice in cognitive measurement: Issues in constructed response, performance testing, and portfolio assessment* (pp. 183–212). Hillsdale, NJ: Lawrence Erlbaum Associates.

Cohen, D. K. (1990). A revolution in one classroom: The case of Mrs. Oublier. *Educational Evaluation and Policy Analysis, 12*(3), 311–329.

Cohen, D. K., Peterson, P. L., Wilson, S., Ball, D., Putnam, R., Prawat, R., Heaton, R., Remillard, J., & Wiemers, N. (1990). *Effects of state-level reform of elementary school mathematics curriculum on classroom practice* (Research report 90–14). East Lansing, MI: The Center for the Learning and Teaching of Elementary Subjects.

Freedman, S. (1993). Linking large-scale testing and classroom portfolio assessments of student writing. *Educational Assessment, 1*(1), 27–52.

Gearhart, M., Herman, J. L., Baker, E. L., & Whittaker, A. K. (1992). *Writing portfolios at the elementary level: A study of methods for writing assessment* (Tech. Rep. No. 337). Los

Angeles: University of California, Center for Research on Evaluation, Standards, and Student Testing (CRESST).

Gearhart, M., Herman, J. L., Baker, E. L., & Whittaker, A. (1993). *Whose work is it? A question for the validity of large-scale portfolio assessment* (Tech. Rep. No. 363). Los Angeles: University of California, Center for Research on Evaluation, Standards, and Student Testing (CRESST).

Gearhart, M., Herman, J. L., Novak, J. R., Wolf, S. A., & Abedi, J. (1994). *Toward the instructional utility of large-scale writing assessment: Validation of a new narrative rubric* (CSE Tech. Rep. 389). Los Angeles: University of California, Center for Research on Evaluation, Standards, and Student Testing (CRESST).

Gearhart, M., & Wolf, S. A. (in press). *The student's role in large-scale portfolio assessment: Providing evidence of writing competency. Part I: The purposes and processes of writing* (CSE Tech. Rep.). Los Angeles: University of California, Center for Research on Evaluation, Standards, and Student Testing (CRESST).

Gearhart, M., Wolf, S. A., Burkey, B., & Whittaker, A. (1994). *Engaging teachers in assessment of their students' narrative writing: Impact on teachers; knowledge and practice* (Tech. Rep. No. 377). Los Angeles: University of California, Center for Research on Evaluation, Standards, and Student Testing (CRESST).

Gitomer, D. H. (1993). Performance assessment and educational measurement. In R. E. Bennett & W. C. Ward (Eds.), *Construction versus choice in cognitive measurement* (pp. 241–263). Hillsdale, NJ: Lawrence Erlbaum Associates.

Herman, J. L. (1994, April). Portfolio assessment: Making the links to improve instruction and learning. In P. Perfumo & R. Calfee (chairs), *Evaluating writing through portfolios: The state of the art* (conference/symposium), Stanford, CA.

Herman, J. L., & Winters, L. (1994). Portfolio research: A slim collection. *Educational Leadership, 52*(2), 48–55.

Herman, J. L., Aschbacher, P. R., & Winters, L. (1992). *A practical guide to alternative assessment.* Alexandria, VA: Association for Supervision and Curriculum Development (ASCD).

Herman, J. L., Gearhart, M., & Baker, E. L. (1993, Summer). Assessing writing portfolios: Issues in the validity and meaning of scores. *Educational Assessment, 1*(3), 201–224.

Hewitt, G. (1991). Leading and learning: A portfolio of change in Vermont schools (Tech. Rep.). Vermont: Governor's Institutes.

Hewitt, G. (1993, May–June). Vermont's portfolio-based writing assessment program: A brief history. *Teachers and Writers, 24*(5), 1–6.

Howard, K. (1990). Making the writing portfolio real. *The Quarterly of the National Writing Project and the Center for the Study of Writing, 12*(2), 4–7, 27.

Koretz, D. (1992). *The Vermont portfolio assessment program: Interim report on implementation and impact, 1991–92 school year* (Tech. Rep. No. 350). Los Angeles: University of California, Center for the Study of Evaluation.

Koretz, D. (1993). *Interim report: The reliability of the Vermont portfolio scores in the 1992–93 school year* (CSE Tech. Rep. No. 370). Los Angeles: University of California, Center for the Study of Evaluation.

Koretz, D., McCaffrey, D., Klein, S., Bell, R., & Stecher, B. (1993). *The reliability of scores from the 1992 Vermont Portfolio Assessment Program* (CSE Tech. Rep. No. 355). Los Angeles: University of California, Center for Research on Evaluation, Standards, and Student Testing (CRESST).

Koretz, D., Stecher, B., Klein, S., & McCaffrey, D. (1995). The Vermont Portfolio Assessment Program: Findings and implications. *Educational Measurement: Issues and Practice, 13*(3), 3–16.

Koretz, D., Stecher, B., Klein, S., McCaffrey, D., & Deibert, E. (1993). *Can portfolios assess student performance and influence instruction? The 1991–92 Vermont experience* (CSE

Tech. Rep. No. 371). Los Angeles: University of California, Center for Research on Evaluation, Standards, and Student Testing (CRESST).

Learning Research and Development Center. (1991). *The New Standards Project: An overview*. University of Pittsburgh, National Center on Education and the Economy, Author.

Learning Research and Development Center. (1992). *The New Standards Project, 1992–1995: A proposal*. Pittsburgh, PA: University of Pittsburgh: Author.

LeMahieu, P. G., & Eresh, J. T. (in press). Comprehensiveness, coherence and capacity in school district assessment systems. *Annual Yearbook of the National Society for the Study of Education*.

LeMahieu, P. G., Gitomer, D. H., & Eresh, J. T. (1995). Portfolios in large-scale assessment: Difficult but not impossible. *Educational Measurement: Issues and Practice, 14*(3), 11–16, 25–28.

Mills, R. P. (1989, December). Portfolios capture a rich array of student performance. *The School Administrator*, pp. 8–11.

Mills, R. P., & Brewer, W. R. (1988). *Working together to show results: An approach to school accountability in Vermont*. Montpelier: Vermont Department of Education.

Novak, J. R., Herman, J. L., & Gearhart, M. (in press). Providing evidence of validity for performance-based assessments: An illustration for collections of student writing. *Journal of Educational Research*.

Prawat, R. S. (1992). Teachers' beliefs about teaching and learning: A constructivist's perspective. *American Journal of Education, 100*(3), 354–395.

Reidy, E. (1992, June). *What does a realistic state assessment program look like in the near term?* Paper presented at the annual ECS/CDE meeting, Boulder, CO.

Saylor, K., & Overton, J. (1993, March). *Kentucky writing and math portfolios*. Paper presented at the National Conference on Creating the Quality School, Washington, DC.

Sheingold, K., Heller, J., & Paulukonis, S. (in press). *Actively seeking evidence: Shifts in teachers' thinking and practice through assessment development* (Tech. Rep.). Princeton, NJ: Center for Performance Assessment, Educational Testing Service.

Stecher, B. M., & Hamilton, E. G. (1994, April). *Portfolio assessment in Vermont, 1992–93: The teachers' perspective on implementation and impact*. Paper presented at the annual meeting of the American Educational Research Association, New Orleans, LA.

Stiggins, R. J. (1991). Relevant classroom assessment training for teachers. *Educational Measurement: Issues and Practice, 10*(1), 7–12.

Stiggins, R. J., Sullivan, P., Aschbacher, P. R., Anderson, E., Flaming, N., Loughron, S., & Van Scoyk, S. (1992, June). *Assessment literacy: The foundation of sound assessment policy and practice*. Paper presented to the ECS/CDE Assessment Conference, Boulder, CO.

Vermont Department of Education. (1990, September). *Vermont writing assessment: The pilot year*. Montpelier, VT: Author.

Vermont Department of Education. (1991a). *"This is my best": Vermont's writing assessment program, pilot year 1990–1991*. Montpelier, VT: Author.

Vermont Department of Education. (1991b). *Looking beyond "the answer": The report of Vermont's mathematics portfolio assessment program*. Montpelier, VT: Author.

Vermont Department of Education. (1991c). *Vermont mathematics portfolio project: Resource book*. Montpelier, VT: Author.

Vermont Department of Education. (1991d). *Vermont mathematics portfolio project: Teacher's guide*. Montpelier, VT: Author.

Webb, N. (1993). Collaborative group versus individual assessment in mathematics: Group processes and outcomes. *Educational Assessment, 1*, 131–152.

Wolf, D. P. (1989). Portfolio assessment: Sampling student work. *Educational Leadership, 46*, 35–39.

Wolf, D. P. (1993). Assessment as an episode of learning. In R. Bennett & W. Ward (Eds.), *Construction versus choice in cognitive measurement* (pp. 213–240). Hillsdale, NJ: Lawrence Erlbaum Associates.

Wolf, D. P., Bixby, J., Glenn, J., & Gardner, H. (1991). To use their minds well: Investigating new forms of student assessment. In G. Grant (Ed.), *Review of Research in Education* (Vol. 17, pp. 31–74). Washington, DC: American Educational Research Association.

Wolf, D. P., LeMahieu, P. G., & Eresh, J. T. (1992). Good measure: Assessment in service to education. *Educational Leadership, 49*(8), 8–13.

Wolf, S. A., & Gearhart, M. (1994). Writing what you read: Narrative assessment as a learning event. *Language Arts, 71,* 425–444.

Wolf, S. A., & Gearhart, M. (1993). *Writing what you read: A guidebook for the assessment of children's narratives* (Tech. Rep. No. 358). Los Angeles: University of California, Center for Research on Evaluation, Standards, and Student Testing; Center for the Study of Evaluation.

PART TWO

GUIDEPOSTS FROM RESEARCH

CHAPTER THREE

A National Survey
of Writing Portfolio Practice:
What We Learned and What It Means

Robert C. Calfee
Stanford University

Pamela Perfumo
University of California, Berkeley

Alternative assessment of student achievement has arrived on the scene during the past decade as a paradigm shift, a fundamental change from earlier reliance on standardized testing techniques (Wiggins, 1993; Wolf, Bixby, Glenn, & Gardner, 1991). Several features distinguish the new alternatives (Calfee, 1992, 1995): production rather than recognition, projects rather than items, and teacher judgment rather than mechanical scoring.

Theory seems far in advance of practice. Teachers are reportedly doing portfolios, reviewing student projects, encouraging exhibitions (Harp, 1991; Murphy & Smith, 1991; Smith, 1991; Tierney, Carter, & Desai, 1991). Psychometricians seem uneasy about these developments, uncertain about how to standardize performance, and concerned about reliability and validity (e.g., Hambleton & Murphy, in press).

This chapter reviews the concept of alternative assessment in a specific situation: teacher assessment of student achievement in the literate use of language in the elementary grades. This domain is interesting as a test case. On the one hand, elementary reading achievement is a centerpiece of the psychometric enterprise; standardized tests are more common in elementary reading and language than any other area of school achievement. Writing achievement in the elementary grades has been less consequential; standardized writing tests do not typically appear until around eighth grade. On the other hand, portfolios and writing journals have found a welcome reception in the elementary grades, building on the tradition of informal assessment (Pikulski & Shanahan, 1982).

As a practical enterprise, the literacy portfolio comprises a folder containing situated samples of student reading and writing performance (Calfee & Hiebert, 1991; Valencia & Calfee, 1991). The student assembles a collection of materials during the school year: lists of books read, reading notes, rough drafts, conferencing memos, final drafts, and published versions. Some tasks are assigned, others are free-form. Some are substantial projects, others a page or less. Each individual assembles his or her own folder, although the contents may include collaborative projects.

The idea behind this activity is that portfolios provide an opportunity for richer, more authentic (i.e., more valid) assessment of student achievement; educators can get a clearer picture of what students can do when they have adequate time and resources. Although the portfolio concept has immediate appeal, questions arise equally quickly, for both researcher and practitioner: What should be included in the folder? What process should be used to evaluate the student's work? What standards should be used to decide on the adequacy of student work? What can the assessments be used for? Some educators have proposed that portfolios replace standardized tests altogether, but what if every teacher approaches the task with different processes and standards?

In this chapter, we first present preliminary findings from a survey of portfolio practice in selected elementary programs throughout the U.S. The survey, designed to answer the preceding questions, suggests that the portfolio movement is broad but thin at the level of teacher practice (the survey did not cover performance-based assessment practices in large-scale testing programs). The second part of the chapter presents a new concept, the Teacher Logbook, designed to support and effectuate the portfolio approach, and to connect portfolios to other facets of teacher professionalization.

THE STUDENT PORTFOLIO: PRESENT PRACTICE

According to articles in outlets like *Education Week* and *Educational Leadership*, regular classroom teachers are taking leadership in the portfolio movement. To be sure, a few states (e.g., Kentucky and Vermont) and a more substantial number of districts have discussed replacing test programs (in part or whole) with portfolios (e.g., Pelavin, 1991). But the movement appears to have the flavor of a revolution: teachers regaining control of assessment policy, tasks that require students to demonstrate what they have learned, "bottom up" rather than "top down" decisions. Under auspices of the Center for the Study of Writing (CSW), we conducted a nationwide survey of portfolio practice to find out what is happening at the level of classroom practice. The goal of the CSW survey was to move beyond headlines (and newsletter reports) to determine what educators mean when they say that they are "doing portfolios." The survey focused on writing assessment, but products often included reading assignments.

What We Found

The survey covered 150 nominated contacts, including states, districts, schools, school teams, and individual teachers. The survey was not random, but can be viewed as an effort to assess best practice. The survey employed a qualitative method, *webbing*, familiar to many elementary and middle-grade teachers. The respondent was instructed to work from a largely blank sheet of paper, which they used to brainstorm and cluster their ideas about student portfolios (see Fig. 3.1). To help the respondents (and to provide some degree of structure to the responses), we divided the survey into distinctive chunks: Background and history (how did you get into portfolios?); Portfolios in your classroom (what does the concept mean in practice?); Portfolio process (how do you do it?); and Portfolio impact (what do you see as the effect of portfolios for your students and for you?). A separate response sheet was provided for each category, along with several starter questions. The complete survey is shown in Table 3.1. The webbing methodology proved quite successful, from our perspective. Respondents provided exceptionally rich and informative data, often filling several pages with notes and reflections. Sixty-eight contacts responded with records that were analyzable.

We employed a complementary strategy for obtaining in-depth information from a group of 24 respondents selected to cover a range of perspectives from the 68 who had sent us materials in the first round. We convened a 2-day working conference for these respondents, during which working groups documented and analyzed their collective experience with the portfolio concept, including episodes from their own situations as well as reports from other projects about which they were knowledgeable. The group sessions were videotaped, and we analyzed the content of these sessions as well as graphic reports prepared by each group. In addition, each individual prepared a post-conference reflective essay, the final entry in the portfolio that each individual prepared before, during, and after the conference.

The data set from this survey comprises 68 complete packets of information. Two state-level projects are represented, along with several districts (about 10% of the sample) and a substantial number of total-school efforts (about 30%). The remainder (almost half) are singletons, individual teachers who had adopted the portfolio process on their own initiative with little support, often developing procedures from scratch. Packets from states and districts were generally quite polished; responses from schools and indi-

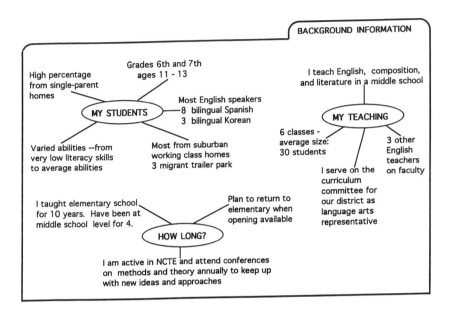

Grades 6th and 7th
ages 11 - 13

High percentage
from single-parent
homes

I teach English, composition,
and literature in a middle school

MY STUDENTS

Most English speakers
8 bilingual Spanish
3 bilingual Korean

MY TEACHING

6 classes -
average size:
30 students

3 other
English
teachers
on faculty

Varied abilities --from
very low literacy skills
to average abilities

Most from suburban
working class homes
3 migrant trailer park

I serve on the
curriculum
committee for
our district as
language arts
representative

I taught elementary school
for 10 years. Have been at
middle school level for 4.

Plan to return to
elementary when
opening available

HOW LONG?

I am active in NCTE and attend conferences
on methods and theory annually to keep up
with new ideas and approaches

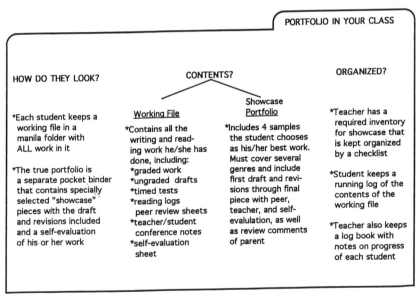

PORTFOLIO IN YOUR CLASS

HOW DO THEY LOOK?

CONTENTS?

ORGANIZED?

Working File

Showcase
Portfolio

*Each student keeps a
working file in a
manila folder with
ALL work in it

*Contains all the
writing and read-
ing work he/she has
done, including:
*graded work
*ungraded drafts
*timed tests
*reading logs
  peer review sheets
*teacher/student
  conference notes
*self-evaluation
  sheet

*Includes 4 samples
the student chooses
as his/her best work.
Must cover several
genres and include
first draft and revi-
sions through final
piece with peer,
teacher, and self-
evaluation, as well
as review comments
of parent

*Teacher has a
required inventory
for showcase that
is kept organized
by a checklist

*Student keeps a
running log of the
contents of the
working file

*The true portfolio is
a separate pocket binder
that contains specially
selected "showcase"
pieces with the draft
and revisions included
and a self-evaluation
of his or her work

*Teacher also keeps
a log book with
notes on progress
of each student

FIG. 3.1. "Webs" for survey teachers' portfolio practices.

66

TABLE 3.1
Categories and Questions in "Webbing" Survey

Basic Information

Who are your students? Grade levels, languages spoken, ability levels, economic status
What do you teach? Self-contained class, subjects
How long have you taught Language Arts? Years, grade levels, professional development

Background and History

How did you begin to use writing portfolios? Who initiated, trained, designed
What purposes are served by portfolios? Goals, scope, instruction, assessment
Who are they done for? You and your students, school, district, state, others
How are they different from previous practice?
Who else on the staff does portfolios and is available for consultation?

Portfolio Process

How did a portfolio get started? How collected, how refined, how reported, how displayed
Who sees it? Who reads it? Who writes in it?
What opportunities for reflection? Student self-reflection, parent, teacher
What happens to the portfolio at the end of the year? Goes to student, next teacher, school files

Portfolios in the Classroom

What are they like? Folders, books, computer disks, videos
Contents? Student selected, teacher selected, "best work," drafts, conference notes, grade versus ungraded pieces
Organization? Checklists, record keeping, updates

Evaluation

What is evaluated? Pieces only, portfolio as a whole
How is it evaluated? Standards, grades, relation to other tests and assessments
Who evaluates it? Student, peers, classroom teacher, other teachers, administrators

Program Impact

How have writing portfolios influenced your classroom? Instruction, curriculum, student attitudes, professional status, department and school programs, collaboration with others
In what ways have portfolios changed your ideas about teaching and learning to write?
What problems have arisen as a result of your use of writing portfolios?

Nuggets and Lumps

Other messages about good things and problems from your experience with portfolios.

viduals were more homespun, but struck us as quite authentic. Most of the sites are suburban (29) or rural (31), with 8 large urban locations. Twelve of the respondents were from low socioeconomic settings, and 11 from locations identified as high on the socioeconomic scale. The majority of the teachers were from primary (15) and upper elementary school (24) settings; 11 were from middle schools and 3 from high schools; most of the remaining respondents held district positions covering the entire grade range. We do not claim that this is a representative sample, but we simply note the trend for nominated respondents to be more often from small suburban than large urban settings, from middle and high socioeconomic levels than from lower levels, and from elementary and middle school grades than from high schools.

Quantitative Analyses

We conducted a quantitative analysis of the surveys by coding the information in each "web" using the categories shown in Table 3.2. We examined the entire protocol for each submission for comments relevant to each category, and rated the submission within that category on a scale of 1 (*not something that we do*) to 5 (*something that we always do*), or 0 (*no mention*). The latter category in the present analysis is coded as missing data. Each category was separately coded for mention of teachers, students, and any others.

Exploratory data analysis revealed several patterns in the codings that attracted our attention. We first look at the simple descriptive statistics for

TABLE 3.2
CODES: Categories and Sub-Categories Used to Cod Information From Respondent Webs

Portfolio Types
    Entire writing portfolio
    Selection of pieces
    Showcase
    Cumulative
    Other

Selection Criteria
    Genre
    Pieces

Standards
    Explicit rubrics
    General guidelines

Audience Functions
    Reads and reviews
    Evaluates and/or grades
    Keeps or owns

Evaluation
    Feedback and comments
    Grades and/or scores
    Individual or group

Purposes
    Curriculum
    Instruction
    Assessment

these patterns, and then discuss the correlations. First is the domain of standards and evaluation in portfolio practice. We combined the codings for teachers and students in the standards categories to create an overall indicator, and the mean rating was 1.74 (*SD* 1.08)—*almost never* on the coding scale. An evaluation indicator was constructed using the same strategy for feedback and grades, yielding a mean rating of 1.94 (*SD* 1.03)—again *almost never*. The bottom line is that in this data set, the informants indicated that they seldom if ever addressed issues related to standards for evaluation of portfolios.

Only one other set of codings yielded a lower rating in the data, and that was mention of students in establishing purpose in portfolio assessment. The category here is mention that students are involved in establishing the purpose of portfolios. The mean value was 1.18 (*SD* 1.15)—*virtually never*, with a few noticeable exceptions. Based on this set of informants, it appears that engagement of students in understanding why they are doing portfolios is not high on the agenda in most of these sites.

The audience category yielded very contrastive patterns. The mean coding for *read and review* was 3.6 (*SD* 1.0), meaning that most respondents indicated that these activities were of high priority. The average for grading was 2.5 (*SD* 1.4), with a flat, almost bimodal distribution in this category; some respondents *never* used portfolios for grading and evaluation, whereas an almost equal number *almost always* reported using portfolios to report grades and evaluations. With regard to the long-term audience for portfolios, again the picture was one of contrasts; the average coding was 2.0 (*SD* 1.27), *mostly not*, reflecting a pattern in which the respondents reported that students often kept their portfolios, whereas teachers generally did not. We do not know, to be sure, what students did with portfolios when these were given to them at the end of the school year, but the passing of portfolios from one teacher to the next did not appear to be common practice in this sample.

We also examined correlations among the various coding categories, and between the categories and the background indicators. The overall category codings were largely independent of one another, except for Audience and Evaluation. Here we found that the more frequently a respondent was explicit about the audiences for writing portfolios, the more likely the webs also contained references to evaluation activities of one sort or another. We conducted several multiple regression analyses to explore linkages among the background factors and the coding variables. These analyses revealed no strong relations. Audience codes were more likely to be mentioned in larger districts ($r = .27$), whereas Purpose codes were somewhat less likely to be made explicit ($r = -.28$) in these locations. Evaluation codes, especially grading, were more likely to be mentioned by respondents in higher socioeconomic sites ($r = .24$).

Qualitative Analyses

The most enlightening information, from our perspective, came from the various qualitative data—the surveys, but also the commentary from the working conference. We reviewed the participant responses for program details, particularly where personal opinions or insights were offered. This analysis provided a way to gather insights about program features and interrelationships. The most informative comments centered around issues related to purpose, which we highlight here.

Portfolios were employed for a broad variety of purposes other than assessment, according to our respondents. Our respondents mentioned a wide range of purposes that related directly to instruction: (a) involving students in the decisions about how to understand what they were learning, (b) giving students ownership of their own learning, (c) informing students about the teaching/learning process, (d) providing a place to honor personal best efforts and celebrate accomplishment, (e) serving as a resource for setting instructional goals and demonstrating abilities, (f) giving individual students identities as writers, (g) developing peer collaboration, and (h) building student self-esteem and pride in their work. Curriculum purposes also covered a wide range: (a) identifying areas of student strengths and weaknesses, (b) helping students identify components of good writing (c) helping establish student accountability, (d) developing students' reflective thinking abilities, (e) developing revision skills, and (f) focusing on writing as whole more than isolated skills.

Looking more closely at respondents' comments about instructional and curriculum purposes, we found some settings where instructional content is shaped or monitored by portfolios. A Indiana primary teacher reported using portfolios to "give students exposure to practicing various writing genre." One Illinois teacher uses portfolios as "a resource for editing and proofreading instruction." Another said, "portfolios allow me to focus on the 'whole' rather than only the skill." A Louisiana teacher, admittedly in the early stages of trying portfolio assessment, said that she saw portfolios "mostly as a source of material for student inventories and revision work."

Several respondents mentioned the importance of developing students' responsibility for their work. A Pittsburgh middle school teacher stated, "Students are given the opportunity to become more responsible, to reflect on what they have created and become more involved." Several teachers from a Georgia site described how portfolios involved their students in "goal setting, making choices, and monitoring their own growth as learners." An Idaho teacher volunteered that "portfolios require students to take more ownership of their writing."

Reflective self-assessment was mentioned by several respondents. An Arizona public school serving Native Americans on a reservation stated that their purpose was "to have students take a more active role in the writing workshops—especially evaluation." The Bay Village (OH) elementary district claimed that "involving students in selection of portfolio pieces and their own assessment is the heart of our portfolio process." A fourth-grade teacher in Central California identified "developing reflectivity" and "increasing student involvement in evaluation and goal setting" as her two primary purposes for using portfolios. An elementary teacher from Arizona employed portfolios to "help children build reflective thinking skills and self-evaluation skills." And from educators in Ohio, a statement that "we now look at a range of student work and empower learners to strengthen their own decision making about standards of quality."

A final instructional purpose emphasized portfolios as a way to develop the student's identity as a writer. A middle school teacher in New Hampshire emphasized that "the purpose of the portfolio is to show who these students are as readers and writers through a range and depth of reading and writing." A Wyoming teacher noted that "letters of self evaluation of a student's writing abilities make up two of the five pieces that go in the district portfolios." Comprehensive records kept by a Southern California district allowed students to "see their own progress as writers."

Purposes grouped around assessment included: (a) making assessment collaborative, (b) seeing growth and change aver time, (c) backing up teacher assessment with hard data, (d) broadening the evaluating scope, (d) improving assessment validity, (e) validating teacher perceptions as complementary to standardized tests, and (f) sharing student progress with parents. A few of the respondents mentioned state mandates. For example, a rural Pennsylvania district supports a portfolio program for all of the more than 8,000 students they serve. The purpose is "to broaden the scope of evaluation, to include multiple measures and multiple observers in assessment, [and] to move away from standardized tests." A rural Ohio district has developed system-wide Literacy Development Files for longitudinal tracking of student and program progress. In a Florida district, portfolios have replaced the state-mandated Reading Management System. In an Alaskan district, the portfolio evolved as an individual assessment tool replacing the report card—a remarkable shift from standard practice.

We found interesting variations in district use of portfolios. In a small rural district in upstate New York, portfolios were "not used for reporting to parents, but to assess programs; not individual students." An Alaskan district serving Native Americans described one of the two primary purposes of portfolios as "tracking district progress in writing." An Indiana district suggested that "Administrators will be able to use grade level products as a purview of content coverage."

Many respondents spoke of the value of portfolios to document change in student work over time, to document an array of skills and abilities, and to identify gaps in student learning to guide instruction. A fourth-grade Iowa teacher reported the main purpose of portfolios was to "assess literacy learning and outcomes." An Arizona teacher stated, "I can use portfolios to look at a student's growth in many areas, for example: spelling development." A middle school teacher from New Hampshire reports: "I look at portfolios to see how kids have grown, how writing has changed, and if goals have been met." An Alaskan respondent: "Portfolios provide an accurate way to measure *and* demonstrate student progress." From an Indiana teacher: "Our primary goal is to use portfolios as an alternate source of assessment of student progress." Other respondents emphasized accomplishment. A middle-school teacher from rural Maine noted that her portfolios serve as a "year-end summary of skills and accomplishments." A Missouri teacher stated that portfolios served many purposes for her, but emphasized the value of portfolios "to show me, my students, and others what they can do." Although these responses are typical, there is a recurrent lack of depth about how these intentions are carried out in practice. Growth and progress are often mentioned, but none of the protocols offers any technical detail on this topic. Validity and reliability were mentioned by no one.

Several programs mentioned parent communication as an important purpose for portfolios. Parent conferencing was noted as a primary portfolio purpose in a Southern California site. An Alaskan teacher responded that child–parent conferences and parent reporting was her "number one purpose." Respondents in both Northern and Central California sites spoke of the value of portfolio assessments for conducting parent–teacher–student conferences; in the words of one teacher, "what I collect, I do to support the child-centered conferences in my class." A Writing Project team in rural Texas turned this arrangement on its head by involving parents in the collection and evaluation of student work; "the parental assessment component leads to more communication with parent and child, . . . and to deeper understanding of school curricula." Elementary schools in Northern California and Georgia asked parents to contribute reflective letters on a regular basis, and at a site in rural Nebraska, parents join teachers and students to "read, reflect, and respond to the contents of the showcase portfolio."

At an operational level, the definition of a writing portfolio is driven by the purposes, stated and unstated, that it is designed to serve. As this review indicates, a wide variety of purposes were mentioned by respondents, reflecting the variety of applications of the portfolio concept. Purpose shapes other dimensions of the portfolio process: collection procedures, instructional roles of the portfolio, and positions on evaluation. We discuss these influences later.

Three Themes

The analysis of the complex array of information presented earlier turned up three themes that appear to us to capture the essence of this admittedly nonrandom sample of contemporary practice. Briefly, (a) teachers who have enlisted in the portfolio movement convey an intense commitment and personal renewal; (b) the technical foundations for portfolio assessment appear infirm and inconsistent at all levels; and (c) portfolio practice at the school and teacher level shies away from standards and grades toward narrative and descriptive reporting.

First, the matter of commitment and renewal. Across wide variations in approaches and definition, the portfolio approach has energized the professional status and development of educators, especially classroom teachers. This response is partly affective; people who often view themselves a subclass report spending enormous amounts of time and energy rethinking the meaning of their work, and they feel good about this renewed commitment. A common theme is ownership. Teachers talk about being in charge of their instructional programs. They describe the benefit to students of taking responsibility to select and critique their writing.

Here are selected verbatim excerpts reflecting this theme:

- By allowing—no, requiring!—teachers to develop their own systems, teachers gained a renewed belief in students and in themselves. Our teachers will fight to keep portfolios in their classrooms.
- Teachers began to toy with portfolios. We wanted a richer portrait of children's overall growth during the school year. Our district used pre-post tests. We found this was not enough information nor the *right* kind of information. Our own teachers have served as mentors to each other as some people are farther along in understanding portfolios.
- I am certain that the power of portfolios lies in helping teachers and students focus on the teaching/learning process.
- Students have begun to claim "ownership" of portfolios and strive to "perform" and do their best. . . . [The process] fosters positive feelings. Everything doesn't have to be perfect the first time. Ideas come first.
- In 19XX the money dried up and the project directors left. . . . As a strong proponent, I decided to take over without monetary compensation.

Second, the surveys, interviews, and associated documents all disclose a lack of analytic and technical substance. For instance, respondents claim that an important purpose of portfolios is valid assessment of student progress and growth, yet nowhere in the packets can we find a clear account of how achievement is to be measured. We pressed for further detail about this point during the working conference, but none was forthcoming. District and state activities generally attempt to incorporate judgments and standards, usually through holistic ratings by external groups; school and classroom projects seldom describe how to convert a folder of work into a gauge of achievement. Also missing is discussion of conventional (or unconventional) approaches for establishing validity and reliability. Validity is assumed to inhere in the authenticity of the portfolio process; reliability is simply not discussed. One state-level project in the sample did employ panel correlation methods for reliability; each portfolio was scored by a panel of two or more teacher-judges to establish consistency. This practice is rare in the districts in our sample, and was not mentioned by any school or teacher respondents.

The most immediate technical concern of most participants was staff development. The emphasis is on learning about portfolio concepts and techniques, and in establishing and refining a workable model for local implementation. Beyond the pragmatics of implementation, the next greatest concern is how to support students in completing portfolios.

The following excerpts demonstrate the intense concern with getting underway.

• We embarked on a year-long research project involving all K–6 teachers [with a consultant]. . . . Involving students in selection of portfolio pieces and their own assessment is the heart of our process. [The portfolios] represent student work over time and are interdisciplinary. We have all levels—working files, teacher portfolios, showcases, cumulative records, and competency portfolios. They show the growth of the student, and demonstrate what the student really can do, does, and knows. Students assess their own growth. Standards are developed within each classroom. . . . Teachers at each grade level work together to score competencies.

• Last year we went to training sessions and struggled over purposes. By the end of the year, five teachers really "tried to do something" with portfolios. . . . We are learners, explorers, teachers!

• The Literacy Portfolio has three components. The Core kept by all District elementary teachers includes the Reading Development Checklist, writing samples, and list of books read. The Core follows each child throughout the elementary grades. The Optional Component varies according to the teacher; I like first drafts, audiotapes of story readings, [etc]. This portion is used to confer with parents, to direct instruction, and for report cards. The Personal Folder, used by teachers for parent communication, includes attitude surveys, work samples (and comments), goals for the next term, [etc]. These go home with report cards.

• Students receive critiques formally and informally at all stages of work. They conference with teachers and peers and share work with the whole class, with the expectation that every child will eventually produce her best quality work. All final drafts are celebrated and displayed for the school or community. They are not graded; they should all be "A" quality work for that child.

• While the portfolio model yielded exciting results, over time it did not transfer as well as I had hoped. The records seemed mechanical and routinized. I think this was largely due to the selection criteria into which students had no input. Now I negotiate with students for the portfolio, for time management as well as of obtaining passing grade.

Third, as foreshadowed earlier, respondents exhibited a definite distaste for evaluation. They did not want to set standards or assign grades for students or programs. This reaction is captured by the remark, "I wish grades would just go away!" Teachers were willing to judge individual compositions and other student work samples, but were uncomfortable about assessing an entire portfolio. The Evaluation section of the surveys received the fewest and briefest entries, but the substance is captured by the following comments.

- Many teachers use criteria written on the report card for giving grades. Others felt grades influenced choices and so did not grade the papers, but noted students' strengths and weaknesses and set appropriate goals.
- Each student sets goals for self at the beginning, which they review and explain to me. Students decide, based on their projects and goals, what grade they should receive. If I had my say, we'd go through the same process but there'd be no grade. A grade is something the school insists on.

What the Findings Mean

Our survey suggests that complex reactions are materializing at the classroom level in response to the portfolio concept. To be sure, these findings hold for selected situations brought to our attention because of their reputation for being unique. We have conducted several informal visits to local sites, and are impressed by the range of implementations, from intensive commitments where portfolios are a dominant feature of the instructional day, to situations where portfolios are little more than manila folders holding an assortment of worksheets.

Complementing the three themes from the findings, we venture three interpretive comments about the portfolio movement. First, the popularity of the portfolio concept often appears as a local reaction to external control. While most elementary and middle school teachers accept standardized tests as the standard, the rebels who do portfolios discover in this concept a way to express their professionalism. It is unfortunate that the movement finds so little undergirding technological support. Teachers cannot call on Cronbach alphas or latent trait theory when asked to reassure policymakers that they know what they are doing, which leads to the second theme.

The portfolio concept amounts to virtual anarchy in many quarters. Most practical articles and newsletters, as well as popular books on alternative and authentic assessment, encourage an anything goes approach. Education is subject to pendulum swings, and portfolios may fall into this category. To be sure, the times call for substantial changes in educational practice and policy, but lacking a technological foundation, the portfolio movement would appear to be in peril.

Finally, what are the prospects that the portfolio movement will sustain its present fervor? Three possibilities come to mind: (a) It will disappear for lack of an audience. Portfolio assessment, if taken seriously, entails an enormous amount of work for teachers (and students). "Who's interested?" will eventually become a compelling consideration. (b) It will become standardized. We have seen examples in our survey artifacts: preprinted folders with sections for (often mundane) entries. (c) It will become a genuine revolution. We consider this outcome likely only if accompanied by other systemic changes in the educational process. The third prospect is compelling, but it remains to be seen whether changes in assessment will become a policy lever for school reform (Newman, 1991). We think that such leverage is likely to require a more systematic role for student portfolios in the teacher's daily life, and toward this end we explore a concept that complements the student portfolio.

THE TEACHER'S LOGBOOK: FUTURE POSSIBILITIES

In the survey responses, classroom portfolios typically rely on the teacher for design and interpretation. The assumption is that collections of student work will automatically assist the teacher in instructional decision making and local feedback. Evaluation by the classroom teacher (accompanied in some instances by student or peer judgment) is the primary technique for converting the collection of artifacts into an explicit judgment.

These conditions leave several questions unanswered about purpose, audience, and procedure in the systematic use of portfolios for assessing student achievement. How to deal with issues of reliability and trustworthiness? How to connect with other assessment methods and outcomes (e.g., grades, parent conferences, standardized tests)? How to manage consistency for students during their years of schooling within and between grades and schools? To be sure, one simple answer to these and related questions is to mandate standardized portfolios as an alternative or complement to existing standardized tests. This possibility merits comment, but we do not address the issue here.

The most serious hurdle in the way of implementing the preceding concepts, for purposes both of research and practice, is the difficulty of sustaining systematic teacher assessment. On the surface, the collecting of student work seems simple enough; difficulties arise in deciding how to select work samples and how to assess these samples in an informative and consistent manner. The Teacher Logbook is designed to address these issues. Figure 3.2 displays the organization of a Logbook designed to accomplish several

THE TEACHER LOGBOOK

Section I: Student Summary

   Fall Entry Level

Student	Reading/Writing/Language				Math . . .
	Vocab	Narrative	Expos	Skills	
Able, J.					
. . .					
Zeno, K.					

Section II: Journal Notes

   Week of _____

Section III: Curriculum Plan/Record

   Plans for Fall Qtr

Sept:	Activities	Vocab	Narr	Expos Skills
	Update			
Dec:	Activities	Vocab	Narr	Expos Skills
	Update			

FIG. 3.2. Design of teacher logbook for documenting student progress and curriculum planning.

interrelated tasks: journal documentation by the teacher of evidence bearing on student performances; summary judgments of student achievement; and a complementary record of curriculum events supporting student learning.

As shown in the figure, student summaries are placed at the beginning of the Logbook, because these play the most critical role in reporting student achievement. The student profiles provide space for the teacher to record ongoing information relevant to student performance; these pages, located in the middle of the Logbook, serve as a working space for the teacher to document observations, informal assessments of student activities and projects, and questions requiring further thought and action (Richert, 1990). The notes are a natural place for comments about student portfolio entries, along with more formal assessments. Curriculum planning is at the end of the Logbook. These entries are quite different from the routinized lesson plans typically completed by teachers to meet bureaucratic mandates. They are long-term working plans organized by curriculum goals, with room for commentary and revision.

Critical to the Logbook technique is the concept of a developmental curriculum, a small set of critical domains with mileposts that serve as targets for the school. For instance, in the literacy curriculum, comprehension and composition in the narrative genre is an important outcome for the elementary grades. Within the narrative form, four outcomes are generally recognized as critical for competence in handling literature: character, plot, setting, and theme. For kindergarteners, appreciating the moral of simple fables might be a reasonable goal. By second grade, students may be expected to identify thematic issues implicit in a work such as *Charlotte's Web*, and to express the meaning of the work in personal terms. Sixth graders should be fully capable of employing thematic elements in their own compositions, and to identify multiple themes in collections of related texts.

The Logbook concept builds on the notion that the teacher, with a developmental curriculum in mind, regularly records brief notes about individual students in the profile section. The comments provide a concrete record for reflection and action. An empty profile sheet is a reminder that the student has slipped from sight. A sheet showing a long list of books read but no evidence of written work is a prod to encourage the student to put his or her thoughts on paper. Teachers keep mental records of this sort; the Logbook is designed as a "memory jogger," and a source of information for reflection and assessment.

The Profile notes are the basis for summary assessments. We imagine a procedure in which, on a regular basis, perhaps once a quarter, the teacher conducts a formal rating of each student's achievement level in the Summary section of the Logbook. The entries reflect the teacher's judgment about each student's location on the developmental curriculum scale, based on analysis of the profile notes, which provide the link to the student portfolios. For instance, a teacher might judge a third-grade student as handling theme at a level appropriate to first-grade expectations; the student is still at the level of mundane morals.

The Profile-Summary combination is designed to address the technical problems that appear in our survey, and that have been raised by psychometrists as concerns about the portfolio approach, without compromising the advantages inherent in the engagement of the teacher in the assessment process as a professional decisionmaker. First, Profile documentation provides a concrete record to serve as a flexible basis for linking evidence to judgment. The journal format fits the realities of the teacher's daily life; standardized approaches to documentation will certainly fail because of the intolerable time pressures endemic to the teaching profession. If a school staff shares a common technical language for curriculum and instruction, then abbreviated notes serve the teacher's individual purposes, but also communicate significant meaning to colleagues.

This linkage is an important consideration in addressing issues of validity and reliability. By what means can the teacher's summary judgments about students be gauged for consistency and trustworthiness. Our answer to this question relies on the concept of panel judgments; much like an Olympic panel, classroom teachers can validate their evaluations through cross-checks (the British refer to this process as the *moderation* task). The workability of this approach relies on the emergence of the teacher as a practical researcher (Calfee & Hiebert, 1988), with the school taking shape as a context for assessment. Several examples can be found to support the practicality of this proposal. In California, for example, panels are incorporated in the Self-Study and Program Quality Review (PQR) process conducted by every school in the state once every 3 years. The idea is also reflected in the frameworks produced by professional organizations (e.g., National Council of Teachers of English and International Reading Association), in the work of grade level teams in many elementary schools, in the maintenance of department standards in secondary schools, and in the shared leadership typical of school restructuring.

Conceptually, the panel-judgment process can call on established methods of generalizability theory as a foundation. To be sure, application of the theory to panel judgments requires the construction of designs that identify significant factors likely to influence the judgment process. As a first cut, we suggest as critical factors the *curriculum domain* (holistic assessment of an entire portfolio is likely to fall prey to the same variability as for writing samples; we think that the teachers in our survey were wise when they resisted holistic judgments), *task conditions* (e.g., standardized vs. open-ended, constrained vs. project-based), *contextual factors* (e.g., individual vs. group, with or without instructional support and resources), and *characteristics of the judges* (e.g., colleagues, administrators, external experts).

The conceptual task of designing and validating the Logbook concept strikes us as no less demanding than the practical issues of implementation. We find in the survey responses little evidence of systematic documentation by teachers, unless this action was externally mandated. Most research on this issue is lacking in authentic purpose and genuine audience; the purposes are primarily for research, and the audience is the researcher. Kenneth Wolf's (1992) research on classroom portfolios (similar to the Logbook) is rich in its accounts of student work samples, but thin on teacher records. Teachers agreed to document the performance of two target students, but ran out steam midway through the school year. In Shulman's (1992) Teacher Assessment Project, teacher logs were an important component in the design of the Literacy component. Beginning teachers compiled professional portfolios during the school year for display during a performance demonstration before an expert panel comprising peers and academics. Collegial meetings during the year provided direction and support. The candidates, third grade teachers, included in their professional portfolio a progress record for four target students within their classroom, a record parallel to the Logbook concept. Although the final report of this Project is still in progress, preliminary findings suggest that with adequate support and purpose, teachers found the documentation task both feasible and informative.

Alternative assessment and student portfolios tend to appear in combination with other elements: whole language rather than basal readers, cooperative instruction rather than didactic teacher-talk, school-based decision making rather than top-down direction, the teacher as professional rather than as civil servant. Many of the survey responses described how externally initiated projects *not* related to portfolios evolved into alternative assessment.

Our sense is that this package offers the opportunity for fundamental reform in U.S. schooling. The various components are seldom connected in a coherent manner, and so teachers are easily overwhelmed by the multiplicity of demands. The enthusiasm and commitment of portfolio teachers is impressive, but the costs and benefits are disquieting. The portfolio movement seems likely to falter and fail unless it is connected to the other supporting components in a manner that continues to meet internal classroom needs (valid data for instructional decisions) while satisfying external policy demands (reliable information for accountability purposes; Fullan, 1991). We have proposed the Teacher's Logbook as a bridge capable of spanning this chasm. For the Logbook to become a reality will require (a) establishment of a serious audience for this activity, and (b) provision of adequate professional development.

Absent such support, our guess is that the portfolio movement will eventually fall of its own weight. Selected teachers will rely on their professional judgment for deciding what to teach and how to teach it, and for rendering assessments to interested audiences. External authorities may entertain the idea of portfolios, performances, and exhibitions, but cost-effectiveness will eventually carry the day (this shift has happened in the past; witness the early years of National Assessment of Educational Progress [NAEP], Tyler, 1969), and another chance to improve the quality of schooling in the U.S. will have slipped through our fingers.

ACKNOWLEDGMENTS

The work reported herein was supported under the Educational Research and Development Center Program (R117G10036) as administered by the Office of Educational Research and Improvement, U.S. Department of Education. The findings and opinions expressed in this report do not reflect the position or policies of the Office of Educational Research and Improvement or the U.S. Department of Education.

REFERENCES

Calfee, R. C. (1992). Authentic assessment of reading and writing in the elementary classroom. In M. J. Dreher & W. H. Slater (Eds.), *Elementary school literacy: Critical issues* (pp. 211–226). Norwood, MA: Christopher-Gordon.

Calfee, R. C. (1995). Implications of cognitive psychology for authentic assessment and instruction. In T. Oakland & R. Hambleton (Eds.), *International perspectives on academic assessment* (pp. 25–48). Boston: Kluwer.

Calfee, R. C., & Hiebert, E. (1988). The teacher's role in using assessment to improve learning. In C. V. Bunderson (Ed.), *Assessment in the service of learning* (pp. 45–61). Princeton, NJ: Educational Testing Service.

Calfee, R. C., & Hiebert, E. H. (1991). Teacher assessment of student achievement. In R. Stake (Ed.), *Advances in program evaluation* (Vol. 1, pp. 103–131). Greenwich, CT: JAI.

Fullan, M. G. (1991). *The new meaning of educational change.* New York: Teachers College Press.

Hambleton, R. K., & Murphy, E. (in press). A psychometric perspective on authentic measurement. *Applied Measurement in Education.*

Harp, B. (1991). *Assessment and evaluation in whole language programs.* Norwood, MA: Christopher-Gordon.

Murphy, S., & Smith, M. A. (1991). *Writing Portfolios: A bridge from teaching to assessment.* Markham, Ontario, Canada: Pippin Publishing.

Newman, F. M. (1991). Linking restructuring to authentic student achievement. *Phi Delta Kappan, 72,* 458–463.

Pelavin, S., (1991). *Performance assessments in the states.* Washington, DC: Pelavin Associates.

Pikulski, J. J., & Shanahan, T. (Eds.). (1982). *Approaches to the informal evaluation of reading.* Newark, DE: International Reading Association.

Richert, A. E. (1990). Teaching teachers to reflect: A consideration of program structure. *Journal of Curriculum Studies.*

Shulman, L. S. (1992). Toward a pedagogy of cases. In J. H. Shulman (Ed.), *Case methods in teacher education* (pp. 1–30). New York: Teachers College Press.

Smith, C. B. (Ed.). (1991). *Alternative assessment of performance in the language arts.* Bloomington, IN: ERIC Clearinghouse on Reading and Communication Skills.

Tierney, R. J., Carter, M. A., & Desai, L. E. (1991). *Portfolio assessment in the reading-writing classroom.* Norwood, MA: Christopher-Gordon.

Tyler, R. W. (1969). National assessment—some valuable byproducts for schools. *The National Elementary Principal, 48*(5), 42–48.

Valencia, S. W., & Calfee, R. C. (1991). The development and use of literacy portfolios for students, classes, and teachers. *Applied Measurement in Education, 4,* 333–346.

Wiggins, G. P. (1993). *Assessing student performance.* San Francisco: Jossey-Bass.

Wolf, D., Bixby, J., Glenn, J. III., & Gardner, H. (1991). To use their minds well: Investigating new forms of student assessment. In G. Grant (Ed.), *Review of research in education* (Vol. 17, pp. 31–74). Washington, DC: American Educational Research Association.

Wolf, K. P. (1992). *Informed assessment of students through the classroom literacy portfolio.* Unpublished doctoral dissertation. Stanford University, Stanford, CA.

CHAPTER FOUR

Dialogue, Interplay, and Discovery: Mapping the Role and the Rhetoric of Reflection in Portfolio Assessment

Kathleen Blake Yancey
University of North Carolina—Charlotte

Tests create that which they purport to measure by transforming the person.

—F. Allan Hanson

We are what we imagine.

—Scott Momaday

Imagination, as Scott Momaday (1992) suggested, can either expand or inhibit what we believe possible, just as by their very nature, tests can likewise constrain or enable what we perceive as within our "ken." At their best, both imagination and (ironically) tests can provide the means through which we can rewrite that ken. Precisely because it is constructivist, the best test, like the best writing assignment, provides a scene where we can achieve in new and original ways. It permits a student to say, "It wasn't until the midterm that I realized that I could pull together what I was learning *for myself.* . . . I could actually tell people what I was learning" (italics mine). In this reflective comment, however, the student touches on some key, related questions: How do we know what we know, what we thought we knew, what we have learned, and what we have accomplished? In the case of writing—both the development and the assessment of writing—what is the role of this kind of knowing, often called reflection? More specifically, what is its role within a portfolio of writing?

INTRODUCTION

In the last 30 years, the assessment of writing has changed dramatically, migrating from the positivist evaluation of indirect measures, for example, multiple choice tests, to a more practice-based evaluation as characterized in direct measures, like first draft essays prompted by external examiners. More recently, particularly in portfolio assessment, the evaluation of writing is said to be moving to a hermeneutically based method (Camp, 1993; Lucas, 1992; Moss, 1994a, 1994b; White, 1994). The portfolio, a set of multiple and diverse samples of behavior that are narrated by the writer in a reflection, offers another text for evaluation entirely, one that is directed by the composer, in its narration of contents and often in the selection of those contents. In the portfolio, then, teachers find multiple contexts for judgment, one of which is always the student's.

Adding reflection to the mix of unlike samples from unlike students, from a psychometric standpoint, makes assessment more complicated. On the one hand, it seems to increase the validity of the measure: We see more samples, we see samples whose construction took place in a naturalistic setting, we use a measure that increases what Moss (1994b) and Camp (1992) have called the *systemic validity of the assessment.* The portfolio links curriculum and assessment in a mutually beneficent way, and the reflection allows the student to make that link personal and specific: to the contexts in which the writing took place, to the student's goals, and to the writings composed before this portfolio was created. On the other hand, the reflective component of portfolio assessment raises multiple questions: What is reflection, anyway? What difference does it make to have it in the portfolio? Does including the reflection in portfolio assessment change our evaluation of our students' work? What forms might the reflection take, and what difference, if any, will the form itself make in our evaluation of student work? What kinds of activities lead to reflection, and what kinds of activities undermine our best efforts?

It is the purpose of this chapter to focus on these questions and to pose tentative answers to them. Briefly, what the chapter will demonstrate is (a) that reflection is most insightful, most generative, when it draws on what Vygotsky (1962) called *spontaneous* knowledge and belief, and when it then juxtaposes these with formal, usually school-based knowledge; and that such juxtaposition is required for the problem-solving that contextualizes and enables learning; (b) that the reflective student, in observing his or her own development and learning, needs to work within a community; that it is only through such communal dialogue and interplay that processes of reflection are learned; (c) that reflection requires both contraries, or opposites (believing and doubting), because it is through balancing these that the perception and insight characteristic of reflection are generated; (d) that in writing the doubting and believing are articulated through a language that is specific; and (e) that including a reflection in portfolio assessment both enhances our evaluation of student writing and problematizes it.

Defining Reflection

One often undervalued and little understood method of identifying what we know and of understanding how we came to know involves what has been called *reflection*. The word itself reflects what Vygotsky would call many senses of the word. It can mean revision, of one's goals, or more often, of one's work (Camp, 1992); it can mean self-assessment, sometimes oriented to the gap between intention and accomplishment (Conway, 1994); it can mean an analysis of learning that takes place in and beyond the writing class (Paulson, Paulson, & Meyer, 1991); it can entail projection (e.g., goal-setting) that provides a "baseline" against which development can be evaluated (Sunstein, 1994); and it can mean all of these things (Black, Daiker, Sommers, & Stygall, 1994).

For our purposes, however, what I mean by reflection is (a) the processes by which we know what we have accomplished and by which we articulate this accomplishment and (b) the products of those processes (e.g., as in, "a reflection"). In method, reflection is dialogic, putting multiple perspectives into play with each other in order to produce insight. Procedurally, reflection entails a looking forward to goals we might attain, as well as a casting backward to see where we have been. When we reflect, we thus project and review, often putting the projections and the reviews in dialogue with each other as we seek to *discover* what we have learned, what we are learning, and what we might learn. When we reflect, we call on the cognitive, the affect, the intuitive, putting these into interplay with each other: to help us understand how something will look when it is completed, how it compares with what has come before, and how it meets stated or implicit criteria.

Reflection, then, is the dialogic process by which we develop and achieve specific goals for learning, strategies for reaching those goals, and means of determining whether or not we have met those goals or other goals. Generally speaking, reflection includes the three processes of projection, retrospection (or review), and revision. For writing, it likewise includes three processes: (a) goal-setting, revisiting, and refining, (b) text-revising in the light of retrospection, and (c) the articulating of what learning has taken place, as embodied in various texts as well as in the processes used by the writer. Accordingly, reflection is a critical component of learning and of writing specifically; articulating what we have learned for ourselves is a key process in that learning.

Defining Portfolios: Five Principles
and Two Characteristics

Reflection is perhaps the most critical feature distinguishing portfolios of writing from simple work folders. The portfolio is more than a set of un-glossed rough and final drafts assembled willy-nilly. Rather, a portfolio of writing embodies five principles and two key features.

- A portfolio is a *collection* of work, but it is a collection that is a subset of a larger archive. Theoretically, the archive is the whole of a student's work, but more practically and more frequently, it is a subset of writing completed in a class, a program, a school.
- The process by which the subset is created is one of *selection*, the second principle of portfolios. How entries are selected varies according to the rhetorical situation contextualizing the portfolio. Is the portfolio's purpose to show development only, or both development and achieve-ment? Who will read the portfolio, an insider like a classroom teacher, or a classroom outsider like a parent, principal, or friend? Who has the authority for making the selections?
- A third principle is *reflection*, the process by which a student explains his or her learning: how the portfolio entries were created, for example, how one compares to another, how writing these has changed the writer, what this learning means to him or her.
- A fourth principle is *communication*, in the sense that the writing port-folio, like any portfolio, will communicate something about the writer, about what he or she values, about the contexts in which the writer has worked, and so on.
- Finally, any portfolio entails *evaluation*, in the sense, again, that it shows processes of valuing taking place, as students make selections, as they arrange them, as they tell the portfolio readers—and them-selves—about the entries and the learning connected with them.

Two features of portfolios, although not universal principles, also con-tribute to this definition of portfolio of writing: portfolios are developmental, and they are diverse. Many writing portfolios are designed to highlight de-velopment; classroom teachers, especially, value the opportunity to see writ-ers develop. Portfolios make that possible (Camp, 1992; D'Aoust, 1992). Equally as important, writing portfolios tend to include diverse samples of writing; it is almost oxymoronic that a portfolio would include multiple pieces of a single genre written for the same readers (Yancey, 1992). In fact, the portfolio as a testing device was initially useful precisely because of its sampling capacity, its ability to accept multiple and divergent kinds of writing, to thus help readers see a writer composing for different audiences and occasions (Belanoff & Dickson, 1991). A benefit of this sampling capacity is also suggested by the word diversity: We see the diversity of our students as perhaps we have not before, particularly when we link the diversity of contents with the reflections students write about them.

PORTFOLIOS AND REFLECTION: MAPPING THE RELATIONSHIP

Ironically, although reflection is the feature distinguishing writing portfolios—it is in part through reflection that folders or collections are transformed into portfolios—reflection, either per se or as a component of the writing portfolio, has in fact received very little attention in the literature. Although reflection is lauded as a valuable practice, few definitions of reflection are provided, few criteria for evaluating it are articulated, and few strategies for fostering it are identified (Belanoff & Dickson, 1991; Graves & Sunstein, 1992). It makes its appearance as almost an afterthought: ah, yes, don't forget, the reflective letter (Conway, 1994).

Two major themes regarding portfolio reflection have emerged, however: the need to practice it, and the need to foster it by way of questions. Camp (1992) for example, commented on how reflection has to be learned and practiced.

> Both teachers and researchers [in the Pittsburgh ARTS PROPEL portfolio project] had noticed that the reflective activities helped students become aware of strategies and processes they had used in writing. In addition, the activities encouraged the students to develop criteria and standards for their work. But we also knew that the practice of looking back was neither familiar to students nor easy for them. . . . [W]e were not terribly surprised that they came into the school year expecting that the teacher would tell them what was good or not so good in their work, and that their job would be to understand and accept the teacher's judgment. (pp. 64–65)

Like Camp, Paulson, Paulson, and Meyer (1991) focused on questions leading to reflection, in their case identifying the kinds of questions that elementary students compiling math portfolios might consider. They have also commented on the sets of texts—a single piece, a pair of pieces, and a body of work—that students might review as they reflect. In the collegiate context, Mills-Court and Amiran (1991) also identified reflection-generating questions, these forming a heuristic that can assist students in understanding their own learning. Beyond this practice-based beginning, however, very little has been articulated. Accordingly, our first task is to consider how this practice is theoretically grounded.

Dewey: Defining and Characterizing Reflection

The work of John Dewey provides a convenient place to begin thinking about reflection and how it helps us learn. Dewey (1993) wrote extensively about reflection, most explicitly in *How We Think: A Restatement of the Relation of Reflective Thinking to the Educative Process*. He defined reflective thinking as "the kind of thinking that consists in turning a subject over in the mind and giving it serious and consecutive consideration" (p. 3). Reflection, he said, is goal-driven; since there "is a goal to be reached . . . this end sets a task that controls the sequence of ideas" (p. 6). Put definitively, reflection is the active, persistent, and careful consideration of any belief or supposed form of knowledge in the light of the grounds that support it and the further conclusions to which it tends (p. 9). Reflection is defined by Dewey (1993) as "goal-directed and sequential, controlled by the learner because he or she wants to learn something, to solve a real problem, to resolve an ambiguous situation, or to address a dilemma" (p. 14). It relies on a dialogue among multiple perspectives, as the learner contrasts the believed and the known with presuppositions and necessary conclusions.

Reflection, Dewey also says, is habitual and learned. "While we cannot learn or be taught to think, we do have to learn *how* to think well," he says, "especially *how* to acquire the general *habit* of reflecting" (p. 34). Because language "connects and organizes meanings as well as selects and fixes them" (p. 245), it follows that reflection is language-specific. Dewey (1993) claimed that there are three uses of language, chronologically developed and applied: first, the attempt to influence others; second, the entering into of intimate relations; and only later, the third: the use of language "as a conscious vehicle of thought and language" (p. 239). The task for the educator is, therefore, to "direct students' oral and written speech, used primarily for practical and social ends, so that gradually it shall become a conscious tool of conveying knowledge and assisting thought" (p. 239).

Vygotsky: The Dialogue of Reflective Thinking

Lev Vygotsky also saw the exchange characteristic of interplay and dialogue as the foundation of reflection. According to Vygotsky (1962), "reflective consciousness comes to the child through the portals of scientific concepts" (p. 171), that is, through the formal concepts typically learned from adults and/or in school, which are juxtaposed with *spontaneous* concepts, those that are unmediated by external language or systematic representation. To illustrate, Vygotsky (1962) uses the task of tying a knot:

> The activity of consciousness can take different directions; it may illuminate only a few aspects of a thought or an act. I have just tied a knot—I have done so consciously, yet I cannot explain how I did it, because my awareness was centered on the knot rather than on my own motions, the *how* of my

action. When the latter becomes the object of my awareness, I shall have become fully conscious. We use *consciousness* to denote awareness of the activity of the mind—the consciousness of being conscious. (p. 170)

Reflection, however, requires both kinds of thinking, the scientific and the spontaneous, the strength of scientific concepts deriving from their "conscious and deliberate character," the spontaneous from "the situational, empirical, and practical" (p. 194).

Speaking generally, Vygotsky said, "the two processes . . . are related and constantly influence each other. They are part of a single process: the development of concept formation, which is affected by varying external and internal conditions but is essentially a unitary process, not a conflict of antagonistic, mutually exclusive forms of thinking" (p. 157). We especially see these processes in dialogue at certain times of development as during the period when children are between seven and twelve. "Then, the child's thought bumps into the wall of its own inadequacy, and the resultant bruises—as was wisely observed by J. J. Rousseau—become its best teachers. Such collisions are a powerful stimulus, evoking awareness, which in its turn, magically reveals to a child a chamber of conscious and voluntary concepts" (p. 165). Learning thus requires scientific concepts, spontaneous concepts, and interplay between them. As in the case of tying a knot, we use this dialogue to focus on the end—the knot—as well as on the processes enabling us to achieve the end.

For Vygotsky, as for Dewey, language is critical for reflection: "The relation of thought to word is not thing but a process, a continual movement back and forth from thought to word and from word to thought" (p. 218). This interplay, then, is both foundational, in terms of our being human, and continuous. It begins at the moment of birth, as the child engages with—interplays with—the others of his or her environment, and according to Vygotsky (1978), it is through this communal play and interaction that the child develops individuality:

> Piaget and others have shown that reasoning occurs in a children's group as an argument intended to prove one's own point of view before it occurs as an internal activity whose distinctive feature is that the child begins to perceive and check the basis of his thoughts. Such observations prompted Piaget to conclude that communication produces the need for checking and confirming thoughts, a process that is characteristic of adult thought. In the same way that internal speech and reflective thought arise from the interactions between the child and persons in her environment, these interactions provide the source of development of a child's voluntary behavior. (pp. 89–90)

In other words, we learn through the explaining of ourselves to others to understand ourselves. To do this, we rely on a reflection that involves a checking against, a confirming, and a balancing of self with others.

Polyani: The Significance of a Problem to Reflection

Knowing and learning—and therefore reflection—occur within the context of a problem. Michael Polanyi, like Dewey before him, identifies the *finding of the problem* as another key feature in reflection. Polanyi (1969) suggested that the problem definition itself is the first critical step in any creative act such as reflection.

> To hit upon a problem is the first step to any discovery and indeed to any creative act. To see a problem is to see something hidden that may yet be accessible. The knowledge of a problem is, therefore, like the knowing of unspecifiables, a knowing of more than you can tell. But our awareness of unspecifiable things, whether of particulars or of the coherence of particulars, is intensified here to an exciting intimation of their hidden presence. It is an engrossing possession of incipient knowledge which passionately strives to validate itself. Such is the heuristic power of a problem. (pp. 131–132)

A scientist, the knower here of whom Polanyi speaks, controls his or her own problem, motivates himself or herself by the questions the self poses, weaving back and forth between the felt and the known, the unarticulated and the explicit, what Vygotsky might call the spontaneous and the scientific, what Carl Sagan has called dual modes co-habiting in the mind.

Collectively, Dewey, Vygotsky, and Polyani thus define reflection as a process by which we think: reviewing, as we think about the products we create and the ends we produce, but also about the means we use to get to those ends; and projecting, as we plan for the learning we want to control and accordingly, master. We learn to reflect as we learn to talk in the company of others. To reflect, as to learn (because reflection is a kind of learning), we set a problem for ourselves, we try to conceptualize that problem from diverse perspectives—the scientific and the spontaneous—for it is in seeing something from divergent perspectives that we see it fully. Along the way, we check and confirm as we seek to reach goals that we have set for ourselves. Reflection becomes a habit, one that transforms.

Reflection and School

Given that reflection is a necessary part of any learning that is learner-directed, it seems to make sense that schools would provide the appropriate context to foster reflection. Ideally, students would be asked to set their own goals for learning, to identify strategies they could use to reach those goals, and to assess how well they have met those goals. Ideally, students in writing classes would apply this protocol to their writing: defining a rhetorical context for writing, with a purpose they cared about and an audience they wished to speak to; generating and collecting material appropriate for such a situation; creating a first draft; sharing it with others to acquire response; redrafting and revising when appropriate; and editing prior to publication. As they moved through these processes, students would reflect throughout: to compare their intentions with those within the text being produced, to evaluate their sense of how well the draft succeeds, to anticipate the response of their readers, to compare their sense of its success with that of their respondents. And on another level, once this specific text is completed, students can reflect on it: to see what they learned about their own writing process as they composed the text; how writing this text changed them, if it did; how the writing of it might help them locate new goals, for another text, and/or for a new direction in which to develop.

The kind of school where this kind of reflection—one defined by Dewey, Vygotsky, and Polanyi—will take place is not the school of the past; it is not the old "good classroom," where "conforming (if not completely passive) students" obey "a teacher who is always in charge" (Greene, 1995), the very teacher described by Camp as the one expected by the ARTS PROPEL students. It is not a school where the teacher's problems are perceived as ones students want to solve (Yancey, 1992). In the old school we do pose problems, but as Mayher (1990) argued in *Uncommon Sense*, too often those problems—what shall I learn, or what shall I write?—have belonged to us, to the teachers, not to the students. In such a school, these questions are not authentic; they are the means to guess what *someone else* wants us to answer, namely, the teacher or a principal. In such a school, writings are not "utterances"; they are "artifacts" (Reither & Hunt, 1994) that do not enliven, precisely because they are not connected to learning. They simply satisfy the need for an assessment that is disassociated from learning and curriculum.

Mayher conceptualized what we call the reflective school as a place where learning would be the *child's* responsibility and where assisting the student to discover and then solve his or her real problem would be the school's aim. Like Dewey, Vygotsky, and Polyani, Mayher (1990) believed that learners "have to set and solve the problems and develop the skills, but they will do so most effectively in an environment which takes their meaning and purposes seriously and which allows them to act as well as to react" (p. 105). A first problem for learners, then, is to set the problem of their own learning, in their own terms, within the context of a school community.

Reflection and the Writing Classroom

What might a writing class in such a school look like? Hilgers gives us at least a start in envisioning this class. Working with four primary students during a 3-year period, Hilgers was interested in seeing whether or not these young children could (a) reflect on their own work and (b) could see their texts and their learning as sufficiently separate from themselves so as first, to see a need for revision and second, to identify strategies for revising: in sum, to use reflection as a means of developing text. During the 3 years Hilgers worked with these students, he observed them, interviewed them, and read their work. What he found runs counter to what is held to be true about young learners, and as important for our purposes, suggests what is needed if a writing classroom is to be reflective.

It is commonplace that very young writers—those in the first, second, third, and fourth grades—find it very difficult if not impossible to separate themselves from their texts; if they cannot achieve such separation, they are unlikely to do much rewriting or even substantial revision, given that such separation is perceived as being necessary for the task (Kroll & Vann, 1981; Murray, 1982; Rubin, 1981). Hilgers discovered, however, that such writers could in fact adopt behaviors of more mature writers, when the proper conditions—the appropriate context—was in place.

Hilgers started with the premise that self-evaluation is an integral part of writing, and that it was something to be encouraged in the children. In observing the children, he noted that when others evaluated their work, the students did not; in other words, to the extent that teachers evaluated student texts, the students deferred making judgments about their texts themselves, preferring teacher judgment to peer response or self-assessment. It is as though there is only a certain amount of space for judgment; if the teacher takes that space, students can or will not, as authors or as peer respondents. On the other hand, when that judgmental space is vacated by the teacher *and* when the students are given the opportunity to develop their own critical standards—through process writing, sharing drafts, and developing personal judgment—even very young writers will do so. It is not enough, then, simply to abandon or vacate judgmental space. Although it first has to be vacated by the teacher, it must then be populated by student discourse oriented to the critical standards governing the student work at the time.

Hilgers (1986) also reported that students developed their reflective capacity over time. When first examining their texts, early in the study, they tended to think in terms of a single criterion: whether or not they *liked* the texts. The second criterion mentioned by the students is length, the longer the better. Still, the trend over time was toward "use of a greater number of criteria" (p. 48): text as understood, craftsmanship, value. As important, students articulated such criteria when they wrote in a classroom that was itself populated with the discourse of composing, where such criteria and such articulations are daily fare, where the spontaneous writing of any text becomes subjected to the analysis of the scientific concept.

Although he cautions against overgeneralizing from such a small study, Hilgers (1986) concluded that "It seems likely that ability to articulate criteria will be found to play an important role, and that conscious verbalization of evaluation criteria and judgments may help students to put evaluations to effective use" (p. 54).

What do these projects tell us about the power of reflection in learning to write, and what do they tell us about the kind of writing classroom where such writing is learned?

1. Students, even young students, can do in school-based writing what Vygotsky claimed for them in speech and thought: internalize the criteria of the community for themselves and use those criteria to evaluate and direct their learning.
2. One way to help students do this is to locate them in a context where they are immersed in such discourse.
3. Providing students with some sense of what helpful reflection sounds like will improve their efforts at reflection.
4. The development of such reflective capacity will take time, especially if we want it to become habitual.

Reflection and Writing Portfolios

Into this environment, the reflective writing class, we introduce portfolios, and through portfolios we introduce four related concepts: (a) the notion (indeed, the gift) of time (Yancey, 1992, 1994); (b) the notion of choice and of making choices that reflect values; (c) the ability to see one text in light of others; and (d) the ability to take a larger view of one's development, to link texts and development, and to chart a coherent course of one's development and achievement as a writer. In other words, the portfolio, because of its framing capability—its ability to showcase different works for different audiences from different time periods that are themselves only a subset of the actual texts created—provides the texts for the reflective questions associated with learning: Looking back at this text, for instance, how does it appear to you now? What does including this text tell you about how you write, about how you assess your work, about how others do, and what lessons there are to be learned there? How does this text compare with others? How do you see all your writing over a certain period of time? When thus queried, students begin to articulate the story of their writing, of themselves as developing writers.

In a first case, that of a single text reviewed later in time, a student—this one from a first-year writing class in a North Carolina college—casts a glance back at a writing completed while she was in high school:

> I guess it does not help my shyness about my writing to start my portfolio off with one of the most personal pieces that I have ever attempted. The poem "Last Bows" was written at the time that I was deciding what college to attend. It seemed like I had to plot out my whole life before high school graduation. The pressures from parents, teachers and peers was formidable.

This piece displays the emotional uncertainty that I was feeling towards my chosen profession (acting). I remember feeling a great sense of relief after I had completed "Last Bows." This was when I discovered that writing could be therapeutic. The curious thing about this selection is, at that time I had not written poetry in years, and since that time [about 6 months] I have not written poetry at all. It seems strange to me that I should turn to such an unfamiliar form when I was feeling so uncertain.

Here we see her thinking about this piece of writing, when it was created, the circumstances that contextualized the writing of it for her. In this reflection, she tells us—her audience—that it is a personal piece, and that she sees herself doing something unusual here, writing poetry, when she feels uncertain and anxious, employing a form that does not call to her at other times. This writer has identified something about her practice she is only able to see with the gift of time and in the context provided by the multiple texts in her portfolio.

In a second case, we hear from a high school student who is talking about her writing and what it and the response it generates can teach her:

I actually didn't have a very difficult time selecting the pieces that would grace my portfolio. There were seven required entries, and that's about how many I turned in this year. I included the essay I wrote on the "Boundaries of Freedom" because I like the introduction so much. Apparently I like it a lot more than any one else does, because I've shared it with several people and I always seem to get a rather comatose response. That's usually when I break into my, "This is good stuff here, c'mon!" whine, but it never really helps. Recognizing one's boundaries and limits is important for operating successfully in our complex society, and ever since I realized mine after writing this paper, I got picked on a lot less.

This writer is engaged here in comparing her assessment of her introduction with that of others, finally acceding to their wisdom. She pictures herself doing what a writer does: writing and getting response and connecting that to her sense of text. Like Hilgers' younger writers, this writer benefits from working in a context that permits reflection, as she writes the text and as she composes her portfolio.

The last example was composed by a fourth grader; it is a letter of introduction to a portfolio of writing that will be submitted to a centralized office as part of a large-scale assessment activity. So the writer knows that he is sharing his documents in a pubic forum, and he knows that he is addressing a fairly wide audience, one with which he is not familiar. He also knows that others' standards will apply, but as we see, he understands his writing and his learning to be highly personal.

Dear Reviewer,

I have changed in many ways since the beginning of the school year along with my writing. I've also growed smarter. And I've growed to love writing. Sometimes I take my writers notebook to lunch and recess. I like to write mysteries and funny stories. One of the things I like to do with writing is to use imagination. At the beginning of the school year I could not spell that many big words. Even though we do not have spelling test, I've learned to use big words in my writing. And I do not misspell the big words. I use words like enormous, tremendous, frightened, and unique. I think writing is fun. It helps me learn. As you can see, I have improved my writing very much.

I have discovered many things about myself as a writer. I know I have improved my writing since the beginning of the school year. I've discovered that I didn't like writing at the beginning of the school year. I've also discovered that I'm capable of publishing my writing. For example, I sent my personal narritive to the ———— and they are going to publish it. Writing doesn't have to be boring. I've also discovered that writing is a way to express my feelings. This is what I have discovered about myself as a writer.

I chose my personal narritive for my best piece. It is called the Big Question. It's about when I when I went to Prestonsburg. And I went to my aunts funeral because she died. Her name is was Juanita. I called it the Big Question because I asked a really big question. What are we born for if we die? That's the question I asked. I chose it because it is the best piece I have ever written. Plus I sent it to the ———. This is why The Big Question is my best piece.

I hope you enjoyed my letter. I also hope you enjoyed my peaces that I put into my writing. I hope you enjoyed reading them as much as I enjoyed writing them.

There is much to discover in this child's reflection. One of the first observations has to do with this writer's sense of discovery and his use of discover as a key word. In a sense, we have to credit his teacher for his use of it, because she, much as the teachers of Hilgers' fourth graders, helped establish the context in which he worked, assisted him to begin to speak in the language of writing, and introduced discover as a word that could lead to insight. But we need to credit the writer as well, for the discoveries he made, for the reflection they motivate. In other words, a reflective classroom fosters the reflection that only a child can compose.

For a fourth grader, this reflection seems both characteristic and exemplary. He does exactly what Hilgers predicted: he likes writing and some of his writings particularly, he likes to write mysteries, and he chooses his best piece in part because it is his best. Taken together, however, these likings form a pattern, signal the development of a writer's identity, especially when we view them in light of the rest of the piece.

He finds that his behavior has changed: "Sometimes I take my writers notebook to lunch and recess." He sees that he is becoming a new writer in his texts as well: he can use "new big words," can identify what some of these are, and can spell them properly, "even though we do not have spelling test." He understands that he is learning in a new way. He is also a new writer in terms of audience; "I'm capable of publishing my writing," for a real audience outside the classroom, and he "hope[s] you enjoy reading" his other pieces in the portfolio "as much as I enjoyed writing them." In the terms of reflective discourse, we have a dialogue here between the old self who did not like writing so much and who had not published and who did not really understand what writing was about, and the new one who uses writing to express feelings and to learn with and to share with a wider audience. The new self has clear standards that he is articulating and meeting: doing what writers do like taking his notebook with him to lunch; using new words and spelling them correctly; publishing his work. We also have a learner who has real problems to solve: he discovers a lot about himself and his writing over the course of the year, when he "growed smarter." Perhaps his most profound discovery is a question generated by a personal event, attending his aunt's funeral: "What are we born for if we die?" Like most big questions, this one traverses both the personal and the public, engages both the cognitive and affect, the intellectual and the spiritual, and resists answers.

The Reflection in the Portfolio: A Return to Assessment

One assumption motivating the inclusion of reflection in portfolio assessment has to do with how it engages the learner, first because an engaged learner is likely to perform better, which is the point of education; and second, because as Hanson (1993) pointed out, the test we construct will construct in turn the person taking the test. If we construct a test requiring a reflective stance and reflective activities, we are more likely to see our students becoming reflective. It is no understatement, therefore, to claim that portfolio assessment is different in kind from earlier tests.

We have included reflection within portfolios, however, without being as reflective about it as we might be. Not surprisingly, there are serious questions regarding portfolios that need better answers than they have received. These questions include: (a) how do we read and evaluate portfolios; (b) what influence does reflection exert in these reading and evaluating processes; and (c) what is it, after all, that we are assessing?

Reading Portfolios

Admittedly, portfolios are multiple texts, so the reading of them would seem to be, again, different in kind than in degree from the reading of earlier single texts. As Murphy and Smith (1992) suggested, the tendency when reading a single text, especially for a classroom teacher, is to read it in the context of the set of texts produced by a group, for example, the class of students. Alternatively, the reading of a student text in the context of his or her own work would seem to be a different matter, not just because the text is embedded in the context of the student's (rather than class') work, but also because it comes without the context of the class. Moreover, the student context does not stand on its own; it is presented and often interpreted by the student. So what we read in the portfolio is unpredictable, multifaceted, and requires interpretation. How we grade or score the portfolio is another and related issue. Burnham (1986) suggested that this grading is itself implicated already in classroom practice, particularly for the classroom teacher:

> Reading a portfolio honestly requires considerable forgetting. Beginning to read a portfolio with preconceptions about a student's ability and potential can lead to reading only to find evidence to confirm those perceptions. This violates the purpose of the portfolio. Instructors need to read the portfolios to evaluate the writing in front of them, not to defend evaluations built up through the semester. (p. 134)

Although Burnham here speaks of classroom teachers who then grade portfolios at the end of a term or class, the same observations obtain when any portfolio is labeled—developmental, basic, ESL. They also suggest questions about what it takes to be a good reader of portfolios—and what would good reading look like?

Scripting Portfolios?

The second question pertains to how reflection engages the reader: The reader presumably is better informed with the student's account of how certain pieces developed, of how the student developed over time, of what the student's strengths and weaknesses are, and the like. But precisely how this information—this necessarily self-interested perspective—affects the reader is unknown. At Miami University, researchers and teachers (Sommers, Black, Daiker, & Stygall, 1993) worked together for several years to design, implement, and revise a model of portfolio of writing used for exemption purposes. The scene they set for reflection is fairly typical of practice. They inform students that their portfolio must begin with a reflective letter.

> This letter, addressed to Miami University writing teachers, introduces you and your portfolio. It may describe the process used in creating any one portfolio piece, discuss important pieces in creating the portfolio, explain the place of writing in your life, chronicle your development as a writer, assess

the strengths and weaknesses of your writing, or combine these approaches. Your letter should provide readers with a clearer understanding of who you are as a writer and a person. (p. 11)

The students have a great deal of freedom with this task, and how that affects the writers is unclear—whether or not they feel that they have enough structure here, particularly given the page limitations (for practical purposes, the reflection has to be confined to two pages). Then there is the reading process; how is that affected by the personal nature of a reflection that invites students to share something of who they are as a person? The Miami researchers believe that it is this inclusion of the personal in the portfolio that readers respond to favorably:

> One reader noted, "I found the reflective letter to often be the most interesting part of the packet, not only because of what it revealed of the individual but because of what it showed about the writer's attitude towards their own work. What a fascinating range of boastfulness, self-effacement, wit, and rambling." Another commented, "The reflective letter fascinates me. It appears to be the place where the student establishes his/her authority as a writer; positions the reader and the writer." A third rather echoes the second: "I liked those reflective letters and narratives which situated the writer and his or her writings best." (p. 11)

There are several observations here worth noting in these reflections on the reading of portfolios. First, they help us understand, at least a little, what goes on when we read portfolios. Second, not unlike Hilgers' fourth graders, we seem focused on what we like in reflection. Seen developmentally, perhaps this is a first step toward establishing a fuller set of criteria that would then be provided to students. Third, and not surprisingly, the attention here is drawn to the writer as much as to the writing, which is to be expected given the personal nature of reflection and the directions given for the reflective letter. Even the genre of reflection—that of a letter—encourages a personal transaction. The question is how our reading and our judgment are affected by such a personal transaction. And fourth, I have to wonder if there is not a script here for the ideal letter of reflection: the script says, albeit implicitly, that this letter shows the writer developing (i.e., getting better), liking writing more, in short, telling us what we want to hear. Would it make a difference, for example, if a writer told us that she hated writing and had not improved or attempted any new strategies or rhetorical situations? Put in Foucaultian terms, as Lester Faigley (1989) argued, we have to consider our own stance: "The authority to determine which truths are universal places the teacher in a position of privilege because the teacher is outside the petty interests of history but within the boundaries of universal truth" (p. 131).

What Are We Assessing?

Underlying the previous discussion is a key question: What is it, after all, that we are assessing? Not that this question hasn't always lurked beneath the surface of all writing assessments; it has. It simply lurks less in portfolio assessment as we see more of a student's work and from more than a single perspective. In part, of course, we seem to be assessing the fit between the student and the contexts in which the writer has been composing; again, that has always been true. In a class or workshop where a writer composes on topics of interest, where he or she receives praise and helpful critique, the fit is said to be good, and the student is likely to do well.

In part, though, I think what we are assessing here—in the portfolio—has to do with two possibilities. On the one hand, we could say that we are looking at a writer's authority, as the Miami teacher said earlier, as constructed through his or her ability to self-assess, to understand when and how he or she performs well and when and how otherwise. In this case, we seem to be assessing two (related) performances: the writing performance and the reflecting/self-assessing performance. Given what we know about the helpfulness, indeed the necessity of self-evaluation, this makes sense, but we then need to indicate that these performances are not co-identical. Or is one embedded in, entailed by the other? On the other hand, it might be that what we are assessing, when we look at reflection, is not performance so much as *knowledge*: self-knowledge about one's writing behavior, but also knowledge about what it may take to be a writer, because that is one context for our own self-assessment. In other words, what we seem to reward here is not just a sense that the writer understands his or her writing strategies and processes, but also that these are appropriate, given the way writers behave. The writer's authority seems appropriate, given the contents of the portfolio; the composer does have the self-knowledge claimed in the reflective letter, and that self-knowledge is consonant with what writing practice. If this is the way we construct portfolios, then it is multi-modal not only in sampling but also in what is being assessed: a process-based measure of outcomes.

Portfolio Reflection as Revealing Our Own Practices

What portfolio assessment is showing us, then, is how our own often tacit assumptions drive both our assessment and our pedagogy. Speaking pedagogically, one case in point has to do with revision, which itself requires reflection. The current prevailing model of composing privileges revision; as Donald Murray says, writing is rewriting. But this model seems to ignore the obvious fact that some writers are single-draft writers (Harris, 1989). Other writers choose, appropriately and from time to time, not to revise. As Tom Hilgers (1986) said, it is possible that evaluation can yield a decision not to revise. Expert writers frequently employ evaluative criteria as goals when they plan a piece of writing (Scardamalia, 1984). When such goals are effectively met in a draft, a decision not to revise may be perfectly appropriate. Even young writers may incorporate relatively simple evaluative criteria as goals in their writing plans, may meet those goals in a first draft, and may thus, appropriately, be moved not to revise. Requiring revision in such instances would be counter-productive. (p. 54)

Glenda Conway (1994) working in a collegiate context, makes a similar observation: "Reagan chose to assign a high status to revision in her cover letter out of her knowledge that revision is necessary and expected in college writing" (p. 86). When we do *require* revision, we invite compliance of the worst sort, as this college student indicates: "I think portfolios put more pressure on me to botch my papers so it looked like I revised, I didn't know how much I needed to scratch out to get a good grade" (Metzger & Bryant, 1993, p. 7). In other words, as we ask students to articulate their assumptions and to reflect, we would do well to do the same.

A second case involves what I think of as the "schmooze" factor in reflection: the temptation to reward students who tell us what we naturally enough want to hear: that they are learning, that they are taking risks, in the most dramatic case, that they have never experienced such pleasure in learning before, that it is in this class where it has taken place. Again, we need, I think, to balance that temptation with some sense of what we know writing requires: hard work, often much redrafting, a sensing of the gap between intent and effect, tolerance of ambiguity, frustration—in short, a good deal of emotion not associated with pleasure or fun.

CONCLUSIONS

As may be apparent by now, this chapter is itself an exercise in reflection. Like many of those working with writing portfolios, I also have been drawn to reflection, engaged by students' accounts of the composing strategies that have worked for them, informed by the rhetorical problems they have en-countered, often surprised by the connections they identify between and among the writings they compose. In some ways, I feel as though a giant window has opened on teaching and learning processes that I have tried to look into for years. But, I am also unsatisfied—wanting more, believing that I can see more, feeling that somehow I am missing something. What that something is has provided the focus of this chapter. Using Vygotsky's method, I've juxtaposed the spontaneous with the school, to learn more about reflection and to reflect on it. The effort has been in context and communal, as I have worked with teachers and students, as I have read variously and widely, as I have shared and rewritten more drafts than right now I care to remember. Finally, like all learning, my quest here is personal.

The questions I have taken up: What, after all, is reflection? On whose philosophies have we been drawing, even if only tacitly? What role does reflection play in learning, in learning to write, in portfolios? What kind of context does one have to create in order for reflection to become habitual and valued? What is "good" reflection, and how does it differ from "inadequate" reflection? How can we communicate this to our students? What impact does it have on portfolio assessment?

In the process, I have learned what we might expect: that reflection has a history, that it is part of a tradition of intellectual thought about thought, that it is intimately connected to learning. It includes central concepts, among them dialogue, language, divergent stances, problem, discovery. It is through reflection, through articulating to others what we think we know, that we learn, through which we compose the past for the present.

In the process, I have learned that there is much still to learn about reflection. We understand generally that it enhances learning, but we still have much to learn: what forms reflection might take and for what effect, how it influences readers and evaluations, what we are, after all, *assessing*. We have much to reflect on, still.

In the process, I have been reminded that, as Scott Momaday (1992) says, constructed in words, we are what we imagine: Reflection helps us imagine who and what we might become. I have been reminded that, as Alan Hanson (1993) asserted, we live in a culture that overrelies on testing, that the transformative effects of our testing can be good or ill, and that when we make reflection a part of an assessment process, we necessarily encourage our students to become more reflective. I have been reminded that since we teachers started asking for reflection, we have become more reflective ourselves; that the tasks we set for others transform us.

I have been reminded that as reflection concludes, it also and necessarily provides a new point of departure.

REFERENCES

Belanoff, P., & Dickson, M. (Eds.). (1991). *Portfolios: Process and product.* Portsmouth, NH: Heinemann.

Black, L., Daiker, D. A., Sommers, J., & Stygall, G. (Eds.). (1994). *New directions in portfolio assessment* (pp. 168–182). Portsmouth, NH: Heinemann.

Burnham, C. (1986). Portfolio evaluation: Room to breathe and grow. In C. Bridges (Ed.), *Training the new teacher of composition* (pp. 125–139). Urbana, IL: National Council of Teachers of English.

Camp, R. (1993). Changing the model for direct assessment of writing. In M. Williamson & B. Huot (Eds.), *Holistic Scoring: Theoretical foundations and validation research* (pp. 56–69). Cresskill, NJ: Hampton Press.

Camp, R. (1992). Portfolio reflections in middle and secondary school classrooms. In K. B. Yancey (Ed.), *Portfolios in the writing classroom* (pp. 61–79). Urbana, IL: NCTE.

Conway, G. (1994). Portfolio cover letters, students' self-presentation, and teachers' ethics. In L. Black, D. A. Daiker, J. Sommers, & G. Stygall (Eds.), *New directions in portfolio assessment* (pp. 83–93). Portsmouth, NH: Heinemann.

D'Aoust, C. (1992). Portfolios: Process for students and teachers. In K. B. Yancey (Ed.), *Portfolios in the writing classroom* (pp. 39–48). Urbana, IL: National Council of Teachers of English.

Dewey, J. (1993). *How we think* (2nd ed). Boston: D. C. Heath.

Faigley, L. (1989). Judging writing, judging selves. *College Composition and Communication 40*, 395–412.

Graves, D., & Sunstein, B. (Eds.). (1992). *Portfolio portraits*. Portsmouth, NH: Heinemann.

Greene, M. (1988). *The dialectic of freedom*. New York: Teachers College Press.

Hanson, F. A. (1993). *Testing testing*. Berkeley, CA: University of California Press.

Harris, M. (1989). Composing behaviors of one and multi-draft writers. *College English, 51*, 174–191.

Hilgers, T. (1986). How children change as critical evaluators of writing: Four three-year case studies. *Research in the Teaching of English, 20*, 36–55.

Kroll, B., & Vann, R. (Eds.). (1981). *Exploring speaking-writing relationships*. Urbana, IL: NCTE.

Lucas, C. (1992). Introduction: Writing portfolios—changes and challenges. In K. B. Yancey (Ed.), *Portfolios in the writing classroom* (pp. 1–11). Urbana, IL: National Council of Teachers of English.

Mayher, J. (1990). *Uncommon sense*. Portsmouth, NH: Heinemann.

Metzger, E., & Bryant, L. (1993). Portfolio assessment: Pedagogy, power, and the student. *Teaching English in the Two-Year College, 20*, 279–288.

Mills-Court, K., & Amiran, M. (1991). Metacognition and the use of portfolios. In P. Belanoff & M. Dickson (Eds.), *Portfolios: Process and product* (pp. 101–113). Portsmouth, NH: Heinemann.

Momaday, N. S. (1992). *In the presence of the sun*. New York: Saint Martin's Press.

Moss, P. (1994a). Can there be validity without reliability? *Educational Researcher, 23*(2), 5–12.

Moss, P. (1994b). Validity in high stakes writing assessment. *Assessing Writing, 1*, 109–129.

Murphy, S., & Smith, M. A. (1992). Looking into portfolios. In K. B. Yancey (Ed.), *Portfolios in the writing classroom* (pp. 49–60). Urbana, IL: National Council of Teachers of English.

Murray, D. (1982). Teaching the other self: The writer's first reader. *CCC, 33*, 141–148.

Paulson, L., Paulson, P., & Meyer, C. (1991). What makes a portfolio a portfolio? *Educational Leadership, 48*, 60–63.

Polanyi, J. (1969). *Knowing and being*. Chicago: University of Chicago Press.

Reither, J. A., & Hunt, R. A. (1994). Beyond portfolios: Scenes for a dialogic reading and writing. In L. Black, D. A. Daiker, J. Sommers, & G. Stygall (Eds.), *New directions in portfolio assessment* (pp. 168–182). Portsmouth, NH: Heinemann.

Rubin, D. (1981, March). *Social cognitive dimensions of composing processes*. Paper delivered at Conference on College Composition and Communication, Dallas, TX.

Sommers, J., Black, L., Daiker, D. A., & Stygall, G. (1993). The challenges of reading portfolios. *Writing Program Administration, 17*, 7–31.

Sunstein, B. (1994). Handout from the New Standards Conference, Palm Springs, CA.

Vygotsky, L. (1978). *Mind in society*. Cambridge, MA: Harvard University Press.

Vygotsky, L. (1962). *Thought and language*. Cambridge, MA: MIT Press.

White, E. (1994). Issues and problems in writing assessment. *Assessing Writing, 1*, 11–29.

Yancey, K. B. (1992). Portfolios in the writing classroom: A final reflection. In K. B. Yancey (Ed.), *Portfolios in the writing classroom* (pp. 102–116). Urbana, IL: NCTE.

Yancey, K. B. (1994). Make haste slowly. In L. Black, D. A. Daiker, J. Sommers, & G. Stygall (Eds.), *New directions in portfolio assessment* (pp. 210–219). Portsmouth, NH: Heinemann.

CHAPTER FIVE

Moving Toward Systemic Coherence: A Discussion of Conflicting Perspectives on Portfolio Assessment

Sandra Murphy
University of California, Davis

Roberta Camp
Educational Testing Service, Princeton, NJ

Over the last 15 years the two of us, separately and together, have participated in hundreds of discussions about the development and use of writing portfolios. We have listened, debated, and shared moments of accomplishment and deep frustration with teachers, teacher mentors, school and district administrators, and researchers immersed in the attempt to make portfolios work for students in individual classrooms and in programs serving a variety of schools, districts, and states. The many conversations we have had with our colleagues in these contexts have allowed us to observe the different and sometimes conflicting perspectives that are brought to the development and practice of portfolio assessment. We have participated in many discussions, for example, in which teachers of writing who see student ownership and learning as the most important elements of portfolio practice find themselves at odds with those who see a need for controlling portfolio contents for the purpose of responsible measurement. In the early years of our work with portfolios, in fact, we found that dichotomies such as these characterized our own thinking as well as the most heated portfolio discussions we witnessed.

In recent years, as a way to think about and discuss issues and disagreements that were surfacing in different political and social contexts of portfolio use, we have developed a framework of perspectives on portfolios (Camp & Murphy, 1989). The continuum in this framework stretches from individual students using writing portfolios to learn and to represent themselves to others, at one end, to government agencies using the information from portfolios to make decisions about policy and the distribution of resources at the other. Because the framework addresses multiple contexts for using portfolios in the assessment of writing, we think it provides a way to uncover and highlight the different and sometimes competing agendas that various parties bring to discussions about portfolios. It has helped us to understand how portfolio participants within each context of use see specific benefits in portfolios but become concerned, and even apprehensive, when their agenda for portfolios has to compete with the agenda of participants operating from another context.

Our purposes in this chapter are to examine and to characterize some of these different perspectives and the tensions that arise from them. Bringing forward and acknowledging the competing agendas will, we hope, move the discussion of portfolio assessment toward an approach capable of preserving the assets of portfolios for all participants, despite their differences in perspective. In particular, we hope to encourage a broadening of the discourse in the development stages of portfolio projects so that the interests of all participants can be better taken into account. In our discussion of the framework, we draw on examples from a limited number of projects, those we know most thoroughly and, in particular, those that are most fully developed and in which the effects of assessment on the educational system can be best observed. What we have learned from these projects leads us to argue for coherence among the components of a portfolio assessment system. When portfolio assessment components are coherent, and when the activities involved in building the assessment create opportunities for informed dialogue among participants, the assessment itself can become an effective means for promoting the kinds of learning it addresses (Camp, 1990, 1992a, 1993b; Eresh, 1990; Howard, 1993; Moss, 1994).

A FRAMEWORK OF PERSPECTIVES ON PORTFOLIO ASSESSMENT

Conditions for generating and procedures for evaluating the contents of portfolios vary widely across portfolio programs. In part, this variation can be explained by the different perspectives of participants within institutional and social contexts that are closer to or further removed from the perspective of the individual who creates the portfolio. Thus, the interests and concerns of students and teachers may be quite different from those of agencies involved in large-scale assessment, such as school districts, state departments of education, or a national reform movement. By the same token, because they are internal to the classroom, the issues of students and teachers are likely to overlap, whereas the external issues of district, state, and nation will similarly overlap. Consider Table 5.1.

TABLE 5.1

A Framework of Perspectives on Portfolio Assessment

Student	Teacher	Parents and Community	School and District	State and Nation
Assets				
• Opportunity for reflection and development of self-awareness • Development of student ownership • Basis for self-assessment and development of standards	• Vehicle for addressing instructional objectives • Richer source of information about students	• Richer, nontechnical source of information about students' learning • Opportunities to support student learning	• Vehicle for curricular reform • Vehicle for teacher development	• Fuller description of student learning • Vehicle for instructional reform
Tensions and Issues				
• Student control over choice versus interpretation outside the classroom • Reflection for learning versus reflection used as a basis for external judgments	• Use for instruction versus use for grades • Alignment between classroom instruction and external goals for curriculum and assessment • Mechanics of implementation	• Familiarity with standardized assessment and lack of confidence in new approaches • Interpretation of results in relation to traditional assessment information	• Competing views about curricular goals • Competing views about purposes and goals of education	• Competing views about purposes of education and theories of learning • Competing views about approaches to reform

Portfolios designed for different contexts may take very different shapes, in part because they appear to offer different assets for those designing them. At the far left end of the continuum, portfolios are likely to be most individualistic in character. Anchored in the curricula of particular classrooms and in the agendas for personal development set by individual students, portfolios here are likely to be more diverse than portfolios at the far right end of the continuum, where the concerns and issues of institutions are represented. At the institutional end of the continuum, because the assessment purposes in these contexts often entail comparisons between individuals or groups for gatekeeping decisions, or decisions about the distribution of resources, there is more likely to be pressure to standardize the portfolio. For example, although portfolio programs at the institutional end of the continuum might require multiple samples, evidence of process and student reflection, features that are common to almost all portfolios, the desire for comparability can easily lead to standardization of the required contents and of the conditions for producing them (Camp, 1993b). As a result, the writing within the portfolios might be generated, collected, and evaluated under conditions like those traditionally associated with the collection of writing samples for assessment purposes, conditions in which writing is done in response to specified prompts, with only limited possibilities for drafting or revising within the constraints of controlled, test-like conditions.

Valencia and Calfee (1991), commenting on this trend, observed that assessment portfolios are all too often

> standardized, with substantial direction from the teacher, administrator, or district. . . . Artifacts are generally authentic and collected over time, but most entries are predetermined, as are criteria for scoring and evaluating performance. Although there is some room for self-selection and reflection, a substantial core of required activities dominates the portfolio. Outside personnel may administer some of the assessments to ensure standardization or consistency. (p. 337)

This trend toward standardization of assessment portfolios, a tendency we have observed in many school- and district-level portfolio projects, reflects honest concern about issues of fairness and a traditional view of the way one goes about arriving at a well-warranted inference in measurement. A central intention of this traditional psychometric approach to evaluation is the control of external variables that might call assessment results into question. This is a serious concern in any assessment with high stakes attached, including most assessments that are external to the classroom. However, although the traditional psychometric approach employed in external assessment may address certain issues of measurement, it may not serve the best interests of teachers and students, the primary stakeholders in the assessment process, or of teaching and learning, the central purposes of education.

We are not the first to comment on the tension between external assessment and assessment internal to the classroom. Other scholars have analyzed the gap between the goals and characteristics of standardized assessments designed for measurement and the goals and characteristics of classroom assessment designed to support instruction (Calfee & Hiebert, 1988; Cole, 1988; Moss, 1994). Standardized assessments are designed with efficiency of time and cost in mind. Characteristic concerns are achieving reliability (arriving at similar results on similar occasions), obtaining data that can be processed centrally, and producing information that is broadly applicable to large numbers of students and useable by large numbers of test givers (Cole, 1988). This kind of assessment is thus typically intended to be independent of any particular curriculum. In addition, standardized assessments are often machine scored and employ a multiple-choice format, although some also include open-ended responses collected under conditions in which tasks, conditions for writing, and scoring criteria are the same for large groups of students, and scoring is done by readers trained for consistency among independent judgments of performance.

Classroom assessment, in contrast, is typically determined by particular instructional goals, mandated by teachers as opposed to external agencies, graded or scored locally by teachers (and sometimes by students), and used to make short-term instructional decisions (Cole, 1988). In addition, the purposes of classroom assessment are often quite different from the purposes of large-scale standardized assessments, which typically compare and sort students into levels of performance. In classroom assessment, the focus is on diagnosis (Calfee & Hiebert, 1988) or on the assessment of knowledge and skills that are subject to change over relatively short periods of time (Cole, 1988). The aims and procedures, then, of many classroom assessments are substantially different from the aims and procedures of most large-scale assessment programs.

The tension between these two purposes for assessment preceded the development of portfolios, but it now fuels debates about portfolio practice. In particular, the push to standardize portfolios reflects a reappearance of the tension between the demands of measurement and the demands of instruction. It is true that standardization addresses traditional measurement issues such as reliability, comparability, and generalizability—issues that are complicated by the variety and diversity of tasks that portfolios can contain. In the case of portfolios, for example, achieving inter-reader reliability is made more difficult because tasks may vary substantially from student to student. Often, the response to this problem has been increased standardization of the assessment. However, standardization may inhibit certain instructional goals. In particular, it may constrain students' autonomy in ways that discourage them from engaging in their own learning. More seriously, the constraints of standardization, especially in the case of writing, may weaken the validity of the assessment, if writing, as current research suggests, is perceived and taught as a process occurring over time and in response to personal, social, and intellectual contexts (Camp, 1993a; Moss, 1994).

One response to this tension has been to argue that the gap between the aims and methods of classroom-based instructional assessment and large-scale assessment is insurmountable (Cole, 1988; Purves, 1993). This stance suggests that separate approaches to assessment should be maintained, one for large-scale assessments that have high stakes attached, and one for classroom purposes. Yet there are hazards and costs associated with this position. Maintaining separate systems can be costly in both time and resources. In addition, there is the real risk that standardized high-stakes assessments, including portfolio assessments, will distort classroom instruction and curriculum.

Research has documented the powerful, often constraining, and sometimes deleterious, effects of standardized assessments on teaching, on curriculum, and on the professional knowledge and status of teachers. Studies have shown, for example, that teachers will base instruction on the content and form of tests, especially when high stakes are attached (Madaus, 1988; Mathison, 1989; Smith, 1991). A number of scholars have argued that curriculum is narrowed and fragmented when teachers rely on multiple-choice tests (Corbett & Wilson, 1991; Haertel & Calfee, 1983; Wells, 1991). Direct assessment of writing has also been shown to impact classroom instruction in powerful ways (Loofbourrow, 1994). Districts, as well as teachers, alter their curriculum to reflect the form and content of tests (Corbett & Wilson, 1991; Door-Bremme & Herman, 1986; Haney, 1984, 1991). In some cases substantial amounts of time are spent preparing students for a particular test, time that is then unavailable for other curricular objectives (Koretz, Linn, Dunbar, & Shepard, 1991). In addition, standardized tests constrain the professional development of teachers and weaken the authority of their professional judgment (Corbett & Wilson, 1991; McNeil, 1988; Shepard, 1991; Smith, 1991). Although previous research has not specifically addressed the impact of portfolios in large-scale assessment endeavors, it seems likely that highly standardized portfolios have the same potential for impact on the curriculum and the culture of schools as do other kinds of standardized assessments, especially when high stakes are attached.

Recognizing the powerful interplay between curriculum and assessment, we see a need for an integrated, systemic approach to portfolio assessment, one that takes into account the impact that assessment necessarily has on curriculum. In an integrated approach, assessment is shaped to fit the goals for learning, not the reverse. The goals for education and the views of learning in such a system are reflected in its assessments, and assessment and curriculum are compatible across different levels, from the classroom to district and state levels. This approach, although difficult to accomplish, resolves the contradictions between the policies now found at different levels of the educational system. To use an extreme but all too prevalent example, it resolves the contradiction between a policy that promotes the development of subject matter knowledge, critical thinking, independence, and creativity at the classroom level, but assesses the results of curriculum at the district or state level with instruments designed to measure isolated basic skills.

To establish an integrated assessment approach with a healthy relationship to the educational system as a whole, the impact on teachers and their professional development must be carefully addressed. There is a growing body of evidence that assessment can have a negative impact on the professional development of teachers, if, for example, the teachers' own creativity and judgment are displaced by externally mandated tests or test-like materials that promote mechanistic kinds of instruction (Calfee & Drum, 1979; Cole, 1988; Haertel & Calfee, 1983; Smith, 1991). Healthy educational systems, however, create situations in which teachers profit from their experience in assessment development. Teachers collaborating with researchers in the development of new approaches to science instruction in Pittsburgh, for example, have devised ways to engage students in "assessment conversations" (Duschl & Gitomer, 1994). Instead of assessing student learning only at the end of an instructional sequence, teachers have designed activities in which assessment is combined with instruction and involves application of criteria based on scientific principles. These teachers, then, are directly involved in the reconceptualization of the relationship between assessment and instruction.

Empirical evidence of changes that can occur when teachers are engaged in meaningful assessment-related activities is provided by work recently completed in California in conjunction with the development of the California Learning Assessment System (CLAS) portfolio assessment. Teachers surveyed in a study by Sheingold, Heller, and Paulukonis (1994) reported substantial changes in their teaching and assessment approaches. In particular, they indicated changes in the sources of evidence they use for assessing student performance, in their expectations for students' responsibility for their own learning and assessment, in their goals for instruction, and in their use of explicit performance criteria to evaluate student work. Like the science teachers in Pittsburgh, these teachers are reconceptualizing the relationship between assessment and instruction. In a healthy educational system, then, teachers' own professional development is enhanced by their direct participation in the development of the assessment.

In recommending a systemic approach, we are suggesting that the well-being of the educational system as a whole be taken into account. That is, considerations such as the potential impact of the assessment system on teachers and their role as professionals should be addressed along with the potential impact on learning and instruction in the assessment design. These considerations, in turn, must be balanced with technical concerns such as the need for acceptable levels of inter-rater reliability, which determine whether assessments can provide meaningful information. The concerns raised by psychometricians about reliability and validity are serious, and the results of statistical analyses of portfolio scoring have so far shown mixed results. Scoring of writing portfolios in the Pittsburgh Arts PROPEL project has yielded high reliabilities across grade levels, dimensions, and raters, even though students are allowed a wide range of choice in constructing their portfolios (LeMahieu, Gitomer, & Eresh, 1995). Vermont's statistics, on the other hand, have been unacceptably low (Koretz, Stecher, & Deibert, 1993). Yet even Vermont's unfavorable results have led to another round of refinement to the scoring procedures and the assessment system. Portfolio assessment, as these examples illustrate, is now at the point at which real world models have been developed and can be examined and refined, a process essential to the generation of new assessment theory (see Snow, 1988).

Calls to standardize the contents of portfolios are frequently based on a tacit assumption that psychometrics cannot change, and that portfolios therefore must be shaped to meet the demands of traditional psychometric approaches. This line of reasoning ignores the work now being done to create new assessment theory (see, for example, Frederiksen, Mislevy, & Bejar, 1993; Linn, Baker, & Dunbar, 1990) and new models for assessment (see, for example, Camp, 1993a; Frederiksen & Collins, 1989). What the new measurement theory suggests is that an assessment should be compatible with the kind of learning it purports to measure. Rather than fit portfolios to the demands of old psychometric models, then, portfolios might well be used to challenge psychometrics to devise new methods for obtaining trustworthy judgments about students, methods that will enhance learning and promote the educational system as a whole. Because scholars are redefining validity to include the consequences of the assessment—the impact on curriculum and participants (Frederiksen & Collins, 1989; Linn, Baker, & Dunbar, 1990; Messick, 1989a, 1989b, 1994; Moss, 1992, 1994)—it is likely, in fact, that an integrated system, if truly coherent, will better meet the requirements of emerging conceptions of validity.

Recent changes in measurement theory, in addition to drawing our attention to technical matters, call for an understanding of the social context in which assessment occurs. Understanding the social context means taking into account, we believe, the perspectives of those who are involved in the assessment. In the pages that follow, we describe and contrast the purposes various individuals and agencies have for using portfolios in different institutional and social contexts—in classrooms, schools, district offices, and state and national arenas—and we analyze the tensions that result from the different agendas within and across these contexts. In the process, we also touch on philosophical differences between theories of learning that underlie the design of portfolio programs in classrooms as well as large-scale assessment programs. Features of portfolio program design (that is, the particular requirements adopted for the portfolio contents, the role of students in making selections, and the procedures employed for evaluation) reveal beliefs about the nature of writing as a theoretical construct, about how children best learn to write, and about appropriate ways to organize the curriculum and to teach (Murphy, 1994a). Tensions arise, we suggest, when the curricular perspectives and assessment goals of participants from different contexts are in conflict. As might be expected, the tensions are especially noticeable when the perspectives and goals internal to the classroom are in conflict with those that inform external assessment systems.

PORTFOLIOS SEEN FROM
THE STUDENT'S PERSPECTIVE

As the framework in Table 5.1 indicates, portfolios provide assets from the student's perspective that are not often found in other, more traditional assessment situations. Certain assets, however, may be perceived as liabilities by parties with agendas different from the student's. The freedom portfolios can give students to choose how they will present themselves to others, for example, may be perceived as a liability by those who have concerns about technical matters such as interrater agreement in large-scale assessment. Thus, the assets perceived by some participants are themselves sources of tension in portfolio design when perceived by others from another context.

Assets

Portfolios allow students to gain some control over the assessment process, to demonstrate more completely and in their own terms what they know and can do, and to set their own goals and assess their progress toward them. Furthermore, a number of portfolio programs have found that portfolios allow students to reflect on their processes for writing, on the products they create, and on their own progress or development over time. Portfolios also encourage students to gauge their own progress and development in relation to standards. In these ways, portfolios encourage students to take greater responsibility for their own learning. Because portfolios offer a way to help children learn how "to assess what they have learned and how they learn best," they help children learn to "become autonomous learners" (Lamme & Hysmith, 1991, p. 632).

From the students' point of view, then, opportunities for reflection and self-awareness, ownership, and self-assessment are the important assets of portfolios. The experience of teachers and researchers observing students working with portfolios have thus led them to incorporate such opportunities into their portfolio guidelines.

Opportunity for Reflection and Development of Self-Awareness.
Recognizing the important role that reflection can play in learning, researchers have emphasized reflection and self-awareness as aspects of performance previously untapped in writing assessment. One of the first attempts to direct attention to portfolios in the early 1980s provided the beginnings of a theoretical description of portfolios emphasizing process and self-awareness (see Camp, 1985). A more recent formulation emphasizing the aspects of performance which are now seen to be essential in the development of writing ability is as follows:

- multiple samples representing a variety of performances and addressing different audiences and purposes;
- evidence of the processes, including interactions with others, used in creating text (brainstorming notes, multiple drafts, etc.);
- evidence of students' awareness of the processes and strategies they have used and indications of what they value in the writing. (Camp, 1993b)

A similar emphasis on reflection and process can be found in the guidelines constructed by Daiker and his colleagues at Miami University in Oxford, Ohio, for advanced placement portfolios (Daiker, Black, Sommers, & Stygall, in press). Daiker and his colleagues have found particular value in the reflective pieces in portfolios because they promote self-assessment and help students assume control of their own development. Highlighting the value of the portfolio for enhancing students' learning, the guidelines they now suggest for portfolio design focus on student reflection and revision in the process of putting together the portfolio:

- Include multiple samples of writing from a number of occasions;
- Require a variety of kinds or genres of writing;
- Provide opportunities for revision;
- Ask students for their reflections—on their portfolio, on their writing process or history, or on themselves as writers;
- Offer important choices to the writer. (Daiker et al., in press)

Research has demonstrated the importance of students' own awareness in monitoring their processes and strategies for writing (Bereiter & Scardamalia, 1987; Flowers & Hayes, 1980, 1981). Awareness is enhanced by reflection.

In fact, Johnston (1983) argued that reflection is central to learning. If students cannot articulate what they are learning, then, he argued, "they are not learning in a way which is conscious and under their control" (p. 3).

Development of Student Ownership. The issue of control from the perspective of students has to do with the amount of latitude they have in (a) the conditions for writing and (b) selecting the contents of the portfolio. Giving students decision-making responsibility in these areas gives them the opportunity to develop agency, that quality Sizer (1992) described as the "personal style, assurance, and self-control that allow [the individual] to act in both socially acceptable and personally meaningful ways" (Sizer, quoted in Posner, 1992, p. 95). Recognizing the potential for students to develop agency by exercising control and responsibility, various groups and individuals involved in the development of portfolio programs have proposed that portfolios be defined to emphasize choice and student ownership. Guidelines proposed by Paulson and his colleagues (1991), for example, which are addressed to portfolios in general, highlight the importance of the students' role in generating the contents of the portfolio and in deciding how their work will be represented to external audiences. According to Paulson et al. (1991), students should have the opportunity to shape the information about themselves that the portfolios will convey. Ownership, in part, is the right to say what *will not* be included in the portfolio:

- Portfolios should provide opportunity for students to engage in self-reflection.
- Students should be involved in selecting the pieces included in the portfolio.
- The portfolio should convey a sense of the student's activities and intentions in generating it.
- The final portfolio should contain only material that the student is willing to make public.
- The portfolio should contain information that illustrates growth.
- Test scores and other cumulative folder information should be included only if they take on new meaning in the context of the portfolio.
- Students should be provided with models of portfolios and of the processes others have used to develop and reflect on them.
- The portfolio may serve multiple purposes, but they should not conflict. (p. 60)

In a similar vein, much of the literature on portfolios indicates that in the process of creating portfolios, students learn to exercise judgment about their own work, monitor their own progress, set goals for themselves, and present themselves and their work to others (see Camp, 1990, 1992b; Murphy & Smith, 1991; Rief, 1990; Tierney, Carter, & Desai, 1991; Wolf, 1989; Yancey, 1992).

Basis for Self-Assessment and Development of Standards. Analysis of recent assessment development work in California also highlights the importance of the student's role and the interchange that is possible in classrooms where assessment is integrated with instruction. Analysis of data collected from a study by the California Assessment Collaborative (CAC, 1993) of 22 pilot alternative assessment projects indicates that elements of assessment programs that focus on the role of students and that are aimed at "developing student capacity to use assessment to improve learning" contribute to sound instruction. Guidelines for assessment development based on the results of the analysis include the following:

- Create opportunities for students to learn and practice self-assessment.
- Give students meaningful feedback on their work.
- Provide opportunities for teachers and students to revisit and improve their work.
- Develop student understanding of the standards on which their work is judged.
- Communicate content standards to teachers, students, parents and the community.
- Articulate the full range of what students should know and be able to do.
- Design a structure for student self-assessment.
- Assure that all students have access to thinking, meaning-centered curriculum and instruction.
- Build community support by demonstrating potential for improved student performance. (p. 2b)

Taken together, these elements describe an educational environment in which students, through their work with portfolios and other assessment activities, become increasingly aware of their progress toward clearly articulated goals.

The three sets of guidelines cited here, coming as they do from a variety of portfolio and assessment projects, indicate the extent to which student ownership, reflection, and self-assessment have been found to be part of the portfolio experience. Portfolios give students opportunities, all too rare in our schools, to assume ownership of assessment, to assess their own work, and to make learning conscious (Howard, 1990, 1993; Reif, 1990).

Tensions and Issues

Student Control Over Choice Versus Interpretation Outside the Classroom. Because students need a degree of control and personal authority in order to develop agency, students who have not had opportunities to practice making choices may be uncomfortable making their own decisions about portfolio selections, and perhaps unwilling to do so. Being unwilling, however, may be in turn the result of a lack of opportunity. The student who says "just tell me what to do" is typically speaking from lack of experience. Having a degree of decision-making responsibility and support while they learn to make their own decisions eventually enhances students' learning and the development of agency.

However, allowing students to make choices in assessment creates problems as well as opportunities. Tensions arise when authority over the way the student presents himself or herself to others is unduly constrained by the demands of external assessment in which portfolios are interpreted and evaluated outside the immediate context of the classroom. These demands often lead to constraints on student choice and to standardization. Flexibility in contents, an advantage from the student perspective, may be perceived as posing substantial challenges when it comes to establishing statistical reliability (see Baker, O'Neil, & Linn, 1991; Nystrand, Cohen, & Dowling, 1993). Reliability appears less difficult to achieve when portfolio contents are uniform (Herman, this volume). Certainly, in the absence of explicitly shared criteria and guidelines and instructional support for assembling portfolios, reliable scoring is difficult, if not impossible to achieve.

Generalizability across contexts is also an issue, as is validity. The variability in content resulting from student choice and differences in classroom instruction makes it difficult to compare portfolios. Concern about this variability has led to ongoing debates as to whether classroom-based portfolios can be used for school- or district-level purposes. In the absence of clearly defined purposes, all alternative assessment techniques, including portfolios, may have questionable validity (Baker et al., 1991). Concerns about the validity of the assessment speak to the need for an integrated portfolio assessment system, one that is based on a coherent view of learning, clearly defined purposes, and explicit criteria that are widely shared among participants in the system.

Our purpose here is not to review the many complex issues surrounding reliability, generalizability, and validity. Nevertheless, these issues are serious. The extremely important measurement problems they involve present substantial challenges for assessment designers. For some, standardization of portfolio contents appears to be required for comparability of results across classrooms or schools for large-scale assessment purposes (Herman, Gearhart, & Baker, 1993; Worthen, 1993). However, it may not be necessary to standardize portfolios in the traditional ways to achieve fair and responsible judgments of student performance.

One example of an alternative procedure is the work that has been done in the Arts PROPEL project in Pittsburgh. Clear and explicit scoring criteria and well-defined assessment purposes that are clearly articulated to everyone involved, including administrators, teachers, students, and parents—not standardized tasks—form the basis for obtaining consistent judgments about the portfolios and for establishing their validity. The Arts PROPEL experience demonstrates that when a clear structure is provided and criteria have become part of the vocabulary of a portfolio "culture," it is possible to obtain respectable statistical indicators of consistency: .72 to .76 for one rating for middle-school portfolios, and .84 to .87 for two ratings, estimates that were calculated through application of the Spearman-Brown prophecy formula to simple correlations (LeMahieu et al., 1995).

The Advanced Placement Examination in Studio Art is a second example of a portfolio assessment that accommodates diversity in student work. Every year, approximately 4,500 students submit portfolios of drawings, paintings and slides to the Educational Testing Service. These portfolios are compiled in response to broad guidelines that allow a maximum range of individual expression. At ETS, a jury method is employed to evaluate the portfolios. This method, widely accepted in other performance fields such as music and sports, substitutes collective judgment for standardization of performance, allowing students multiple options for demonstrating achievement (Mitchell, 1992).

In alternative models of this kind, judgments about dimensions of performance are based on collections of evidence in portfolios, and the criteria on which the judgments are based are public—shared with students as well as evaluators (Camp, 1992a). For example, in the Arts PROPEL model, teachers, looking at the entire portfolio, evaluate on three dimensions: accomplishment in writing, use of processes and resources for writing, and development as a writer. In the Advanced Placement Studio Art general portfolio model, judges evaluate three dimensions of performance: breadth, original work, and single theme concentration. These more flexible models of large-scale assessment seem preferable to standardized portfolios, because they can accommodate a high degree of student ownership (Mitchell, 1992).

Although it may not be necessary to streamline and standardize collection procedures in order to achieve fair and responsible judgments of student performance, certain other kinds of regularization do seem required. It seems reasonable to expect, for example, that the principles used to shape the portfolio project be reflected in both the conditions for generating and the procedures for evaluating the contents of the portfolios. This regularization may come in the form of consistent application of a particular learning theory in structured classroom activities. In the Arts PROPEL project, for example, portfolios include diverse kinds of writing, but the requirements for particular kinds of reflective entries are regularized both in classroom instruction and in the frameworks for putting together the portfolios.

Another way to achieve coherence is to match the requirements for contents and the criteria for evaluating the contents. Some projects use the criteria for evaluating portfolios as guidelines for assembling them. For example, instead of asking students to submit particular types of writing or other specified pieces of evidence, teachers ask students to demonstrate particular strategies or habits of mind. Many different kinds of evidence might be offered, as long as the particular strategy or habit of mind is demonstrated. The CLAS portfolio framework reflects this approach. Students are asked to demonstrate their accomplishments in relation to broad dimensions of learning in the English language arts: "constructing meaning" by reading and by listening, and "composing and expressing ideas" in speaking and in writing (CLAS, 1994). A similar approach, but one more focused on specific disciplinary concerns, has been adopted by teachers at San Diego High School, where teachers provide explicit criteria to guide students in assembling their interdisciplinary portfolios (Murphy & Smith, 1991). In social studies, for example, students are asked to take into account criteria such as:

- Uses historical evidence to support arguments and ideas.
- Uses creativity to approach and convey ideas.
- Expresses ideas clearly.
- Connects historical periods with today.
- Demonstrates an understanding of cause-and-effect relationships.

Establishing congruence between requirements for contents and criteria for evaluation offers definite advantages. It makes explicit the goals of the educational experience to be demonstrated by the portfolio, bringing criteria and expectations into public dialogue and debate. For some students, it is true, particularly those who have not had opportunities to become familiar with the language of the criteria, these kinds of guidelines for portfolios may be relatively inaccessible. It must be acknowledged, further, that even when there is coherence between elements of the portfolio assessment (for example, between principles used for shaping the portfolio, conditions for generating the contents, and procedures for evaluating them), there are major problems still to be solved. One is the challenge of making criteria specific enough to be useful as tools for learning, yet generic enough to accommodate diversity in the way they are met within the system. This challenge is being addressed in several recent portfolio projects that are described later in this chapter.

***Reflection for Learning Versus Reflection Used as a Basis for
External Judgments.*** Like student ownership, student reflection has created some debate among portfolio practitioners, both in and out of the
classroom. Outside the classroom, experts debate what part reflections should
play in the evaluation of student performance. Some educators, like the
teachers in Webster Groves, Missouri, highlight reflection by making it part of
the requirements for portfolio contents. Some believe reflection should be
scored; others believe that for assessment purposes it should be ignored. Some
present evidence that certain kinds of reflection (postwrites) in conjunction
with a writing sample may provide a more accurate picture of a student's
abilities than a writing sample alone (Allen & Roswell, 1989). Others worry
that reflection, along with other contextual information, will influence the
scoring process in ways that would make the assessment unfair. In some cases,
researchers who investigate the validity of writing portfolios have stripped
portfolios of their contextual information before conducting readings (Herman, Gearhart, & Baker, 1993). They argue that if such information was
included, the scoring task would take the reader "into another complicated
area—the feasibility of adjusting ratings based on differences in support and
assignment difficulty" (p. 220). The raters in the study, however, like portfolio
readers in other projects, "felt the need for more information about both the
nature of the instructional context and the nature of the assignments that
students were given to inform their ratings" (p. 220). Teachers of writing also
argue that, in some cases, a piece of writing in a portfolio should be judged
on its merits alone, apart from student reflection.

What these disagreements highlight are the different agendas of participants in the portfolio process and different beliefs about how to create a fair
and trustworthy assessment. It seems reasonable to suggest, however, that, in
an integrated assessment system designed to enhance learning and students'
development of agency, one could look at both the work itself, for the
evidence it yields about students' accomplishments, and at the students'
reflections for evidence of metacognition or awareness of process and
product. Looking across both makes it possible to gauge the match between
the work itself and the student's assessment of it. This, in fact, is the approach
taken in the Arts PROPEL writing portfolio assessment (Camp, 1993b).

Within the classroom, the debate continues. It is not uncommon to hear
teachers say they are dissatisfied with the perfunctory attempts at reflection
their students produce. Some teachers decry the self-serving comments of
students engaged in sales jobs ("I just love this class!"). Others point to the
metronome lists in what may be a fast developing new genre—the fill-in-
the-blanks portfolio letter. (The list goes something like this: "I put this piece
in because. . . . I put this piece in because. . . . Finally, I put this piece in
because. . . ."). Teachers who are in the early stages of portfolio use seem
most likely to be dismayed at such comments, even as their students seem

most prone to making them. Experienced teachers, on the other hand, treat perfunctory reflection as a challenge. Many experienced teachers, especially those who adopt a workshop or studio approach to the teaching of writing, have been quite successful at encouraging their students to assume responsibility for their learning, to set goals for themselves, and to reflect on their learning processes (Beach, 1989; Gadda, 1991; Howard, 1990; Johnston, 1983; Kirby & Kuykendall, 1988; Rief, 1990).

What this debate demonstrates, we think, is that thoughtful reflection is like most other challenges in the teaching of writing: it takes hard work, courage, honesty, support from teachers, and a classroom climate that encourages it, whether it is part of assessment or not. The climate that encourages thoughtful reflection takes time to evolve. Its key components, according to teachers who have worked to establish it, are also critical to the development of student agency:

- a freedom to discuss issues central to writing and to literature-as-writing;
- an environment in which everyone's opinion is equally valid. (Howard, 1993, p. 90)

These components work to establish a class as a "community of learners" and to create a supportive climate that "allows students to take risks" (Howard, 1993, p. 91).

Thoughtful self-evaluation is, as Johnston (1989) has said, "the most effective evaluation for learning" (p. 523). For this reason alone, we need to find ways to encourage students to attempt it, and to avoid discouraging them by doing it for them. Given opportunities to develop agency and practice in evaluating their own work and work processes, and the guidance of thoughtful teachers, all students can learn to be more articulate about how they want to present themselves in their portfolios, about the kinds of things they want to include, and about the processes that help them do their best. In time, as Howard (1993) has observed, "The portfolio and the classroom culture in which it is produced provide the forum within which [students] can learn to speak with clarity, confidence, and understanding" (p. 94).

PORTFOLIOS SEEN FROM
THE TEACHER'S PERSPECTIVE

Portfolios offer teachers opportunities to help their students become more aware of how they are developing as writers and thinkers. Teachers who use portfolios value the opportunities they provide to help students reflect, assume ownership and responsibility, and practice self-assessment (Yancey,

1996). Thus, the teachers' perspective on the assets of portfolios overlaps with that of students. In addition, from the teachers' perspective, portfolios offer richer and more useful sources of information about students. The additional information provided by portfolios may be perceived, however, as a liability, if its collection is mandated by outside agencies and the task of collecting it is perceived as an unnecessary burden. Again, assets perceived in one context can produce tensions in portfolio design if they conflict with purposes arising from another context.

Assets

Vehicle for Addressing Instructional Objectives.   For teachers, portfolios provide a vehicle for addressing important instructional objectives in writing, such as using writing to learn, discovering writing strategies that help the writer, and writing for diverse audiences and purposes. In some schools teachers ask their students to select a piece for their portfolios and reflect on something they learned or discovered during the process of writing it or on their purpose for writing the piece. This kind of approach allows teachers to emphasize that writing is not just a product, or something writers complete after all their thinking is finished, but a process that contributes to thinking and learning. In this way, portfolios help teachers accomplish a unique instructional objective—increasing students' awareness of the uses of literacy processes in learning.

In other schools, teachers have taken advantage of the opportunities portfolios offer to encourage students to write to diverse audiences for diverse purposes, and thus, to put a premium on versatility. In Hickson Junior High School in Webster Groves, Missouri, for example, teachers distribute guidelines for putting portfolios together that ask students to demonstrate and analyze their own versatility as writers. Teachers at Hickson ask students to create portfolios that demonstrate their ability to write to different audiences for different purposes and in different genres and forms. In addition, teachers encourage the students to compare and contrast features of the different kinds of writing their portfolios contain. As a guiding characteristic of a rich writing program and an explicit instructional objective at Hickson, versatility has become a criterion for students to meet, to document, and to analyze.

Richer Source of Information About Students.   Portfolios also offer teachers a richer source of information about their students than do scores from tests. They give teachers a detailed portrait of a student's strengths and weaknesses, accomplishments, and areas that need further work. Teachers perceive information garnered from portfolios as more useful for developing instructional plans than information from discrete standardized measures. In one study, teachers receiving portfolio data "were able to design specific instructional strategies for students" with limited proficiency in English, while "teachers receiving only the traditional assessment data requested additional information and were unable to recommend specific instructional plans" (Garcia, Rasmussen, Stobbe, & Garcia, 1993, p. 431).

In addition to concrete evidence of student performances, portfolios provide opportunities, when students are asked to reflect, for teachers to learn what students think they know, and what lessons, current or past, they consider important. Portfolios also make visible important aspects of learning: processes, purposes, and values. Consider the following excerpts, which are taken from letters written by middle school students in Oakland, California, to introduce their portfolios.

Reflection, these letters suggest, can give teachers valuable information about students' knowledge of particular writing strategies. The following excerpt indicates, for example, what the student knows about strategies for developing characters in stories:

> "My strength as a writer is my descriptive language. I usually write paragraph after paragraph on how a character in my story looked, talked, walked, and even sleep. That is also a weakness of mine."

The teacher who has access to this reflection can follow up on the student's interest in the problem with conciseness by providing models of effectively developed character description and by responding to the student's own writing with focused suggestions for deletion of irrelevant or redundant details.

Reflection can also show what students know about genres. The following excerpt, for example, indicates what the student knows about poetry, as well as her personal aims in writing it:

> "Poetry, to me, is a way of expressing your feelings without really *telling* them."

Reflection can also show teachers what their students think good writing is:

> "I'm not really a good writer except I try to do my best. That's why all the writings I do or have done have a lot of mistakes. I'm not good at punctuations, sentence structures, and tenses."

Knowing that the student conceives of good writing as writing free of mechanical errors, the teacher is better equipped to help him discover other ways to judge quality in writing.

Reflections such as these address an important loose end in the teaching of writing—the extent to which students gauge effectiveness in their own writing. Thus, reflections offer unique assessment information that is essential to learning and that can help teachers design appropriate instruction. Even when teachers have the means to assess the writing itself, it is difficult for them to know whether students are consciously aware of what makes a piece of writing successful unless they also have information from reflection. Equally important, reflections such as these create opportunities for response to student writing that is more focused on what individual students are attending to in their work. They promote dialogue between teacher and student that is anchored in the student's agenda for learning.

Portfolios can tell teachers about many aspects of student learning that might be difficult to discover otherwise. We know that systematic observations of students' use of language recorded in portfolio-like assessments such as the Primary Learning Record have been extremely useful, for example, in helping teachers understand how students perform in their home language and how that performance differs from performance in school language tasks. Thus, portfolios can help teachers explore and understand how language varies across situations. Using portfolios to look explicitly at how language varies with audience and purpose and across situations is particularly helpful for teachers of students who need to learn how English used for academic purposes in school differs from other kinds of writing and from language used at home. Because portfolios contain multiple pieces of writing, they invite teachers to help students take a closer look at how texts differ from one another and to compare and contrast rhetorical strategies used in different languages and situations (Murphy & Smith, 1992; Murphy, 1994b). In this respect, they offer a unique teaching opportunity.

Tensions and Issues

Use for Instruction Versus Use for Grades. Portfolios can provide a basis for grades, although not all teachers choose to use them for this purpose. Some teachers are reluctant to make portfolios part of a formal evaluation process, even in the classroom, much less in the arena of large-scale assessment. These teachers seem to feel that students learn from the process of creating a portfolio, but that grading portfolios would undercut their value. Other teachers, however, see portfolios as a way to help students understand the grades they receive and as a way to engage them in a dialogue about criteria for evaluation. Roussea (1996), for example, involves her students directly in the evaluation process. Believing that portfolios encourage each student "to take greater responsibility for his or her own growth as a writer," because "each had to review patterns and determine ways in which he might improve," Roussea asks her students to generate criteria for their writing that she can use when she evaluates it. Students initially do this individually. Then small group and full class discussions follow, and finally a vote to determine criteria for the class. In Kathryn Howard's classes, students produce "wall charts containing revisable lists of those qualities the students perceive to be essential to the creation of a good piece" (1993, p. 91). Howard believes these lists are important "because they are student-generated and because they provide a foundation for personal standards and criteria for good writing as well as an internalized and personalized writer's vocabulary" (p. 91).

In all of these scenarios, evaluation is negotiated among teachers and students, a radical change from the traditional scenario, in which the teacher makes all the decisions. The issue of grades is not a stumbling block for portfolios in these classrooms, where portfolios are part of a rich mixture of information gained through a variety of classroom interactions. When evaluation becomes part of classroom dialogue, the issue of grades becomes secondary. Portfolios can be used in combination with whatever other information is available.

Alignment Between Classroom Instruction and External Goals for Curriculum and Assessment. As we have argued elsewhere, portfolio assessment systems are vulnerable to many of the same implementation problems that beset other kinds of assessment. From a teacher's perspective, performance assessments can be as much an interruption to day-to-day teaching as any multiple-choice test if they take time away from teaching or if they interfere with curricula and routines already in place in the classroom. Tensions arise when the curricular goals of the teacher are not in line with the curricular goals and instructional approaches reflected in the design of the large-scale assessment system. When discontinuity exists, teachers may experience loss of authority and pressure to conform. Smith (1991) observed that teachers whose curricular programs are not well matched with the contents of mandated testing, and who resist changing their programs, are "likely to be subject to frequent demands to defend their programs on other grounds, and to fears that they will suffer sanctions and loss of autonomy because of low scores" (p. 10). Similarly, 67% of the teachers in the Hatch and Freeman (1988) study of kindergarten classrooms reported distress because of discontinuity between instructional methods that were in part dictated by accountability pressures and their own views about children's learning needs. Case studies of portfolio assessment implementation are now drawing attention to teachers' resistance to these new assessment approaches when their views about curriculum are different from the views on which the assessment program is based. Lamme and Hysmith (1991), for example, writing about one elementary school's "adventure into portfolio assessment," described the conflicts that can occur when teachers hold different philosophical approaches from the ones associated with the particular portfolio practice being introduced. At this elementary school, teachers who did not embrace whole language philosophy and practice "became disillusioned about what they perceived as additional work requirements" (p. 639).

Mechanics of Implementation. From a teacher's perspective, rapid implementation of any innovation by an external agency is disruptive. When teachers experiment on their own with any new approach or curricular innovation, including portfolios, they can introduce the approach at their own pace, try it out, and revise it, shaping it to suit the existing curriculum, their views about learning, and their general instructional approach, style, and needs. But when new approaches are introduced to meet the needs of agencies outside the classroom, teachers may not have the same flexibility of pace or the same freedom to adapt and experiment. In our experience, because teachers are ultimately responsible for introducing and managing portfolios in the classroom, they are often concerned about procedural issues such as manageability (i.e., the procedures involved in collecting materials, making the selections, and interpreting the portfolio contents). Teachers are also concerned about the compatibility of the portfolios with existing classroom activities. They worry about the time portfolios will require, and they wonder whether portfolios will interfere with or add to what they are already doing in their classes. These issues are raised by teachers experimenting with portfolios within their own classrooms. They become even more critical when portfolios are part of large-scale assessment.

Management becomes especially burdensome if portfolios require significant amounts of record keeping on the part of the teacher. Portfolios that include records of teachers' observations of children's progress along with collections of student work can provide useful information for instruction and lead to significant changes in the way teachers perceive students and their own role in students' learning. However, these kinds of portfolios present difficult management problems for teachers. Cheong (1993), the author of a recent study of the California Learning Record (CLR), a record-keeping system for teachers which in many ways resembles a portfolio, reported that

> All teachers interviewed expressed concern about expanding the use of the CLR to more students and finding classroom time to do the observations and fill out the paperwork (forms). . . . In particular, teachers said that they spent too much time transferring their own observation or interview notes onto the "official form," a process one teacher described as "redundant" and "a waste of time." (p. 14)

Teachers in the pilot study made a number of suggestions for improving the CLR and supporting its use. Several suggestions focused on the issues of time and flexibility. Teachers advised, for example, streamlining the forms, integrating the records of observations with portfolios, and allowing teachers to attach writing samples rather than requiring summary descriptions of the children's writing on the official form. Teacher research studies conducted at other grade levels confirm the difficulties teachers have in managing the CLR (McCall, 1994; Wood, 1994). Teacher-researcher Wood (1994) wrote:

> While the information that came out of each of the three records I kept this year was very helpful, I am daunted by the idea of doing thirty such records every year. I am afraid this type of time requirement of teachers could cripple the average classroom. . . . To do this on a regular basis for an entire classroom would become a full-time job on its own. (p. 5)

Lamme and Hysmith (1991) also have warned about the burden of port-folio data collection, if it is not well integrated with instruction. Commenting on the ways data collection can take time away from instruction, they pointed out that "it is important for teachers not to waste time copying notes over or transcribing them onto different forms" (p. 635). The time issue is a matter of serious concern to teachers. In another study of one teacher's experience with portfolios in an elementary school, portfolios that included student products as well as forms for the teacher's observations, researchers con-cluded that "the use of portfolios required significant amounts of both in-class and after-school time" (Gomez, Graue, & Bloch, 1991, p. 627). Gomez and her colleagues cautioned that "the reality of portfolio assessment . . . tells us that the responsibility of making this restructured assessment work falls squarely on the shoulders of already overburdened teachers" (p. 628).

Studies such as these indicate some of the problems that are likely to occur when assessment is not well integrated with instruction. It is clear that teachers resent and resist assessments that take time away from instruction. Data collection procedures should be set up so that they are useful to teachers in day-to-day instruction. Wherever possible, techniques used should be compatible with teaching practices currently in place and should not require busy work such as recopying. As much as possible, students themselves should be responsible for collecting and shaping data, for these are the activities that integrate assessment with learning.

Assessments that require new approaches to curriculum and teaching are likely to evoke resistance, especially if they are mandated externally (Callahan, 1994; Gipps, 1993; Gomez, Graue, & Bloch, 1991). Lamme and Hysmith (1991) recommended that provisions be made to support teachers in the transition to new approaches. When new techniques are introduced, time and support should be provided for experimentation, and entry points should be provided for all teachers, novices as well as experts, with a variety of instructional approaches. The studies cited here suggest that lack of flexibility in the implementation process may increase resistance. An evolutionary process, one in which new approaches to assessment integrated with instruction are introduced, then modified and added to as teachers become familiar with the new techniques, appears more likely to succeed. The Mt. Diablo High School

Portfolio Project, for example, has evolved over the past 6 years from a highly prescriptive, menu-driven approach to specifying portfolio contents toward a more open-ended approach that accommodates diversity and encourages experimentation on the part of both teachers and students (Murphy, 1994a). Flexible approaches to design and implementation that allow room for evolution, as opposed to highly specific, fixed requirements in portfolio design, may also provide room for and encourage participation in assessments on an even larger scale. They allow entry points for teachers with diverse instructional approaches. The broad dimensions of learning in the framework adopted in the CLAS portfolio pilot described earlier, for example, accommodate a wide variety of curricular approaches at both the school level and at the levels of individual classrooms and students.

It is difficult to argue for the time needed for an assessment system to evolve. From an institutional perspective, an evolving process of development may appear to signal a lack of leadership and clear vision about the new system. Because concern exists about the expense of putting a new assessment system into place, the temptation is to take an immediate stand and implement the new approach quickly. However, wherever possible, teachers need to be allowed to adjust to new systems at their own pace and in their own way. If the new portfolio assessments now being created are to be effective, they must be developed and implemented in ways that are sensitive to the impact they will have on teachers and students. Although many educational reformers look to alternative assessments as instruments of educational reform, it is unwise to assume that their impact will be invariably or uniformly positive or that the new assessments will not disrupt good practices as well as bad.

PORTFOLIOS SEEN FROM THE PERSPECTIVE OF PARENTS AND MEMBERS OF THE COMMUNITY

The perspectives of parents and members of the community toward assessment are perhaps less well understood than those of other parties in educational systems. We are just beginning to get a sense of the issues that are important for these groups, in part because the practice of consulting parents and community members about educational issues is not widespread, and in part because parents and members of the community have been, so far, less likely to be consulted in the early stages of developing assessments. Although the importance of involving parents and the community is becoming more obvious as new assessments become more fully established, much work remains to be done to better engage these groups and to understand their perspectives on educational assessment. Nevertheless, some assets can be inferred, and some information about parents' views is available from classrooms where portfolios are in place.

Assets

***Richer and Nontechnical Source of Information About Students'
Learning.*** From the perspective of parents and other members of the
community, portfolios offer new sources of comprehensive and nontechnical
information about student learning, achievement, and development. The
benefit is a more focused understanding of a child's work habits, accomplishments, and progress in schooling. Research conducted in Colorado on parents'
opinions about standardized tests, information provided by teachers, and
performance assessments, although not specifically focused on portfolios,
indicates that third-grade parents consider seeing graded samples of student
work to be "much more useful in learning about their child's progress than
standardized tests" (Shepard & Bliem, 1993, p. 23).

When parents examine children's portfolios, they see real samples of
writing and other work that may be more immediately intelligible to them
than are traditional forms of assessment information, such as stanines and
percentiles. Portfolios give parents a richer sense of the curriculum and the
students' learning environment than any grade or score presented in isolation. From the student's written reflections, and when they are present, from
the teacher's written comments on the student's writing, portfolios can give
parents a view into classroom instruction and learning and a sense of the
interactions that occur in the classroom, as well as insights into the criteria
and language used by the teacher for evaluation. Once parents have that
kind of insight, they can meaningfully enter into a discussion of student
learning with the teacher and with the child. In turn, they can bring their
own perception of the child into the conversation.

Opportunities to Support Student Learning. Parent interactions
around portfolios can also aid student learning. In some of Pittsburgh's Arts
PROPEL classes, for example, students take their writing folder home and
ask parents to read their writing and answer a set of open-ended questions
about what they see in it. Kathryn Howard, a teacher who uses this procedure, asks parents to comment on what they learn about the strengths of
their children's writing from reviewing their portfolios, to identify the children's needs as they see them, and to suggest ways to address those needs
so as to aid the children's growth and development as writers (Howard &
LeMahieu, 1995). Because the questions asked of parents require no special
knowledge or particular expertise, parents can enter the conversation about
their children's writing, bringing "a perspective on the student that is not
always available from within the classroom" (Camp, 1992a, p. 257). Moreover, when students return to the classroom, they reflect on what they
learned about themselves as writers from discussions with their parents. In
this way, the exchange between parent and child has a direct impact on

the student's learning in the classroom. Portfolios can thus involve parents directly and positively in their children's learning.

Tensions and Issues

Familiarity With Standardized Assessment and Lack of Confidence in New Approaches. Like other participants in the assessment process, parents and members of the community have opinions about how assessment should be conducted. Some parents, like some teachers, believe that in order to be trustworthy, information must come in the form of "hard data" collected under controlled, standardized conditions. In the Shepard and Bliem (1993) study mentioned earlier, despite the parent's overall valuing of student work samples, several parents indicated that they thought "standardized tests were more objective in contrast to performance tests that would be either difficult to grade fairly or more time consuming to grade" (p. 22). Many parents and members of the community have confidence in the "objectivity" of psychometrics and statistical indicators. Johnston (1989) has commented on the persuasive power and the danger of this kind of technical verification: "Psychometrics, because of its roots in positivistic empiricism, prevents the expression of stance because that suggests subjectivity. In so doing, it eliminates the expression of counter-stance" (p. 511). Because of its claims to objectivity, information collected by traditional scientific methods carries powerful weight. It should not be surprising, then, that parents might be reluctant to give up the security of that "weight," for new and relatively untried procedures. Parents and members of the community have been conditioned over the last 50 years to expect the kinds of information that come from traditional assessments.

In the Shepard and Bliem study, although there was evidence that parents preferred performance assessment, especially for the purpose of learning about their child's progress, many parents (46%) favored requiring schools to use standardized tests to measure student achievement. According to results of the annual Phi Delta Kappa/Gallup poll, there is even more widespread and consistent support among the general public for the "use of standardized national tests to measure the academic achievement of U.S. students" (Elam, Rose, & Gallup, 1993, p. 147). In 1976, 65% of respondents favored the use of standardized national tests for this purpose. Twelve years later in 1988, support rose to 73%, and by 1989 to 77%. In 1992, 71% of respondents favored using standardized national tests to measure student achievement. In a recently published poll (1993), 92% of public school parents approved of the use of standardized tests to "identify areas in which students need extra help," and 87% "to identify areas in which teachers need to improve their teaching skills" (Elam et al., 1993, p. 147). There appears to be widespread support from both parents and the general public for using standardized assessments, however they are conceived, to monitor individual student progress and to hold schools accountable. Although approval of standardized tests does not imply disapproval of performance measures, such widespread public approval makes standardized assessment an attractive and, on the face of it, more cost-effective alternative for public agencies engaged in large-scale assessment.

Interpretation of Results in Relation to Traditional Assessment Information. Parents are also concerned about the comparability of standards underlying different kinds of assessment. They may worry that performance assessment represents a lowering of standards. Some groups, for example, fear that focusing on complex kinds of learning may result in lack of attention to the basics. Others, familiar with the format and requirements of standardized, multiple-choice tests, may distrust alternative forms of assessment. These issues can be particularly acute for parents of minority children.

Such concerns present substantial challenges for administrators who are responsible for communicating information about students' performance in ways the public finds credible. The problem for the administrator is to find ways to educate parents and other members of the community about the value and trustworthiness of data collected in alternative assessments and the positive impact such assessments can have on the curriculum at the school. Like other participants, parents and members of the community need to learn that it may not be necessary to standardize collection procedures, in the sense of requiring identical activities produced under identical conditions, in order to achieve fair and responsible judgments of student performance.

Administrators and teachers also face the challenge of dealing with parents who may feel disenfranchised in the school environment, who feel their interests are not well represented, or who feel uncomfortable talking about their children's work. These difficulties speak to the need to develop an assessment system in which the views of all participants are addressed and in which standards and information about assessment methods are distributed, in nontechnical terms, to all participants. The challenge for administrators is to set up interactions that are accessible and meaningful to parents, carried out in ways that do not require specialized knowledge or language. These interactions will need to take the concerns of all participants into account, and to draw on the interests and expertise of all parties in the assessment.

When the assessment system is fully developed, confidence in it can be enhanced by inviting members of the community to participate in an audit. In Pittsburgh, for example, teachers and administrators from surrounding school districts and representatives from business and foundations visited the Pittsburgh School District to audit the portfolio assessment system. The assessment was validated in the community in which its students are likely to reside, work, and apply for post-secondary education (LeMahieu, Eresh, & Wallace 1992; Rothman, 1992).

PORTFOLIOS SEEN FROM THE PERSPECTIVE
OF THE SCHOOL OR DISTRICT

From the perspective of the school or district, portfolios offer particularly attractive opportunities for curricular reform and for teacher development. These opportunities are relevant, of course, to the agendas of parties in other levels of school governance—for instance, at the state and national levels. We are introducing them here, though, because administrators at this level are responsible for implementing and coordinating reform initiatives, especially those intended to encourage site-based management. Particularly attractive assets are the opportunities portfolios provide for collaborative projects in which teacher inquiry grounded in focused discussions of student work becomes the basis for teachers' development of the skills they need to systematically observe and analyze their students' learning processes. These kinds of discussions form the basis for more thorough-going curricular reform and professional development than do programs that merely impart methods and procedures. Tensions arise, however, when individuals within the school or district hold competing views about approaches to professional development and curricular reform, or about the structure and educational goals of the curriculum.

Assets

Approaches to professional development and curricular reform vary widely. Some districts adopt a very top-down approach, spelling out specific methods and procedures for teachers to follow. In this approach, the teacher's role is to implement decisions that have been made elsewhere. In other districts, teachers take an active professional role in the life of the school or district and in the decision-making process. Professional development programs in such districts attempt to create a collegial climate in which teachers participate in the development of curriculum and instructional methods. In such districts, the dialogues about student work in portfolios that occur among teachers at the school site and between teachers and teacher mentors at the district level can become the basis for reform that actually changes the classroom climate. Further, in districts that are moving to site-based management in restructuring, dialogue about student work in portfolios helps to ensure that changes occur not only in managerial structure but also in curriculum and instruction.

Vehicle for Curricular Reform.   At the school and district level, portfolios offer opportunities for accomplishing a number of objectives with curriculum, from making constituents aware of it, to shaping and enhancing it, implementing it, and revising it as necessary. For programs that focus on critical thinking, complex learning tasks, and learning processes, portfolios can mirror and inform the curriculum in ways not possible with other assessment methods. For example, portfolios can include exemplars of problem-solving activities along with reflections on the processes used in the activities. They can represent work accomplished in long-term curriculum-embedded projects that integrate language processes—reading, writing, listening, and speaking. In short, they can accommodate complex and authentic activities, the kinds of activities that a school or district might want to encourage as contributing to learning and making visible the thinking processes of students.

When teachers are encouraged to share exemplars drawn from portfolios, they learn how to engage their students in learning activities similar to those that produced the student work. Discussions of exemplars also force concrete questions about what students are to learn and what constitutes adequate evidence that they are learning. Such discussions encourage a specific and grounded sense of curriculum and goals for learning because they are anchored in the work of individual students. They invite teachers to ask: "Is this what we want?" and "What do we want next?"

From our experience working with teachers in a number of portfolio projects, it has become clear that teachers have an intense interest in discussing the practices behind the work they see. A school or district engaged in curriculum reform is well advised to take advantage of the powerful impact that the talk surrounding portfolios can have on teachers, and thus on curriculum. In one instance, teachers from the social studies department at Bret Harte Junior High School in Oakland, California, helped their colleagues in English see new ways to scaffold writing assignments with classroom activities in which students generate ideas and content for their writing (Murphy & Smith, 1990). Using exemplars from the students' portfolios, the social studies teachers described assignments that worked well, and explained how the assignments had been supported by instruction. Such discussions provide a mechanism for encouraging curricular change. Discussing successful teaching and learning strategies revealed in student work is a powerful way to encourage groups of teachers to attempt new methods (Hansen et al., 1993).

Vehicle for Teacher Development. Discussions that focus on student work in portfolios offer a powerful mechanism for teacher development. They encourage teachers to engage in collaborative action research. Teachers in Pittsburgh's Arts PROPEL, for example, engage in collaborative assessment conferences—small group discussions in which they look closely at the work of one student, describe what they see, and talk about what to do next (Camp, 1992a, 1993b). In this way, teachers share their insights about students' needs. At the same time, they sharpen their own perceptions of student learning. Teachers' shared insights and perceptions then become the basis for a district-wide portfolio climate that is carried directly into the classroom.

Portfolio-like assessments that ask teachers to observe and summarize student performance also enhance teachers' understandings of their students' needs and abilities. Use of the California Learning Record, with its emphasis on teacher observations of students' activities, led teachers to reassess their teaching practices and to experiment with new strategies (Cheong, 1993).

Reports from the Pittsburgh portfolio project indicate that teachers become more curious about students' thinking and learning when they discuss student portfolios together, an observation confirmed by students (Arla Muha, personal communication). This enhanced awareness of and curiosity about the elements of student work invites teachers to assume the stance of inquiry, to become researchers of their students' learning processes and of effective instructional practices. These insights in turn can be refined in discussions with other teachers and other colleagues. When this happens, teacher development can become an ongoing and to some extent self-sustaining process.

Portfolios have also been used in collaborative projects in which groups of teachers learn to conduct systematic investigations of the ways students revise their texts, respond to different writing topics, and react to conditions for writing (Murphy & Smith, 1990). Teachers who engage in these collaborative investigations of their students' portfolios learn how to scaffold student performance with effective teaching and how to design effective writing assignments.

Benefits to the school and district also accrue in other kinds of discussions about portfolios. Conferences between teachers and language arts mentors in Pittsburgh, for example, which focus on a selection of portfolios from the teacher's class, lead to rich conversations about student learning and effective teaching practices (Camp, 1992a). These conversations help to establish expectations for collegial discourse within the district, they create district level understanding of teachers' concerns, and they inform district decisions about teachers' professional development needs. The benefits of such conversations can be amplified by group evaluation of portfolios. The setting of shared standards for performance, as exhibited in judgments of sample portfolios, helps teachers to understand school or district standards in tangible terms. It also helps them see their own students' work in relation to those standards and to performance by students in other classrooms.

Tensions and Issues

Portfolio selection guidelines embody priorities and views of learning even when they are not structured around particular content, a particular taxonomy of discourse, or a particular curriculum for writing. Some are very prescribed and directive, some very open. Those that are tightly prescribed tend to be more closely associated with a specified curriculum. Those that are more open-ended often assume that students and teachers will take active roles in shaping not only the portfolios but the course of students' learning in general. Reflecting the philosophy of Dewey (1938), with his emphasis on the active role of the individual and of individual experience in learning, these more open-ended portfolios put less emphasis on pre-scribed content and they accommodate cooperative development of cur-riculum by teachers and students. In addition, they complement constructivist theories of language use and development. Instruction based on construc-tivist theory, according to Applebee (1993), becomes "less a matter of trans-mittal of an objective and culturally sanctioned body of knowledge, and more a matter of helping individual learners learn to construct and interpret for themselves" (pp. 199–200). Thus, open-ended guidelines for portfolios assume a constructivist perspective on learning.

In one way or another, what is prescribed, however narrowly or broadly, becomes a statement about what is valued. Tensions arise when differences about curriculum and educational values implied in portfolios have not been addressed. A major challenge for decision makers, then, is to help the de-signers of school and district portfolios become aware of the assumptions about curriculum and education implied in portfolio design. A second chal-lenge is to promote discussion and resolution of differences likely to cause conflict once the portfolio design is used by large numbers of teachers in a variety of classrooms.

Competing Views About Curricular Goals. Although portfolios offer attractive opportunities for curricular reform, not everyone agrees about how portfolios should be designed and used. Within any single school, if faculty have not agreed on specific parameters, portfolios will take very different shapes to represent the curricular perspectives and theories of learning held by different individuals. Because they embody different beliefs about cur-riculum and learning, portfolios will then vary in the ways they represent content, and they will promote different ideas about the purposes for edu-cation. Contrasting, and sometimes conflicting, perspectives on the purposes and content of curriculum can in this way become the fuel for debates about portfolio practice. Some curricula, for example, focus on the transmission of certain kinds of knowledge, whereas others highlight the development of the individual and the capacity of the individual to learn. Schools and districts need to take into account the views of curriculum implied in the portfolio designs they adopt.

In some projects the contents of portfolios are defined in ways that reflect theoretical conceptions of how the discipline is or should be structured—what should be taught. In Ann Roussea's class, for example, students include an in-class response to a prompt and their best examples of expressive, essay, and poetic writing (Roussea, 1996). In specifying this framework, Roussea is drawing on the work of James Britton, a major discourse theorist in the teaching and learning of writing, and his colleagues at the University of London. This British research team, departing from traditional rhetorical categories, based their framework on an analysis of school as opposed to writing (Britton, Burgess, Martin, McLeod, & Rosen, 1975). Their scheme of the functions of written utterances includes *transactional* writing (e.g., essays, writing to inform) *expressive* writing (language close to the self) and *poetic* writing (patterned verbalization of the writer's feeling and ideas. Roussea's portfolio content framework, with its categories of essay, expressive, and poetic writing, thus reflects one formulation of the structure of the discipline of English language arts.

In other schools or districts, different ways of organizing the portfolio have been developed. In several California schools, for example, where the new canon (for some) was for a time the set of writing types that appeared on the state-wide writing test, teachers asked their students to fill their portfolios with the identified types of writing. In these California schools, students were asked to include in their portfolios one autobiographical incident paper, one speculation about cause and effect, one interpretation paper, and so on. These lists of portfolio contents, known as "menus," put the spotlight on the rhetorical characteristics of particular products of student work, but not necessarily on the processes by which they were created or on the students' development as writers. Students picked the best exemplars of particular types of writing from their working folios to put in their portfolios. The selection guidelines for these kinds of portfolios allow some freedom of choice (best from a particular category), but they are clearly not as wide-open as guidelines that allow the student to select the genres to be put into the portfolio. Some decisions have already been made for students—decisions that emphasize certain types of writing and thereby discourage students from taking the initiative in describing themselves as writers. Clearly, this kind of portfolio organization has implications for the kinds of learning and writing promoted in the schools and districts using it.

A modified and somewhat less prescribed "structure of the disciplines" approach can be seen in Vermont's specification of requirements. Students are asked to include five major pieces. Among them must be (a) a poem, short story, play, or personal narration, (b) a personal response to a cultural, media, or sports event, to a book or current issue, or to a math problem or scientific phenomenon, and (c) a prose piece. In addition to writing in these discourse categories, students in Vermont must include a "best piece" (of any type) and a letter from the student to the portfolio reviewers explaining why the student chose the "best piece" and how it was composed (Vermont Department of Education, 1991). Students' choice of what to put into their portfolios is thus constrained by guidelines that specify particular categories of discourse, but it is open to several types of writing within those categories. An implicit goal underlying these guidelines is to encourage a rich and diversified curriculum in Vermont schools. A school or district wishing to encourage a degree of student choice and diversity in classroom curricula might use similar portfolio guidelines.

Competing Views About Purposes and Goals of Education. Other portfolio projects also encourage diverse writing experiences for students, but are more open-ended in the way they specify portfolio contents and the freedom they allow students to set their own educational agendas and to decide how their abilities will be represented. In the Webster Groves project referred to earlier, the guidelines for the Hickson Junior High School portfolio do not require a particular set of tasks, but they do require students to demonstrate their versatility. Students are free to select any of several different ways to demonstrate the breadth of their abilities by including, for example, different topics (subjects), genres, modes, audiences, purposes, particular writing strategies, styles, and/or points of view. Other portfolio projects ask students to demonstrate habits of mind or particular abilities as opposed to mastery of particular rhetorical strategies or genres. For example, at Central Park East Secondary School (CPESS) students are expected to create projects which are intelligible (employ appropriate conventions), encompass a wide knowledge base, make connections so that the whole is greater than the sum of the parts, provide credible and convincing evidence, and engage the reader (CPESS, 1992).

In Pittsburgh Arts PROPEL, guidelines for contents do not require specific types of writing or writing within particular discourse categories. Rather, students are asked to engage in a set of reflective activities in which they make choices for their portfolios. The portfolios are then evaluated with a rubric whose dimensions apply to both the pieces of writing selected and the students' reflections. As indicated earlier, students are asked to demonstrate their accomplishments in writing, their use of processes and resources for writing, and their development as writers, aspects of writing performance that are spelled out in detail in the rubric for scoring. The portfolio guidelines give students and teachers both the responsibility and the authority to make choices about how to best demonstrate these broad dimensions of performance. This approach is similar to the one developed in the California Learning Assessment System pilot portfolio project, where students and teachers choose pieces that demonstrate broadly defined dimensions of learning (Sheingold et al., 1994).

Clearly, important philosophical differences about the purposes of education underlie differences in the design of portfolio programs in large-scale assessment programs as well as classrooms. These differences present a challenge for individuals in policy-making positions who make decisions about the shape of an assessment. To identify and address these differences requires an approach to assessment development that gives all participants voice in the process and honors their different perspectives. With the recognition of competing views, the task of developing a portfolio assessment becomes in large part one of consensus building.

PORTFOLIOS SEEN FROM THE PERSPECTIVE OF THE STATE OR NATION

To some degree, concerns of participants at the level of the state or nation mirror those of parties at other levels. Like their local counterparts in schools and districts, decision makers at the state and national level see the potential of portfolios for providing a fuller description of student learning and for playing a role in educational reform. At this level, as at others, portfolios are attractive because they offer an opportunity to encourage and to assess higher level skills and abilities that have not been encouraged or assessed with other methods. At state and national levels, in addition, portfolios fit in with a broader concern for reforming education in order to meet national education goals. Of particular relevance to this discussion is National Education Goal 3: "Student Achievement and Citizenship" cited in "Raising Standards for American Education: A Report to Congress, the Secretary of Education, the National Education Goals Panel and the American People," by the National Council on Education Standards and Testing (NCEST, 1992):

> By the year 2000, American students will leave grades four, eight, and twelve having demonstrated competency in challenging subject matter including English, mathematics, science, history, and geography; and every school in America will ensure that all students learn to use their minds well, so they may be prepared for responsible citizenship, further learning, and productive employment in our modern economy. (p. 2)

To meet this goal, among others, members of NCEST call for the development of national standards, including content, student performance, school delivery, and system performance standards, as well as the development of a system of assessments for students consistent with those standards. They argue that "high national standards tied to assessments" are critical to the nation in three primary ways: "to promote educational equity, to preserve democracy and enhance the civic culture, and to improve economic competitiveness" (p. 3). They also acknowledge, however, that "the country is engaged in a national debate on what students should know and be able to do and on how to measure achievement toward those ends" (p. 8). Thus, although there may be a fair amount of agreement about the need for national standards, there is less agreement about what those standards should be and how progress toward them should be evaluated. Similarly, there is disagreement on how to go about reaching the standards, once they are defined.

Assets

Fuller Description of Student Learning. From the perspective of a legislator or state department of education, portfolios offer many of the same assets as they do at other levels of educational governance. Like participants at the school or district level, representatives of state departments of education and national agencies value the potential of portfolios for providing a more complete picture of student accomplishment, one that includes information about student learning and addresses aspects of performance such as process and metacognition that have been relatively neglected in other kinds of assessment. Equally important, portfolios can be shaped to address important instructional and curricular goals that might not be easily assessed by other means—for example, students' ability to carry out complex and long-term projects aimed at developing critical thinking skills and problem-solving abilities. In this, portfolios speak directly to concerns at state and national levels about the preparation of a new generation of students to participate in and contribute to an increasingly complex society.

Vehicle for Instructional Reform. At a state or national level, portfolios may also be particularly attractive as a vehicle for instructional reform. Certainly, they are compatible with the kinds of learning valued by many of the individuals who want to accomplish reform. In addition, they can provide the kind of flexibility that is critical to participation across a wide variety of schools and districts, while also providing a basis for judgments that are comparable from one student's portfolio to another. Portfolio selection guidelines and criteria based on broad categories can also address a need for consensus on large issues or important values while accommodating local diversity.

At the same time, portfolios offer possibilities for encouraging the kinds of changes in professional power structures that many educational reformers advocate. They offer rich opportunities for the professionalization of teaching. For example, in the recent work of the New Standards Project, a consortium of several states and school districts involved in the development of performance assessment systems, teachers have been taking the lead in developing guidelines for compiling and scoring portfolios. Teams of teachers (more than 900 total) from each state and district who participated in professional development sessions in the spring and summer of 1994 are acting as lead teachers in their own states and districts in field trials in following years (NSP, 1994a).

Tensions

Competing Views About Purposes of Education and Theories of Learning. Tensions in assessment development at this level come about in part because of differences in beliefs about the purposes and goals of education and theories of learning, just as they do at other levels of school governance. Many policymakers in Washington and in state departments of education have the same sorts of concerns as do teachers in classrooms and scholars in universities. Some scholars examining assessment at the national level are apprehensive about the models of communication that national goals will embody when they become operationalized in assessments. For example, Witte and Flach (1994) express concern that when the National Assessment of College Learning is put in place, communication may be reduced, "for the sake of efficiency and expediency in measurement," to a "set of isolatable but 'basic skills' for which commercial test-makers could generate items or prompts to elicit performances independently of any naturally occurring contexts . . . for producing or using language" (p. 9).

Emphasis on "basic skills" in curriculum and in assessment is based on a psychology of learning derived from behaviorist principles (Resnick & Klopfer, 1989). A basic assumption underlying this view of learning is that learning is "an accumulation of pieces of knowledge," which can be analyzed into components and transmitted to students "through practice and appropriate rewards" (p. 2). In an educational system informed by this view of learning, activities such as reasoning and problem solving, at the top of hierarchies of objectives like that of Benjamin Bloom (1954), are viewed as separate from more "basic" activities such as the accumulation of facts and skills (Resnick & Klopfer, 1989). In turn, an approach to teaching is adopted in which teachers engage in a teach–test–reteach instructional cycle intended to monitor individual progress toward mastery of sequential skills (Smith, 1986). Translated into school practices, this view of learning results in programs of mastery learning in which all students are expected to learn the same skills and to learn lower-level skills before progressing to the skills at the next level in the hierarchy.

Although some educators and many individuals in the community at large see basic skills programs as a way to reform schooling, others want to forge new paths to reform that reflect different views of learning. One of these new paths, based on the cognitive perspective, has steadily gained ground in the last decade at the national level. Resnick (1983) summarized the theory of learning associated with this perspective as follows:

> First, learners construct understanding. They do not simply mirror what they are told or what they read. Learners look for meaning and will try to find regularity and order in the events of the world, even in the absence of complete information. This means that naive theories will always be constructed as part of the learning process.
>
> Second, to understand something is to know relationships. Human knowledge is stored in clusters and organized into schemata that people use both to interpret familiar situations and to reason about new ones. Bits of information isolated from these structures are forgotten or become inaccessible to memory.

Third, all learning depends on prior knowledge. Learners try to link new information to what they already know in order to interpret the new material in terms of established schemata. (pp. 477–478)

In a cognitively oriented curriculum, the spotlight is on the acquisition of internal mental structures and processes that are necessary for successful performance and are broadly enabling for learning. A key concept of this theoretical perspective is the idea of learning as a cognitive apprenticeship in which learners engage in "contextualized practice of tasks, not exercises on component skills that have been lifted out of the contexts in which they are to be used" (Resnick & Klopfer, 1989, p. 10). At least one multi-state assessment reform project reflects the influence of this perspective. Under the leadership of Lauren Resnick, the New Standards Project (NSP) incorporates on-demand tasks, curriculum-embedded assessments, and portfolios (NSP, 1992, 1993). The open-ended guidelines in the pilot handbook for secondary portfolios in English language arts in this project call for students to demonstrate technical control, range and versatility, use of literacy processes, and reflective analysis (NSP, 1994b).

Competing Views About Approaches to Reform. In addition to competing views on theories of learning and curriculum philosophy, however, debates at the state and national level focus on the processes of instructional reform. In interesting ways, these debates parallel the tensions seen in portfolio design between standardization and flexibility. On one hand, there are calls for national standards and national testing. On the other, there are calls for school restructuring and site-based decision making. The opposition between these trends is readily apparent. Tye (1992), for example, describing the growth in state power and bureaucracy which has occurred since the 1970s, noted that "educational decision making is more 'top-down' and hierarchical than it has ever been," and he argued that changing the behavior of state and district board members from "directing" to "serving and supporting" is "absolutely necessary if restructuring is to be successful" (p. 14). He suggested that if decision making is decentralized, "testing will probably change from being a measure of accountability and a means of directing what is to be taught to being what it was originally intended to be: a means of diagnosing weaknesses and strengths in learning" (p. 14). Authority, in Tye's scheme, would no longer flow from top to bottom, with the state dictating to the district and the district to the school. Rather, he argued, teachers and school principals, "working with their communities," will have to assume new responsibilities and "learn to make collective decisions and to take collective actions" (p. 14). In a restructured education system, he said, "everyone will be accountable, not just teachers and administrators" (p. 14).

Clune (1993) also challenged the current trend toward reforming instruction in schools "through a centralized strategy of mandatory curriculum frameworks, high-stakes student assessments, and coordinated teacher training" (p. 237). Clune pointed out that the problem with centralization in assessment is the possibility that curriculum could become standardized. He argued that a common curriculum may be inequitable because "low-income schools and students . . . need a curriculum that is well adapted to produce dramatic gains in learning for their particular students, not a curriculum that is identical to and imported from somewhere else in the country" (p. 237). What both of these authors suggest, then, are systems of assessment that allow much more freedom of choice at the local level and less standardization and direction from the the top. An issue here is how to provide the same kinds of challenges for all students but present them in contextualized terms that are appropriate for particular students.

As noted earlier, models that incorporate a good deal of flexibility do exist. In a number of schools, promising portfolio programs are in place that allow students and teachers flexibility in putting together their portfolios within guidelines that enhance learning—schools we have described here, such as Mt. Diablo High School, Hickson Junior High School, Central Park East Secondary School, and schools in the Arts PROPEL project, among others. The challenge now is to create assessment systems that will accommodate, even encourage, these promising practices, yet also address the need for information at the state and national level.

Here too, promising work is underway. Large-scale portfolio systems such as the CLAS Portfolio Assessment Pilot and the New Standards Project have been designed to (a) encourage desired learning, (b) to move all students toward higher standards for learning, and (c) to allow schools and teachers collectively to define standards and performance in terms that are compatible with their local contexts. Moreover, in each of these programs, large numbers of teachers have been involved directly in the assessment development process, in articulating guidelines for portfolio selections, in developing criteria for evaluation, in piloting materials, and in analyzing results. The development processes adopted in these projects, then, are providing powerful professional development experiences for teachers, as well as new models for assessment development that take into account the views of important stakeholders in the assessment. In addition, these systems are attempts to accommodate diversity and decentralization within a larger framework that recognizes the legitimate needs of policymakers at state and national levels for information about the general level of achievement of the country's students.

CONCLUSION

Creating a portfolio assessment system that is workable both in classrooms and beyond them requires that several major hurdles be faced. A central one is the matter of ownership. If a system is to accommodate diversity, it will need to allow ownership for all parties in the assessment, each with different hopes and concerns for portfolios and with different responsibilities, knowledge, and power. The different perspectives of participants in the varied contexts of assessment, we believe—students, teachers, school and district personnel, parents, members of the community, and leaders at the state and national levels—need to be taken into account.

To be workable and effective, a portfolio approach also needs to be systemic. The assessment, that is, needs to be consistent with curricular goals and educational purposes. It needs to be supported with professional development for teachers. It needs to address the desire of parents for information about their children and of school and district personnel for information relevant to decisions about allocation of resources and necessary for monitoring performance. It should also be compatible with desired reforms at the school, state, and national level.

Envisioning a system such as this means casting everyone, but especially teachers, in new roles. In the past, the classroom teacher has been cast primarily as the recipient of policy decisions formulated by outside experts and as an implementer of initiatives designed by others—or as Darling-Hammond (1990) has said, as a "conduit for instructional policy, but not as an actor" (p. 233). If teachers are to have ownership in any new assessment system, they will need to be included in ways that assume their responsibility as promoters of standards, of student achievement, and of accountability. They will need to be actors, not recipients, and to make informed decisions about assessment—its purposes and content—just as they need to make informed decisions about teaching and learning. Students, too, will need to assume new roles. Like teachers, students in the past have been cast as the recipients of assessments designed and implemented by others. If assessments are to be compatible with new views of learning that highlight self-assessment and reflection, then students will have to assume more responsibility for making decisions about their learning and assessment.

Portfolio systems aimed at reform require time and support for students and teachers to become accustomed to new roles and to new approaches to instruction. During this time school and district personnel need to encourage the development of a collaborative, inquiry-based environment for teachers, as well as students. As Darling-Hammond and Snyder (1992) have pointed out, this will require new institutional capacities in schools: "Organizational supports for collegial work and learning are critical for the implementation of new educational practices" (p. 23).

Parents, members of the community, administrators at all levels of the educational system, and policymakers, like teachers and students, need to be brought into the dialogue about assessment and their concerns need to be addressed. To bring about a portfolio assessment system in which all parties are full participants requires time, so that the concerns of all parties can be expressed and consensus can develop. An additional hurdle in assessment reform will be to establish the credibility of the assessment with parents and the community at large. In part, this will require a concerted effort to educate these constituencies about new forms of assessment such as portfolios. In addition, development of new measurement theory and new methods for evaluating the effectiveness of assessments should be given high priority. Technical concerns that bear on the reliability and credibility of information provided by these new approaches to assessment cannot be ignored. Routine application of psychometric procedures designed for traditional forms of assessment will not suffice to establish the credibility of the new approaches.

At the state and national level, efforts should be made to promote assessment systems that will accommodate diverse approaches to curriculum while encouraging high-quality educational programs and intellectual accomplishments. Ideally, such systems would not attempt to dictate good practice in the schools by imposing prescriptive requirements. Rather, they would build on good practices and systems already in place. At district, state, and national levels particularly, there is a need for a flexible but coherent approach to assessment reform. Standards, mandates, and reform initiatives currently proliferate at these levels of the educational system, sending conflicting messages to schools and frustrating teachers and administrators charged with implementing them.

The challenges outlined here are inherent in all assessments, but are made explicit in a systemic approach. They must be attended to if portfolios are to be used successfully for assessment reform. The new assessments will need to move from an emphasis on standardization to focus on coherence of the system—in the relationship between principles for selecting portfolio contents and criteria for evaluation, for example, and in the ways the system is developed. They will need to integrate thinking about learning with thinking about assessment at every level, within classrooms as well as in our state capitols and in Washington. They will need to serve learning and instruction, but also the needs of audiences outside the classroom. All parties in the assessment will need some ownership of the assessment process, if these new assessment approaches are to succeed. But ownership is only possible with knowledge and shared understanding through which all participants can own the assessment in the sense that is important to them. To build this kind of ownership, the new portfolio assessments will have to incorporate definitions of accountability in which everyone has both voice and responsibility, and in which all parties can learn from their experiences and contribute to improvements in the system.

ACKNOWLEDGMENTS

The ideas in this chapter have taken shape through many years of dialogue with teachers, administrators, and fellow researchers about the potential of portfolios in assessment. This dialogue began in 1986 in the Writing Portfolio

Project funded by the California Assessment Program and in the Writing Portfolio Study Group sponsored by the National Writing Project. It expanded through the years to include colleagues engaged in portfolio development work in a number of projects throughout the United States. During one of those conversations several years ago, we drafted the initial outline version of the framework of perspectives on portfolio assets and tensions presented in this chapter. Subsequently, we have each used the framework as a starting point for many discussions about portfolios. We hope this chapter will be one more "turn" in our continuing conversations with our colleagues. We would like to express our appreciation to Robert Calfee and Pamela Perfumo for their thoughtful comments on earlier versions of the chapter.

REFERENCES

Allen, M., & Roswell, B. (1989, March). *Self-evaluation in holistic assessment.* Paper presented at the annual Conference on Composition and Communication, (ERIC ED 303-809), Seattle, WA.

Applebee, A. N. (1993). *Literature in the secondary school: Studies of curriculum and instruction in the United States* (National Council of Teachers of English Research Report No. 25). Urbana, IL: National Council of Teachers of English.

Baker, E. L., O'Neil, H. F., & Linn, R. L. (1991, April). *Policy and validity prospects for performance-based assessment.* Paper presented at the annual meeting of the American Psychological Association.

Beach, R. (1989). Showing students how to assess: Demonstrating techniques for response in the writing conference. In C. Anson (Ed.), *Writing and response: Theory, practice and research* (pp. 127–148). Urbana, IL: National Council of Teachers of English.

Bereiter, C., & Scardamalia, M. (Eds.). (1987). *The psychology of written composition.* Hillsdale, NJ: Lawrence Erlbaum Associates.

Bloom, B. S. (1954). *Taxonomy of educational objectives. Handbook 1: Cognitive domain.* New York: Longmans, Green, & Co.

Britton, J., Burgess, T., Martin, N., McLeod, A., & Rosen, H. (1975). *The development of writing abilities (11–18).* London: Macmillian Education.

Calfee, R. C., & Drum, P. A. (1979). How the researcher can help the reading teacher with classroom assessment. In L. B. Resnick & P. A. Weaver (Eds.), *Theory and practice of early reading* (pp. 173–204). Hillsdale, NJ: Lawrence Erlbaum Associates.

Calfee, R. C., & Heibert, E. (1988). The teacher's role in using assessment to improve learning. In E. Freeman (Ed.), *Assessment in the service of learning* (pp. 45–62). Princeton, NJ: Educational Testing Service.

California Assessment Collaborative (CAC). (1993). *Charting the course toward instructionally sound assessment: A report of the alternative assessment pilot project.* San Francisco: Author.

California Learning Assessment System (CLAS). (1994). *Phase I orientation materials working draft.* Educational Testing Service, Center for Performance Assessment, Emeryville, CA: Author.

Callahan, S. (1994, November). *Trying to dance in the glass slipper: Portfolios and accountability.* Paper presented at the annual meeting of the Conference on College Composition and Communication, Nashville, TN.

Camp, R. (1985). The writing folder in post-secondary assessment. In P. Evans (Ed.), *Directions and misdirections in English evaluation* (pp. 91–99). Ottawa, Canada: Canadian Council of Teachers of English.

Camp, R. (1990). Thinking together about portfolios. *The Quarterly of the National Writing Project and the Center for the Study of Writing, 12*(2), 8–14.

Camp, R. (1992a). Assessment in the context of schools and school change. In H. H. Marshall (Ed.), *Redefining student learning: Roots of educational change* (pp. 241–263). Norwood, NJ: Ablex.

Camp, R. (1992b). Portfolio reflections in middle and secondary school classrooms. In K. B. Yancey (Ed.), *Portfolios in the writing classroom* (pp. 61–79). Urbana, IL: National Council of Teachers of English.

Camp, R. (1993a). Changing the model for the direct assessment of writing. In M. Williamson & B. Huot (Eds.), *Validating holistic scoring for writing assessment* (pp. 45–78). Cresskill, NJ: Hampton Press.

Camp, R. (1993b). The place of portfolios in our changing views of writing assessment. In R. E. Bennett & W. C. Ward (Eds.), *Construction versus choice in cognitive measurement: Issues in constructed response, performance testing, and portfolio assessment* (pp. 183–212). Hillsdale, NJ: Lawrence Erlbaum Associates.

Camp, R., & Murphy, S. (1989). *A framework of perspectives on portfolios.* Unpublished manuscript.

Central Park East Secondary School (CPESS). (1992). *Central Park East Secondary School (CPESS) portfolio assessment rubric.* New York: Author.

Cheong, J. (1993). *A first look: Report of the 1992–93 pilot study of the California Learning Record.* Unpublished manuscript. Davis, CA: University of California, Center for Cooperative Research and Extension Services for Schools.

Clune, W. (1993). The best path to systemic educational policy: Standard/centralized or differentiated/decentralized? *Educational Evaluation and Policy Analysis, 15*(3), 233–254.

Cole, N. S. (1988). A realist's appraisal of the prospects for unifying instruction and assessment. In E. Freeman (Ed.), *Assessment in the service of learning* (pp. 103–117). Princeton, NJ: Educational Testing Service.

Corbett, H. D., & Wilson, B. L. (1991). *Testing, reform, and rebellion.* Norwood, NJ: Ablex.

Daiker, D., Black, L. Sommers, J., & Stygall, G. (in press). The pedagogical and political implications of college writing portfolios. In E. White, W. Lutz, & S. Kamusikiri (Eds.), *The practice and politics of assessment in writing.* New York: Modern Language Association.

Darling-Hammond, L. (1990). Instructional policy into practice: "The power of the bottom over the top." *Educational Evaluation and Policy Analysis, 12*(3), 233–241.

Darling-Hammond, L., & Snyder, J. (1992). Reframing accountability: Creating learner-centered schools. In A. Lieberman (Ed.), *The changing contexts of teaching. Ninety-first Yearbook of the National Society for the Study of Education* (pp. 11–36). Chicago, IL: University of Chicago Press.

Dewey, J. (1938). *Experience and education.* The Kappa Delta Pi Lecture Series. New York: Collier/Macmillan.

Door-Bremme, D., & Herman, J. (1986). *Assessing student achievement: A profile of classroom practices.* Los Angeles, CA: Center for the Study of Evaluation.

Duschl, R., & Gitomer, D. (1994). *Strategies and challenges to changing the focus of assessment and instruction in science classrooms.* Pittsburgh, PA: Learning Research and Development Center.

Elam, S. M., Rose, L. C., & Gallup, A. M. (1993). The 25th annual Phi Delta Kappa/Gallup Poll of the public's attitudes toward the public schools. *Phi Delta Kappan, 75*(2), 137–152.

Eresh, J. (1990, November). *Balancing the pieces: Content, teachers, tests, and administration.* Paper presented at the annual meeting of the Conference for Secondary School English Department Chairpersons, Atlanta, GA.

Flower, L., & Hayes, J. R. (1980). The dynamics of composing: Making plans and juggling constraints. In L. W. Gregg & E. R. Steinberg (Eds.), *Cognitive process in writing* (pp. 31–50). Hillsdale, NJ: Lawrence Erlbaum Associates.

Flower, L., & Hayes, J. R. (1981). A cognitive process theory of writing. *College Composition and Communication, 32,* 365–387.

Frederiksen, J. R., & Collins, A. (1989). A systems approach to educational testing. *Educational Researcher, 18*(9), 27–32.

Frederiksen, N., Mislevy, R., & Bejar, I. (Eds.). (1993). *Test theory for a new generation of tests.* Hillsdale, NJ: Lawrence Erlbaum Associates.

Gadda, G. (1991). Writing and language socialization across cultures: Some implications for the classroom. In F. Pietzman & G. Gadda (Eds.), *With different eyes: Insights into teaching language minority students across the disciplines* (pp. 55–74). Los Angeles: University of California at Los Angeles Publishing.

Garcia, E., Rasmussen, B., Stobbe, C., & Garcia, E. (1990). Portfolios: An assessment tool in support of instruction. *International Journal of Educational Research, 14*(5), 431–436.

Gipps, C. V. (1993, April). *Reliability, validity and manageability in large scale performance assessment.* Paper presented at the annual conference of the American Educational Research Association, Atlanta, GA.

Gomez, M. L., Graue, M. E., & Bloch, M. N. (1991). Reassessing portfolio assessment: Rhetoric and reality. *Language Arts, 68,* 620–628.

Haertel, E., & Calfee, R. C. (1983). School achievement: Thinking about what to test. *Journal of Educational Measurement, 20,* 119–132.

Haney, W. (1984). Testing reasoning and reasoning about testing. *Review of Educational Research, 54*(4), 597–654.

Haney, W. (1991). We must take care: Fitting assessments to functions. In V. Perrone (Ed.), *Expanding student assessment* (pp. 142–163). Alexandria, VA: Association for Supervision and Curriculum Development

Hansen, R., Johnson, J., Marlink, J., Medina, K., Murphy, S., Myers, C., Nicolls, B., Samuels, D., Scheeline, P., Shoemaker, E., Stokes, L., & Watterson, P. (1993). *The secret knowledge of teachers: Case studies of teacher-initiated change in classrooms and schools.* Unpublished manuscript. Davis, CA: University of California, Center for Cooperative Research and Extension Services for Schools.

Hatch, A., & Freeman, E. B. (1988). Who's pushing whom? Stress and kindergarten. *Phi Delta Kappan,* 145–147.

Herman, J. L., Gearhart, M., & Baker, E. L., (1993). Assessing writing portfolios: Issues in the validity and meaning of scores. *Educational Assessment, 1*(3), 201–224.

Howard, K. (1990). Making the writing portfolio real. *The Quarterly of the National Writing Project and the Center for the Study of Writing, 12*(2), 4–7, 27.

Howard, K. (1993). Portfolio culture in Pittsburgh. In R. Jennings (Ed.), *Fire in the eyes of youth* (pp. 89–102). St. Paul: Occasional Press.

Howard, K., & LeMahieu, P. G. (1995). Parents as assessors of student writing: Enlarging the community of learners. *Teaching and Change, 2*(4), 392–414.

Johnston, B. (1983). *Assessing English: Helping students to reflect on their work.* Philadelphia: Open Court Press.

Johnston, P. (1989). Constructive evaluation and the improvement of teaching and learning. *Teachers College Record, 90*(4), 509–528.

Kirby, D., & Kuykendall C. (1988). *Mind matters: Teaching for thinking.* Portsmouth, NH: Heinemann.

Koretz, D. M., Linn, R. L., Dunbar, S. B., & Shepard, L. A. (1991, May). *The effects of high states testing on achievement: Preliminary findings about generalization across tests.* Paper presented at the Annual Meeting of the American Educational Research Association, Chicago.

Koretz, D., Stecher, B., & Deibert, E. (1993). *The reliability of scores from the 1992 Vermont portfolio assessment program* (Tech. Rep. No. 355). Los Angeles: University of California, the Center for Research on Evaluation, Standards, and Student Testing and the Center for the Study of Evaluation.

Lamme, L. L., & Hysmith, C. (1991). One school's adventure into portfolio assessment. *Language Arts, 68,* 629–640.

LeMahieu, P. G., Eresh, J. T., & Wallace, R. C. (1992). Using student portfolios for a public accounting. *School Administrator, 49*(11), 8–13.

LeMahieu, P. G., Gitomer, D. H., & Eresh, J. (1995). Portfolios in large-scale assessment: Difficult but not impossible. *Educational Measurement, 14*(3), 11–28.

Linn, R. L., Baker, E., & Dunbar, S. B. (1990). Performance-based assessment: Expectations and validation criteria. *Educational Researcher, 20*(8), 15–21.

Loofbourrow, P. (1994). Composition in the context of the CAP: A case study of the interplay between composition assessment and classrooms. *Educational Assessment, 2*(1), 7–49.

Madaus, G. F. (1988). The influence of testing on the curriculum. In L. Tanner (Ed.), *Critical issues in curriculum, Eighty-seventh Yearbook of the National Society for Study of Education* (pp. 83–121). Chicago: University of Chicago Press.

Mathison, S. (1989, April). *The perceived effects of standardized testing on teaching and curricula.* Paper presented at the Annual Meeting of the American Educational Research Association, San Francisco, CA.

McCall, K. (1994). *Can anecdotal records work in junior high?* Teacher Research Report. Davis, CA: University of California, The Center for Cooperative Research and Extension Services for Schools.

McNeil, L. M. (1988). Contradictions of control, Part 3: Contradictions of reform. *Phi Delta Kappan,* 478–485.

Messick, S. (1989a). Meaning and values in test validation: The science and ethics of assessment. *Educational Researcher, 18*(2), 5–11.

Messick, S. (1989b). Validity. In R. L. Linn (Ed.), *Educational measurement* (3rd. ed., pp. 13–104). New York: American Council on Education and Macmillan.

Messick, S. (1994). The interplay of evidence and consequences in the validation of performance assessments. *Educational Researcher, 23*(2), 13–23.

Mitchell, R. (1992). *Testing for learning.* New York: The Free Press.

Moss, P. (1992). Shifting conceptions of validity in educational measurement: Implications for performance assessment. *Review of Educational Research, 62*(3), 229–258.

Moss, P. (1994). Can there be validity without reliability? *Educational Researcher, 23*(2), 5–12.

Murphy, S. (1994a). Portfolios and curriculum reform: Patterns in practice. *Assessing Writing, 1*(2), 175–207.

Murphy, S. (1994b). Writing portfolios in K–12 schools: Implications for linguistically diverse students. In L. Black, D. Daiker, J. Sommers (Eds.), *New directions in portfolio assessment* (pp. 140–156). Portsmouth, NH: Heinemann.

Murphy, S., & Smith, M. A. (1990). Talking about portfolios. *The Quarterly of the National Writing Project and the Center for the Study of Writing, 12*(2), 1–3, 24–27.

Murphy, S., & Smith, M. A. (1991). *Writing portfolios: A bridge from teaching to assessment.* Markham, Ontario, CA: Pippin Publishing Ltd.

Murphy, S., & Smith, M. A. (1992). Looking into portfolios. In K. B. Yancey (Ed.), *Portfolios in the writing classroom* (pp. 49–61). Urbana, IL: National Council of Teachers of English.

National Council on Education Standards and Testing (NCEST). (1992, January). *Raising standards for American education: A report to Congress, the Secretary of Education, the National Education Goals Panel, and the American people.* Washington, DC: Author.

New Standards Project (NSP). (1994a). Let the field trials begin. *The New Standard, 2*(7). Author.

New Standards Project (NSP). (1994b). *Student portfolio handbook: High school English language arts, mathematics. Field trial version.* Author.

New Standards Project (NSP). (1992). Rochester, NY: National Center on Education and the Economy. Author.

New Standards takes close look at portfolios. (1993). *The Council Chronicle, 3*(2). Author.

Nystrand, M., Cohen, A. S., & Dowling, N. M. (1993). Addressing reliability problems in the portfolio assessment of college writing. *Educational Assessment 1*(1), 53–70.

Paulson, F. L., Paulson, P. P., & Meyer, C. A. (1991). What makes a portfolio a portfolio? *Educational Leadership, 48*(5), 60–63.

Posner, G. (1992). *Analyzing the curriculum.* New York: McGraw Hill.

Purves, A. (1993, August). *If it's a new bottle, the wine had better be new too.* Unpublished manuscript distributed at the meeting of the New Standards Project Portfolio Pilot, Minneapolis, MN.

Resnick, L. B. (1983). Mathematics and science learning: A new conception. *Science, 220*(4596), 477–478.

Resnick, L. B., & Klopfer, K. (1989). *Toward the thinking curriculum: Current cognitive research. 1989 Yearbook of the Association for Supervision and Curriculum Development.* Alexandria, VA: The Association for Supervision and Curriculum Development.

Rief, L. (1990). Finding the value in evaluation: Self-assessment in a middle-school classroom. *Educational Leadership, 47*(6), 24–29.

Rothman, R. (1992). Auditors help Pittsburgh make sure its portfolio assessment measures up. *Education Week, 11*(40), 1–4.

Roussea, A. (1996). From the inside out. In K. B. Yancey (Ed.), *Voices from the field: Portfolio practice in middle and secondary school contexts.* Unpublished manuscript.

Sheingold, K., Heller, J., & Paulukonis, S. (1994). *Actively seeking evidence: Shifts in teachers' thinking and practice through assessment development.* Princeton, NJ: Educational Testing Service.

Shepard, L. A. (1991). Will national tests improve student learning? *Phi Delta Kappan, 73,* 232–238.

Shepard, L. A., & Bliem C. L. (1993). *Parent opinions about standardized tests, teacher's information and performance assessments.* Paper presented at the annual meeting of the American Educational Research Association, Atlanta, GA.

Smith, F. (1986). *Insult to intelligence: the bureaucratic invasion of our classrooms.* Portsmouth, NH: Heinemann.

Smith, M. L. (1991). Put to the test: The effects of external testing on teachers. *Educational Researcher, 20*(5), 8–11.

Snow, R. (1988). Progress in measurement, cognitive science, and technology that can change the relation between instruction and assessment. In E. Freeman (Ed.), *Assessment in the service of learning* (pp. 9–25). Princeton, NJ: Educational Testing Service.

Tierney, R. J., Carter, M. A., & Desai, L. E. (1991). *Portfolios in the reading-writing classroom.* Norwood, MA: Christopher Gordon.

Tye, K. A. (1992). Beyond the rhetoric of restructuring. *Phi Delta Kappan, 74*(1), 8–14.

Valencia, S. W., & Calfee, R. C. (1991). The development and use of literacy portfolios for students, classes, and teachers. *Applied Measurement in Education, 4,* 333–345.

Vermont Department of Education. (1991). *"This is my best": Vermont's Writing Assessment Program. Pilot year 1990–1991.* Montpelier, VT: Author.

Wells, P. (1991). Putting America to the test. *Agenda, 1,* 52–57.

Witte, S., & Flach, J. (1994). Note toward an assessment of advanced ability to communicate. *Assessing Writing, 1*(2), 207–246.

Wolf, D. P. (1989). Porfolio assessment: Sampling student work. *Educational Leadership, 46,* 35–39.

Wood, E. (1994). *A review and analysis of my experience with the California Learning Project.* Teacher Research Report. Davis, CA: University of California, Center for Cooperative Research and Extension Services for Schools.

Worthen, B. (1993). Critical issues that will determine the future of alternative assessment. *Phi Delta Kappan,* 444–454.

Yancey, K. B. (Ed.). (1996). *Voices from the field: Portfolio practice in middle and secondary school contexts.* Unpublished manuscript.

Yancey, K. B. (Ed.). (1992). *Portfolios in the writing classroom.* Urbana, IL: National Council of Teachers of English.

CHAPTER SIX

Sailing Ships: A Framework for Portfolios in Formative and Summative Systems

Miles Myers
NCTE Executive Director

After 10 years (1980–1990) of reforming K–12 schools by decentralizing the hiring, purchasing, and management decisions of the district's central office, we have begun attempting to reform K–12 schools by changing the curriculum content that could guide those administrative policies. For 75 years K–12 schools have quite successfully taught a curriculum of basic skills, but contemporary social needs call for descriptions of a new K–12 curriculum content of higher-order thinking skills for all students and new assessments to measure and report on those skills (Myers, 1996).

Descriptions of the new curriculum content in K–12 schools take several forms: course descriptions—for example, the College Board's Pacesetter Project; standards documents or frameworks—for example, the standards documents of the National Council of Teachers of Mathematics (NCTM) and the National Council of Teachers of English and International Reading Association (NCTE/IRA); and the various subject area frameworks of the states—for example, the California Writing framework. Alternative assessments to report student achievement of the new curriculum are being developed by private companies, a few states (Vermont and California), and state coalitions like the New Standards Project. In this chapter, I focus on the development of portfolio assessment within the literacy unit of the New Standards Project.[1]

---

[1]Members of the New Standards Project are the states of Arkansas, California, Colorado, Connecticut, Delaware, Iowa, Kentucky, Maine, Massachusetts, Missouri, New York, Oregon, Pennsylvania, Texas, Vermont, Washington; and the cities of Fort Worth, New York, Rochester,

First, let us review briefly the overall framework of the descriptions of curriculum content being developed in English/English language arts. In the "new" English of contemporary classrooms (Myers, 1996), the content (what students know) comes from the three worlds of human experience (Popper & Eccles, 1977): the external World-1, which includes, along with animals, vegetables, and minerals, the physical structure of books (Where is the index, name of author?), tools (How do computers work?), cultural artifacts (How are libraries organized?), and rhetorical situations (What is the physical distance between audiences and reader?); the internal World-2, which includes cognitive processes (predicting), states (attention), schemas (organization charts), internalized voices, and self-images; and the concepts and technical structures of World-3, which include the philosophy, logic, structure, and theories of numbers and language, including textual knowledge (oral and written genres), ideas (justice), themes (reason vs. feelings), and the structure of disciplines (literature, history, physics).

The content of English standards, then, tends to take the form of rhetorical principles (speaking and writing to diverse audiences), cognitive processes (strategic use of metacognitive skills), and conceptual structures (understanding literary and nonliterary structures and issues). To learn to write or speak, to listen and read, to communicate, to discover ideas, and to solve problems in the content of this new English—speakers, listeners, writers, and readers engage in the rhetorical acts of distancing, collaboration, internalization of voices, and role reversal, speakers pretending to be listeners of their talk, writers pretending to be readers of their own materials; engage in the conceptual acts of modeling in which the structures of genre shape the evolving text and the structures of logic shape the evolving ideas; and engage in the cognitive act of interpretation and comprehension, appreciation and criticism. To assess the breadth and depth of this kind of curriculum content requires new kinds of assessments that do not rely exclusively on traditional school-designed, short answer questions or machine-scored, norm referenced tests. The kinds of assessments being called for are authentic, real life, cognitively complex, and embedded in real time and actual situations.

The New Standards Project, a coalition of two dozen states and several school districts, is one of the largest organizations attempting this formidable task of developing an alternative assessment system for this new content.

San Diego, and White Plains. Together they enroll about 50% of all U.S. public school children. New Standards is a joint undertaking of the Learning Research and Development Center at the University of Pittsburgh and the National Center on Education and the Economy in Rochester, New York. It is funded by grants from the Pew Charitable Trust, the John D. and Catherine T. MacArthur Foundation, the U.S. Department of Education, and the dues of the Partners. The Literacy Unit of the New Standard Project is housed at the National Council of Teachers of English, Urbana, Illinois. Miles Myers and David Pearson are co-directors of the Literacy Unit; Liz Spalding is the on-site coordinator; and Sally Hampton is the unit manager.

Using an NCTE/IRA content standard such as "The student learns to write to multiple audiences," the New Standards project has developed a set of assessment tasks in which students write to different audiences on particular subjects, has selected from responses to those tasks student papers at different levels of performance and has prepared rubrics and interpretive summaries for these papers. But evidence of student achievement cannot rely solely on a national pool of on-demand tasks providing primarily end-of-process products within set time limits. As a result, the New Standards Project has turned to the development of portfolios as the key instrument in NSP's alternative assessment system, and in portfolio assessment tasks are only one part of the system.

My experience over the last 4 years as codirector (with David Pearson) of NSP's effort to develop a national portfolio assessment system for English/English language arts has led me to the conclusion that we need an overall conceptual framework to guide our work in portfolio assessments. Portfolio assessment often seems to be guided by a conglomeration of psychometric principles from machine-scored tests and personal growth issues from clinical psychology. Portfolios are obviously not just another version of machine-scored tests, and they are not just another private collection of an individual author or reader. Where are we to find the conceptual framework that could productively be applied to portfolios in the new literacy? Latour's (1987) description of data collection in the Golden Age of Geographic Exploration—the Age of Columbus, Cortes, Magellan, Drake, and Cook—gives us, I think, an interesting and potentially valuable conceptual framework for designing portfolios both as an accountability instrument for public consumption and as a learning instrument for classroom use.

The basic metaphor of this framework is portfolio-as-sailing-ship. For more than 300 years during the Golden Age of Geographic Exploration (1300–1800), sailing ships were the portfolios of a data collection system that enabled government officials to account for growth in geographic control and trade and that enabled researchers to learn how the world was organized. The first key part of LaTour's conceptual system is that in the data collection system of sailing ships the work of the private artisan and the public adventurer had to be joined:

> In modern times, as never before, adventurer and artisan have been assimilated into a single community of questing mankind. Western progress since the eighteenth century has dramatically mixed and unified their roles. Modern discourse and modern inventor have been drawn together by forces beyond their control in an undeclared, sometimes involuntary partnership. (Boorstin, 1994, p. 34)

The discoverer was largely public, political, and policy-directed, and the inventor was largely private, guild-centered, and problem or learning-directed and their partnership dates "from about the beginning of the eighteenth century" (Boorstin, 1994, p. 32–34). Captain Cook, for example, acting as a public policy leader, had to secure public funds from politicians to find the Great Southern Continent and then he had to report back at the end of his long voyage (1772–1775) with Summative Evaluations on his success or failure. Incidently, Cook had to report back to his financial backers that he had not found the Great Southern Continent, which every policymaker hoped would bring enormous wealth to the country. In addition, Cook had to be a teacher and learner just to organize and to carry out successful voyages. For example, by experimenting with a diet of lemon, orange, and other fruits on his long voyage to find the Great Southern Continent, Cook ended up not losing one sailor to scurvy, a remarkable achievement at the time (Boorstin, 1994). Thus, in a Formative Evaluation of what Captain Cook learned on his voyage, Captain Cook did quite well, losing no one to scurvy and adding to geographic knowledge, but in a Summative Evaluation of whether Captain Cook reached his policy goal of the Great Southern Continent Captain Cook did not do well.

The need to bring together inventors and discoverers in geographic exploration is comparable, I think, to the need in portfolio assessment to bring together Formative Evaluation for learning and personal growth and Summative Evaluation for accountability reports to the public (see Scriven, 1967, for Formative/Summative terms). In portfolio assessment, it is essential to have a partnership between the Formative purposes of assessment, which monitor teaching and learning, and the Summative purposes of assessment, which monitor pass–fail certification and policy accountability (see Bertisch, 1993). For example, portfolio systems need to have one or two portfolios for a student's personal growth, another one or two for teacher research, several for different types of public certification (grades, graduation, college advanced placement), and another for public policy reports (see Table 6.1).

Portfolios developed for Formative purposes must have an interactive relationship with the portfolios developed for Summative purposes. Within a portfolio data collection system, there should be a consistent effort to use Summative results to test the claims of teaching and learning and to use Formative results to test the completeness and authenticity of Summative claims. For example, the Summative claim that Cook's voyage was a failure needs to be offset by the recognition that Cook did discover that the Southern Continent did not exist, and the Formative claim that Cook may have found a cure for scurvy needs to be offset by the recognition that Cook's financial backers had no return on their money.

There is a tendency among some to oppose the use of portfolios in Summative Evaluation. Lucas (1992), for example, called for "turning our energies from perfecting the external test toward improving evaluation in

TABLE 6.1
Contrasts Between Formative and Summative Applications of Performance-
Based Assessments

Formative Purposes		*Summative Purposes*	
Portfolios and tasks used in classroom for learning and teaching		Portfolios and tasks used in public for certifying students and establishing policy claims	
I	*II*	*III*	*IV*
Student's personal portfolio (private for student)	Teacher's portfolio of student work stays in classroom	Portfolio of student used for graduation/ applications	Samples of student portfolios to show policy makers
Personal growth portfolio	Teacher research portfolio	School graduation certification portfolio	Policy portfolio

the classroom," for replacing "accountability testing" with "ecological evaluation" (p. 9). Yancey (1992), similarly, argued that "teachers need to design their own portfolio projects relative to their own curricular demands and concerns" (p. 107), and apparently concluded that portfolios cannot be used to provide accountability to a distant public: "A second guiding principle has to do with the nature of portfolio projects: they are not portable" (p. 108). This, too, was the position of Patricia Carini and her colleagues at Prospect School, one of the few sites where the practice of teacher research and formative assessment was seriously pursued for many years (Carini, 1975).

However, Daiker, Dubinsky, Helton, and Wilson (1993), argued just the reverse, in 1990 at Miami University (Oxford, OH), introducing the use of portable high school portfolios to award to entering students college credit and advanced placement. Classroom elementary teachers in South Brunswick, New Jersey and high school teachers at Central Park East in New York City have also argued the reverse. At Central Park East in New York City, teachers are developing Summative Portfolios as a key part of the student's course grade and certification for graduation from high school, and elementary school teachers in South Brunswick have developed an Early Literacy Portfolio for students in Grades 1 and 2 to produce Summative scores twice each year to meet state and local testing requirements. Of course, both the Central Park East and South Brunswick portfolios are also used for formative purposes. In fact, the South Brunswick District Manual for the Early Literacy Portfolio says that the portfolio provides "data to support and inform decisions about daily teaching" (South Brunswick Board of Education, 1992). I endorse the position taken by Freedman (1993) when she said, "Portfolios do, however, fit naturally with good writing instruction—and portfolios can be used for large scale testing. The challenge is to make the links" (p. 47). This linking of Formative and Summative evaluation, a linking of the roles of artisan and discoverer, is the first key part of LaTour's conceptual framework.

The second key part of LaTour's (1987) conceptual framework is the need for government sponsorship. In his examination of data collection and analysis during the Golden Age of Geographic Exploration, LaTour shows us the importance of government funding to build sailing ships as data gathering devices, to design instruments like sextons and compasses to sample particular kinds of data, and to "bring things back to a place for someone to see it for the first time so that others might be sent again to bring other things back" (p. 79). To "bring things back," to make data transportable and mobile, the Portuguese government had to fund the development of large ships that could carry large cargoes and not come apart in heavy storms, fund the development of instruments, and fund the building of centers for collecting data.

Portfolio projects also need government resources to develop portfolio instruments like tasks and double-entry journals and build centers for data collection. Support at the federal level for portfolio development was enacted on March 31, 1994 when the Congress in Public Law 103-227 established a National Institute on Student Achievement, Curriculum, and Assessment to undertake, among other things, "a comprehensive, coordinated program of research and development in the area of assessment," a program which addresses, among other things, "developing, identifying, or evaluating new educational assessments, including performance-based and portfolio assessments . . ." (p. 4).

The law also specifies that "The Council shall certify State assessments only if a State can demonstrate that all students have been prepared in the content for which such students are being assessed" (Section 213,[f], [C] of Public Law 108 STAT.145, 1994). In the long term (over 5 years), portfolios could be used for grade promotion, graduation, and assessment within federal programs.

It is possible that many sections of this law will not be funded by the new Congress. Nevertheless, the passage of this law represents a new national attitude toward federal involvement in public education, and a new national attitude toward the machine-scored tests and alternative assessment. The public wants a different standard of minimum literacy, and it wants appropriate tests to go with those standards. It seems certain that if the federal government does not fund portfolio development, many states will need to do so.[2] States will continue to support the New Standards Project as long as they receive particular services necessary for an alternative assessment system: an opportunity to reduce development costs by pooling costs for alternative assessment with other states; use of a national auditing system that could certify comparability of scores and standards across state lines; use of national performance standards mapped to content standards; and use of a mastery certificate, based on standards, to pair with diplomas, based on grades.

The third key part of LaTour's conceptual framework for sailing ships is the way government-funded discoverers and inventors had to invent ways to organize the visibility, mobility, stability, storability, and combinability of data: "(a) render [data] mobile so they can be brought back; (b) keep them stable so they can be moved back and forth without additional distortion, corruption, or decay, and (c) [make them] . . . combinable so that whatever stuff they are made of, they can be cumulated, aggregated, or shuffled like a pack of cards" (LaTour, 1987, p. 223). Later LaTour adds: "The history of technoscience is in large part the history of all the little inventions made along the networks to accelerate the mobility of traces, or to enhance their faithfulness, combination, and cohesion, so as to make action at a distance possible" (p. 256).

The questions that are a critical part of LaTour's conceptual framework for the Age of Geographic Exploration are the same questions that can be used to guide the development of portfolios, and, thus, in the Age of Cognitive Exploration with portfolios, methods have to be developed that will make portfolio data visible, mobile, stable, storable, and combinable: Is it visible (Can I see or track the data?), mobile (Am I able to transport it from one place to another with some ease?), stable (Is it still visible and not decomposing?), storable (Can the data be easily stored after delivery?), and combinable (Can the data be combined and categorized for analysis?).

It is important to remember the need for visible, stable, mobile, storable, and combinable data did not begin in school testing with portfolio assessment. These needs had a major impact on educational testing from the very beginning. For example, oral recitations and disputations could be used for testing in the 18th century as long as the subjects of schools were rhetorical, the teachers and students were very few in number, and the data on oral recitations did not have to be sent to a central location for analysis, summarization, and reporting. But by the end of the 19th century, the subjects taught in schools had changed, the number of students and teachers had increased, and the number of centers of calculation or accountability had

---

[2]California is certainly the largest effort in the country, spending over $28 million per year on developing an alternative assessment. NSP's total budget per year is not over $9 million.

increased. One of the most notable changes in subjects was the addition of mathematics to the K–12 curriculum. Teachers could not hear mathematics the way they could hear rhetorical language skills. To see mathematics, teachers needed visible calculations on paper. In addition, the number of students and teachers in publicly funded English classes increased, and more and more regional centers for public accountability were established. Thus, oral recitations became more difficult to use for data collection about English, and written records (tests) had to be introduced (Madaus & Tan, 1993).

To make data on ships visible and stable during the Golden Age of Geographic Exploration, the government developed numerous experts and instruments (clocks, compasses, sextants, quadrants, telescopes) with visible codes for time, direction (north, east, and so forth), size of land, astronomy, botany, minerals, and so forth. On July 17, 1787 Jean-Francois Laperouse (or La Perouse), captain of L'Astrolabe, landing on what some of his books and maps said was a peninsula connected to Asia and what other books and maps said was an island separated by a strait, found a native who drew a map in the sand showing that "Sakhalin" was an island. But a rising tide erased the map. Captain Laperouse then found another native who drew in Laperouse's notebook a similar map, thereby solving the problem of making data visible and stable (LaTour, 1987). This is a critical problem in both sailing ships engaged in geographic exploration and in portfolios engaged in cognitive exploration.

The loss of visible and stable data is an enormous problem in portfolio assessment. The first step in the development of visible and stable data in portfolio assessments is to identify the methods used to analyze or make visible the content standards of English/English language arts—such matters as the students' in depth use of rhetorical distancing (How well did the student write to a particular audience?), cognitive processing (Did the student use an appropriate strategy like prewriting?), and logical modelling (Did the student understand the conventions of a particular genre?; see Table 6.2). One could also examine breadth of writing structures in rhetorical distancing (How many different audiences did the student write to?), processes (What was the range of available strategies?), and logical modelling (How many different logical structures did the student attempt?). Reading analysis could also examine rhetorical distancing (What is the range of points of view and "person" in materials read?), cognitive processing (What is the depth of processing in reading, from gist to elaborated comprehension, to interpretation, appreciation, and criticism?), and logical modelling (What is the range of genres read and what is the depth of the reader's understanding of the logic of what is read?). All of this is summarized in Table 6.2.

Portfolio assessment of the higher-order thinking skills in Table 6.2 faces numerous visibility and stability problems: How does one make visible self reflection, the prewriting process, the editing process, and reading responses?

TABLE 6.2
Curriculum Matrix Displaying Literacy Domains, Performance Standards, Typical Assessment Tasks, and Content Standards

Topics in content Standards: What students should know (content) and be able to do (use)	Performance Standards/Traditions of Analysis (possible)			Performance and Data for Assessment	Content Standards Statements
	Performance Standards in Rhetoric / *Distancing to audience (Dialectical Knowledge)*	*Performance Standards in Logic (philosophy)* / *Modeling (Logic/Concepts Metaphors/Modes)*	*Performance Standards in Cognitive/Science* / *Processing (Metacognition/ Procedural Knowledge)*	*Suggested items in inventory for student portfolios*	*The standards below come from the NCTE/IRA standards for English language arts*
I. Effective speaking and listening	Lead small group discussion (or participation)	Outline logic of group discussion	Find evidence of questioning and summarizing in discussion	I. Give speech to class on public issue (video)	Students should be able to speak, listen, and respond in large and small groups including different audiences and different purposes
	Give large group speech (or listen to)	Identify diverse modes used in speech	Drafts show use of multiple sources in development of speech	II. Packet with drafts of speech	
II. Writing - Fluency/conventions		Show evidence of editing conventions	Show automaticity in handwriting	III. Writing fluency certificate from teacher	Students should know editing conventions and develop fluency

TABLE 6.2
(Continued)

III. Writing-Breadth					
A. Literature	Uses dialogue to "show" point --------------- Show ability to shift point of view of work in writing	Show ability to write in different literary forms	Use writing processes in development of piece (see IX)	III. Rewrite literacy piece in two other forms (lyric, sonnet)	IV. Write fictional story	Students should write in a variety of genres for a variety of purposes to a variety of audiences
B. Public discourse	Write to three different audiences on public issue	Write in four different newspaper forms (report, editorial, letter	(see above)	V. Write news report VI. Write editorial	VII. Write letter-to-editor VIII. Write ad using computer	Students learn to use computer
IV. Writing - Depth						
A. Literature	Has sense of theme, place and character in writing of literary selection	Shows effective use of narrative form	Drafts show revisions at word, sentence, and other levels	VIII. Write story, attach drafts, plot visuals	IX. Enclose learning log reflecting on strategies in writing	Students should be able to synthesize multiple sources and to show conclusions
B. Public discourse	Is able to write argument in third person or first person	Shows effective use of argument form and is able to translate argument into plan of action	Drafts of argument (4) show strategies of questioning, believing, disbelieving, summarizing, clarifying	X. Write argument on public issue XI. Prepare plan of action for implementing conclusion	XII. Attach drafts of argument ----------- Participates in a public forum on public issue (no direct data)	Students should be able to write in a variety of genres for varied purposes and audiences

TABLE 6.2
(Continued)

V. *Reading-Fluency/conventions*			Show automaticity in reading	Reading fluency certificate from teacher		Students should learn the reading conventions/cues
VI. *Reading-Breadth*						
A. Literature	Reads a range of points of view from culture, history, and subject	Reads with a range of responses---impressionistic, interpretive, reflective ---------- Reads a range of forms---poems, novels, short stories	Shows use of self-correction in reading log, expanding range of fiction and interpretive readings	XIII. Include certified reading record from school/public library showing range of reading	XIV. Prepare reading log reflecting about reading problems, reading successes	Students should read contemporary and classical literature from diverse cultures and times
B. Public discourse	Reads a range of opinions by different "persons"	Reads a range of forms---magazines, newspapers	Shows comprehension and interpretation in reading log	XV. Story retelling records	XVI. Complete reading review of nonliterary texts	Students should read a range of nonliterary texts
VII. *Reading-Depth*						
A. Literature	Shows understanding of differences and similarities in point of view	Recognizes & understands intertextual relationships (how two different works compare)	Uses prediction of plot, guessing about thoughts of characters (4)	XVII. Write comparison and contrast of two novels or two stories	XVIII. Prepare double entry journal on two literary selections	Students should recognize and reflect on the aesthetic dimension of literature

159

TABLE 6.2
(Continued)

B. Public discourse	Shows understanding of different points of view	Identify details supporting generality	Use questioning and summarizing in discussion, is able both to criticize and appreciate same piece	XIX. Leads reciprocal reading group on two public discourse selections	XX. Write personal summary of one's reciprocal reading group	Students should be able to analyze and evaluate what they read, write, hear, say, and view
VIII. Content						
A. Language conventions	Exercixe: Rewrite paragraph as first person	Exercises: Write simile and metaphor	Exercises: sentence combining Invented spelling activity	XXI. CLOZ Test XXIII. Oral reading records	XXII. Concepts about print test (Clay, 1982) XXIV. Editing assignment	Students should learn the structure of English
B. Literature conventions	Why is a narrator unreliable?	How does a work mix genres?	Where in story does plot reach crisis?	XXV. Act in two scenes from two dramas from two periods. Write three essays on three questions of content and form in literature		Students should use a variety of literary forms
C. Public discourse conventions	What is the contrasting opinion from Middle Ages to now?	How is argument organized now? What are the core issues of the day?	How are debate expectations changed from beginning to end?	XX. Participate in three group discussions of three critical issues in public discourse (No data in portfolio)		Students should understand how language and ideas vary across cultures and time

TABLE 6.2
(Continued)

IX. Viewing and composing multimedia work	View CNN news and NBC news ------ Write radio script with narrator, and two characters	View three different types/genres of TV shows and write review ------ Write critical dialogue for scene	Save drafts of radio script and write caption summarizing revisions	XXVI. Discuss difference of CNN news and NBC news on TV (taped) ------ XXVII. In groups of three, prepare radio script to be played for class XXVIII. Write review of three different types of TV shows, analyzing scene in each	Students should be able to interpret and to critique in their viewing and listening.
X. Reflection	Write letter inviting reader to read portfolio ------ Write review for teacher of one's life-time development	Put captions on each piece showing where piece belongs in portfolio inventory.	Introductory letter shows evidence of belief/disbelief ------ Evaluation of best pieces	XXIX. Review one's development as reader and writer in writing ------ XXX. Write introductory letter for portfolio listing inventory of your portfolio and commenting on strengths and weaknesses.	Students should be aware of one's own processes and strategies in reading and writing

Note. The standard for English language arts are available from the National Council of Teachers of English, 1111 Kenyon Road, Urbana, IL., 61875.

The need for visible and stable data showing reading and writing processes has led to the invention of new genres of response: double-entry journals, two column contrasts (character's word in one column; character's thoughts in others), drawings of a situation and their explanations, Venn diagrams showing different and overlapping attitudes, organization charts (story trees, charts of family relationships), learning logs recording strategies and miscues in reading and writing, narratives about one's literacy development, value-scales, and meaning scales (semantic differential scales).

However, there are a number of performances and processes that remain invisible in most portfolios—speeches and the oral reflections of students being two notable examples. But new computer programs and CD-ROM technology are beginning to reduce the magnitude of some of these problems. Several teachers in the New Standards Project are beginning to use CD-ROM technology to gather visible data on speeches, drama, a student talking aloud in self reflection, and writing-in-process. In a frame in one corner of the computer screen, the student talks aloud about the thinking processes reflected in a piece of writing shown on another part of the screen. Reilly (1994) has made a major contribution in this area with his work at Bell High School in Los Angeles. The results of teacher observations are also difficult to make visible and stable in most portfolios. The California Learning Record is an example of one attempt to make teacher observations of learning visible, and the Literacy Profiles of Ministry of Education in Victoria, Australia is another.[3]

One way to enlist the students in the effort to make the content of English curriculum visible is to ask students to prepare a table of contents listing the items in the portfolio and then to write notes and check cells in a matrix to show which items provide evidence for a given performance standard.[4] Table 6.3 provides one example of a selection from the possibilities in Table 6.2. This allows some student choice and, at the same time, reduces the portfolio items from 30 to 7.

The performance standards in Table 6.3, of course, are mapped to content standards, which guide performance in portfolios like the maps that guided the performance goals or routes of sailing ships. The sailing ships brought

---

[3]Some commentators have announced that Australia's literacy profiles are an "assessment report." These profiles do not meet the requirements for an assessment/summative report in the United States. For one thing, the levels, as far as I can tell, have never been tested by having teachers together, in one place, to rank common pieces. These literacy profiles do, however, serve a Teacher Research or formative function, and some parts of the profile are used in both NCTE's standards and in the portfolio scoring rubrics of the New Standards Project. Finally, information on the California Learning Record is available from Dale Carlson, State Department of Education, Sacramento, California.

[4]The idea for the student checks on matrix comes from a conversation with David Pearson (1994), who tried out the idea in a class. The 30-item matrix for portfolio assessment in Table 6.2 is my invention.

TABLE 6.3
Portfolio Matrix Displaying Contents and Categories of Evidence

Table of Contents

	Rhetoric	Logic	Cognitive
(1) Introductory letter	√ Purpose and audience variety	√ Writing different modes	√ Self-reflection on processes
(2) Tape of speech to class on public issue	√ Purpose and audience variety	√ Speaking-logic	
(3) Editorial on public issue	√ Purpose and audience variety	√ Logic of public discourse	
(4) Collection of my poems		√ Logic of literary understanding	
(5) Search paper			√ The problems I ran into preparing editorial
(6) Learning log			√ Record of reading process
(7) Library reading recored-breadth		√ Breadth in reading modes	√ Breadth in reading strategies

back data about the performance goals *and* about the world. Portfolios bring back data about student performance and about cognitive development in general. In Table 6.3, the library reading record (7) (see XIII in Table 6.2) provides evidence about the performance standard of breadth in reading, and the performance standard can be mapped to the reading content standard of reading in different modes. Sometimes content standards reveal gaps in performance standards. For example, in the early work of NSP, the content standards provided a map showing that not enough public discourse, which means general informational reading was being sampled in the performance standards for reading tasks. One might argue that Table 6.3 is short on rhetorical data.

In addition to the problem of visibility and stability of data, there is the problem of mobility and storability of data. One of the problems in an authentic assessment is that the most authentic data are not mobile and storable in Summative Portfolios used for certification at a distant site. Some data, which are valuable for Teacher Research and student reflection, can only be stored in the classroom or at home and are not transportable to a center of calculation—and they need not be anything else. Some interdisciplinary history and science projects and some field trip reports with artifacts from the field trip site, which could be part of a Summative report for graduation from middle school or high school, are far too large for inclusion in a certification or policy portfolio sent off to a distant center of calculation.

The selection of data for Summative Portfolios always deals with the tension between low-cost, storable, and mobile data and the most authentic samples of performance, which are high cost, not easily storable, and often not mobile. Table 6.4 illustrates these degrees of difference (Myers, in press; adapted from Shavelson, Baxter, & Pine, 1992). Notice that A and B on the validity-storability-mobility scale involve the extended processes of different forms of writing (letters of inquiry, drafts of the editorial) prior to the final product. Some authentic writing, such as preparing a grocery list, is, of course, not all that costly or time consuming or unstorable or unmobile, but most writing in A and B takes up more storage space than E and F, and may not be that mobile. We could ship everything somewhere, but no one at the other end could make sense of it without a large investment of time and money. Standardized tests at E and F, however, are given a low validity rating (and a high storability and mobility rating). For one thing, these tests at E and F usually assume that all children should be able to do the same tasks in the same amount of time, and, therefore, these tests ignore the intelligence of students who take their time; students who have a slower pace. Assessments at A, B, and C work better for most students because, for one thing, these assessments collect data on the achievement of students who work at different speeds. Teachers must decide what range of authenticity, time, mobility, and storability is tolerable in a Formative Assessment for the classroom and what range is tolerable for policy makers in a Summative Assessment for public accountability. Similar decisions need to be made about reading.

Teachers reviewing some of the early tasks of the New Standards Project found that some of the reading tasks were too authentic. That is, they took up too much class time, as much as 4 or 5 days in a few cases, and/or they had so many sources of information (brochures, video tapes) that administration and scoring at a distant site became too complicated. The issues of storability and mobility can lead to the elimination of data. One proposal for showing breadth in reading was to ask that the student bring to the class a stack of books that had been read and the teacher would interview the student about each work. This might work for Summative Evaluation in the school, but it is

TABLE 6.4
Relations Between Cost/Time and Validity in Writing Assessment

A Costs and Time Scale for "Higher Order Thinking" in Writing

High Costs and Time	*Medium Level Costs*		*Low Costs and Time*
Writing an editorial for a local newspaper after an actual investigation and report	An editorial written in class after a week of development	An editorial written in one hour without prior preparation	An editorial written in 15 minutes without prior preparation	A short written description of an editorial	A multiple choice test on skills used to write editorials

A Validity Scale for "Higher Order Thinking" in Writing

High Validity				*Low Validity*
A	B	C	D	E	F

Note. From Myers (in press). Adapted from Shavelson et al. (1992). Reprinted with permission.

impractical for off-site Summative Evaluation. Here is a place where parts of some portfolios may not be mobile in other portfolios used for other purposes.

One way to solve some of the data storability and mobility problems is to introduce a certification process into Summative and Formative Portfolios. Let us say that the performance standard "breadth in reading" calls for storable and mobile data on the reading of as many as 30 books each year.[5] Thirty, one should note, is quite visible, although some adjustments between length and complexity are needed. To store this data in any portfolio requires some kind of shorthand system of data collection. One cannot put in the portfolio 30 books and all the teacher interviews with students on those books. One suggestion is the inclusion in the portfolio of a Certificate from a teacher or librarian certifying that the student read a certain number of books.

The certificate process provides visible, mobile, and storable evidence on a performance standard difficult to verify. A similar verification problem is the storing of adequate, visible data on a child's developing fluency and concepts of print. Eight weeks of drawings and print from the average preschooler can sometimes nearly fill up a footlocker. To show literacy development in more efficient storage units, some teachers are including in Summative Portfolios teacher administered tests like the decoding and comprehension test of Calfee and Calfee (1981), the concepts of print test of Clay (1979), or a Certificate of Fluency test given in the classroom. Another example of verification problems might be data on development of the writing process and various conventions of older students. In the California assessment, teachers decided to use a machine-scored editing test to gather data on editing conventions. The score on the machine-scored test reduces the problem of visible, mobile, and storable evidence. This kind of test also enables low-scoring students to make visible their editing knowledge. They are not always able to show this knowledge in a writing performance. The point here is that storability and mobility, particularly in Summative Portfolios, requires a range of devices to shrink and to store data, including short tests and Certificates of Completion.

---

[5]The 30 books per year base-line for breadth in reading was arrived at in the following way. First, several researchers found that the growth in recognition vocabulary of the school age child typically exceeds 3,000 words per year (Nagy & Anderson, 1987; Miller & Gildea, 1987). Then several researchers found that basal readers (Calfee & Drum, 1986) rarely exceeded 500 new words per year and that classroom reading instruction rarely focused on vocabulary instruction (Durkin, 1979). Therefore, where did students get their new words? Those that get 3,000 new words per year appear to get them from out-of-school and literature-based reading of about 1 million words (or 30 books) per year (Nagy, Anderson, & Herman, 1987; David Pearson, personal communication, 1994). Independent reading or non-basal reading is, thus, the primary source of new words for all students. But some students read very little, and some read a lot—the students at the top reading 200 times more than those at the bottom (Nagy, Anderson, & Herman, 1987). One conclusion here is that the performance standards of reading must be explicit about what "breadth of reading" means or else those at the bottom will be left out or, at least, their goals left vague and unexplicated.

Computers are another way to shrink and store data. Teachers are beginning to use new computer programs to increase the storage capacity for reading and writing data and, at the same time, to increase the speed of keyword searches. One teacher showed me a single disk with 4 years of portfolio data and an indexing system that allowed her to skip from one year to another in seconds. Her data included photographs of projects, filmed segments where the student talked about work in an adjacent window, drawings, writing samples arranged in sequence of development, and so forth.

Another requirement in data collection and analysis is combining data. To make data combinable in the Golden Age of Geographic Exploration, various governments funded thousands of conferences of experts and asked them to agree on ways to combine data, preparing, for example, common maps and log books. The problem of combinable data is primarily a conceptual problem. Let me illustrate this problem with Captain Laperouse's notes on Sakhalin from his naturalists, geographers, and others. These notes were delivered by De Lesseps to Versailles, and the cartographers at Versailles were able to add data on Sakhalin's shape and location to their maps of the area. These cartographers, of course, were able to combine this map data with other map data because they had a standardized conceptual system for combining location data.

To make location data combinable, King John II of Portugal, in 1484, convened a commission of cartographers and other disciplinary experts in mapmaking to reach agreement on standardized locations throughout the world. Using the stable reference points of the sun and the North star to determine location and time throughout the world, the Commission put together a handbook on how to use various instruments to find the angle of the sun and stars, created log books to show time and date at various locations, and plotted latitude and longitude lines on new maps (LaTour, 1987). This combined data, creating a new currency of geographic knowledge, gave centers of calculation new power. For example, it enabled Captain Martin to be in the powerful position of seeing Sakhalin for the second time when he landed his ship Neptune at Sakhalin on November 5, 1797, 10 years after Captain Laperouse (LaTour, 1987). He saw Sakhalin for the first time while in London reading "Laperouse's notebooks and considering the maps engraved from the bearings De Lesseps brought back to Versailles" (p. 217).

The combining of data also made it possible for centers of calculation throughout the world to store more and more information in a smaller space. For example, by the 1800s, one map of England, showing the location of 200 towns and combining 400 longitude and latitude calculations and a potential 20,000 itineraries from one town to another, could easily be held in the hand and examined (Polanyi, 1974). The combining of data also revealed gaps and inconsistencies in knowledge. For example, chemists agreed at their first international meeting in Karlsruhe in 1860 that atomic weight was the dimension they would use to combine and categorize chemicals, but they were hardly out the door of the conference when dissatisfied chemists were already trying other approaches. Mendellev, 9 years after the conference in 1869, proposed a table that listed chemicals horizontally by atomic weight and vertically by valencies, but Mendellev's tables produced some empty cells. Then chemists began to fill those empty cells. Lecoq de Boisbaudran added gallium to fill "the box left vacant in the table under the name eka-aluminum" (LaTour, 1987, p. 236). Conferences had to be called again and again to standardize the classification of plants, animals, minerals, geography, and even time, which had to be standardized in different ways in geology, biology, and astronomy.

The first step in the development of combinable data in portfolios is to describe the intellectual domain one wishes to assess. The New Standards Project, National Council of Teachers of English (NCTE) and International Reading Association (IRA) have all sponsored conferences and meetings to develop a professional consensus about the categories and common language of domains in English and English language arts. For example, NCTE has held two meetings with the Modern Language Association on content standards, and others are planned. Domains represent the subject from which content standards are a sample, and performances represent samples of content standards. An example of a domain matrix for writing genres in English is shown in Table 6.5. The writing domain, for example, includes office memos, but memos are not explicitly called for in the content standards, and they do not appear as required performances for assessment in most projects (see Tables 6.2 and 6.5).

In the New Standards Project, the effort to standardize and combine data from portfolios has led to dozens of meetings to design a menu showing the choice of contents for portfolios at Grades 4, 8, and 10, a student handbook telling students how to decide what to put in the portfolio, an inventory list describing what teachers should look for in the portfolio, a rubric for scoring the level of performance exhibited in the contents of the portfolio, exemplar portfolios at different performance levels for each grade level (4, 8, & 10), and interpretative summaries or commentaries showing how each exemplar portfolio reflects the features at different levels in the rubric.

The menu raises the question of "What is the evidence that an item on the menu is present?" (see Table 6.3 for an example of a list of items on a menu). Teachers using the menu need to have decision rules on what counts as an argument or narrative or a project, what counts as writing to multiple audiences in a letter of introduction, what counts as fluent reading or a range of cognitive strategies or depth in reading and thinking processes or components of Narrative (see Table 6.6). Using these decision rules at the school site, the teacher should be able to combine several items in the portfolio into one category on the menu and to combine several standards into one item on the menu.

On-demand tasks are necessary exemplars of the kinds of items one might include in portfolios and can be used to monitor the scoring and the

TABLE 6.5
The Domain of Writing genres

Speech Events	The Modes: The Cognitive Dimension--What are the cognitive ways we organize "knowledge"?				
	Expressive Mode	The Synthetic Mode Prototype Categories, Case Knowledge		The Paradigmatic Modes/Analytic Modes Classical Grid Categories, Feature Knowledge	
What are the social ways we organize knowledge?	*Chunking ideas with "Free" Associations* EXPRESSIVE Mode	*Chunking with Time Line* NARRATION	*Chunking with Spatial Image* DESCRIPTION	*Chunking with Types, Sets, or Containers* EXPOSITION	*Chunking Parts Toward Thesis* ARGUMENT
What are the social dimensions: What are the audience (interpersonal), subject (ideation), and text (textual) relationships in discourse/knowledge production?	To associate things, focusing on expressive purpose, using freely whatever comes to mind.	*To recount factual events or tell stories* (semi-factual events) focusing on historical purpose using a cause-effect process time line. The kinesthetic experience arranged over time.	*To describe and portray,* focusing on ethnographic purpose, using the contextual hypotheses. The image experience arranged in space at a moment in time.	*To define* forms and types, focusing on the topological/ definitional purpose, using the types/categories hypothesis. The container experience of things in a category.	*To argue,* to persuade, focusing on system of proof, editorial purpose using the machine/hypothesis system of parts and wholes, developing an idea/position.
Notational Speech Events: The discourse of lists	Clinical word association test, a "stream" of associations.	List of events, calendar, steps in *a recipe,* simple directions, sequential grocery list, usually has an implied or stated goal	Classified want ad, police wanted poster/list, resume, census statistics, weather statistics.	Types, grocery list, notes toward report, clustering ideas-telephone directory, stock market, tables, lists of type of things, the reading of the list of dead at a memorial, the message on a tombstone.	Proverbs, maxims, list of predications, system listing.

TABLE 6.5
(Continued)

Conversational Speech Events: The discourse of close social relations and common sense concepts	Pouring it out to a friend; letting is all out in a journal	Anecdotes, gossip, joke, an informal biographical sketch, social exchange, social exchange over sequential steps in a procedure, personal letter with story, sharing time, stories, dinner-time conversation.	Causal descriptions of place, travel ads, personal letters describing someone in context.	Journal or diary reports, learning logs and memos describing definitions of things, types of things, categories of things.	Personal letter of opinion, informal letter to editor, a draft of problem solutions, an informal debate.
Presentational/Public Speech Events: The discourse of public transactions	Public "confession" on Oprah, public mono-logue about one's feelings about an issue.	A biographical event, myth, autobiographical incident, a formal story, a fable, policeman's accident report, newspaper reports of events, an elaboration of a cause-effect or direction/procedures.	Newspaper description of weather damage; a magazine sketch portraying a person or place.	Magazine report on world economy or elections; showing types of voters or businesses or heroes in novels.	Formal letter to editor, editorial/ proposed solution, analysis of reasons for an event, movie review, evaluation of a candidate, a commentary.
Academic/Sacred Speech Events: The discourse of specialized knowledge, rituals, and scientific concepts.	N/A see below	Academic history paper, books of historical research.	Ethnographic study: Research report from Gertz or Becker or Margaret Mead.	Technical summaries, summary of laws or types, Popper's world hypothesis (four types of hypothesis), Botany studies, Chomsky's types of syntactic structures.	Papers from disciplines: social science disciplines, scientific summary of experiments, philosophical argument on critical theory, research report on medical experiment.

The expressive has no publicly "accepted" form in presentational or academic speech events. The examples in the cells are forms of discourse/writing shaped by speech events and modes. From Myers (1996). Reprinted with permission.

TABLE 6.6
Components of a Narrative

Genre	Traditionally, genre is a classification system for organizing literature. It chunks stories with common elements together, although the categories are the subject of much debate. More recently, genre is seen as social action used to accomplish particular purposes.
Theme	Theme is the message of the story--an idea of comment about life. Theme illuminates the emotional content of the human condition.
Character	Characters are actors in the story whose actions, intentions, and motivations interact with what others do, say, think, and feel. Characters can be people, animals, or personified animals, objects, or creatures.
Setting	The basic elements of setting are the place, time, and situation of the story. The setting can be simple or effect the characters, plot, and mood either directly or symbolically.
Plot	The plot is a series of events which occur in a specific order. Not necessarily linear, the sequence represents the author's decisions for moving the story along.
Point of View	Point of view is the view of the action the reader follows. It is often signaled by insights into the thoughts and feelings of particular characters.
Style	Style is the use of language that reflects the spirit and personality of the writer through specific literary devices. Authors make purposeful stylistic choices to create images, set mood, and reveal character.
Tone	Tone is the manner of expression which conveys (through stylistic choices) the author's attitude toward his or her subject.

Develop a Common Language

Genre	Fantasy: traditional folk, myth, fable; high fantasy; science fiction; reality; problem realism; historical fiction, animal realism
Theme	Universal; moral; implicit & explicit; primary & secondary
Character	Major/minor; protagonist/antagonist; Features: emotional, physical, intellectual; Character development, revelation, intention
Setting	Time; place; situation; historical context; mood
Plot	Story graph; episode analysis: problem, emotional response, action, outcome; flashback, conflict, suspense, foreshadowing, climax
Point of View	First person (often the protagonist); omniscient (spread across characters); focused (usually on one character); objective (actions reveal motivation)
Style	Imagery; allusion; puns; hyperbole; figurative language, personification, metaphor; sound devices, alliteration, assonance, rhythm
Tone	Humorous; affectionate; angry; condescending; didactic; ironic

TABLE 6.6
(Continued)

Explore the Text

Genre	Identify characteristics of certain genres. For example, fairy tales tend to have stock charters. Historic fiction relies heavily on the development of setting. Fables offer specific rules to live by. Identify the genre you prefer and analyze why you like it. Discuss the author's choice of genre for delivering the theme of the story. Debate how you could stretch or fracture the genre to accomplish different purposes.
Theme	Identify the theme(s) in the text. Describe the relationship of the theme(s) to your life. Compare/contrast other pieces of literature with similar theme(s). Describe how our understanding of character, setting, & plot enhance your understanding of the theme(s). Decide on the universality or unique qualities of the theme(s); who is most affected by the message(s)?
Character	Identify the major & minor characters in the story. Compare and/or contrast the story characters to you or people you know. Trace the development of a character through the story. Analyze the intentions behind the actions. Trace the relationships between characters. Analyze how the character is revealed through other characters' eyes.
Setting	Explain the relationship of the setting to the story. Relate the time, place, & situation to your own. Explore the historical & cultural significance of the setting. Describe how the setting reflect the characters. Compare/contrast two or more settings in the story (e.g., How do the different settings effect the characters or mood of the piece?).
Plot	Compare the plot to events that have occurred in your own life. Identify an episode in terms of problem, emotional response, action, & outcome. Outline several episodes relating the outcome of one episode to the problem of the next episode. Explain the effect of characters' intentions & motivations on the plot or vice versa.
Point of View	Identify who's telling the story. Analyze how the point of view reveals the characters' motivations and intentions. Justify the effectiveness of the point of view. Criticize the author's choice or point of view. Would the story have been better served by an alternative? What might that look like?
Style	Describe the stylistic choices of the author and how they enhance the story. Describe how the author's style reveals character, setting, & plot. Which words create vivid images? How? Compare/contrast stylistic choices within one author's work or between authors. Reflect on the stylistic choices you will incorporate in your own speech and writing.
Tone	Evaluate the tone(s) of the narrative voice. Describe the influence of tone in relation to the characters (e.g., affectionate, condescending). Analyze how stylistic choices reflect the tone. Compare/contrast choices in tone within one author's work or between authors. Discuss how tone will vary depending on the author's purposes.

Note. Wolf, Shelby A. and Maryl Gearhart, " Writing What You Read: Narrative Assessment as a Learning Event." *Language Arts,* Volume 71, Number 6, October 1994, Pages 425-444, NCTE.

172

classification of inventory items in the portfolio assessment system. In NSP, on-demand reading and writing tasks are approximately 3–5 days in length, they have been piloted in classrooms of Grades 4, 8, and 10 across the country, and have been scored by teachers across the country for reading and writing at four levels of performance. Rubrics, exemplar portfolios, and interpretive summaries or commentaries are prepared for each task to show adequate performance. Using the rubrics, the exemplars, and summaries/commentaries, teachers attempt to identify explicit indicators of performance levels in the student response. These on-demand tasks, in addition to giving teachers exemplars of reading and writing tasks with high degrees of authenticity, provide some evidence that portfolio scoring and many classifications are or are not basically consistent across the country.

Like much of the data that came back on the early sailing ships, the data from early writing records in NSP has not been consistently combinable. For one thing, agreement among teacher judges who were scoring the responses to reading and writing tests has been lower than the NSP staff of the literacy unit expected. The first scoring of NSP tasks generally produced dead-center agreement among the judges in the .55 and higher range. In the Vermont Portfolio Project, raters had correlations from .39 to .52 on writing in portfolios and correlations from .49 to .60 on all dimensions combined (Koretz, Stecher, Klein, & McCaffrey, 1994). Most school districts report reliabilities at the .80 level (8 out of 10 times judges agree and 8 out 10 times the student's score on a particular item does not change from one administration to another).

NSP's discrepancy happened for two reasons. The first reason is that NSP set very high scoring standards. NSP staff was aiming for dead-on agreement, a much higher standard than most states. Most states allow a one point disagreement and count that as agreement. Some school districts have decided that when two judges differ by one point on a point scale, the two scores together should produce a mid-point or .5 scale point. In other words, if on a 4 point scale, one judge gives a 3 and another gives a 4, then the score is recorded as 3.5. In this way, one point of differences are not counted in reliability correlations, thereby raising the statistical measures of agreement. Some agencies accomplish the same goal by having papers with one point difference read by a third reader who drops one score and doubles the other, again producing high reliabilities.

The second reason for lower than expected reliability correlations is that very few states—maybe not more than four states: California, Oregon, Kentucky, and Vermont—have attempted tasks as complicated as NSP tasks. NSP tasks include the reading of a whole piece (article, story, poem, and so forth), five to eight questions about the reading (including diagrams and pictures), a discussion period, and a writing topic with 1 class hour for prewriting and another hour for the final draft. One problem of complexity in some NSP tasks was that the more open-ended questions, which were wonderful for instruction, made reliable scoring difficult if not impossible. Teachers could not predict how students might answer an open-ended question, and, therefore, preparing good scoring rubrics before reading papers became more problematic.

One way to correct the situation is to do two full readings—one for a rubric development and another for scoring. This double reading increases costs and reliabilities. Another way to raise agreement among judges is to reduce task complexity by narrowing options on task questions, thereby closing off options that increase the unreliability of scoring. Closing off options also increases bias, adding to equity concerns. No one who has attempted to design authentic text will be surprised by this story of tension among validity, reliability, and bias (Camp, 1989, 1992). Many of the most authentic tasks were great for instruction and lousy for assessment—lousy, at least, in the view of assessment principles being proposed by some technical advisers (Wainer, Wang, & Thissen, 1994).

A critical question facing portfolio assessment is whether increasingly complex tasks and projects, both possibly necessary to get good data on higher order thinking skills, will make traditional standards of reliability in scoring untenable. As noted earlier, several studies have shown that if rubrics and exemplars can be adequately standardized, writing samples can be scored with high rater reliability, reaching interrater correlations of .70 and higher (Dunbar, Koretz, & Hoover, 1991). In the National Assessment of Educational Progress (NAEP; 1990) study on portfolios, Gentile (1992) reported scoring reliabilities on individual pieces at .76 or higher and in a summary of Pittsburgh portfolio scoring, LeMahieu (1993) reported approximately .80 agreement among raters on scores for such dimensions in the portfolio as growth and development as a writer. Gentile (1992) reported incidently, that "coefficients above .80 are considered strong, and above .65 are considered good" (p. 24).

But how much reliability is possible in the scoring of a portfolio with complex material? Delandshere and Petrosky (1994) argued that when typical reliability procedures are applied to the scoring of complex materials, the usual correlation standards cannot be reached and then the materials are often trivialized to get high reliabilities (Delandshere & Petrosky, 1994). Similarly, Zadeh (1973), father of fuzzy set theory, has argued that in humanistic systems, people reason by approximations of fuzzy sets, not by precise, quantitative terms:

> . . . [A]s the complexity of the system increases, our ability to make precise yet significant statements about its behavior diminishes until a threshold is reached beyond which precision and significance (or relevance) become mutually exclusive characteristics (Zadeh, 1973, p. 28; see also McNeil & Freiberger, 1993).

Some parts of the Summative Portfolio system may require entirely new approaches to scoring. For example, Moss (1994) suggested that assessment devices like portfolios may need new alternatives to the present standards for reliability, suggesting hermeneutic approaches like panels of judges and consensus decisions as one alternative. The reliability issue could certainly sink portfolio assessment in some states if the alternatives to portfolios—machine-scored tests—were not so unattractive. Mills and Brewer, leaders of the Vermont Portfolio Project, warned us more than 6 years ago that portfolio assessment would require a long period of development (Mills & Brewer, 1988).

One of the problems of combinable data, in addition to reliabilities in scoring, is the absence of a common vocabulary. For example, the effort to find combinable data in portfolios—almost 4,000 classroom teachers were trying NSP portfolios in October 1994—has revealed that across the country, there are a number of different ways of classifying types of writing. NAEP, to use one national example, proposes combining writing samples into three types: Information, which emphasizes the subject; Persuasion, which emphasizes the readers; and Narration, which emphasizes the imagination (Applebee, Langer, Mullis, Latham, & Gentile, 1994). Although every Information topic for the writing report card used the word "describe," these Information topics named a variety of required forms—an article for a newspaper reviewing a program, descriptions of school lunchtime, and descriptions of a favorite object (Applebee et al., 1994). NAEP's classification of information is not consistent with that of most states. Some states call a newspaper movie review Exposition, the lunchtime description a Narrative or Exposition, and the description of a favorite object a Description.

Most states would also disagree with the way NAEP limits narration to imaginative writing. All except one of NAEP's Narrative topics were imaginative or fictional, using words like "pretend," "imagine," "write a story about an adventure as a space traveler," "create a dream car and write about an adventure with your imaginary car," and "choose any person from history and imagine that you spend a day together. Write a story about what happens" (Applebee et al., 1994, p. 68). Most states focus the majority of their Narrative topics on events that actually happened, and most school districts do not assign much importance to imaginative or fictional writing after 6th grade. Only one of the NAEP Narrative topics focuses on something that actually happened: "think about an embarrassing situation you have been in and describe what happened" (Applebee et al., 1994, p. 68). To combine data, we must have common terms. Figure 6.6 is an example of a 3-step process used by teachers to get to common language.

Thus far, I have presented the story of the Age of Geographic Exploration as if it were the story of progressive advances in data collection, analysis, and dissemination and as if it never encountered a basic contradiction between Formative and Summative evaluation. However, the Age of Exploration did encounter that contradiction. In the process of collecting data, most of the centers of calculation ended up with trash and unusable data that could not be classified or somehow combined with other data on a chart. Sometimes this material was put on display in museums, but more often this material was simply discarded. Examples of this kind of trash and unusable data included human beings who were brought back to the centers of calculation, put on display in museums, and often donated to other institutions or sent home.

One example is Ishi, the last of the Northern California Indians, who was brought to the anthropology museum at the University of California, Berkeley, put on display, and finally hired as a custodian at the museum. Toward the end of Ishi's life, he was taken back to his native area, accompanied by two researchers. The two researchers reported that seeing Ishi in his natural environment for the first time made visible and combinable the meaning of some of his words, the uses of some of his tools, and the appearance of some of his skills for hunting and living in context. In other words, the center of calculation at the anthropology museum was able to make much information visible, stable, storable, mobile, and combinable, but the museum was fundamentally unable to see and to combine the knowledge made visible and combinable watching Ishi in his natural setting. At the end of the Age of Geographic Exploration, many researchers were already leaving the centers of calculation and returning to South Pacific Islands like Sakhalin to make visible and storable new data about people living in their native areas. This data was expected to capture individual portraits of a people in process in particular cultures, and, in time, the data of Goffman, Turner, Geertz, Meade, and other ethnographic researchers became part of the Summative data used by government agencies for government purposes.

At the end of the New Standards meeting in San Francisco in 1994, when we tried to find an inventory system accounting for contents we all agreed were there, we had interesting collection of odd material leftover that did not fit the menu for literacy: beautiful paintings, chalk drawings, sketches of people, rough charts, pieces from interdisciplinary projects, personal diaries, lists. Some of these items (lists, personal diaries) appear on almost any chart of the domain of English and English language arts (see the notational band in Table 6.1; Myers, 1996). But some of the items did not appear to belong on any of our charts. These items obviously have value in Formative Evaluation—what I call portfolios for teacher research and for student reflection. Furthermore, these items have local display value. They can be displayed in the museums of Cognitive Exploration that could be established at every school site, creating a place for teachers, parents, and students to see these materials from portfolios as well as other student work. But at the present time we have no way to make these leftovers meaningful outside the school site. One suggestion is to use narrative to restore the context for portfolio items by asking students and teachers to explain how items were developed and why were they included in the portfolio. The beautiful drawings, for example, were part of book report project in a particular teacher's classroom. Centers of data collection cannot account for these drawings without finding some way to restore context, and once context is restored, we may find we can combine the description with other things.

There was a time when countries only measured their wealth by the amount of fertile land they owned—the currency of the Age of Geographic Exploration. But transportation and agricultural science changed the value of that currency. There was a time when amount and location of financial capital determined a nation's wealth. Then nations found they could transport money from one place to another, and even create international spending on credit cards. Today nations are measuring their wealth by the amount of human and social capital they have. The concept of human and social capital turns education into an investment and turns the higher-order thinking skills of the population into an essential resource. At this point in our history, portfolios have become an essential data collection device for tracking the location, amount, and developmental needs of this essential human resource in an Age of Cognitive Exploration.

REFERENCES

Applebee, A. N., Langer, J. A., Mullis, I. V. S., Latham, A. W., & Gentile, C. A. (1994). *NAEP 1992 writing report card.* Washington, DC: Government Printing Office.

Bertisch, C. A. (1993). The portfolio as an assessment tool. In K. Gill (Ed.), *Process and portfolios in writing assessment* (pp. 54–59). Urbana, IL: National Council of Teachers of English.

Boorstin, D. J. (1994). *Cleopatra's nose.* New York: Random House.

Calfee, R. C., & Calfee, K. H. (1981). *Interactive reading assessment system (IRAS),* (rev.). Unpublished manuscript, Stanford University, School of Education.

Calfee, R. C., & Drum, P. A. (1986). Research on teaching reading. In M. C. Wittrock (Ed.), *Handbook of research on teaching* (3rd ed., pp. 804–849). New York: Macmillan.

Camp, R. (1989). *Arts propel: Suggestions for creating writing portfolios.* Pittsburgh, PA: Educational Testing Service.

Camp, R. (1992). Portfolio reflections in middle and secondary school classrooms. In K. B. Yancey (Ed.), *Portfolios in the writing classroom* (pp. 61–79). Urbana, IL: National Council of Teachers of English.

Carini, P. (1975). *Observation and description: An alternative methodology for the investigation of human phenomena.* North Dakota Study Group on Evaluation, University of North Dakota.

Clay, M. M. (1979). *The early detection of reading difficulty* (3rd ed). Portsmouth, NH: Heinemann.

Daiker, D., Dubinsky, J., Helton, E., & Wilson, S. (1993). *The best of Miami University's portfolios.* Oxford, OH: Department of English, Miami University.

Delandshere, E., & Petrosky, A. (1994). Capturing teachers knowledge: Performance assessment (a) and post-structuralist epistemology, (b) from post-structuralist perspective, (c) and post-structuralism, (d) none of the above. *Educational Researcher, 23,* 11–18.

Dunbar, S. B., Koretz, D. M., & Hoover, H. D. (1991). Quality control in the development and use of performance assessments. *Applied Measurement in Education, 4,* 289–303.

Durkin, D. (1979). What classroom observations reveal about reading comprehension instruction. *Reading Research Quarterly, 14*, 481–533.

Freedman, S. W. (1993). Linking large-scale testing and classroom portfolio assessments of student writing. *Educational Assessment, 1*, 27–52.

Gentile, C. (1992). *Exploring new ways for collecting school-based writing: NAEP's 1990 portfolio study.* Washington, DC: Office of Education Research and Improvement.

Koretz, D., Stecher, B., Klein, S., & McCaffrey, D. (1994). The Vermont portfolio assessment program: Findings and implications. *Educational Measurement: Issues and Practice, 13*(2), 3–16.

LaTour, B. (1987). *Science in Action.* Cambridge, MA: Harvard University Press.

LeMahieu, P. (1993, April). Data from the Pittsburgh Writing Portfolio Assessment. In J. Herman (Chair), *Portfolio assessment meets the reality of data.* Symposium conducted at the annual convention of the American Educational Research Association, New Orleans.

Lucas, C. (1992). Introduction: Writing portfolios—changes and challenges. In K. B. Yancey (Ed.), *Portfolios in the writing classroom* (pp. 1–11). Urbana, IL: National Council of Teachers of English.

Madaus, G., & Tan, A. (1993). Growth of assessment. In G. Cawelti (Ed.), *ASCD Yearbook.* Alexandria, VA: Association of Supervision and Curriculum Development.

McNeil, D., & Freiberger, P. (1993). *FuzzyLogic.* New York: Simon and Schuster.

Miller, G. A., & Gildea, P. How children learn words. *Scientific American, 257*(3), 94–99.

Mills, R. P., & Brewer, W. R. (1988). *Working together to show results: An approach to school accountability in Vermont.* Montpelier, VT: Vermont Department of Education.

Moss, P. (1994). Can there be validity without reliability? *Educational Researcher, 23*, 5–12.

Myers, M. (1996). *Changing our minds: Negotiating English and literacy.* Urbana, IL: National Council of Teachers of English.

Myers, M. (in press). *Writing assessment and the shaping of professionalism.* In L. Odell & C. Cooper (Eds.), Urbana, IL: National Council of Teachers of English.

Nagy, W. E., & Anderson, R. C. (1984). How many words are there in printed school English? *Reading Research Quarterly, 19*, 304–330.

Nagy, W. E., Anderson, R. C., & Herman, P. A. (1987). Learning word meanings from context during normal reading. *American Educational Research Journal, 24*, 237–270.

Polanyi, M. (1974). *Personal knowledge: Towards a post-critical philosophy.* Chicago: University of Chicago Press.

Popper, K., & Eccles, J. C. (1977). *The self and its brain: (Parts I and II).* New York: Springer International.

Public Law 108, Statute 139 and 145. Passed by Congress, March 24, 1994.

Reilly, B. (1994). *The video portfolios CD ROM.* Los Angeles, CA: Bell High School.

Scriven, M. (1967). The methodology of evaluation. In R. E. Stake (Ed.), *Curriculum Evaluation: AERA Monograph Series on Evaluation, No. 1* (pp. 39–55). Chicago: Rand McNally.

Shavelson, R. J., Baxter, G. P., & Pine, J. (1992). Performance assessments: Political rhetoric and measurement reality. *Educational Researcher, 21*, 22–27.

South Brunswick Board of Education. (1992). *Early childhood education: A guide for parents and children.* South Brunswick, NJ: South Brunswick Board of Education.

Wainer, H., Wang, X-B, & Thissen, D. (1994). How well can we compare scores on test forms that are constructed by examinee's choice? *Journal of Educational Measurement, 31*, 183–199.

Wolf, S. A., & Gearhart, M. (1994). Writing what you read: Narrative assessment as a learning event. *Language Arts, 71*(6), 425–444.

Yancey, K. B. (1992). Portfolios in the writing classroom: A final reflection. In K. B. Yancey (Ed.), *Portfolios in the writing classroom* (pp. 102–116). Urbana, IL: National Council of Teachers of English.

Zadeh, L. A. (1973). Outline of a new approach to the analysis of complex systems and decision processes. *IEEE Transactions on Systems, Man and Cybernetics, 3*, 28–44.

CHAPTER SEVEN

The Metaphor of the Portfolio and the Metaphors in Portfolios: The Relation of Classroom-Based to Large-Scale Assessment

Sarah L. Jordan
Alan C. Purves
State University of New York, Albany

Most of this chapter is, like many research papers, a simple recounting of our experience working with teachers who were beginning to use portfolios in their literature classrooms. It is, for the most part, practical, because the research, conducted through the National Research Center on Literature Teaching and Learning, uses a case-study approach in investigating how teachers use portfolios. But the research—and the arguments stemming from the research—become more complex, because the use of portfolios in classrooms takes on a metaphoric or symbolic role in education.

Metaphors are used to name one's place in the world and to help find meaning for one's life. Using metaphors to explain what portfolios do is also a way of conceptualizing one's reasons for teaching and one's expectations for students. But the portfolio is more than an object—it is also a metaphor itself. If metaphors are so powerful, and if they are individual, then a serious problem arises for those who wish to make large-scale generalizations about portfolios. Large-scale generalizations can get very messy, as we found out when we made an attempt to expand the implications of individual teachers' metaphors to include the role of the district, if not the nation.

In this chapter, therefore, we abandon the practical research base and jump into a discussion about hypertext as a possible metaphor for the portfolio, the classroom experience, and educational systems in general. We feel that this discussion is necessary because of the impact that computers have on our conceptions of text. *Hypertext* is the confluence of text segments (or spaces) that may be recombined by the reader, who must then make sense of the original. A hypertext is "nonsequential" writing—text that branches and allows choices to the reader, best read in an interactive sense. As popularly conceived, a hypertext is a series of chunks [of text] connected by links that offer the reader different pathways.

We offer this metaphor because both portfolios and hypertexts have appeared at a time when challenges have been made to traditional ways of thinking about writing, about the teaching of writing and literature, and particularly about the assessment of learning. These challenges are evident in a number of guises: whole language, process writing, response-based literature, third-generation evaluation; challenged are notions of generalizable skills, drill-and-practice activities, and authorized interpretations. Although the use of hypertexts is not commonly found in schools, we believe that one day teachers will feel comfortable with computerized texts that can be connected in any order and still make sense, just as we hope that one day students might perform a classroom activity and not worry about the grade received.

BACKGROUND

Imprecise definitions and indeterminate effects of schooling have plagued the field and have led to a persistent antagonism between the professional teacher and the professional assessor. Each time a test has been produced, it has been attacked as being narrow or limiting by some teachers. Psychometricians have thrown up their hands at the fuzzy-headedness of the teachers; teachers feel that no external test can ever measure what really is being learned in the classroom. Another aspect of the antagonism has arisen from the differences between the practice in a single classroom and the curriculum definition of the district, state, or country. The antagonism has been exacerbated as the educational system has opened its doors to include people who would have been excluded from schooling on the basis of race, ethnicity, social class, or disability. Such an opening has been attended by a broadening of the curriculum and an emphasis on processes rather than rote knowledge.

Portfolio assessment entered into this historical situation in the 1980s. The portfolio as a collection of representative pieces of an individual's work had long existed for artists of various sorts, including writers. Its entry into school-level assessment also began with the arts when a single test did not make much sense. The portfolio serves as an assemblage of the student's work over time. It contains a number of individual pieces, both rough and finished, in an arrangement established by the student in collaboration with the teacher. Both the separate pieces and the assemblage can be rated by a jury. The idea of a portfolio was quickly adopted by teachers of writing, first at the college level, where single tests or writing samples were suspect, and later at the primary level, when students produced a variety of disparate works.

In the 1990s, the idea of raising the performance portfolio to the state or national level emerged. But can portfolios satisfy the demands of large-scale assessment? Freedman (1993) scrutinized four attempts at large-scale portfolio assessment: Arts PROPEL from the Pittsburgh school district, the Primary Language Record for elementary students in England, Vermont's statewide assessment of fourth and eighth grade portfolios, and a large-scale national examination for the completion of secondary schools in Great Britain. While applauding all of these experiments, Freedman also pointed out that they are troubled, that portfolios are hard to rate with any degree of reliability, and that it is hard to standardize the collection of material and to guarantee that all submissions are a student's own work. Her questions are also raised by Daniel Koretz of the Rand Corporation, who investigated Vermont's inter-rater reliability and found it wanting, and who noted that teachers who use portfolios often want to accomplish two things: to improve what goes on in the classroom and to assess student progress accurately (Black, 1993). In this way, portfolios are used by teachers as formative assessment; they provide teachers with information about the student that is then used to create a new understanding of the student's knowledge and abilities so that learning goals can be modified. This purpose carries with it the implication that the portfolio will be localized and accommodated to the classroom if not to the student; it is also in direct conflict with the purpose of large-scale assessment, which is to standardize the measurement of student accomplishment.

So there is an apparent discrepancy between the purposes of portfolios at the classroom level (how teachers use them) and the district or state levels (how portfolios can be used to measure learning). The appeal of portfolios is that they are a grass-roots movement on the part of teachers to gain control over the process of assessment and to offer something back to their students that, unlike externally created tests, takes into consideration the context of the classroom. Research on the effects of large-scale portfolio assessment focuses on the reliability between raters (clearly an important concern) without looking at either the change in classroom interaction or how portfolios function across sites to enhance teaching (Baker, Haman, & Gearhart, 1993). Although portfolios are created by individual students, which means that they will contain individual differences in terms of perception of learning, large-scale portfolio assessment cannot take into account the individual nature of portfolios. In fact, the purpose of large-scale assessment is to weed out individual differences, a top-down statistical approach that is at odds with the bottom-up appeal of portfolios. Theoretically, then, there appears to be a mismatch between portfolios and large-scale assessment.

Within this larger context, this study was undertaken by the National Research Center on Literature Teaching and Learning. Following a survey of the current uses of portfolios (Kolanowski, 1993) as well as of the literature on portfolios, the project focused on a series of teacher-initiated studies within the context of state-mandated assessment. The two states chosen were Connecticut, where the emphasis is on program assessment, and New York, where the emphasis is on individual assessment. Our aim was to follow the teachers as they worked out the answers to the questions they had about implementing portfolios in their classrooms. In this project, the teachers themselves are the research team; the Center's function is to assist them, to enhance communication among the researchers, and to explore any common threads, particularly as they might shed light on the concerns of larger entities like the state educational agency.

THE STUDY

We wished to document how different teachers in different contexts used portfolios in their literature classrooms, with an eye to exploring implications for large-scale uses. We worked with 14 teachers at seven different sites, with a fairly equal distribution of middle- and high-school-level classes and a variety of communities (rural, urban, suburban). For the most part, the teachers joined the project because they were interested in portfolios and because they believed that portfolios might be one way of helping effect the kind of changes in their teaching practices that they desired. They did not see the project as focusing on assessment only, but on the structure of the classroom and the shape of instruction.

We innocently assumed that the portfolios produced at the end of the year by the teachers would be fairly similar, and that what differences did occur would be due in large part to the communities that house the schools. What we found, however, were differences in approaches to portfolios that were more complex than community differences or lack of consensus about what it means to be a good student. We found that different "frame factors" (Dahloff, 1971) or contexts created fundamentally different metaphors for the portfolio and that, ultimately, these metaphors were not compatible.

The idea for metaphoric analysis emerged as we examined both the literature on portfolios and the case-study reports described later. We found that different people used different metaphors to explain their use of the portfolio. Some followed the basic artistic metaphor, but other metaphors emerged: the log, the diary, the certificate, the exhibition, the anthology, the museum, the mirror, the title (we explore the implications of these later).

Case-Study Methodology

The data for the case study part of this report come from interviews and classroom observations with the four teachers from New York participating in the Portfolios in the Literature Classroom research project. The original purpose for the case study was to provide one graduate student with an opportunity to practice her qualitative research skills. The four portfolio metaphors provided by these teachers proved so irresistible, however, that we conducted a critical analysis of the year-end reports of an additional nine teachers (one teacher dropped out of the project). Teachers and schools who participated in the assessment are listed in Table 7.1. These teachers are all either junior high or high school English teachers in Connecticut and New York. Data for this particular analysis were collected during the project's first year. The teachers selected for case study represent a range of contexts and experiences. Nancy Lester and Anne Kuthy are from a suburban high school with a population that is mostly White and college-bound; Carol Mohrmann works in an inner-city middle school with a large minority population; and Joseph Quattrini teaches in a small and quite rural high school, of which almost the entire population is White and from a low-income bracket.

Before the project officially began, teachers were visited and interviewed about their interest in portfolios in the literature class. They were then asked to answer questions about program assessment, about their own methods of assessment, about their 3-year plan for the project, and about what they expected to gain from the experience.

TABLE 7.1
Teachers and Schools Participating in the Portfolio Project

School	Teachers	Target Grade
Connecticut		
Danbury	Rich Harris	12
	Suzanne Heyd	9
	Charles Phelps	9
Groton	Deane Beverly	6
	Marian Galbraith	8
	Pam Keniry	8
	Carol Mackin	7
Old Saybrook	John Hellelly	12
Plainville	Christine Sullivan	10
New York		
Canajoharie	Joe Quattrini	10
Schenectady	Carol Mohrmann	8
Shaker	Anne Kuthy	10
	Nancy Lester	12

We sought to work with teachers on articulating their own theories of teaching and learning, rather than impose a theory on classroom practice. Most of the first year of this study was, for the teachers, spent in trying to answer the question "What am I trying to accomplish with this portfolio?" Then, during mid-year interviews, initial expectations and statements were modified as teachers grew more comfortable in their classes and with the researchers.

Most data for the case study came from the original goals as articulated by the teachers, from discussions at quarterly meetings of all the teachers in the project, and from interviews and classroom observations scheduled after the mid-year marking period. The researchers also collected anything that the teachers wanted to share in terms of reports, speeches, evidence of student learning, and journal entries. Because one of the goals of this project was to articulate what it is about portfolio assessment that makes it so appealing to classroom teachers, any information that the teachers could offer was noted. The interviews focused on what was going to go into the portfolio, who would select the pieces, and who would see the portfolio.

Report Analysis Methodology

All of the teachers in the project wrote reports of their work in the first year. Some of these were jointly written and some were written by each teacher in a school. In addition to the four case-study teachers, there were six other teachers who reported. These were analyzed by the second author using the technique of content analysis and in particular, we were looking for a guiding metaphor or set of metaphors in each report. For the case-study teachers the analysis was simply to confirm the findings of the case study; for the other reports, the analysis was to generate additional metaphors and construct the framework outlined later in Table 7.2.

RESULTS: THE CASE STUDIES

The following case studies of 4 of the 14 teachers involved in the Literature Center project show, in part, how diverse are the expectations they placed on portfolios. They also show how a framing metaphor emerged over time in each context. This is not to say that the teachers are oblivious to the concerns of large-scale assessment. On the contrary, the four teachers are primarily interested in how portfolios affect policies and procedures first in their classrooms, then their schools, and finally their districts. The possibility of using portfolios to create programmatic changes in instruction cannot be ignored; although it is often seen as secondary to the demands on student assessment, it becomes primary in the eyes of the teacher.

The following descriptions are perhaps overly brief, due to constraints on the length of this chapter. We provide what we hope is just enough detail about expectations, community, and outlook to explain each teacher's metaphor.

Teachers and Their Frames

Suburban. Both Anne Kuthy and Nancy Lester worked for the same school district. Anne Kuthy indicated that standardized tests were very important in the district: "Budgets have been sold on the basis of test scores. There's a lot of pressure." Nancy Lester, however, admitted to being much less aware of test pressures and, therefore, much less constrained by them.

Anne Kuthy worked with a 10th-grade class "of above average ability." Being both a teacher and an administrator (she is Supervisor of English for the district), she has only one class. She indicated that, when evaluating student work, she looked for originality, interest, and personal growth. She indicated that reader-response theory underlay her evaluations of student work: "The exciting thing about reader response is that it allows for such a high degree of individuality." As we worked with Anne Kuthy during the year, it became clear that she never forgot the importance of those mandated tests; perhaps this is why she placed so much value on individual response.

At first she was not sure about how she would create a portfolio. When asked about her vision of a portfolio in literature, she wrote:

> I don't know if I can answer this completely. I think the literature portfolio will evolve as we progress through the year. I will begin with reading logs, reader response journals, and critical essays. I would like to include my narrative about each student's classroom participation, self evaluations, parent responses, creative pieces related to the literature, art work, and some type of alternate assessment project culminating the year's work.

Anne Kuthy was concerned with the how-to of creating a portfolio, the real structure that could be produced at the end of the year. She was also concerned with consistency of grading across projects, and she wanted a unique and interesting final project. Anne Kuthy's goals were to figure out what would go into the portfolio and how the portfolio would be different from regular grading—what would make the portfolio special?

What is consistent in all her answers is the word "assessment," which is something that teachers struggle with on their own. They do not talk to each other about criteria or new methods of grading. Perhaps because she holds an administrative position, she is well aware that "changing the assessment strategy will have a major effect on a program. Thus, if we have high quality assessment that looks at many aspects of student learning and that encourages critical thinking, we will have curriculum that does the same." Even though this was not on Anne Kuthy's agenda as an area to be investigated, it was clear that she was interested in curriculum changes that would be a result of portfolios.

At the initial interview Nancy Lester was bothered by the lack of guidance on the part of researchers. Finally she asked, "Oh, so this is a grading project?" It was hard for her not to have clear goals; in her own classroom, she is very clear on her expectations and standards. Nancy Lester chose to work with a 12th-grade advanced placement class. She also indicated that she was unaware of the impact of standardized testing in her district, although she was aware of state demands to justify grades and to remain accountable to parents.

The initial perusal of Nancy Lester's answers gave us an indication that she valued text-centered reading and writing, and the development of writing skills. She did not indicate that her students would have any responsibility in the evaluation of their own work, although she mentioned the possibility of including peer editing and self-evaluation without any concrete examples of how she would include these. Months later she said that she was not the sort of teacher who thought up "cute little activities" for her class. She is, quite simply, intensely academic. Her only classroom tools were reading, writing, and talking.

Nancy Lester's goals were rather introspective. She wanted to work out a rubric to evaluate class participation, "since discussion of literature is integral to the course." She also wanted to "focus on defining and documenting the 'fudge factor' that most English teachers I know implicitly include in their evaluating of English students. I hope that in defining mine, we can strive for consistency in standards and expectations in all our classes." Another goal involved communication. She said she tried to call parents "when their children have said or done something noteworthy, in addition to when they have fallen below expectations." But, she said, "communication with teachers is more difficult, and I would like to come up with ways of sharing my students' work with them."

Rural. In his answers to the initial questions, Joe Quattrini said that what he looked for in student reading and writing was development of writing skills, mastery of conventions, and critical stance. After scrutinizing his answers, it became clear that what he valued would be the ability to make connections and to look at a text from more than one perspective— depth, not breadth, of coverage. And something else that became clear is that, for Joe Quattrini, portfolios were not an answer to the problem of assessment, but an experience in themselves.

Unlike both Nancy Lester and Anne Kuthy, Joe Quattrini expressed little interest in how parents would perceive portfolios or how they could participate in the experience. At first it was not clear as to why this was so, but in

November Joe wrote in his notes, "Some parents were less than enthusiastic about responding to their kids' poems and short stories. Regarded as home-work for THEM, I guess. Others were happy to see their kids' work." Then in December, "Most parents are working, and aren't interested in spending time reading things, even if their kids wrote them. A little disappointing, but not really a problem." Perhaps his earlier lack of concern with parents was actually an intuitive understanding of his community.

Joe had the support of his administrators. Anne Kuthy and Nancy Lester had token support from theirs, with the clear understanding that as long as test scores were not affected, new classroom practices could be tolerated (However, Anne Kuthy's superintendent also told her, "Be careful what you model, because other teachers will think they will need to do what you do."). Joe, on the other hand, reported both to his principal and his superintendent about progress on the portfolio project. Like Anne Kuthy, Joe understood this new tool to have the potential to shape instruction and to change programs, and Joe was very clear on the changes he wanted. He wrote, "For a change, assessment will guide instruction, and may even help to change instruction toward large-scale integrated activities. In this way, the portfolio can be an agent of change." This is the heart of Joe's involvement with the project. He was dissatisfied with state-controlled exams and competency tests, which tested on decontextualized knowledge and which (he felt) were insulting to teachers' professional ability and knowledge. He wanted to see portfolios bring about school-wide change in terms of instructional and assessment activities. In addition, Joe expressed the hope that "collegiality might go past morning nods to actual activities that require collaboration." Joe's goals were to effect changes and to get his students to engage in the work, not to perform for a grade.

Urban. During the year prior to the commencement of the project, Carol Mohrmann's school district was in the process of reorganizing—merging the two high schools into one and reducing the number of middle schools from five to three in the hopes that they would be more equitable. Because Carol Mohrmann was so involved in this process, she was not as thorough as the other teachers in examining her goals for the project. Her response to the initial questions was to hand in the newly devised scope-and-sequence chart that the middle-school English teachers in her district had just completed. Carol Mohrmann wrote, "Prior to [the reorganization], each school did pretty much as it pleased regarding language arts. All of the middle school English teachers in the district have been meeting to try to come together on a mutually agreed upon curriculum for [the] middle school English classes. Remarkable enough we seem to have done just that."

It is in the reorganization of the district that Carol Mohrmann placed her hopes for the portfolio project. She wrote that "there seems to be a great deal of interest in the topic of portfolio assessment in all of the middle schools. This seems to be a prime time for initiating such a change. . . . [P]erhaps we can develop this procedure in all of our middle school classrooms. I intend to keep other teachers informed of our progress in the hopes this will occur."

Carol Mohrmann, like Anne Kuthy, was also concerned with the brass tacks of portfolios. At the end of the summer, just as the project was starting, she wrote, "I have purchased hanging file boxes with color coded files. I am hoping to have access to the computer room so the students can do some of their writing on disks." At this point, it appeared that Carol Mohrmann envisioned portfolios as a collection, and she was more concerned with the actual collection and storage of the material than with the evaluative choices that would need to be made (the *how* rather than the *what*).

Context has shaped the goals and expectations of these four teachers. It is clear that Nancy Lester and Anne Kuthy, with their high-achieving classes, can take for granted mastery of basic language skills. This permits them to reflect on their own values about what is good teaching and how learning is demonstrated, and how choices are made. Joe, too, has a similar choice because of his decision to work with above-average 11th-grade students. But he can also afford to think in terms of district-wide changes because his district is small and relatively stable. Carol Mohrmann, however, cannot take mastery of language skills for granted. She is working with a younger set of students in a school that is racially, socially, and economically diverse. For her, the basic questions—How do I collect these things? How do I store them?—are as important as Nancy Lester's questions about how she grades, or Anne Kuthy's questions about how to make the portfolio different enough to impact curriculum.

A further differentiation is that of focus. Nancy Lester might be said to value knowledge and to be interested in issues of maturity; Anne Kuthy, in her desire to help students develop a voice, would prefer "the practice of quality"; Joe Quattrini, in pushing for depth, would prefer "the practice of maturity." Carol Mohrmann, by basing her work on the scope-and-sequence chart, indicated that the acquisition of skills is what she values over the other domains, although at a much younger level.

If we were to stop here and guess what the portfolios of the students of these teachers would look like, we might conjecture that the portfolios of Anne Kuthy's students would contain plenty of responsive essays and perhaps some narratives; Nancy Lester's students would have produced several critical essays; Joe Quattrini's students would have produced a variety of responses to a single piece of literature; and Carol Mohrmann's students would have produced writings and activities to demonstrate a mastery of skills. But our guesses would be wrong, because the portfolio project, shaped by teachers, also shaped the teachers and their teaching.

Changes During the Year

Nancy Lester's Advanced Placement (AP) English students read a great deal, wrote critical essays, and talked a great deal about literature. Because the entire class was being trained to take the AP exam at the end of the year, she had decided that their outside reading would be relatively unstructured. She required her students to read at least six books outside of the classroom during the school year and to keep a response journal. This response journal became the portfolio, measuring what critical essays and a final exam could not: how the students were evolving as readers. It captured what was at the heart of Nancy Lester's teaching, what she had written earlier (but had not thought could be included in a portfolio) about getting students hooked on books. But she expressed doubts about this being a portfolio because it was just what she would have done even if she was not involved in the project.

Anne Kuthy was still trying to decide what to put in the portfolio. The work that students had done during the year had been graded when turned in, and she didn't seem to want to use the portfolio as a final assessment device. In fact, she was waiting until the end of the year to put the portfolios together, and was wondering what would be included. Just the student's best work? All of the student's work? Would the portfolio show growth or would it be a snapshot of the student at the end of the year? Anne Kuthy was still struggling with the idea of using the portfolio to communicate her goals to both students and their parents; she really wanted the parents to see them and to comment on them. It seemed that she, too, wanted the portfolio to convey to parents what test scores and report cards could not. She toyed with the idea of having a special parents' night but was discouraged from doing so by her superintendent. It was at this point that Anne Kuthy's district began to plan for a pilot project that would use portfolios in certain grades. Because the plan was that the portfolio would be reviewed not just by the student's then-current teacher but by the student's prospective teacher as well, Anne Kuthy decided that a portfolio should show the student's current ability. Still, months later, she once again indicated a wish to share the portfolios with parents.

At the beginning of the project, Joe Quattrini had outlined his first-year plans. The question that concerned him was: How can we make evaluation and assessment part of the learning, rather than either a byproduct or the sole purpose of other activities? He started by not assigning grades for the first quarter of the year, and when report cards came out, students submitted grade proposals. By the third quarter, he was experimenting with alternate evaluative procedures and asking for student feedback about various methods of grading, although he eventually decided to return to the original process of stating quarter goals and then asking for grade proposals. Joe Quattrini also looked at state, district, and departmental guidelines and requirements; school population; and his own ability to invest in a new idea in terms of time and energy. By the middle of the year he was satisfied that he was meeting curriculum guidelines, pushing his students to take more responsibility for their own learning, and stimulating conversation with colleagues and administrators. He wrote: "Language arts outcomes keep coming up in our discussions, and that's a good thing. It keeps us looking at performance and growth, rather than at grades."

By the middle of the year, Carol Mohrmann was thinking of starting to pull the portfolios together. During the fall, she had worked with her students to prepare for the regional competency tests. She felt quite bound to those tests, she said, "in fairness to the kids. They get tracked by the results. Our scores were high." But spending a semester teaching to a test brings up an interesting question: Should the business letters and persuasive pieces that were taught be included in a portfolio? Carol Mohrmann was trying to figure out whether a portfolio was everything or just final products. Like Anne Kuthy, Carol Mohrmann was unsure whether a portfolio should measure growth, or whether it should be a demonstration of ability. She indicated more of a bent toward portfolios as a document of growth in both skills and in thinking. She talked about the introductory letter as an example of metacognitive work— thinking about thinking. "In thirty-six years," she said, speaking of her teaching career, "we have rarely asked 'What are you thinking?' " The metacognitive writing included in a portfolio would address student thinking.

It should be clear by now that portfolios are more than just a classroom assessment device that demonstrates a teacher's view of the domain of English. And they are more than the product of classroom context and teacher ideology; they are also political tools and professional communication devices. How and why teachers choose to use portfolios in their classrooms is a combination of several factors—not just teacher values, but perceptions of need in the district and community play a part in defining a portfolio's use. It was at this point in our research that we realized that there were no simple answers to describing how portfolios are used, and that the large-scale implications of portfolios were nonexistent. So we looked beyond differences between these teachers to one remaining common point: the need to name what one is doing and to find a metaphor for one's work. The preceding details illustrate how such metaphors emerge.

Metaphors

Metaphor becomes "a set of terms that permit one to speak of experience and possibilities, and the mystery and hiddenness of their fundamental reality" (Denton, 1974). Because a teacher's world is essentially a world of action, teachers are not often in a situation when they must put terms on their actions. Consequently, beliefs are expressed in practice before they are expressed in words (Clandinin, 1986). After watching and talking with Anne Kuthy, Carol Mohrmann, Nancy Lester, and Joe Quattrini, we worked together to express in words what each was trying to do.

Nancy Lester wanted to help her students create an autobiography of a reader. It is true that she was not using portfolios, because portfolios are a collection of work. But the purpose of a portfolio is to present the creator to the outside world (Purves, 1993), and to this ideal Nancy Lester held true. Her students were readers, they interacted with texts, they talked to each other about books. Their response journals were valid and valuable auto-biographies of themselves as readers.

Anne Kuthy wanted the portfolio to be a vehicle of communication be-tween parents, teachers, and students. Perhaps her metaphor would be "portfolio as agenda for a conference," in that three people would have an opportunity to view and discuss an event without necessarily having to see it together. The student, in viewing the event, would have some distance on his or her work and this distance could perhaps permit critical thought.

Carol Mohrmann focused on her role as a teacher. In a speech delivered to her district colleagues about the nature of portfolios, she said, "We are no longer gurus with all the knowledge of the world to hand down. Rather we are mediators who encourage creative thought, value judgments, critical thinking, and decision making along with other cognitive skills." Earlier she had said, "I am no longer captain of [the] ship, rather admiral of [the] fleet."

Joe Quattrini's metaphor could be "portfolio as certificate of membership in a community." He wrote that students "need to be able to use metacog-nitive language of the discourse community they belong to, but first they must be aware that they're in one, but first they have to be in one—as full-fledged members." Embedded in the portfolio is the language used by the community of the classroom, as created by its members. The common thought created by a classroom should be evident in a student's portfolio.

So we have four metaphors: Portfolio as an autobiography, an agenda, the log of a ship that the student sails, and a certificate of membership in a community. These metaphors are products of individual classrooms working with specific teachers in specific school districts. What could they have in common? If the issue is the use of portfolios in large-scale (summative) assessment, then we need to find commonalties in how teachers use portfolios.

RESULTS: THE SELF REPORTS

In order to explore further the idea of metaphors, we undertook an analysis of the written reports of the other teachers in the study. There were six written reports prepared in the summer of 1993. These came from teachers in four schools in Connecticut.

John Hennelly was, at the time of the study, lead English teacher at a small high school serving a population that was primarily White and of mixed socioeconomic status. The class he was working with was a senior English course. He felt that the function of the portfolio was to challenge the students to take control and negotiate responsibility for their learning and their assessment. In his report, he wrote:

> The common denominator and recurring focus in my instructional growth has been challenging students to assume greater control and responsibility for their growth as writers and learners. The challenge is not so much an "I dare you" as it is negotiation: negotiation among student, teacher, and curriculum.
>
> Recently, I asked two groups of students to review their portfolio submissions and identify the elements or criteria that they valued in good writing. [The list included words and phrases like "developing ideas/organization," "focus/purpose," "detail," "paint a picture," "transitions," "be passionate/convincing/inspired."] What this list reflects . . . is understanding and appreciation of writing, but goes beyond to note the importance of style, voice, attitude, and belief. As such, it represents students' heightened awareness of what makes writing effective.

John's description suggests that the portfolio, and particularly the self-evaluations and self-statements, are an indication that the students have become part of the community. It gives evidence that they have adopted the language of the community to talk about themselves and their colleagues. In this sense, taking control is showing how one has assimilated into the community that is the classroom, or in Applebee's (1994) terms, how one has become a full participant in the conversation that is the classroom.

Christine Sullivan teaches at a high school in a poor industrial community with a mixed European and Latino population. Her target group was a 10th-grade mixed-ability class. She writes of this class:

> Many students knew of each other, even if they hadn't been in class before. That familiarity may have been helpful in the groups on the one hand, but on the other hand, any long-standing animosities and perceptions could have and did cause some difficulties. Over the years together, a "pecking order" among these students had grown. This project was designed to help students define for themselves what they could and should do. With regard to this aspect, the declarations of achievement in each semi-public evaluation session helped challenge this informal but nonetheless rigid system. Often, once a student's perception of his or her own work changed, he or she tried very hard to gather evidence to influence others to change their perceptions as well . . .
>
> One primary skill that was a predicate to informing those learning or assessment occasions was self-reflection. The ability of high school sophomores, of distinctly different ability levels and attitudes toward school, to become objective quantifiers and qualifiers of their own learning guided much

of direct instruction and practice in the classroom. For many students, the acquisition of this skill represented the single largest hurdle of the entire year.

Later in the report, she writes again of the principle of objectivity and how difficult it is to achieve:

> The project looked into the effects of maturity and the ability to be objective on each student's assessment. For several students, including those who performed very well, the final evaluation sessions revealed that although the students "talked" a good game, their permanent, written self evaluations reveal their uncertainty about personal performance and suggest that issues of closure need to be addressed more directly . . .
>
> For those students to whom their own education had long been a thing of mystery, assurance and involvement meant that they could exercise control over the process and over themselves as they charted their progress. This internalization of the process provided an intrinsic motivation for each student and focused the responsibility for learning on the learner.

It would appear that Christine Sullivan's use for the portfolio is one of developing objectivity and the capacity for self-assessment. She does this within the metaphor of the portrait, which she uses differently from Anne Kuthy in the case study. She is concerned with developing the self-awareness and the satisfaction that comes with it, a set of qualities that Anne Kuthy's students appeared to have gained.

Marian Galbraith, Pam Kiniry, Deane Beverly, and Carol Mackin comprise the reading staff at a middle school in an industrial community with a mixed population. The school is one of three in the district and the one that has students from the lowest socioeconomic group. They submitted a common report, for theirs is a program in which the four teachers work together in a 3-year sequence of learning. They reported that the portfolio served their reading program by allowing the students to show evidence of growth over time (both in the single year and across the three years of the school). Their first step was to have each student establish goals and to move beyond the simple goal of passing or getting a good grade:

> As much as we wanted students to determine their own goals, we also wanted those goals to reflect the goals of the curriculum. As a guide we provided a simplified version of the curriculum goals and asked the students to choose goals from that list which they felt ready to attempt . . .
>
> Ownership has always been a cornerstone of our reading program. Students make decisions about what they read and the ways they respond to what they read. Now students were taking ownership of not only the portfolios, but the curriculum. The program goals were becoming student goals . . .
>
> In sixth grade, the concept of goal setting is one with which the students were unfamiliar. In subsequent grades, we realized we needed to help students to think of their work as more than a reaction, to see it as evidence of change, and to make choices about their work. Beyond that we wanted to help students

to reflect on themselves as readers, thinkers, interpreters, to begin to understand and consider the types of thinking they bring to a piece of literature and the kinds of thinking in which a piece engages them.

It would appear that the guiding metaphor of the portfolio for these teachers is one of a deed, or a means of giving title and ownership to those who had been tenants or leaseholders.

Still another approach to portfolios is that reported from the fourth school. Suzanne Heyd, Charles Phelps, and Rich Harris teach at a large urban high school with a large number of Hispanics and other ethnic groups. They issued separate reports on their 9th, 9th, and 12th-grade classes, respectively. Harris's report speaks of his attempt to get a group of college-bound seniors to undertake self-assessment and of the near revolt it produced. Charles Phelps, an experienced teacher returning to a 9th-grade class after some years with older students, also found the experience a contest of wills. What he sought in the project was to have the students participate in the class: "My goal was to have them read short stories thoughtfully and talk and write about them intelligently, using as a framework the organization of the text around literary concepts. Their goal seemed to be to do the very minimum amount of work necessary to pass."

Later in the semester, in discussing a unit on the novel, Charles Phelps reported:

> [I] asked each class to produce, as a class project, the equivalent of a Cliff's Notes study guide to the novel, working in groups. Predictably some groups produced better work than others, and some group members did very little while others did quite a bit. . . . Most important, however, was that, for the first time, some of the students seemed to take some visible pride in work of quality which they had produced.
>
> [In the end-of-the-year self-evaluations] the papers seemed to me to be honest and thoughtful, and, while I am sure that at least some of the work reflected parental assistance, the voices were clearly those of the students and not someone else. Furthermore, to a much greater extent than at any other time during the year, the writers were beginning to make specific references to the work in their portfolios. Finally the papers were interesting. . . . I sense that in this final project there is evidence of a lessening of the adversarial relationship between students and teacher, and that in English classes at least, some students are now ready to take responsibility for their own learning.

Charles Phelps uses some of the same language as do other teachers, but the metaphor of participation in the class is one that overrides that language and differentiates his classroom and his use of the portfolio from those others who also see it as evidence of growth.

Suzanne Heyd, the final teacher of the group, approaches the portfolio much differently. Her report is entitled "Assessment as Awareness," and she uses as reference points such writers as Natalie Goldberg, Peter Elbow, and

Christine Feldman, all of whom take a meditative approach to writing, literature, and the classroom. She opens her report by saying that she took a meditative spirit to her work on portfolios. She asked her students to do a learning analysis of each piece they submitted. This was a reflection on the process and on the strengths and weaknesses of the writing:

> What happens when we are open, receptive, and curious? Each one of us knows that feeling—it is the beginner's mind . . . and it evokes in us a sense of possibility. Openness as opposed to defining, grading, or labeling, connects us to the present moment, giving us the power of awareness and the freedom from our preconceptions and judgments . . .
>
> Instead of grades and goals for the fourth quarter, each student kept a daily observation log, written in during the last five minutes of each class. The log was a vehicle for students to record the things they noticed, learned, and were aware of in the classroom. I asked them to work on "bare awareness" and record what they actually observed without coloring it with value judgments . . . I kept one, too. . . .

The word "awareness" pervades Suzanne's report. Awareness is a quality that is to become internal to each student; it is an awareness of themselves, of the classroom, of the subject, and of the standards that are expected of them. As they acquire greater awareness and reflect on it, they become meditative and more passionate about their performance. She concludes: "Perhaps assessment isn't about judgment, it is about knowing ourselves intimately, it is about deepening in the kind of wisdom that only we can know: the wisdom of self-knowledge. It would seem that this turns the notion of assessment around on its heels."

Summary of Metaphoric Constructs

Earlier in this chapter we discussed the conflict between educational practice and educational assessment. We would like to point out that much of the tension lies in a conflict of metaphors. Educational assessment often uses factory and industrial metaphors: the school is a factory, the student is a product; teachers work on an assembly line. With this metaphor, learning is linear, and the image of an assembly line or conveyor belt carries a concept of unidirectional learning, stopping only when the four o'clock whistle blows or the belt breaks or the product falls off the line ("drops out").

But practice uses completely different metaphors. Previously, teachers, if pressed, might have used the metaphor of an artisan's workshop for what schools actually were: teachers were the masters, students were the apprentices. This metaphor grants some autonomy to the student, although it still carries with it the concept of some final judgment made about either the student's abilities or the work produced. But the metaphors that the teachers in this study used indicate that no one metaphor will suffice, that instead a list of metaphorical categories is needed. The specific metaphors we have traced are samples of larger metaphorical groups, which we might designate as in Table 7.2.

Table 7.2 is by no means complete. It is primarily a set of metaphors for the portfolio as artifact, and not for the process of creating a portfolio, which might be likened to the writing of a script, the culling of a scrapbook, or any one of a number of metaphors related to assembling and creating. Further, in any one class, portfolios can take on many metaphors, depending on their use and the context in which they are being reviewed. The roles of student, teacher, and system change as the metaphors change, or even as the purpose of the portfolio changes, meaning that the evaluation criteria and evaluators change. Although there may be some common threads among the teacher reports, and some common language, particularly the use of the word "responsibility," one should not be blinded by this commonality to the differences that persist and differentiate the teachers and their classrooms. As we suggested earlier, each metaphor contains within it an implicit drama

TABLE 7.2
Categories of Metaphors for Portfolios

When the portfolio is a(n) . . .	The student's role is to . . .	The teacher's role is to . . .	The district's role is to . . .
agenda	select	respond	arrange
portrait	outline gain perspective	guide	provide background
summary	select	define	judge
certificate of membership	select and define	administer and set the norms	set bounds
log or diary	compile	file	measure change or growth
evidence, testimony	amass	defend	bring change
mirror	participate	question	honor
museum/gallery anthology	create and collect	curate	view
meditation	gain awareness	encourage and guide	affirm
title or deed transferring or conferring of power or responsibility	claim	validate	affirm

(and in Table 7.2 some of the characters suggested) with an intended narrative (that the characters act).

National roles and metaphors are more ambiguous because, at this point, there is no national portfolio assessment device. But because there are movements toward national standards for judging portfolios, then we need to consider what a national role and metaphor would be. If the student is using the portfolio as evidence of having participated in a program (the certificate metaphor) then the student and the teacher become co-presenters and the district itself either recognizes or denies the evidence in the portfolio. With this metaphor, the national focus would not be on the student but on the district and whether or not the district's certificate is worthy at the state level (This was the original purpose of the Vermont Portfolio Project: to see if writing programs in schools were indeed having students write.).

The next section investigates the use of computer metaphors for portfolios. More specifically, the concept of hypertext is applied to schools and school activities. Readers who are more interested in the practical aspects of portfolios than in theoretical frameworks may wish to skip to the concluding remarks.

PORTFOLIO AS HYPERTEXT

As we pondered the messiness of creating a system of metaphorical categories, we came to see that computers may have permitted a new metaphor for the portfolio, one that honors both the individuality of the creator, the characteristics of the work produced, and the changing roles of student, teacher, program, and system. This metaphor is that of the hypertext, that which is signaled by the storage and search capacities of the computer and the diskette. This metaphor has come to us to be seen as superordinate to the others in that it speaks to the newness of the portfolio and to the challenge it presents to previous ways of thinking about testing and teaching. The portfolio is not simply a collection of papers. It takes on a radically new character that is similar to (perhaps identical to) the radical character of hypertext in relation to traditional views of text.

The Portfolio and Hypertext as Transforming Agents of the Schools

In a hypertext system, there is a writer who produces a web of text spaces, the features of which are such that although they may be read in a linear fashion (like a novel) with difficulty, the web invites and rewards the person who moves around text spaces from space to space following one of a number of logical or analogical chains. The organization of the text has a number of hierarchies and connective points put in by the author. But the reader also puts in other connections as he or she moves from idea to thought to imagination. Some primitive forms of hypertext include the cento or commonplace book, the volume of essays, the newspaper (including supplements), the omnibus catalog, the comic book, and perhaps the encyclopedia. The distinction between author and reader diminishes, because the reader is in effect a co-creator of the text. In the minds of some critics (Lanham, 1994) the hypertext has become an emblem of the postmodern view of text.

Hypertexts are entering the curriculum in a number of ways (Bolter, 1991; Landow, 1992; Lanham, 1994). They are becoming a part of the instructional milieu and in many cases they are becoming the creation of students themselves. The things students are producing for their courses leap beyond the bubble test or even the term paper or research project. The students are creating and participating in games and simulations; making programs, tapes, document files, stet hypertexts, and constructing hypermedia performances as well. The portfolio is the best, if not the only, vehicle for the summary picture of this new world of student performance. As the disputation fitted the ideal academic performance in the age of scholasticism, and the dissertation or thesis the ideal of the age of print, the portfolio fits the postmodern age of hypermedia.

The portfolio is a hypertext in the sense that it is an assemblage or collage of text and nontext materials that purport to give a portrait of the portfolio creator as (in the case of schools) a student in a particular institution. The portfolio is an individual creation and it is intended to be read and recreated by the teacher/reader/judge/employer/critic. It is not read necessarily from beginning to end; it is certainly not linear. In Marshall McLuhan's language, it is a "cool" medium in which the audience has to participate fully. The reader may look at the portfolio and recreate a portrait of the creator as student, as writer, as human being, as artist, or as employee. Each reader is expected to make something different out of the portfolio. There is no thought of similarity of readings. Each reading depends on the context in which creator and reader fall. There may be advice; there may be judgment; there may be a job offer; there may simply be encouragement.

If the portfolio is a hypertext, then it is difficult to talk of the reader—there are individual readings. It is difficult to talk of a grade or a measurement of the portfolio—the grade is simply a linear response to a nonlinear document. We do not know what the appropriate response of a judge or a jury to the portfolio is, except perhaps acceptance or rejection, which are admittedly subjective responses. It is important to note, however, that in research on performance assessment in writing, the subjectivity of the judgment has been lurking beneath all of the psychometric attempts to create an objective measure, and it is finally unleashed and cannot be put back (Baker et al., 1993; Purves, 1992). It is also difficult to talk of comparability except in the head of the person looking at a number of portfolios. It is also difficult to talk of competence as an abstract concept; there is only the observed performance. And each observation implies a different performance. The portfolio, like the hypertext, depends on context.

Implications for Education

What this means for schools and education is that the school serves the student in construction of that student's portfolio. It serves to provide something common for all students but to allow the student to present his or her unique performances, as a member of both the school community and the larger community, in a form that can show the totality of a student's accomplishment in the way in which the student wants to present himself or herself. The school is both democratic and unforgiving, for its task is to shift the burden of responsibility for education and the presentation of the self to the student. It is the student who is accountable. The school and teacher are primarily accountable for helping, serving, guiding, facilitating. The school and the teacher encourage various forms of cooperation among students and between students and teachers in order to allow each individual to be self-sustaining and part of the community, to create each student's hypertext which becomes part of a larger hypertext.

This seems utopian, and it is. It is radical and serves to transform the school from a factory to a marketplace of ideas and activities. It will probably be resisted, and various people will seek to take portfolios and make them look like a complex form of a multiple-choice test. Such a linear psychometric approach will only serve to vitiate the portfolio and destroy the potential of the schools for enabling each student to achieve his or her maximum performance.

Although one can reach a consensus or accommodation between what is desired by the individual teacher and the individual student on the one hand and the state system on the other, the interests of the two are fundamentally opposed. People in assessment and education have tried to blur this opposition, particularly through such slogans as authentic assessment, performance assessment, and even portfolio assessment. The portfolio represents, we believe, not a blurring but a sharpening of the distinction.

CONCLUDING REMARKS

If the portfolio of each student is a hypertext, for a class the students' portfolios are spaces or nodes in a hypertextual web; the portfolios are individual but linked through common assignments, common readings, common metaphors. If we were to place the classroom in a school, we might see similarities and common points, but also differences. In the multiteacher middle school where Marian, Pam, Deane, and Carol teach, there is more similarity among classroom portfolios and their metaphors than in the high schools where Nancy Lester and Anne Kuthy or Charles Phelps, Suzanne Heyd, and Rich Harris teach. Were we to extrapolate to a network of schools, the web expands and the links become attenuated. Each of the classroom or possibly school webs of portfolios might be seen as having some of the characteristics of a community (Berry, 1993; Tinder, 1980). That is to say that the classroom contains a set of shared assumptions and a shared language (Applebee, 1994). But such a community is necessarily small and evanescent. For a given teacher, no two classes form similar communities. Although the metaphor may be constant, the drama of the metaphor will be played out differently.

Is there, then, no role for the state or national agency in portfolios? We think there is. Although one would expect and desire a low intraclass or intraschool correlation of portfolio scores rated by a single rater or a group of raters (the variation among performances might well be high, just as the variation of performances within a single portfolio might be high), one could treat the school as a portfolio of portfolios. Using some form of matrix sampling that would draw a number of portfolios without identifying the student by name or even by teaching, one can assess, and perhaps rate, the performance of the school (but not of any single student within that school). One could not, however, make comparisons across schools, again because comparability is not the expectation. Again, one could make a portfolio of schools without comparisons among the schools in the sample. The purpose of these aggregate portfolios might be to attempt a portrait of a school as a learning environment or of a segment of a state or the nation. The aggregate would be a large hypertext, perhaps as large as some of the rooms or groups in the electronic world of multiple user groups on the Internet. The assessment would necessarily be hermeneutic (Moss, 1994).

Such an assessment, however, would be expensive, would require large numbers to serve on the jury, and would be virtually impossible to report out to the press. Would it be worth the expense? It may be that for whatever purpose large-scale assessment serves (and we think there are legitimate purposes), some form of domain sampling and assessment is appropriate, but not a portfolio or a portfolio of portfolios. The portfolio is a time-honored way for the individual to make himself or herself presentable and desirable to an outside jury. A portfolio refers to external standards and is usually judged in the light of those standards. But the judgment is normally individual, perhaps involving some form of head-to-head competition, but often not; unlike the portfolio, large-scale assessment does not deal in individuals, communities, or even classrooms (see Table 7.3).

This fundamental difference between the node on the web and the web, the community and the larger entity, and the local and the national, speaks

TABLE 7.3
Differences Between Individual Assessment and Large-Scale Assessment

Individual Assessment	*Large-Scale Assessment*
Selects from the domain	Covers the domain
Seeks unique accomplishment	Strives for comparability
Focuses on the whole individual	Focuses on school effects
Is the responsibility of the student	Is the responsibility of the assessor

to the impossible and counterproductive consequences of assuming that portfolios can and should become a part of a large-scale assessment project. This does not mean, however, that there should not be a national movement in support of portfolio assessment as a way of viewing the individual student. Portfolios are a superior way of certifying the performance of individuals, of showing the breadth and depth of the student as a student and, in our case, as a user of the language. And they are consonant with the sea change in the nature of knowledge storage, transmission, and retrieval. They are the best classroom assessment device for the foreseeable future. They should be supported for the classroom, required by employers, and accepted as an integral part of admission to higher education in all fields, not merely—as is current practice—in the arts.

These differences appear bland, but if taken seriously they represent a major shift in thinking about schooling and education, and particularly about students. This is a shift that may prove too difficult for the system of a state or a nation to accept. The shift, however, seems to be consonant with the shift that is already occurring with the emergence of hypertext and hypermedia in education.

REFERENCES

Applebee, A. N. (1994). *Toward thoughtful curriculum: Fostering discipline-based conversation in the English language arts classroom* (Report No. 1.7). Albany: State University of New York, National Research Center on Literature Teaching and Learning.

Baker, E., Haman, J., & Gearhart, M. (1993). Assessing writing portfolios: Issues in the validity and meaning of scores. *Educational Assessment, 1,* 201–224.

Berry, W. (1993). *Sex, economy, freedom and community.* New York: Pantheon.

Black, S. (1993). Portfolio assessment. *The Executive Educator, 15*(1), 28–31.

Bolter, J. D. (1991). *Writing space: The computer, hypertext, and the history of writing.* Hillsdale, NJ: Lawrence Erlbaum Associates.

Clandinin, D. J. (1986). *Classroom practice: Teacher images in action.* London: Falmer.

Dahloff, U. (1971). *Ability grouping, content validity, and curriculum process analysis.* New York: Teachers College Press.

Denton, D. E. (1974). That mode of being called teaching. In D. E. Denton (Ed.), *Existentialism and phenomenology in education* (pp. 37–52). New York: Teachers College Press.

Freedman, S. W. (1993). Linking large-scale testing and classroom portfolio assessments of student writing. *Educational Assessment, 1,* 27–52.

Kolanowski, K. (1993). *Use of portfolios in assessment of literature learning* (Report No. 3.7). Albany: State University of New York, National Research Center on Literature Teaching and Learning.

Lanham, R. (1994). *The electronic word.* Chicago: University of Chicago Press.

Landow, G. P. (1992). *Hypertext: The convergence of contemporary critical theory and technology.* Baltimore: Johns Hopkins University Press.

Moss, P. (1994). Can there be validity without reliability? *Educational Researcher, 23,* 5–12.

Purves, A. C. (1992). Reflections on assessment and research in written composition. *Research in the Teaching of English, 26*(1), 108–122.

Purves, A. C. (1993). Setting standards in the language arts and literature and the implications for portfolio assesment. *Educational Assessment, 1*(3).

Tinder, G. (1980). *Community: Reflections on a tragic ideal.* Baton Rouge: Louisiana State University Press.

CHAPTER EIGHT

Tensions in Assessment: The Battle Over Portfolios, Curriculum, and Control

James M. Wile
Miami University of Ohio

Robert J. Tierney
Ohio State University

Ms. Smith and Mr. Jones both teach the fourth grade. Both are excited about implementing portfolios in their classrooms. They have read some of the current literature and both agree portfolios will enable them to collect information about their students' progress that would be unobtainable through traditional norm-referenced achievement tests. What's more, both teachers believe the information they get from students' portfolios will enable them to provide instruction more in line with their students' developmental levels.

Ms. Smith begins to organize her portfolio program with a checklist of objectives she feels fourth graders should accomplish. Her checklist is a composite of recent statements on standards published by two national literacy organizations, along with curricular guidelines published by the state board of education, local school board policy, and the grade report card she is required to send home every 9 weeks.

From this checklist of learning objectives, Ms. Smith has decided that the students' portfolios will showcase various literacy products: a reading log, samples of narrative and expository writing, book reviews, and vocabulary lists. Ms. Smith reasons that because these products grow out of the daily classroom experiences, they provide an authentic or ecologically valid picture of students' abilities. She then analyzes these products according to the features she has created to gauge students' mastery of the curriculum.

At the end of each grading period, Ms. Smith collects the portfolios and evaluates them using a holistic scoring guide. The rubric she uses is based on the five-level grading system used to report student progress. Working from the checklist of competencies she developed, Ms. Smith has devised benchmark criteria for each level. She has separate sets of benchmarks for reading, writing, and language development. As she reviews each student's portfolio, Ms. Smith evaluates individual pieces and measures them against the benchmark characteristics. Finally, she evaluates the overall appearance of the portfolio, its cover, and general quality of organization. From this analysis, she determines a grade she feels accurately represents the student's progress toward mastery of the curriculum.

Mr. Jones is also aware of the standards and performance objectives recommended by national, state, and local agencies. He also uses these standards as a framework for the curriculum in his classroom. Mr. Jones believes portfolios are ideally suited to represent students' interaction with the curriculum.

Mr. Jones introduces the portfolio to his fourth grade class by comparing it to a personal museum. He explains to the students that the portfolio is the place where they can keep any objects of meaning to them. He points out that these objects can be things they create, like stories, book reviews, and drawings—or they can be things created by others such as poems, favorite books, and comments by peer editors. He reminds them that because they are all different, he expects the contents of their portfolios to be different, too.

Mr. Jones and the students use the portfolios in a variety of ways. Students compare reading logs with their partners as they organize author studies or explore new topics. A piece from last week's writing becomes the text for this week's mini-lesson. Breakthroughs are celebrated publicly during group portfolio shares.

At the end of the grading period, Mr. Jones schedules individual portfolio conferences with his students. Prior to the interview, students select several key artifacts from their portfolios and use these as the foci of reflective narratives they write. During the 10-minute session, each student discusses with Mr. Jones his or her work since their last formal conference. Mr. Jones listens attentively, asks probing questions, and offers positive comments and encouragement. With a new understanding of the child's interests and achievements, Mr. Jones helps the student articulate a self-evaluation and set new goals.

The portfolio practices just sketched share some important similarities. Both focus evaluation on students' actual classroom experiences, and both contribute to informed instruction. However, the subtle differences between the way these teachers approach portfolio analysis represent huge differences in orientations. While one teacher struggles to harmonize the student to a curriculum of a priori objectives and standards, another teacher sees the portfolios as a way to harmonize the curriculum with the students' emergent needs and interests. Where one approach strives for reliability and consistency, another acknowledges the idiosyncratic nature of learning. Where one teacher assumes the role of judge, another teacher assumes the role of audience. One approach views the portfolio as a product to evaluate, another sees the portfolio as a vehicle for self-evaluation. One encourages students to move toward convention, another enables students to set goals toward personalized targets. Where one procedure encapsulates learning, another enables students to construct meaning from their experiences.

Pressure to focus the discussion of assessment in terms of matters of best practice is real, especially given the general high stakes nature of assessment and our national passion for efficiency. However, debates over technique sidestep more substantive and critical questions pertaining to theories of learning. Just as with instruction, assessment procedures divorced from theory, even though technically sound, are pedagogically and ethically bankrupt.

The differences illustrated by the practices of our hypothetical teachers are at the heart of critical touchpoints in the developing national dialogue concerning the role portfolios might or ought to play in contributing to instruction, assessment, and the development of appropriate curriculum (Tierney, Carter, & Desai, 1991). Central to this discussion are issues concerning the way portfolios might be analyzed and their overall reliability as techniques for collecting information and the matters of analysis (Herman & Winters, 1994; Linn, Baker, & Dunbar, 1992).

Portfolios raise critical issues—questions about standardization, validity, reliability, as these pertain to practices of curriculum, instruction, and assessment. Unfortunately, the decisions affecting areas of instruction and assessment can be incongruous when they are made in ad hoc fashion or without returning to fundamental principles. Most notably is the application of positivistic theories of assessment to the constructivist theories of learning. What is particularly unsettling is that while matters of instruction are dominated by constructivist perspectives, assessment remains rooted to its positivist tradition.

Those who use portfolios in an innovative manner often find themselves under pressure to develop procedures that conform to traditional positivist theories of measurement and evaluation. These pressures can lead to a moral schizophrenia, ultimately compromising both innovative and traditional points of view of assessment. The quandary over how portfolios might be incorporated into the mainstream of American education reflects diverse and conflicting conceptualizations about the relationship between the assessors and the clients of assessment, and between assessment and learning.

The strength of portfolio evaluation is that it allows educators to engage in a form of assessment that is consistent with constructivist tenets. This view suggests a different orientation to what is done in the way of assessing, who does it, and for what purposes. Portfolios not only provide authentic answers to traditional questions about achievement, they dramatically shift our thinking about assessment, ask different types of questions, and answer those questions in different types of language.

The intersection of these important issues forms the starting point for considering ideas about ways to analyze portfolio data. In an effort to develop a theoretical framework to guide the decision-making process, we consider portfolios in light of several fundamental orientations.

As instruments of data collection and analysis, portfolios resonate with three theoretical themes: client service, qualitative inquiry, and constructivism. Portfolio practices that abandon these fundamental themes and retreat to traditional positivist definitions of assessment risk generating information that is less meaningful, useful, or relevant.

The connection between constructivist views of curriculum, instruction, and assessment is natural (Paris, Calfee, Filby, Hiebert, Pearson, Valencia, & Wolf, 1992). This view suggest an educational context that is open-ended and divergent. It reaffirms the value of the individual, and places a premium on the student's ability to derive meaning out of his or her experience.

The chasm between constructivist and positivist orientations is itself situated within a larger, more political context. Attempts to write these orientations with their ideological counterweights: production, quantitative inquiry, and positivism are ethically untenable. To disregard the political aspect of assessment is to decontextualize portfolios. This can result in the use of portfolios for ends other than those intended—ends that are estranged from constructivism.

Further, we address those who direct criticism at portfolio practice (Gearhart, Herman, Baker, & Whittaker, 1992; Herman & Winters, 1994; Linn, Baker, & Dunbar, 1992) using criteria that should not be applied to constructivist portfolios. Much of what amounts to the misapplication of portfolios originates from a confusion over theoretical and ethical concerns.

PORTFOLIOS ASSESSMENT AND CLIENT SERVICE

Contemporary notions of assessment reflect the diversity that characterizes the nature of classroom relationships between teachers and students. Marxist theories (Apple, 1986; Fine, 1991; Shannon, 1989) have described this relationship essentially as struggles over the control of productive energy. Schools operating as production facilities, with all of the ramifications of authority, power, and purpose would be expected to devise evaluation procedures sensitive toward shifts in productivity.

Cultures entrenched in large-scale, norm-referenced assessments—assessments derived from orientations of production and quality control—might be expected to apply similar notions of standardization to portfolio assessments. Such portfolios, despite heralding banners of authenticity, eventually manipulate students rather than empower them by monopolizing the curriculum and discouraging diversity.

What if schooling were a service rather than a production process? What would be the implications for assessment and evaluation in such a shift in orientation? Applying notions of client service to schooling recasts some key features of the education landscape. The more crucial topography is represented in Table 8.1. The history of the factory/production orientation toward education is rooted in the industrial reforms of the early part of this century (Callahan, 1962). With efficiency measured in levels of productivity, school leaders were able to bring statistical data as evidence of their good work and worth. The publication and subsequent impact of the report of the National Commission on Excellence in Education, *A National at Risk* (1983) reminds us of the hegemony of the production orientation of schooling.

What's puzzling is that the reform movement of the 1980s spawned by documents such as *A Nation at Risk* cast doubts on the effectiveness of schooling (e.g., a rising tide of mediocrity) while continuing to propose solutions and measures seemingly aimed at improving the efficiency of schooling.

In a production orientation, decisions regarding curriculum, instruction, and assessment revolve around productivity. To this end, positivist analysis procedures serve three functions: they provide general information about the school's overall level of productivity; they identify students with special needs; and, to sort students into manageable classifications. These functions are carried out in ways that are deductive rather than inductive, standardized versus divergent, quantitative rather than descriptive, periodic rather than ongoing, and summative rather than formative. The teacher's role as analyst is reduced to managerial tasks: modeling prescribed experiences, devising rewards and punishments, and keeping accurate accounts.

Traditional standardized, norm-referenced assessments provide information about the efficiency of schooling and the quality of products in terms

TABLE 8.1
The Lineage of Assessment Issues

Assessment Issue	Traditional View	Constructivist View
Orientation	Production	Client service
Values	Productivity	Customer satisfaction
Measurement focus	Efficiency/quantity	Effectiveness/quality
Theoretical frame	Positivistic	Constructivist
Conception of student	Student-as-product	Student-as-client
Assessment audience	Public constituencies	Individual students
Assessment aims	Broad view/simplistic	Narrow view/complex
Curricular goal	Uniformity	Diversity

of preset guidelines. Portfolios used to facilitate human service, that is, intended to capture patterns of experiences for the purpose of providing students with a time and place for revisiting these experiences and reflecting on their meaning. Once students become viewed as the clients of education, they also become the principle stakeholders of assessment.

PORTFOLIOS IN THE SPIRIT OF QUALITATIVE INQUIRY

Positivistic traditions of quantitative assessment operate along assumptions of hypothesis-testing. These traditions assume that literacy occurs in predictable ways, and that these ways are closely connected to the introduction and virtual mastery of specific benchmark conventions. Periodic sampling of students on annual achievement tests—prized for reliability and validity—assume generalizeability and predictability. Unfortunately, even periodic positivistic snapshots of student performance fail to account for the learning context, learner motivation and personal investment, time and space constraints, and other factors that contribute to the complexity of the development of literature behavior. Some portfolio procedures place a premium on the qualitative explanations individuals give as they revisit their own experiences. Those who utilize qualitative assessments eschew the temptation to use portfolios to direct students' learning experiences. Schemes that are flexible offer open-ended dialogue between students and teachers and contribute to the understanding of students across a fuller and more representative range of situations.

Assessment procedures that sacrifice personal autonomy to the positivistic pursuit of experimental control and objectivity inevitably create an ethic of manipulation. We find ourselves ready to abandon analytic strategies that constrain learning and penalize risk taking. Students' experiences are not uniform and constant. They vary across time and by event and situation.

As educators pursue new analytical alternatives—alternatives grounded in the data of literacy learning—they become faced with the difficulty of dealing with complexities. For a variety of reasons, traditional analytic procedures retreat from dealing with complexity, idiosyncrasy, and emerging data. The result? Rigid continua and categorical descriptions which, in themselves, fall short of representing the full range of student learning and development. Attempts to impose a priori schemes on personal experience fail to provide analyses that are sufficiently clear and meaningful.

This lack of clarity has important implications. Data analysis schemes that employ homogeneity—simple additive models of overall achievement tied to consistency versus accuracy and integrity—may serve to overshadow or displace what could be assessed, should be assessed, and acted on. Unable to access the language of positivism, a form of displacement may occur.

This marginalization conveys one clear message—that students are often subjugated by assessment rather than empowered by it.

A key criterion for portfolio analysis is that it be true to its qualitative roots. Shared characteristics between qualitative inquiry and portfolio practice are summarized in Table 8.2.

Patton (1990) described 10 themes permeating qualitative inquiry. This framework also serves to characterize the design and utilization of portfolios. Analytic procedures need to be discovery-oriented, offering opportunities to capture actual events as they unfold and to hold them for reflection.

Unstructured portfolios cast wide nets, collecting events of differentiated value and meaning. Turning away from a priori analysis schemes, they place the student at the center of the evaluation process. Students become obligated to develop a language of reflection and goal setting. Open-ended portfolios provide an opportunity for learners to organize their own experiences, explore categories, and develop labels. Management of the analysis process invites the learner to bring meaning and value to the learning/assessment cycle.

The role of participant observer seems particularly apt here. Not only does this characterize the teacher, but accurately captures the active nature of the learner's role as well. The collaborative aspect of qualitative inquiry encompasses not only past experiences, it promotes goal-setting as an ongoing component of curriculum, instruction, and assessment.

Formative analyses enable teachers and learners to clarify where learning is headed. Students ask, "Why am I doing this thing? Where do I want to expend my energy?" As diagnostic inventories, portfolios attempt to guide students in reclaiming control over their own learning. Students set priorities based on data emerging from the portfolios.

The portfolio process, like other aspects of truly qualitative inquiry, point out the importance of the neutrality of the data analyst. The analysis process invites participants to adopt a stance of empathic neutrality.

Portfolios integrate assessment within the teaching-learning dynamic and the analysis is situated within the everyday conduct of that dynamic. Although quantitative assessments strategies stand outside this dynamic, they rely on constructs of consensus, uniformity, and simplicity to obtain credibility. Unfortunately, these attributes may displace what might have been measured or should be measured. Because they are understood as being imposed rather than emerging—they are viewed as more invasive than inviting, more colonial than empowering.

Portfolios designed to achieve constructivist aims contain data grounded in the student's experiences. Their reflections on this grounded data enable students to link formal classroom learning with their past learning both in and out of school.

TABLE 8.2
Relation of portfolios to Qualitative Inquiry

Theme	Qualitative Inquiry	Aspect of Portfolios
Naturalistic	Lack of predetermined constraints on outcomes	Discovery-oriented
Inductive	Open-ended questions result in the discovery of important categories, dimensions, and interrelationships	Patterns emerge across portfolio elements
Holistic	Phenomenon under study is understood as complex, more than the sum of its parts	Recognized literacy as the orchestration of complex behaviors
Qualitative data	Detailed, thick descriptions, in-depth inquiry; incorporates direct quotation to capture people's experiences	Data sources include dialogue, observation, and examination of products; especially the learner's interpretation as "overlay"
Personal contact/insight	Investigator has close contact with person under study; investigator's perspectives and experiences part of the inquiry	Participant observer status; insider perspective
Dynamic systems	Attention to process; assumes change is constant and ongoing	Emphasis on facilitating improvement; provides formative analysis
Unique case orientations	Inquiry is being true to respecting, and capturing details of the individual being studied	Emphasis on rich description, multiple elements and individual outcomes
Context sensitivity	Findings are placed in a social, historical, and temporal context; dubious about the possibility or meaning of generalizations across time and space	Because they are customized assessments, no attempt to generalize across cases
Empathic neutrality	Objectivity is impossible; the inquirer includes personal experience and empathic insight while taking a nonjudgmental stance toward emerging content.	The goal of the process is for both teacher and learner to better understand their lived experiences; empathic stance places teachers in supportive roles
Design flexibility	Open to adapting inquiry as understanding deepens and/or situations change; avoids rigid designs that eliminate responsiveness; pursues new paths of discovery as they emerge	The structure of the portfolio unfolds as a reflection of the emerging nature of literacy development

THEORETICAL FRAMEWORK

Portfolios are an outgrowth of a constructivist framework of literacy and the way literacy develops. We compare this orientation with traditional positivist notions in Table 8.3.

A central tenet of the constructivist perspective is the notion that the process of learning varies among individuals, even among individuals who have shared common experiences. Important learning breakthroughs and insights are, more often than not, serendipitous rather than predictable.

Some portfolio procedures are more than well-suited to obtain the kinds of information valued in a constructivist perspective—but only if they afford opportunities for formative self-evaluation and capturing nuance. When theoretical orientations to instruction and assessment are compatible, as in the case of constructivism, portfolio analysis techniques merge instruction and assessment until they become inseparable.

TABLE 8.3
Comparing Positivistic Portfolio Approaches With Constructive Approaches

	Positivistic	*Constructive*
View of learning	Learning believed to develop in uniform, predictable, and linear sequence	Learning believed to develop as a result of personal construction of meaning in consequence of interaction with various experiences
Purpose of assessment	To evaluate learning, facilitate sorting and classifying individuals	To guide learning, to document personal development and facilitate personal goal-setting
Control of Assessment	Directed by assessor operating on a priori expectations	Directed by client operating on the need to interpret personal experience
Contents of portfolio	Specified and predetermined; limited to materials created by client	Varied and idiosyncratic; may include materials *collected* as well as *created* by the client
Focus of analysis	Secondary analysis: rubrics & checklists Artifacts in portfolio	Primary/grounded analysis Client's interpretation of artifacts in portfolio
Units of analysis	Portfolio artifacts measured against a priori standards and preset categories and characteristics	Portfolio artifacts related to grounded analysis of personal experience, with emergent categories and characteristics
Trustworthiness	Claims to represent single "truthful" interpretation; correspondence to conventional abstract notions of development	Recognizes multiple interpretations which may shift across individual perspectives and times; correspondence to grounded data

Analysis schemes developed out of a constructivist framework share characteristics such as making meaning, the collaborative relationship between the teacher and learner, tester and testee. They foster and maintain the distinctive flavor of a community of learners.

Because the constructivist curriculum is flexible and emergent, procedures that drive analysis aim to be emergent. Built into constructivist procedures are frequent opportunities for students to express personal insights that are explanatory and evaluative. Constructivist portfolios acknowledge the learner's role as codeterminer and cointerpreter of his or her own educational experience.

Portfolios are ideally suited to maximize opportunities for customization and personalization of curricula, instruction, and assessment. However, the application of positivist analytical strategies may reduce the likelihood of this sort of customization.

A constructivist portfolio analysis plan would be expected to serve the purposes just outlined: to capture and build on the processes of learning. More specifically, a portfolio analysis plan built on the theoretical frameworks of service, qualitative inquiry, and constructivism might be distinguished by four features: open-ended, elemental, perspectival, and purposeful.

Student-centered learning is expected to be unique. Literacy portfolios intended to collect information about that process need to be *open-ended* to accurately capture a full range of real and often fortuitous individual experiences. Appropriate analytical schemes need to be flexible to accommodate the variety in students' background experiences, interests levels, and purposes. Such plans must emerge from the learning experience not imposed onto that experience.

Constructivist analytic plans would encourage students to document their experiences, much like an archaeologist piecing together fragments of evidence. The contents of a student's literacy portfolio might not be limited to original products created by the student, and actually contain a range of artifacts.

A constructivist analytic scheme focuses on discrete elements rather than wholes. Positivistic plans assume relationships between elements which may not be accurate. The *elemental* character of constructivist analysis excuses observers from trying to force elements that are emergent and diverse into a priori and static categories. An emphasis on elements as the unit of analysis invites risk taking and exploration of new areas, particularly if both students and teachers share the understanding that not every effort will result in success. Constructivist portfolio analytic schemes reinforce this understanding by building in a record of false starts, blind alleys, and disasters. Students' critical reflection on these incidents become opportunities for learning and add value to that experience.

Although holistic assessment has somehow captured the moral high ground in contemporary discussions of classroom practice, this position reflects curious ideas about curriculum, instruction, and assessment. First, it reinforces the view of assessment as a form of measurement rather than intelligence generation. Second, it risks excluding or discounting experiences that do not coincide with curriculum guides or checklist descriptors. Third, it reinforces the perception of the portfolio as a product of the curriculum, rather than as a vehicle connecting the student to his or her interaction with the curriculum.

The power of a constructivist portfolio analysis plan is illustrated in the way historical researchers use the concepts of primary and secondary source documents. Historians term *primary source documents* various first-hand accounts—letters, diaries, oral texts, and so on—through which an individual attempts to make sense of his or her personal experiences. Historians, consider *secondary source documents* those materials that serve as outsider interpretations.

The elemental character of constructivist analysis plans contribute toward an oral portrait of an individual that is more primary than secondary, more emergent than imposed. It is an evaluation that refrains from demanding a single-minded, predetermined ordering of elements and how they relate to one another but one that allows this order to develop and shift over time.

During individual portfolio conferences, participants may be given openended prompts such as "What can you tell me about what you have been doing? Use items in your portfolio to illustrate or clarify your comments." In this way, the entire portfolio becomes a type of primary document, an auto-narrative, through which the individual constructs his or her own interpretation of experience. Contrast this approach with the traditional holistic scoring plans that retreat to notions of consistency in order to persuade teachers and students to accept standardized interpretations of their individualized and complex experience.

Constructivist analysis of portfolios are *perspectival*, that is, they invite multiple perspectives and are open to multiple interpretations. This may proceed along various lines: bringing multiple observers into the analytical dialogue and encouraging each observer to adopt multiple stances in the analysis process.

Attempts to address the notion of multiple perspectives appear simplistic and crude. Analysis procedures that are ongoing challenge participants to confront their own perceptions and come to grips with alternative perspectives and interpretations.

Constructivist analysis schemes are *purposeful*, in the sense that they generate information that is complex yet useful to students as well as teachers. Evidence of usefulness might be the extent to which the analysis process contributes to and supports students' growth. The process serves to keep in tact the relationship between event and interpretation, between students and teachers in a community of learners.

SOME LIMITATIONS OF PORTFOLIOS

Portfolio analysis schemes that reflect a constructivist orientation are exceptionally valuable. They extend the ability of portfolios to reveal complex data. However, there are some limitations pertaining to this perspective as well.

The strength of the constructivist portfolio is also one of its weaknesses. Personal portfolios may be less amenable to outsider, or secondary, interpretation. The portfolio conference, a necessary ingredient of the dialectic between teachers and students may be affected by traditional conceptions of evaluation and grading, as ways of doing business in school. Students might feel pressured by the prevailing social conventions and unequal distribution of power and authority to alter their perceptions to conform to the teacher's agenda.

Because the constructivist notion of portfolio analysis resists standardization, the entire process is sensitive to influences caused by the way in which it is introduced and maintained. The rich relationships between students and their teachers may play key roles in making up for the lack of a priori guidelines and determine the success of the analysis process.

Students' ability to take responsibility for developing their own criteria, for collecting and organizing elements, for reflecting on their development and setting goals needs to be determined and nurtured. Our instructional conventions have traditionally identified the culmination of the learning cycle as application. Constructivist theories suggest that the learning cycle is incomplete until students have demonstrated evidence of an ability to monitor the quality of the goals they set, the personal literacy strategies they choose, and their perception of the outcomes of specific learning experiences.

The development of a metacognitive framework, essential for independent learning, is reflected in the usefulness of the portfolio analysis. Naive learners may not have sufficiently well-developed understanding of a complex issue to collect and organize experiences appropriately. They might discount or neglect important data. The portfolio may offer misleading evidence of the student's ability vis à vis various specific literacy goals. Sophistication in the collection and analysis of intelligence might be inevitable. Fenner (1994), for example, found that participation in the process of portfolio analysis affected the ways students think and talk about their learning.

The constructivist analysis process is embedded in the learning context. However, this limits the meaningfulness of the analysis to the degree to which the student and the assessor share contexts. Insider information may be essential to develop rich understanding. If the connection between shared experience and interpretation is vital, the application of portfolio schemes to inquiry requiring wide-scale assessment seems problematic.

Finally, the portfolio has the inescapable appearance of a product. The portfolio is presumed to contain evidence of student learning. For classroom teachers who continue to focus on this product nature of the portfolio, their positivist analysis will describe the quality of these products rather than approaching these as shadows cast by far more-interesting processes, attitudes, and complex understandings. Unfortunately, such abstract notions labor in the compelling appearance of the portfolio-as-product.

The analytic guidelines offered here are fundamentally true to their qualitative roots. As such, we consider the rich, descriptive nature of the intelligence generated through these procedures reasons to reexamine the way portfolios are being introduced and utilized in school literacy curricula.

We find ourselves perplexed with the positivistic leanings of psychometricians perseverating on reliability, consistency, and generalizability as key qualities when trustworthiness, interpretability, situation specificity and empowerment seem more appropriate. With assessment intimately linked to elements grounded in an individual's experiences, constructivist analytic approaches offer stakeholders a level of trustworthiness rare among analytic techniques.

Finally, while the production orientation that continues to characterize schooling calls out for ways to make analysis more uniform, perhaps even more specific and certain, there is equal room to argue for a view of information gathering that is individual, indefinite, and ongoing. After all, this seems more in line with the way learning occurs.

REFERENCES

Apple, M. (1986). *Teachers & texts: A political economy of class & gender relations in education.* New York: Routledge.

Callahan, R. E. (1962). *Education and the cult of efficiency.* Chicago: The University of Chicago Press.

Fenner, L. (1995). *Facilitating the development of higher quality work through reflective portfolios.* Unpublished doctoral dissertation. The Ohio State University, Columbus, OH.

Gearhart, M., Herman, J. L., Baker, E. L., & Whittaker, A. K. (1992). *Writing portfolios: Potential for large-scale assessment.* Los Angeles: University of California, Center for the Study of Evaluation.

Herman, J. L., & Winters, L. (1994). Portfolio research: A slim collection. *Educational Leadership, 52*(2), 48–55.

Linn, R. L., Baker, E. L., & Dunbar, S. B. (1992). Complex, performance-based assessment: Expectations and validation criteria. *Evaluation Comment,* Winter, 2–9.

National Commission on Excellence in Education (1983). *A Nation At Risk: The Imperative for educational reform.* Washington, DC: Government Printing Office.

Paris, S., Calfee, R., Filby, N., Hiebert, E., Pearson, P. D., Valencia, S. W., & Wolf, K. P. (1992). A framework for authentic literacy assessment. *The Reading Teacher, 46*(2), 88–99.

Patton, M. Q. (1990). *Qualitative evaluation and research methods* (2nd ed.). Newbury Park, CA: Sage.

Shannon, P. (1989). The struggle for control of literacy lessons. *Language Arts, 66*(6), 625–634.

Tierney, R. J., Carter, M. A., & Desai, L. E. (1991). *Portfolio Assessment in the Reading-Writing Classroom.* Norwood, MA: Christopher-Gordon.

PART THREE

THE VIEW
FROM THE FIELD

CHAPTER NINE

Video Visits: A Practical Approach for Studying Portfolios

Pamela Perfumo
University of California, Berkeley

Portfolios have captured the limelight in the recent wave of assessment reform as a new tool for assessing student performance. Stories and examples of portfolio projects in classrooms around the country abound in educational reports, newsletters, and trade papers. The pictures are quite varied. To more fully characterize and understand the nature and purposes of portfolios, The National Center for the Study of Writing and Literacy conducted the research project explained in chapter 3 of this volume.

Despite the rich array of information available from the surveys and working conference described in chapter 3, the picture lacked the multidimensional information needed to bring the images to life—the detailed texture and interactional context of the projects. To gather this type of information, we needed an opportunity to hear and see teachers as they grappled with the issues of portfolio implementation. Site visits would have been ideal, but a shoestring budget and limited time made these an impossibility.

Necessity became the mother of invention. We devised a technological strategy for investigating portfolio applications in context that we have dubbed the video visit. The basic idea was to ask teachers, individuals, and groups to videotape a discussion session centered around their use of portfolios, which could then serve for viewing and analysis. The intention was that the teacher would walk around the classroom (without students present), display various artifacts related to portfolio assessment, and discuss the story of their implementation of the portfolio concept. This chapter describes our sojourn into this new strategy for data collection. The findings illuminate some aspects of portfolio use, and also show the possibilities and problems of the video-visit methodology.

THE QUEST

Video visits were designed to alleviate several limitations of the other strategies that we had employed in the project. For instance, despite efforts to create an open-ended framework for the survey, respondents tended to stay fairly close to the initial questions, offering little in the way of expansion or additional information. We hoped that the video visit would expand the boundaries of the responses by opening a path for more direct communication, one that provided some scaffolding but invited participants to shape their answers more actively. The discussions at the working conference showed the value of collegial interaction in leading participants to reflect on their own processes, but lacked the immediacy of the participant's classroom and school context. We hoped that respondents, offered an opportunity for discussion and reflection on their "home territory," would be more outgoing about matters like teacher decision making, organizational choices, and professional thinking. Finally, we hoped that the video visits would provide richer images of the local context than were possible with either surveys or conferences.

Specifically, by collecting video excerpts of staff meetings and presentations around portfolio assessment, we hoped to flesh out our data in several specific ways:

- To capture the context of the portfolio projects. Survey responses typically offered little detail about how materials were organized within individual portfolios, within the classroom, and throughout the school day. Some respondents chose to send samples of organizational pieces used in their portfolios, but often the surveys came with sparse explanation. Seeing actual student work, in a complete context, offered the prospect of more complete understanding and interpretation of other data sources.

- To capture more in-depth information than is possible with written forms. Time and space constraints limit the detail that respondents can provide on surveys. Time demands on teachers are a barrier when it comes to reporting the details of classroom practice. The majority of our surveys were completed by single respondents, and these solo presentations did not include the feedback and commentary from colleagues that can spark expanded discussion and detail. With no one to challenge, question, or extend the information a teacher offers in the survey, the data can be rather flat and uni-dimensional. Bringing together a faculty team for discussion of portfolio practices seemed an ideal way of jump-starting discussions with questions and comments.

- To capture different information than what is available on written forms. Our aim in the survey web was to provide open-ended questions, but what we included and excluded in phrasing our questions undoubtedly shaped the responses we received. Teachers and administrators may have had many other things on their minds. Some of these thoughts might inform their descriptions in significant ways. Sometimes the only way to discover the right question is to listen longer.

- To capture the professional context of portfolio projects. Professional connections and collaborations are difficult to represent on paper, especially when they involve input from a variety of personnel—administrators, consultants, professional development staff, and faculty. Also, when more than one teacher has been involved in a portfolio project, it can be difficult to appreciate the between-class variation in approach and process. A team-based video visit offered an opportunity to hear a variety of perspectives, and to learn about differences between classrooms.

"IMAGE," PROCESS, AND DESIGN

We began to design our video visit concept by imagining what an ideal visit might look like. What would it include, and how would the information be conveyed? How would the visit be different from just videotaping a classroom? As we thought more about the matter, we realized that we were actually suggesting to teachers that they prepare a portfolio on portfolios.

For instance, reflection and selection quickly came to the fore as important features of the video visit. Unlike a typical classroom observation, the aim was for teachers to prepare a collection of artifacts ahead of time that would go beyond exemplification to an understanding of the portfolio process. This move would involve outlining the key features of the portfolio program, and selecting artifacts to explain how those features worked.

The ideal video visit began to take shape as a retrospective. It might resemble an interview in some respects, but on home territory with the participants structuring the presentation, determining what was important to highlight, what was working, and where the challenges lay. In the natural settings of the school and the classroom, teachers would walk the viewer through their arenas. Unlike more traditional data sources, participants could take the opportunity to reflect and respond to one another candidly as the presentation unfolded. Unique classroom approaches could be contrasted with schoolwide or district plans. Genuine unfettered discussions about choices, differences, and perspectives would highlight the underlayers that define a program.

As a vision of the ideal video visit emerged, we also began to recognize the learning potential for the participants. By constructing a video visit, schools had an opportunity to reflect on their own processes and progress with portfolios. Data from surveys and the working conference made it abundantly clear that teachers yearned for more time to talk to one another, to explore for themselves what they were doing and why, and to examine and consider options and choices. Asking a teacher team to sit down together for a presentation of their portfolio program required group planning and discussion around the themes and topics central to their approach. To expand the learning potential for participants, and to provide an example for the exercise, we decided to prepare a model of how a video visit might be planned and conducted. Later in this chapter we describe these support materials.

The Sample

From the larger sample of survey sites, we invited 24 schools and districts that had portfolio programs to participate in the video visit. These programs were chosen because they demonstrated a relatively advanced level of progress in using portfolios at their sites. Criteria for selection included (a) a history of one or more years of portfolio use, (b) a minimum of three teachers at the site involved in using portfolios, and (c) explicit district-level investment in the portfolio project. Our letter described the task of creating a video visit and explained its role in the research project.

We asked participating sites to return a finished video to us in 4 months. After several follow-up calls to encourage completion of the project, we finally received nine video visits. Of the original 24 sites, 7 declined participation, 5 did not respond, and 3 agreed to participate but later were unable to complete a video due to unforeseen problems.

Of the nine video visits we received, four sites included completed evaluation forms along with their videos, and two sites sent along copies of artifacts discussed in their videos. Four sites sent videos that had been created for other purposes—dissemination of program information, materials for parent education, and so on. These tapes covered many of the questions pertinent to the project, and so are included in the analysis even though they are not exactly in the spirit of the video visit. The response rate was lower than we had expected, a matter that we discuss later in the chapter.

Support Materials

We formulated a fairly extensive set of materials to explain the concept of a video visit to participants and to assist the sites in preparing their videos. We fixed on several basic guidelines: (a) the kit needed to be short and demand little time, (b) the material needed to be attention-grabbing, and (c) the task needed to be explained simply and directly. To accomplish these goals, we developed four components: (a) a brief outline of the video-visit process, (b) a list of suggestions of topics and themes that a video-visit tape should address, (c) a model video to illustrate what a video visit might look like, and (d) a program profile and evaluation form.

The outline (Fig. 9.1) was designed to be simple and user friendly, to suggest a casual and open process. The entire production comprised seven steps, which were connected to the model video. We think that this part of the process was solid, and recommend it to others.

The list of suggested topics and themes (Fig. 9.2) included many topics and questions that appeared in the original survey, not surprising, because they sprang from the conceptual framework presented in chapter 1. We tried to open the way for a wide range of possibilities, a springboard for ideas.

We are looking forward to a video visit with you and your colleagues, in which you share your own experiences with portfolios. The following outline may help you plan your production.

1.   BUILD YOUR MESSAGE
   Think about a handful of important themes and principles that you want to focus on during the visit. A list of suggestions is included.

2.   CHOOSE YOUR PARTICIPANTS
   In our model tape, we arranged for samples with a single teacher, with a teaching team, and with a faculty group and administrator. We used an "interviewer" for some of the segments; you may find that helpful to keep the visit on an agenda of sorts.

3.   ASSEMBLE YOUR ARTIFACTS
   The more concrete examples you can provide, the better for our purposes. Don't worry about capturing the details on video--that turns out to be more trouble than it's worth, and you can send copies along as separates. But the artifacts give you something to talk about, help to illustrate your ideas, and can help to guide your presentation.

4.   CREATE AN ENVIRONMENT
   In the sample tape, we selected a classroom with lots of "action," typifying a literate environment. There was room to "set up" for interviews and to move around to look at classroom items. Another approach (not exemplified in the tape) is to place artifacts at different locations around the classroom or school and move from one to another of these during the visit.

5.   COLLECT EQUIPMENT
   You don't need a high tech video camera, but it will help to move up from the "handy cam" models made for home use, if possible. A tripod will help keep the picture stable. Remember that sound is more important than sight. If you have a camera that can connect to a remote microphone, we highly recommend that you use a remote mike set up near the participants.

6.   START WITH A SCRIPT . . . AND THEN EXTEMPORIZE
   In the sample tape, we talked for a while about the main points to cover, and jotted down key ideas on butcher paper that we hung near the camera before we began filming. But once the camera was rolling, we used the list only for guidance, and went with the flow of discussion.

7.   MAIL THE MATERIALS TO US
   When you're done, send us the tape, as is. Don't worry about editing for our purposes. Send along your "script notes" to help document your process, and copies of any artifacts you may have referred to in your tape. And please take a moment to complete the evaluation form we have sent along.

FIG. 9.1. Video visit outline sent to prospective participants.

Possible Discussion Questions and Themes

Please address as many of these questions as you can when you work on the video visit. Please add other questions or issues which are pertinent to your program.

- How did you get started with portfolios? What was the motivation to begin using them?
- What are the purposes of your portfolio assessment system?
- Is the portfolio design uniform, or unique to each class? How was the design developed?
- Do all teachers use them in your school or district, or only some?
- Discuss what collaboration between teachers, if any, exists around using portfolios.
- Discuss the procedures of what goes in to a portfolio, and why?
- How are the portfolios evaluated? What standards are used to judge the quality of student work in the portfolio? How were the standards decided upon?
- Discuss the student's role in evaluating work which is present in the portfolio.
- Is the portfolio used in grading? If so, how?
- Have portfolios replaced any other assessment tool?
- How has portfolio assessment influenced instruction or curriculum?
- How has portfolio assessment influenced the professional development of the teachers involved?
- What have been the problems or snags in implementing portfolio assessment?
- What is the best thing about using portfolios?

FIG. 9.2. List of questions sent with video visit kit.

Finally, we included a Program Profile and Evaluation form, in which we asked about the site and the participants, as well as the process of creating a video visit, and the value, if any, that the process held for them. We wanted to learn if attitudes about the exercise changed after the video was complete, and we asked respondents to evaluate their initial willingness to participate and their ultimate opinion about participating.

The Model Video

Preparation of the model video was perhaps the most important component we crafted in this project. The model had to be engaging, had to cover the information needed to make an effective product, and had to energize the participants.

The model offered participants three different models, along with the suggestion that they explore those options most comfortable for them. The options included (a) a show-and-tell episode, in which a teacher showed portfolio artifacts from her classroom while she discussed how she used each of them, (b) an interview episode in which two teachers from the same school discussed the school portfolio program, and (c) a panel discussion, in which several teachers from different schools in the district review their use of portfolios with a district administrator.

In pursuit of an authentic model, we conducted an actual video visit with local teachers from the Redwood City School District. We discussed the three variations with the teachers, who then decided on assignment to the different segments. The classroom was arranged to provide a comfortable setting, as well as reasonably high quality sight and sound. After these preparations, we filmed the three episodes. We did not rehearse the teachers, relying instead on their spontaneity (and editing) to convey the message.

The model video visit was then edited for the final version. Of almost an hour of footage, 18 minutes wound up in the model tape. The model begins with a brief introduction by Calfee, who discusses the purpose of our project and the goals of the video visit concept. The three video visit segments are then presented, with a sample excerpt from the actual video visit inserted to illustrate each style. Finally, production tips are listed for the viewer based on the outline in Fig. 9.1—suggestions for organizing the participants, questioning strategies, setting up a comfortable seating arrangement, and assuring that microphones and lighting are adequate.

Because the teachers were discussing real processes, purposes, and issues around their use of portfolios, the segments in the model video were both authentic and lively. The model video ran just over 30 minutes, offering viewers guidelines for creating a video visit by offering them views from an actual portfolio project.

RESULTS AND DISCUSSION

As noted earlier, we received 9 responses from the 24 sites that were invited to contribute videotapes. We analyzed the responses along three dimensions: (a) the conceptual framework for the respondent's portfolio program, (b) critical issues identified by program participants, and (c) judgments and attitudes about what is happening in practice and what might or should be happening.

Based on the questions used in our portfolio survey, a list of descriptive statements was generated to describe the various components included in each project, spanning the definitions, purposes, processes, and applications. The range of options for each field came from the variety or responses represented when survey data were analyzed. After repeated viewings of each video, a summary of the content was written describing the technology and issues highlighted in the tape. Variations particular to the program, along with variations from class to class or grade to grade was also noted. Information from the video visits was then aggregated with program information in the written survey. We searched for consistencies and discrepancies in the information, along with novel insights from the video visit.

Synopses

A description of each video visit we received follows, showing the range of programs, from the single-class project to the large districtwide program, from small rural schools to big urban districts. Considerable variety is present in the definitions, purposes, and processes described in the different portfolio projects. Similarities, particularly with assessment actions and comments relating to student ownership and professional development are also evident (see Table 9.1 for a summary of the information).

Deciding on the order of presentation of the synopses was a puzzle. We finally decided on the dimension of project-relatedness. The first visits in the collection are clearly identified with external projects, whereas the latter visits are local efforts. The small number of protocols makes it impossible for us to establish that this is the dominant dimension, but it seems to capture some significant contrasts. In any event, this report is best viewed as a collection of case studies, capable of being recategorized in a variety of ways.

Program CRESST (CLA) submitted a short, already-prepared video describing portfolio writing assessment in high technology classrooms. The report, a collaboration between UCLA's Center for Evaluation and the Cupertino, CA Apple Classrooms of Tomorrow schools, is quite professional, with voice-over descriptions and brief excerpts by researchers and teachers. The main message is the importance of reaching consensus about what is valued and why, if portfolio collections are to serve for assessment. Eva Baker, Co-Director of the Center and spokesperson for the project, put it this way: "Writing portfolios can be a powerful tool for review and assessment, but only if there is agreement about what kids should be learning, what should go into the portfolio, and how the material is assessed."

Sections of the video illustrate teachers discussing standards, and the difficulty of accomplishing this task. In this project, the program implementers were interested in evaluating the effectiveness of the technology, which led to considerable emphasis on portfolio use for accountability and instructional improvement. Including technology introduced an additional challenge mentioned in the video. "The importance of developing assessment standards and methods applies to any area of instruction. How do we develop standards for innovative multimedia products when there are not, as yet, any standards established?"

The ancillary themes revolved around issues that turn up in many discussions of portfolio use: the enthusiasm of teachers for more valid assessments of student achievement, the information provided about student growth, and the value of portfolios in provoking student self-assessment and dialogue with teachers and parents. The presentation concluded with a final caution: "Just collecting work for a portfolio doesn't accomplish the task of setting standards and measuring progress. Good assessment remains based on well established standards as a basis for measurement, and the design of what those standards are and how they are to measure progress are a continuing challenge."

Program Pittsburgh, PA (PPA) sent a lengthy, 90-minute presentation made especially for our project by the Arts PROPEL group in the Pittsburgh schools.

TABLE 9.1
Profile of Video Visits

site	Video Type	Format	Participants	Purposes	Comments
PPA	For project	large group	20 faculty from middle school & high school	-- Enhance student writing -- Students responsible for own learning -- Help teachers & district assess instruc.	-- Collection and evaluation uniform across district -- Student reflection is highly valued
SAK	For project	6 small panels	14 faculty from same primary school	-- Help with conferencing -- Develop self-eval. skills -- Collect info across years	-- Grassroots initiation by teachers seen as critical -- Student reflection & ownership highly valued
OCA	Other purpose	Voice-over description	Students and teachers from same primary school	-- Help students to monitor & reflect on learning -- Help students set learning goals -- To inform parents	-- Students use their portfolio collection to lead parent conference -- Collection & eval. uniform across school
MTX	For project	Panel	8 faculty from same district	Purposes varied school to school, but included - Devel. reflection skills - To show growth - To inform parents	-- Voluntary pilot study encouraged innovation -- Uniform evaluation by rubrics across district
NFL	For project	1 interview and 1 panel	5 faculty from same district	-- To show growth -- To provide alternative assessment information	-- Pilot project encouraged innovation, so little uniformity present -- Student reflection valued by all programs
RCA	For project	1 interview and 2 panels	4 faculty from same district	Purposes varied school to school, be included - Devel. reflection skills - To show growth - To inform parents	-- Processes used varied to reflect different purposes
SMA	Other purpose	Interview	1 teacher & interviewer	-- Used to hold project work "in progress" -- Create a project "history" from first draft to final	-- School embraced "portfolio culture," but some differences in process exist across grade levels

(Continued)

TABLE 9.1
(Continued)

site	Video Type	Format	Participants	Purposes	Comments
CLA	Other purpose	Voice-over description	Students & teachers from same elem. school	-- Accountability -- Instructional improvement	-- Emphasized need for site agreement about what is valued, and why -- Just collecting work isn't enough--must be judged against standards
PMA	Other purpose	Interview	1 teacher & interviewer	-- To document teacher judgments about student achievement	-- Spoke only for own class--no information about school or district efforts -- Teacher chooses contents to justify grades

The video included a large-group discussion of 20 teachers sitting in a faculty area. Individual teachers took turns addressing specific questions from our list of suggestions. A few artifacts were shared, but the individual tended to address the question as a spokesperson for the entire group. There was considerable uniformity and consensus, with little questioning or debate. The participants paid considerable attention to the topic of purposes for portfolio assessment: to enhance student writing, to lead students to become responsible for their own learning, to help teachers assess instruction more effectively, and to provide the district with more trustworthy evidence about student achievements. In discussing purposes, a teacher mentioned the limitations of simply grading student work: "I would get frustrated because students just look at the grade and don't read the thousands of comments I write to help improve their writing. The grade was the thing, and we needed to break away from that."

For district purpose, growth criteria were laid out in the form of checklists, with children involved in the generation of the criteria. In discussing the process, a teacher shared how student feedback helped him reflect on his own teaching choices. "Recently, we were picking an 'unsatisfactory selection.' 80% of the kids picked the same assignment! It was my assignment, which made me question 'What's wrong with this assignment?' "

Portfolios were graded as a whole, with the processes for collection and evaluation quite uniform across the district. Student reflection and responsibility were mentioned as distinctive and critical features of portfolios, but in describing the processes of reflection, a teacher confessed that this was one of the more challenging aspects of the portfolio program. "It's not easy to help children reflect. The first thing to do is to help children define 'reflection.' On reflection sheets, children must justify their decisions. It's intimate and difficult, but when children do it, they gain a confidence in what they can do."

Program Provincetown, MA (PMA) was created as part of an educational television project by Project Zero staff in Provincetown, MA. The tape includes an interview of a first-grade teacher who discusses her approach to portfolios. It is a highly personal account, in which the teacher shares a rich array of artifacts and experiences from her class. She does not address issues of how or whether portfolios might be used in a broader context in her school or district, but in her remarks can be found a variety of important insights for a broader audience. Her primary purpose in portfolio assessment is to document the basis for her judgments about student achievement and progress, providing "evidence to back up comments and ratings on student report cards."

She does not lay out general criteria for gauging growth, but recounts her comparisons of work over time. Yet she appears clearer than most on her criteria for judging progress. She looks piece-by-piece for evidence of change, such as fine motor development, fewer orthographic reversals, increased length, and so on. As examples, she shares the tape recording of student reading, which she collects four times over the year to document growth in fluency as well as reading choice. She also shared the writing in a student's journal from September to October, pointing to additional length and detail as signs of progress.

She mentions student reflection as an important component, although students are not involved in choosing portfolio contents. "I meet with students once a week, usually on Friday mornings, for some reflection work one-on-one. This is a very important part of the process for the child, because they *see* their own changes." The teachers who called in with questions were very interested in the details of her class management to accomplish individual conferencing, which the teacher handled by having other students do independent work and writing about their own reflections. One caller asked why the portfolio did not replace the report card. She replied, "I don't think parents or teachers are ready to give them up. They are a concise way to convey a lot of important information. Portfolios are useful because they can support grading judgments."

Program Shutesbury, MA (SMA) was similar to Provincetown, in that the video was developed as part of an educational television program. It centered around a 20-minute interview with a teacher who was using portfolios in his school, followed by call-ins from listeners interested in the topic. The teacher described a "portfolio culture" that had been established at his school. The teachers had designed the curriculum around thematic projects rather than textbooks and worksheets, and student work went through many drafts and revisions. In this culture, high quality was the standard. As described by the teacher, "If a student hands in something that isn't A+ material, it isn't judged as bad—just unfinished." Portfolios housed the drafts and critiques of work-in-progress, while finished projects were put on display, put into use for reference or entertainment, or archived in the library.

Emphasis was high on peer review and critique, and an example was shown of a student's progress in drawing a cave map when peer review was included. "After she received feedback, (her map) made a real leap in ability. Now you can tell above ground from below, and more labeling appears as a direct result of the feedback she received." Teachers who called in their questions where very interested in how to teach children skills to review and critique one another's work, and the process was described around helping children build a vocabulary. "Initially, I model critiquing. I bring in a former student's work or something of my own and begin critiquing it, explaining the words and descriptions I use. I use a sample to help kids build the vocabulary to critique, whether its an art piece or a science piece or whatever. The rule is to start with something you like, or something you think works. Then you can add suggestions for improvement."

The teacher seemed to speak for the entire school, suggesting considerable uniformity across teachers and grades, although he emphasized that it was the philosophy of learning and the project-based curriculum that tied the portfolios together. Differences in the details of compiling and critiquing portfolios did exist from room to room, even in this small portfolio "community."

Program Susitna, AK (SAK) in Anchorage, AK submitted a very detailed presentation prepared especially for our purposes. The tape comprised six small-group segments, in which small teams of teachers and administrators discussed various issues centering around portfolio use. The teachers, all of whom were from the same school, spoke with unity about the purposes of the portfolio, which began as a tool to better inform parents. "We were frustrated talking about letter grades at parent conference time. We began to collect samples of (student) work and got a little away from grades, and began feeling better about conferences because we were talking about children and not grades!" As portfolios began to evolve, the purpose also shifted, focusing on child-centered conferencing, and the development of self-evaluation skills. "It's really interesting that parent reporting was our first concern, but now it has moved way down the list. Now we want to get children more involved in their learning and taking more responsibility for it."

The participants reported on plans to collect information across years, and ultimately to replace the report card. They distinguished between *working portfolios* used to assess work during a particular school year and *progressive portfolios* that were selective for passing on from year to year. They saw grassroots portfolio assessment as critical, and mentioned teacher reflection and ownership of work as important features of their project. "We started out thinking portfolios would do all these things for the kids—and they also have done something for us teachers. By creating those rubrics and internalizing that information, I'm much more able to assess children and I know what objectives I want my lessons to meet." The district coordinator concluded with a strong case for not trying to transplant portfolio programs from one school or district to another, arguing that teachers needed to work out their own ways to make the concept work.

Program Midland, TX (MTX) also sent a detailed production made especially for us by a team of seven teachers and one administrator. The district language arts coordinator began by explaining how the team had conducted a voluntary pilot study involving teachers from different district schools. Each participant addressed in turn one of the questions from our list: how the portfolio got started, what purposes it serves, who it is for, how it is done, how it is evaluated, and the snags and successes they have encountered. The discussion became more natural and animated as teachers from different schools explained how they dealt with the specifics of each of their programs, with staff collaboration a key theme throughout. "We began to meet once a week and discussed how to do prewriting, how to do revising, how to do different aspects of the process all the way through. As we got student work, we would get together as grade levels and discuss what we were doing with our classrooms. We tried to go out to other writing projects as much as possible to research process, and still to this day we are talking about process!"

In most schools across the district, criteria for growth was determined with rubrics. However, one school felt it was important for students to set their own goals, because they saw student reflection as an especially critical component for evaluation. "We develop a rubric before they write a piece, and if they choose that piece we sit together and review the piece against the rubric. This makes them realize the value of assessment rather than just passing work in to the teacher and not knowing what the assignment means. From this, they choose what they want to learn next—whether a skill or a craft of writing. In this way they set their own goals."

Teachers of the same grade level from different schools worked together to review work at the end of the first year as a way to evaluate the curriculum. One teacher shared her satisfaction in adopting process writing and portfolio assessment: "I could finally sleep at night knowing I did not have to worry about comparing my kids' progress to others. I could compare them against their own progress to see how far they had come."

In the Naples, FL (NFL) video production, prepared especially for our purposes, the tape was divided into two separate segments. In the first segment, two teachers from the same school discuss the similarities and differences in their portfolios in kindergarten and fifth grade. At this school, each grade level made their own decisions about portfolio use, so the two participants were learning from each other about their different approaches. Several samples were shared, such as a project called *A Book About Me*, a mini-portfolio that the child adds to over the school year that shows changes in drawing and writing abilities.

The second segment involved three teachers from primary classes at three different schools. They discussed their own programs but also discussed general issues around using portfolios in the classroom. The purpose for using portfolios was to show growth and to provide alternative assessment information. Criteria for growth were not outlined. Instead, a comparison of work was considered piece-by-piece for change, such as handwriting, paragraph structure, and story length. One teacher shared a clever method for annotating portfolio entries. "I put Post-it note observations inside their portfolios to note their engagement, processes, and weaknesses. Parents enjoy reviewing the notes. The little things tell a lot."

Portfolio use is voluntary in this district and teachers were encouraged to try out their own ideas, so there was wide variety between classes. Despite the lack of uniformity, student reflection was mentioned as an important component by every participant. When discussing the practical aspects of fostering reflection in their students, a teacher offered, "I like the idea of the 3, 2, 1. List 3 things I want to remember, 2 ways I will remember, and 1 more question I want answered."

Program Redwood, CA (RCA) submitted a 45-minute tape made especially for our video project describing a pilot project with three schools that were exploring quite different purposes and designs for their portfolio projects. Representatives from the three schools met together during the taping, and it was apparent that they had relatively little time together beforehand to discuss their activities. The purposes were focused and quite distinctive: to show student growth, to increase the student's role in their own assessment, and to inform parents of student progress. In describing how her school reviewed past practice to determine their purposes, one teacher shared, "The amount of risk taking among the staff was really tremendous. There was such an ability to share the pitfalls as well as the successes, and that's where a lot of growth happens."

The processes each school used to reflect different purposes varied. For example, at one school students were responsible for selecting portfolio pieces to reflect on their progress, whereas at another school teachers se-lected most of the portfolio samples to show parents how students were improving over time. They found consensus, however, when discussing snags in their programs. Teacher 1: "We struggle with how to keep it so that the child decides 'I want to put this in because I like what it shows about me,' when teachers and schools and districts need something consis-tent to compare to standards." Teacher 2: "Yes! Doing it with first graders, when they finished a journal we'd ask them to select a piece they liked and tell why. Of course it's not always their 'best' or something that shows a lot of progress, but if we encourage them to explain why they chose it, it helps." The teachers fairly bubbled with questions for one another, and discussed plans to show a copy of the video visit at upcoming faculty meetings.

Program Orion, CA (OCA) provided a short, already-prepared video describing student–parent conference use of portfolios at their school (cf. chapter 10 by Klimenkov and LaPick for more details on this program). The tape had been prepared for other interested schools in the district. It relied on extensive voice-overs to describe vignettes of children sharing their work with their parents at different grade levels. It emphasized the value of the portfolio as a vehicle for students to monitor and reflect on their learning, which enabled them to inform parents about their progress during the student-facilitated conference. Because this process was carried on at every grade level, students developed proficiency as they progressed through school. To take advantage of the older student "experts," a Kinderbuddy program was set up to allow kindergarten children to practice setting goals and reviewing their progress with sixth-grade students who could provide support and suggestions.

The teachers saw enormous importance in having children set their own goals and evaluate their own progress. Explicit growth criteria were not laid out in the program. Instead, students compared work done at different points in time piece-by-piece, looking for evidence of change and improvement in skills. Teachers offered advice on the evaluation process to students beforehand, but the parent conference was completely led by the student. One vignette showed the type of support a teacher might offer a child during a parent conference: Teacher: "How will you know if you've accomplished a goal?" Child: "When the teacher says I'm finished." Teacher: "How will I know?" Child: "I'll show you."

As noted at the outset, this collection of video visits is marked by considerable variability, and is best viewed as case studies. Nonetheless, we have identified several interesting substantive patterns in the collection, and have learned several lessons about the video-visit methodology from the experience. We turn to these matters in the following sections of the chapter.

Patterns

The video visits contributed substantial new information to our understanding of portfolio assessment at the different sites. First, there were disparities between the information we gleaned from surveys and what we learned from video visits. For example, Program MTX reported a unified purpose for the portfolio in the survey, stating they were developed to "show growth and development over time." However, the video discussion revealed that different teachers saw different purposes for the portfolio, and ranked their importance differently from class to class. In the video, different teachers identify parent conferencing, improving student self-esteem, aiding curriculum development, and transferring the responsibility of learning to students as primary purposes.

An important piece of information shared on video but not mentioned in the survey response from Program MTX was that each class was encouraged to experiment with their use of portfolios to compare systems that were more or less successful. It is likely this experimental cast on the project accounted for the differences of purpose, but the survey did not convey this important contextual feature of the project. We are not suggesting that a unified purpose was necessarily desirable for the project; indeed the project directors did begin with a vision, but in working out the details, different teachers highlighted different features as important for them in the portfolio process. The possibilities for flexibility and individualization are a positive feature of portfolios, unlike standardized tests, in which uniformity of purpose often springs from the uniformity of procedure.

Another video visit turned up disparities in the process of creating portfolios. The survey information from the curriculum director for Program RCA described the process of creating and using portfolios as proceeding consistently across district schools. However, as teachers compared and discussed their activities during the video, differences in the selection process and the degree of involvement with student reflection became evident. We learned that some teachers exerted considerable control in selecting work for the portfolio, whereas the survey described this as a student-controlled process. In one particularly candid exchange, it became apparent that this disparity was neither known nor intended. The curriculum director pointed out the importance of greater staff sharing (including activities like the video visit) to ensure more coordination across classrooms.

Disparities were also apparent around the issue of time commitments required for portfolio assessment. Six of the nine surveys from video visit participants raised concerns about the time involved in using portfolios. Survey respondents described the extra time needed to design and analyze portfolios as problematic, even when they saw benefits from the process. The survey from Program SAK reported that extra release time for portfolio activities had been an issue of contention in recent contract negotiations. The survey from Program RCA noted teachers had put in "a lot of their own time" to ensure success of the portfolio project. And the Program CLA survey listed "Time!" as the main snag they faced in their portfolio project.

In contrast, the video visits painted a more positive picture about time. In the video from Program SAK, rather than framing the issue negatively, teachers reported that they "used their time differently." Video participants from Program RCA did acknowledge greater time demands, but stressed that the benefits of portfolio assessment largely outweighed the extra time needed to manage portfolios. They spoke of their motivation to devise creative solutions to time demands to accommodate further development of portfolio programs. The video from Program CLA was an informational video created for another purpose, but it made no mention of teacher burnout or overload.

Second, there was a difference in the type of information available when participants describe practice in written form compared to a group discussion of the program. An example is found in the areas of the role of collaboration and staff communication. In surveys, the importance of collaboration and discussion among teachers was often stressed, leading to the impression that opportunities were adequate for this purpose. According to their survey, Program PPA "places a high value on the personal and professional development that has resulted from the collaboration required to use portfolios." Program SAK reported that "the power of portfolios lies in helping teachers focus on the teaching/learning process together." From Program MTX, "reviewing our curriculum and identifying what we value has been the foremost benefit of our portfolio pilot." Program NFL stated that "this project has brought on a new level of collaboration between us that we've never had before." Program RCA, still in the developmental stages of their project, nonetheless claimed that "communication and sharing between teachers is what keeps our project alive and evolving all the time."

In the videotapes, however, several projects mentioned that preparing for the video visit had been a first or rare opportunity to talk together about their portfolio practice. It is possible, of course, that there had been previous collaboration, but that these had been confined to grade-level peers or other small groups. As teachers talked about their work on camera, however, it seemed that many were learning for the first time about the details of their colleagues' work at the schoolwide or districtwide level. In their video, Program PPA brought together middle school and high school teachers to discuss their program. When talking about collection and evaluation procedures, middle school teachers were interrupted twice by high school teachers who noted that things were done a bit differently at their level, which was apparently news to the middle school group.

Programs SAK, MTX, NFL, and RCA set up panels with teachers from different grade levels or schools, and in these spontaneous discussions they had many questions for one another about issues, procedures, and priorities. The teachers from Program SAK did not realize that their definition of portfolio varied from one level to another, with some including standardized tests and others not. The NFL video began when a kindergarten teacher told a fifth-grade teacher how happy she was that they would now have a chance to learn about one another's portfolio programs. Teachers from Program RCA did a comparative presentation, showing artifacts from different grade levels to compare programs; there were frequent comments of "what a good idea," or "I did not know that," further indications that the teachers were exchanging information for the first time. The discussion format validated the importance of staff collaboration that had been indicated in the surveys, but broadened the definition to include the need of collaboration with a wider scope of professionals.

Another type of information found in the video data but not apparent from survey data centered around problem-solving processes. For example, in the video from Program MTX, a teacher asked for ideas about extending the student's portfolio beyond a single grade level. The district curriculum coordinator suggested a plan for cumulative portfolios that would follow the child through their entire academic career. This spurred a discussion among the teachers concerning the problems with making assumptions about a student based on past performance. The group decided to investigate alternative models for cumulative assessment before moving ahead, and a teacher volunteered to look into the matter.

The information captured on the videos also served to reinforce certain points in the survey data. Program PPA used the survey to list features valued in student work. In the video, teachers also spent considerable time discussing individual perspectives on what they valued in student work and how those perspectives helped determine curriculum goals. A common theme found throughout the survey and video data concerned the increased ownership and pride students felt about their work as a result of their involvement with portfolios. For example, Program OCA identified student ownership of work as a major purpose for their portfolio project in their survey response. Their informational video highlighted excerpts of students talking with their parents about the pride they have in their work. Program CLA survey participants commented on the improved motivation and ownership students showed in their writing when discussing the benefits of their program. The video highlighted this feature with vignettes of students planning and collaborating on reports without teacher guidance.

Enhancements

The preceding comparisons were drawn from programs that reported on their portfolio use with both a completed survey and a video visit, showing how the new and different information obtained through video visits can add a new dimension of understanding to descriptive studies. The videos ultimately served to illuminate certain points raised in the surveys and challenge others, accomplishing much that we had set out to do. But on reflection, there are some changes we would make in our methodology.

For example, one thing we did not learn as much about as we had hoped was the environmental context for using portfolios. We should have made this point more clearly in preparing the participants. The model video showed a teacher walking us through her class with a show-and-tell of the artifacts she and her students used, but none of our video participants chose this format as an option. Although several brought student samples to show in group discussions, we did not get a look inside the actual classrooms in most instances. Instead, most visits were filmed in conversational groupings, typically in a staff lounge area or other equally "antiseptic" settings that revealed little or nothing about classroom configurations and student artifacts.

In looking back, we can now see that our model video was biased toward the more formal format. Only one brief segment (approximately 5 minutes), showed a class "walkabout;" the rest of the tape (more than 15 minutes) portrayed conversational groupings. Also, the discussion questions we sent along as prompts were more focused on purposes and structures of portfolios than on classroom organization and routines. This experience points out the careful planning that must go into preparing the "video-visit kit" for this methodology. Clearly, our modeling shaped our results and imposed limits in ways that we did not intend.

Providing ample time and support for programs to complete the project is another methodological feature that we would change. We obtained a participation rate of only one in four invitees, but if we were to only count the videos specifically created for our study, the rate drops significantly. Telephone invitations and discussions are critical for explaining the process and encouraging participation. Planning for a second round of recruitment that builds on results from the first round might also contribute to a higher participation rate.

In addition to the matters just mentioned, we have become aware of other limitations to the video-visit process. For instance, it is difficult to ensure a random sample. The rigors and commitment involved for a participant to agree to produce a video visit limited the data pool to those participants favorably inclined toward the project or process under study. It seems unlikely that a project experiencing difficulty with portfolios would be inclined to complete a video visit. The methodology relies on volunteerism to construct a public display of the program's competence, leading to a tendency to put your best foot forward.

On the other hand, the video-visit concept has possibilities that may prove very useful beyond the borders of research. With staff development time at a premium, it has potential as a communication tool for professional development. The reality of teachers and students working on actual programs offers the prospects of more lively workshops, and would seem to be quite valuable for the induction of new teaching staff. A video visit might be framed in which a mentor teacher and a novice review the particular needs of the new teacher. We also see possibilities in this methodology as a teacher evaluation tool for examining classroom practice; indeed, some of the techniques being considered by the National Board of Professional Teaching Standards capture the flavor of the video visit. Finally, novel programs might be effectively conveyed to parents and community members through this approach.

Substantively, and despite the limitations, we believe that we learned some important lessons about portfolio practice from the current collection of video visits. Looking through different lenses brought some new issues to the forefront and cast others in a different light. Just as moving beyond a typical rating survey to a more open-ended webbing style in our written surveys opened new avenues for participant response, so adding an inter-active video provided more options, and suggested the potential value of video technology for documenting interaction and reflection.

REFERENCE

Calfee, R. C., & Perfumo, P. A. (1993). Student portfolios: Opportunities for a revolution in assessment. *Journal of Reading, 36,* 532–537.

CHAPTER TEN

Promoting Student Self-Assessment Through Portfolios, Student-Facilitated Conferences, and Cross-Age Interaction

Margaret Klimenkov
Nina LaPick
Orion Elementary School, Redwood City, CA

This chapter presents the story of two teachers engaged in a schoolwide portfolio project to involve students in self-assessment. Together with our colleagues, we employ portfolios and student-facilitated conferences as vehicles to give students greater ownership of their learning. By using portfolios to organize their work, our students are learning to set personal learning goals, engage in self-evaluation, and present their accomplishments to teachers and parents. Students also learn to conduct conferences with their parents, using portfolios to discuss past goals, propose future goals, and answer parents' questions. Between us, we cover a broad spectrum of practice; Margaret Klimenkov (MK) works with fifth and sixth graders, while Nina LaPick (NLP) teaches a kindergarten–first grade developmental class. This chapter shows the possibilities across this spectrum.

As our evaluation practices have evolved, it has been a natural extension to include cross-age interaction, in which more experienced students tutor younger, less experienced learners in the development of self-assessment skills. Along with the ownership and pride that children gain from the self-assessment process, we have observed that younger students gain communication skills and confidence in presenting their work and older students are given the opportunity to role play the part of the parent, gaining insight into the parent's point of view. Additionally, in learning how to help their little buddies explain their growth and learning, older students have become better able to explain their own progress during the conference.

Our work with portfolios and student-facilitated conferences has evolved over a 3-year period, and over time has come to involve all members of the school community—students, parents, and teachers. Through trial and error, parent feedback, and staff development, we have made many changes in the format of the portfolio, the length and format of the conference, and the process of student preparation for the conference. This chapter will examine the questions and issues that prompted our project, the purposes and processes that influenced the evolution of the program, and the challenges ahead. Here, then, we chart for you where we began, where we have come from, and where we hope to go as our inquiry continues.

THE HISTORY AND PHILOSOPHY OF PORTFOLIO ASSESSMENT AT ORION SCHOOL

Orion School is a public alternative school within the Redwood City School District in Redwood City, California. The philosophy of Orion School stresses the development of the whole child and of individual learning styles through the use of hands-on experiential learning and cooperative activities. Instructional strategies encourage children to participate at their own maturity level, and to assume responsibility for their own learning as appropriate. We particularly value the ability of students to set their own learning goals and to self-evaluate progress toward those goals.

In an effort to align assessment processes with school philosophy and instructional practices, Orion began by using a written narrative to report a child's progress to parents. Each teacher maintains a set of working files for each student. Each of these files contains samples of student work along with informal assessment notes, anecdotal records based on observations and interactions, and other relevant information for assessing student progress. The information in these working files provides the basis for the teacher's written narrative to parents.

The Orion School community had never considered traditional letter grades reflective of the student as a whole person; as an alternative, the written narrative offered a one-page summary of the child's academic, physical, and social growth. Parent–teacher conferences were held three times per school year for 20 minutes. At the conference, the parents received the written narrative and a checklist of skills showing their child's growth in those skills.

Gradually, the staff decided to involve students more fully in the evaluation process. In 1989, two Orion teachers attended a professional conference about alternative assessment techniques. "Evaluation: A Perspective For Change," a presentation led by Terry Johnson and his associates, described a method that shifted the focus of student assessment away from the teacher and distributed it more equally among all participants in a child's education. The presentation offered ways to help teachers empower students by allowing students to have direct involvement in their own assessment.

The Orion staff adapted and expanded Johnson's basic format to fit the philosophy and practices of Orion school. First, we discussed what we saw as important to help make each student a successful learner. The following statement captures the essence of our goals for students at Orion School:

> The capability and willingness to assess their own progress and learning is one of the greatest gifts students can develop. Those who are able to review their own performance, explain the reasons for choosing the processes they used, and identify the next step have a life long head start. Learning power comes with knowing how much we know and what to do to learn more.

With this goal in mind, the staff envisioned a student portfolio that contains a body of work demonstrating the students' progress toward achieving learning goals. Together, we developed the following objectives for the use of portfolios:

1. To promote a stronger understanding of what the child does in the classroom.
2. To empower children by giving them some control over their own education.
3. To open communication between children and their families.
4. To help students develop a sense of standards for their own performance, and to allow them to set goals.
5. To create an understanding by students that they are accountable for their efforts.
6. To help students understand and communicate where they are, and to lay out the steps they have to take in order to move ahead.
7. To have students help evaluate one another by constructive comments on one another's work.
8. To develop life skills in goal setting, self-evaluation, and creating focus in order to achieve a goal.

To assure that these goals and objectives were shared by the school community, the plan was brought before the Orion School Site Council (the parent–teacher governing body of the school). The council officially voted to institute the student portfolio program during the 1990–1991 school year as part of the school's assessment program.

CURRENT PORTFOLIO PROCESSES: DESIGN AND USE

Following the objectives just defined, the staff developed the Orion portfolio design with the three components shown in Fig. 10.1. Some modifications were dependent on the student's grade level, and the showcase component was added over time. The portfolio assessment plan includes three basic components. Students have primary responsibility for the binder and show-case components. Each student has a three-ringed binder where he or she keeps all of his or her work. The binder is divided into sections according to subject matter: language arts, social studies, math, science, handwriting, and "other." A list of student-generated goals is kept in the front of the binder. The students take the binder portfolio home with them at regular intervals during the school year to keep parents informed and involved in their child's schooling. It also provides a vehicle for parent feedback.

The philosophy and process underlying the Orion portfolio is spelled out in plain language in Fig. 10.2, which shows the letter to parents that explains the role of the parent in reviewing the binder portfolio. This letter goes home with the binder in October. The letter briefly reminds parents of the purpose for the portfolio and the process of the Orion self-assessment plan. The questions are designed to stimulate conversation and open communication between the child and his or her parents. The child has an opportunity to discuss the self-assessment process and share his or her accomplishments with parents. Teachers use this information to assess the degree of communication between the child and parent concerning the work the child is doing in school and in the self-assessment.

The portfolio process has changed throughout the years as a result of our experience. For instance, we quickly discovered that children were overwhelmed by the large amount of paper that accumulated in the binder. They needed a mechanism for identifying those pieces that they considered to be exceptional and particularly reflective of their growth. Just as in the real world, a professional portfolio must be selective to appropriately represent individual skills and accomplishments. Teachers moved to help the

Binder Portfolio	Showcase Portfolio	Teacher Records
*goals checklist	*goal card	*skills checklist
*work from various curricular areas (all that can fit into the binder)	*self-evaluation worksheet	*anecdotal notes
	*student selected or teacher suggested pieces from each section of binder with student rationale: "Why I am proud" (K/3) or "Signs of improvement"(4/6)	*performance-based assessments
*parent feedback letters		*writing samples
*past showcase pieces		*cassette tape of monthly reading and writing (K/1)
	*current monthly writing sample	*videotape of presentations (5/6)

FIG. 10.1. Design of Orion portfolio.

Dear Orion Parent,

  The student portfolio is an important piece of the Orion assessment process. The binder portfolio allows the child to be included in the process of self-assessment, goal-setting and monitoring his/her own growth throughout the school year. During our second parent-teacher conference in March, your child will run the conference, presenting the "showcase" pieces of his/her work and discussing the progress made on the goals he/she has selected for him/herself.

  Hands-on learning and cooperative activities are emphasized at Orion, so the portfolios can not possibly hold all the school work that your child does. We invite you to come into the classrooms, look around the walls, ask your child questions, peek in your child's binder, writing folder, cubbie, desk, and so on.

  Before each conference, please take some time with your child to go through the binder, discuss what you see, and think about the following questions:

*How well can your child explain the process of self-evaluation and the goals that he or she selected?
*How well does your child recognize his or her progress or areas of need at this point?
*How did your child feel when he or she shared the portfolio with you?
*What experiences have stood out for your child this year?
*What is your favorite piece in the binder? Why?

FIG. 10.2. Letter to parents describing Orion portfolio.

students select a few "showcase" pieces with care and thoughtfulness, keeping in mind purpose and audience. The showcase portfolio is a large, expanding accordion file holding four or five self-selected pieces of high quality work covering the entire curriculum. Staff and students have found the showcase an invaluable addition for several reasons. First, the process of selecting their highest quality work becomes a concrete and valuable activity for students' self-assessment. Second, it allows the students to focus on the quality rather then the quantity of work. Third, students can focus during the conference itself, creating a more coherent presentation for parents by using the showcase pieces rather than the entire bulky binder.

SETTING GOALS AND SELF-ASSESSMENT

Assessing myself gives me a chance to take a step ahead in learning, lets me choose my own challenges, lets me choose the pieces I think I worked hard on. I get to choose things I think were fun. And I get to choose pieces that I learn a lot on. I think it really benefits students to be able to assess themselves. (sixth-grade boy)

The process that students use to assess themselves, set goals, and choose appropriate showcase pieces for the conference begins with developmentally appropriate expectations established by the Orion staff, each teacher adding his or her own distinctive flavor to the process. Our expectations reflect not only the district's standards for specific grade levels, but also the ability of students to understand and articulate their own growth. For example, younger students just learning the process are asked to judge their abilities with simple "yes" or "not yet" responses, whereas older students are asked to rate on a

5-point scale the degree to which they have mastered the skill. Older students are asked to incorporate a greater number of pieces in their showcases, and to prepare written comparisons of early and late works. In the early grades the teacher is primarily responsible for establishing criteria, whereas in the later grades the students give input. Detailed examples of the process are discussed in the two following sections.

Primary Grades

In the primary classroom, the teacher guides the students through the process of self-evaluation early in the school year, using a pictorial checklist of skills and behaviors appropriate to the grade levels (see Fig. 10.3, which is adapted from a form presented during a 1990 workshop by Barbara Rothman of Bellevue, WA). Skills are divided into physical, social, and academic sections, in alignment with the Redwood City District Scope and Standards. Using the checklist with groups of students, the teacher shows the students how to think about the skill or behavior and to thoughtfully consider themselves in deciding "Yes, I can do that" or "No, not yet."

The teacher gives examples of each skill and behavior with the class, as the children carefully consider their own abilites.

Categories:
 Personal Information:
  examples: *I know my phone number*
               I can tie my shoes
               I know my address

 Social Skills and Work Habits:
  examples: *I can solve my own problems*
               I follow directions and signals
               I keep hands to myself

 Physical Skills:
  examples: *I can jump rope*
               I can catch a ball
               I can skip

 Math Skills:
  examples: *I can make a pattern*
               I can count to 100
               I can write numerals 0 - 10

 Language Arts Skills:
  examples: *I know beginning consonant sounds*
               I chant and read aloud with the class
               I write a story with pictures

Checklist examples:

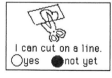  

FIG. 10.3. Kindergarten self-evaluation checklist.

The concept of self-evaluation can be new and difficult for young learners. A safe environment where students can learn to be honest with themselves when considering their own abilities is essential. The teacher stresses that "not yet" is a perfectly acceptable response, because it can give direction in deciding on future goals. As strengths and shortcomings are identified, the classroom climate needs to be respectful and appreciative of student differences.

In LaPick's kindergarten–first-grade classroom, each student selects three goals, one from each of the learning areas—physical, social, academic. These are recorded on a 5″ × 8″ card in both print and picture (see Fig. 10.4). The goal cards are placed in a pocket chart where the children can easily reach them and review them. They can also see who else in the class is working on

Katherine's Goals
(October)

1. To know my address:

123 Adam St.
Redwood City

2. To jump rope 2 x

3. To raise my hand

Katherine's Goals
(February)

1. To label pictures in my stories with one important word

2. To jump rope 10 x

3. To use words to solve problems with others

FIG. 10.4. Kindergarten goals card.

similar goals. The goal card is part of the package used in the conference. The skills checklist remains in the child's binder as a working document. Goals are highlighted and then checked off and dated as the child completes them. Specific time slots are allocated during the week for students to work toward accomplishing their goals, either individually or in groups. The teacher may also suggest goals as the year progresses. Katherine chose her October goals from her "not yet" responses to her self-evaluation checklist. In February, she moved from using random letter strings and scribble writing in her stories, to connecting letter sounds to her words. Her first goal was a result of a writing conference with her teacher.

Throughout the school year, students check in with the teacher or a parent volunteer when they feel that they have reached one goal and are ready to pick a new one. They are asked to show evidence that the goal has been accomplished. Evidence may involve showing completed work kept in the binder portfolio or doing a demonstration. When a goal is judged completed, the child works alone or with the teacher to generate a new one. The new goal is then added to the skills checklist and to the goal card.

Upper Grades

The process of goal setting in the upper grades begins on the first day of school and continues throughout the school year. The initial step for goal setting includes a whole class brainstorming session in which students identify the qualities that make a good student and the steps necessary to achieve excellence. The following example is a list of goal definitions created by Klimenkov's sixth-grade class of 1993.

- Something you're not too good at that you work on so you can get better.
- A tool that makes you feel good about yourself when you can use it to accomplish something.
- A point to get to.
- A standard you set for yourself that you try to reach.
- You're not afraid to learn something new.

The class also creates a list of concepts and skills they may choose to learn around each subject area. Again, criteria for determining the quality of the work is discussed by the entire class. The lists are posted around the classroom for students to refer to easily. Figure 10.5 shows an example of responses that third through sixth graders gave to the question, "What makes a good writer?" The process of self-assessing began with the students creating definitions of good writers. Through teacher modeling, peer discussions,

FIG. 10.5. Student criteria for "what makes a good writer."

and cross-age activities, students compared their work to the definitions. The results were used to set new goals. As students progressed through the year, they gained a stronger understanding of the writing process and definitions became more specific and developed.

In the second step of the goal-setting process, students identify personal strengths and explain why they have made these judgments. They create learning goals that build on these strengths. They are also encouraged to create goals that will develop new skills. The teacher provides students with information about district and state expectations for fifth and sixth graders as a foundation for choosing academic goals. The students then discuss their goals with parents.

The students are given specific class time to work on their goals. However, many of the goals also fit naturally into the curriculum. As a whole class, students review and choose new goals approximately every 4 to 6 weeks during the school year. Individually, students choose new goals as soon as they accomplish their current goal. As the school year progresses, the goals become more specific and specialized. Figure 10.6 shows an example of one 6th grader's progress toward making her goals more specific over the school year.

Another component of upper grade self assessment and evaluation is learning to use scoring rubrics. The rubrics are designed by the class as a whole or by the teacher at the onset of an assignment. When a project has been completed, students evaluate their work comparing it to the expectations listed on the rubric.

Rubrics are used throughout the curriculum, primarily for long-term projects. Figure 10.7 depicts application of a rubric for assessing a writing project. After studying biographies, students and the teacher arrived at the list of

September	November	January
To write stories that won't need much editing.	To have a good beginning, middle, and a good end. I like writing a good story, but you can't have a good story without a beginning, middle, and end.	To develop characters that are interesting. A well-developed character has attitude, does action, has an appearance that is their own, and a unique speaking style.

March	May/June
To use more similies and metaphors in my descriptions because it makes my writing interesting.	To write during the summer. To put quality time into revising so my stories are not full of unnecessary words.

FIG. 10.6. Goals adopted by a sixth grader during an entire school year.

expectations that served students as a guideline when writing their own life history. The rubric comprises three levels of accomplishment: distinguished, commendable, and apprentice. For this assignment, the students decided that to achieve distinguished level they had to complete all 6 of the expectations, 4 to 5 expectations for commendable level, and 3 or fewer for apprentice level.

The top panel of Fig. 10.8 shows how Doneva responded to her work using the self-assessment sheet, which provided questions directly related to the expectations that assist students in assessing their work along the way. Doneva, a sixth-grade student, considered each of the expectations in judging her piece. This level of attention to detail will be a plus for her in future assessment tasks.

The bottom panel of Fig. 10.8 is from a student who had difficulty both with writing and with self-assessment. He judged his work to be commend-

1. Your paper must be detailed.
    A. no lists of facts
    B. facts written within paragraphs
2. Your paper must be nicely written or typed.
    A. paper should not be wrinkled
    B. no smudge marks
3. Your paper must demonstrated that it was carefully edited.
    A. no misspellings
    B. full and complete sentences
    C. logical organization
4. You paper must demonstrate evidence of revisions.
    A. expansion of detail when necessary
    B. elimination of non-necessary or redundant information
5. You must ask a minimum of fifteen questions.

You must decide which expectations you have met. In this process you must be able to clearly state how you know you have met these expectations.
    Ask yourself questions that are related to the expectations. For example; "How do I know that my paper is not just a list of facts?" (Expectation #1) or "Do I say the same thing twice?" (Expectation #4)

FIG. 10.7. First hand biography writing expectations.

First Hand Biography Self-Assessment

Name: D . . .

Distinguished: Has met all six expectations
<u>YES</u> No (underline one)
WHY?
Expectations that I accomplished.
Q. Is your paper detailed? A. It is not just a list, it has many paragraphs.
Q. Does my paper demonstrate careful editing? A. If you look on the sloppy copy you can see all the editing marks. My paper follows a logical pattern. When you read it you learn a lot about D.
Q. Is my paper nicely written or typed? A. You can see the cursive when you look at it.
Q. Your paper must demonstrate evidence of revisions. A. Look on the sloppy copy and you can see how I crossed out words and added words.
Q. You must ask a minimum of 15 questions. A. I have two pieces of paper that have the questions and answers I asked.
Q. Was my paper turned in on time? A. Yes I turned it in on time.
I met all the expectations. I did better than a commendable. This is going in to my showcase!

First Hand Biography Self-Assessment

Name: L . . .

Commendable: Has met 4-5 of the expectations
YES NO (underline one)
WHY? I had good detail and organization. It was in on time. It had full and complete sentences.

FIG. 10.8. Example of a commendable assessment using biography.

able, but without demonstrating the critical thinking skills that Doneva managed. His responses are simplistic and he is unable to point out where in his piece of writing he accomplished "good detail and organization." This student needs more time and exposure to quality writing.

Using a rubric teaches students to examine their work objectively. In addition, the practice of self-evaluation is a critical part in preparing for the student-facilitated (SF) conference. As the SF conference approaches, students can review progress toward their goals by looking for correlations between their work and their goals. The process, including the self-assessment forms, makes the task very explicit.

Some indication of students' reactions to the process comes from interviews obtained by Sara Smith, a graduate student at the University of California, Berkeley, who talked with two students from Klimenkov's upper elementary class about their perceptions of self-evaluation, goal setting, and the student-facilitated conference. Their responses, samples of which are shown in Fig. 10.9, demonstrate a sense of empowerment as well as an understanding and enjoyment of the process. The sixth-grade boy is clearly more involved in the process than the fifth-grade girl, but both are able to talk knowledgeably about their level of achievement. Their reactions to the SF conference, which we discuss later, are particularly interesting—a sense of apprehension beforehand, followed by relief and satisfaction afterward.

Student Interview: Sixth-Grade Boy

What kind of a student do you think you are? A good student, because I turn in all my work on time and I enjoy it and my teacher likes it too.

What do the words "evaluation" and "assessment" mean to you? To tell myself how good I'm doing, how I feel about my world; and the changes that have happened in my world.

How do you feel about assessing yourself? It is really hard but I guess it's getting easier this year because we are working harder at it.

What do you do with your portfolios at the end of the year? We take them home so we can just have them later, for like later in the future to look back at them. (laughs) I have never looked back at them though.

What is it like setting goals for yourself? It is sort of fun because you get to choose things that you want to do and accomplish them instead of having just your teacher saying that you're going to do this by the end of the year, even if you don't want to do it.

What do your friends feel about portfolios and self-assessment? Everyone sort of feels during the conferences like, sort of afraid, but once you are done then they really like them and understand what they've done and how they are doing in school.

What do you think your portfolio says about you as a student? That I have a lot of good talent in the subjects and I enjoy the school and learning about stuff.

What do you think people can learn about you from your portfolio? That I try in school and that it's not that hard for me to be a good student and learn a lot.

What goes into a showcase portfolio? The work that either my teacher likes a lot or you like a lot and, you know, you can choose anything you want that you liked. You put in one piece that you don't feel is your best and one that you're really proud of and compare them. My favorite ones I usually choose and then I just choose one I don't really care about but one that was still, you know, pretty good. It's sorta hard comparing them because you can't always see the differences or the similarities and improvements. But I mean, once you see one then they all appear — at first it's kind of hard to figure out but then you get it.

What kind of differences do you look for? Descriptions or character development or setting or plot in writing and then in, like reading, we look for the things that we recognize in the book, like mood and tone and stuff.

If you had your choice and could take either multiple choice tests and get scores from them, and have grades or do what you're doing here where you assess yourselves, which would you prefer? To assess myself —I mean—because I learn most from doing it.

What are the conferences like; can you describe one? You get your showcase, and first of all you show your goals and your self-evaluation sheets, and then you show them your good pieces and you compare them, and then you just show your other ones, just the ones you didn't compare. The parents have a list of questions they could ask, or they can think of their own. My teacher had to say something like, "See how much he's improved" or put something out and then they'd ask a question and I'd answer it.

How do you feel about working with your "little buddy" when preparing for conferences? It's fun, I mean, the little buddies are fun but it's sort of weird because they don't always understand everything and the things that you understand, they don't, so it's really hard to get them to understand what you're doing. But after you get them to understand it really feels good inside.

Student Interview: Fifth-Grade Girl

What kind of a student do you think you are? Just an average student—I don't think, like, I'm really good or really bad, just normal.

What do the words "evaluation" and "assessment" mean to you? Like, seeing how good I am at things by having to look, at the stuff in my portfolio.

How do you feel about assessing yourself? Sometimes it's sort of hard to think of things to say but then like once I get one idea they all just come. So, it's hard at the beginning but then I just know what to say.

Do you think you learn a lot about yourself when you look at your portfolio? Yeah. (In what way?) Umm, (laughs) let's see... (Do you see big differences when you see work-that you did early on in the year compared to work that you've done now?) Yeah. Like my hand writing is different.

FIG. 10.9. *(Continued)*

What is it like, setting goals for yourself? Um, let's see. Well, for lots of them it's really easy because I know what I need to do but some of them, like my physical goals, um, I don't know what to say and I like think and think and think.

How do you feel about talking about your strengths or things you are good at? Um, well sometimes I don't like to say it because sometimes I'll think that everyone is better than me at this, but sometimes I'm really proud of myself and I'll say it over and over again. So it depends on if I'm proud of myself or not.

What about the things that you don't like, or you don't feel you are that good at? I can talk to my friends about it but I can't really talk to the whole class about it. Like, sometimes I don't like reading my stories to the class because I don't feel like they were real good but sometimes I want to read my stories over and over again to the class.

What do your friends feel about portfolios and self-assessment? They don't really care and I don't really care either. It's just sometimes fun to do it and sometimes it's not because I want to be finishing up my other work. Sometimes my friends and I will have to finish it before it's due and we'll ask each other what we think; and I like that.

How do you feel about keeping a portfolio? I think it's a good idea to have the really good stuff separated from the normal stuff. I like it because I can look in there and go, "Oh yeah, I remember this." I like looking at what I've done before. Sometimes I'll forget to put it in my binder, but then I'll put it in my portfolio and go "wow!"

What happens to your portfolios at the end of the year? We'll take the work home but give the binder to our teacher so we can use the actual folders next year, and if we're graduating we just take it with us. (Have you kept your work from past years?) Yeah. (Do you ever look at it?) I have it all in a certain drawer in my desk that I keep all my other work that I've done from other years and one day I'll just look at it and go "oh yeah, I remember this" and I'll go through the whole drawer and it's really fun. I like looking at what I used to do. And I think it's funny when I can't read what I wrote before.

What kinds of questions do your parents ask about your portfolio? "How did you figure this out? Why did you do this? This is great. Who taught you how to do this?" (laughs) I have the best mom in the world.

How does she feel about the portfolios? I think that she thinks it neat because she likes it when I bring it home and she gets to look at it and stuff. And at conferences she likes to look; at it. Sometimes she's surprised on the work I've done, like if it's really, really good she'll be surprised or sometimes she'll be surprised if it's really, really bad. Sometimes she won't be surprised at all, she'll just be like "I knew this would be good."

What kind of differences do you look for when you are comparing pieces in your portfolio? Sometimes we compare pieces that we like and ones we don't really like and sometimes we'll compare ones from the beginning of the year and ones from the end of the year or our showcase pieces to our binder pieces. The differences I look for are the handwriting and the spelling and the words, like if I've described it a lot better or a lot worse.

What is it like running your own parent/teacher conference? I am really nervous at the beginning like, "oh no I'm going to do something wrong," but at the end it turns out to be really good and I'm proud of myself.

What are the conferences like? Can you describe one? We'll go in and show our stuff and then we will like, then the parents will ask us questions about it and then the teacher will like, say how she thinks we are doing, what's going on and what area I may need to work on.

Who sits down to review your portfolio with you at home? My mom usually does—my dad's at work really late. Sometimes in the morning if we have time he'll take a look at it though.

How do you feel about working with your little buddy when preparing for conferences? It's fun, and I like how my buddy will talk to me. Some of my friends don't like it at all. They don't want to be with their buddies. They think they're annoying. But I like my buddy.

Do you think your buddy understands what is going on? Sometimes she does. Sometimes she doesn't listen to my suggestions and she won't listen to the instructions and she'll do something wrong but we'll fix it. She'll sort of tell me how they did something but she has a hard time telling why she likes it. She'll sometimes say,"Cause it was fun" or "Because I worked hard on it."

What kinds of things do you think she should be saying instead? I learned this and it was fun learning this because, instead of this was horrible. But she is a little kid and I don't mind hearing her say that. My teacher wants us to take it a step farther. I don't care if my buddy says something like that but I'll correct her sometimes.

I don't know you very well so if I were to look at your scores or your portfolio which do you think I'd learn more from? Probably my portfolio, because with that you'd be able to see my work and how I did it. You'd actually be able to look at it instead of just saying "oh you got this (score) or you did this so well or did this so horrible—that would be really judging me." You can't really judge a person by their scores.

FIG. 10.9. Student interviews on portfolios and student-facilitated conferences.

CROSS-AGE INTERACTION:
PREPARING FOR THE CONFERENCE

> Working with my little buddy is fun, exciting, frustrating, and gets baby sitting jobs. We help our little buddies organize their binders. We play games with them. They feel like their big buddies are their best friend. Mark (one of my little buddies) asked me to read *Garfield* to him. It felt good inside. I love having little buddies and hope it continues through the years. (fifth-grade girl)

During the first year of student-facilitated conferences, we discovered that students had some difficulty explaining to parents what they knew and had accomplished. They also had difficulties explaining to their parents their goals and why they chose them. We concluded that giving the students more opportunity to communicate their strengths and weaknesses would increase motivation and confidence in preparing for the conference. With her younger students, NLP discovered that she needed to help students choose pieces of work, take dictation about their reflections of showcase pieces, and update their goals. It was difficult to assure that each student was fully prepared for the conference, because she did not have the time to meet with them individually. It became clear to both of us that we needed to give the students more opportunities to model and practice for the conferences.

As kindergarten–first grade and fifth–sixth grade teachers, we decided to turn this problem into an opportunity for establishing a cross-age interaction program. In the classroom, children are partnered with a cross-age buddy with whom they go through the process of self evaluation and preparation for the conferences.

The cross-age interaction program begins 2 months prior to each conference. To ensure success of the partnership, the pairing of students is carefully considered. As teachers, we consider such factors as learning styles, behavior, social maturity, language skills, personalities, and common interests. We first lead students through an initial series of experiences unrelated to the conference as a time for bonding and building of relationships. These activities include ice breakers, cooperative games, paired reading, and hands-on math. Teachers oversee the process to ensure an adequate level of comfort and good communication skills between the partners.

The buddies begin to prepare for the conference 1 month in advance. Part of the preparation process involves helping the younger students select their showcase pieces. A great deal of time is spent teaching the big buddies how to guide the little buddies through the process of selecting and assessing their work. The older students learn what kinds and how many pieces should be chosen from each section of the portfolio. The older students talk with the younger students about their accomplishments and signs of growth. The younger student then dictates to the big buddy his or her reasons for each selection. Big buddies are directed not to accept responses like "I worked hard" or "I like it" without further qualification. The response is then printed onto a paper titled "I am proud of this piece because . . ." This paper is then attached to the showcase piece. Together the buddies stamp the piece of work with an official "showcase" stamp. These pieces are then housed in the showcase portfolio.

The selection process is often the first experience in self-assessment for our younger learners. Reviewing class guidelines for good work and comparing their efforts to class standards takes practice for most children. The modeling that their older buddies provide when showing their own showcase selections has proved most valuable in helping the younger children understand the process and purpose.

The process of helping their little buddies choose showcase pieces is beneficial for the older students as well. It gives them insight into how their parents may react to their own work. They develop communication skills by asking questions of their little buddy. They discover that articulating how they are learning is essential to communicating their own improvement. They discover that they need concrete examples that will support their self-evaluation.

A second part of the conference preparation involves big buddies helping little buddies identify three specific things that they "can do well in school." These specifics are then recorded on a self-evaluation worksheet. This step is important in helping the younger student feel like a successful learner by identifying their strengths as a foundation for further development. In the conference, the self-evaluation form is compared to a similar form prepared earlier in the school year, allowing parent, child, and teacher to note progress in the student's abilities. This page is also kept in the showcase portfolio along with the previously selected showcase pieces and the goal card.

Figure 10.10 presents a sample self-evaluation worksheet. In October, Sammy, a kindergarten student, was asked to list three things he felt he could do well. His answers are broad and simplistic. He again listed his

Three Things I Do Well in School (October)

1. drawing
2. writing
3. counting

Three Things I Do Well in School (February)

1. I can pay attention well.
2. I play nicely with other people.
3. I can swing really high.

FIG. 10.10. Kindergarten self-evaluation worksheet prepared with buddy assistance.

strengths in February when his big buddy, Susy, helped him prepare for his conference. Here he demonstrates a greater understanding of his abilities and how to communicate his strengths to others. His February reflections emphasize his strength in social skills rather then academic skills. It appears that Sammy has come to realize the importance of social skills because considerable time is spent in the fall of the kindergarten year learning how to get along with others and solve problems independently. His October self-assessment was more academically based because that is what beginning kindergartners at Orion tend to think school is all about. Sammy's responses are typical for students in the first year of the self-assessment process. Their word choice by the second self-assessment activity is often reflective of the experience with the goals checklist.

For the older students, the process of choosing showcase pieces is lengthy. Students' first task is to review their current goals. As they review each goal, they record the degree to which they have accomplished it, along with evidence to support their claim. They then go through their portfolio, subject by subject, and choose pieces that reflect growth toward accomplishment of each goal. Finally they choose pieces from their binder portfolio to compare with the pieces they have chosen for their showcase portfolio. The comparison process requires them to cite similarities, differences, and signs of improvement in their work. They report improved skills and progress toward goals to parents, using this comparison paper as evidence.

Figure 10.11 illustrates the process for a typical student. Tyler completed his comparison report after he examined a piece of writing from his binder and compared it to a showcase piece. Both writing pieces were fiction. His task was to find signs of improvement using the class definition of "what makes a good writer," along with other information about good writing that he had collected during the school year.

When I (MK) examined Tyler's self-assessment, I was pleased to see Tyler incorporating the literary elements that had been taught in class. Tyler's assessment is typical of students who made the connection between their own work and the concepts taught in class. My next step was to ask Tyler how he knew that "Jeopardy has a lot more rising and falling action," and to ask him for examples to support this claim.

*Jeopardy has a lot more description and more understanding of paragraphs then Time Traveler.

*Jeopardy has a lot more rising and falling action.

*Jeopardy is neater then Time Traveler because it is easier to read and doesn't have as many errors.

*Jeopardy has a line of events and Time Traveler is scattered.

FIG. 10.11. Self-assessment by upper-grade student comparing works from early (*Time Traveler*) and late (*Jeopardy*) in school year.

Students of this age level often assess their writing according to volume rather than quality of writing. For example, one student wrote, "Summary of *Where the Red Fern Grows* is a lot longer than *Animals of the Rain Forest*." My question to this student was "Can you identify the other improvements in your writing?" I asked her to think about the lessons we had worked on recently in class and how these influenced her writing. Her response indicated that she could indeed identify improvements in her writing. She wrote, "In the summary of *Where the Red Fern Grows* I put my writing into paragraphs. The paragraphs have more description then in *Animals of the Rain Forest*."

The final preparatory step for the conference is a practice session in which students present their showcase folders and the self-evaluation derived from its contents. The older students are given a checklist of steps to follow with their little buddies. They are trained not only how to guide their little buddies through the conference steps, but also how to play the role of parent. The checklist includes questions that parents may ask to guide the big buddies. Of course, these questions prepare the older students for questions that their own parents may ask of them.

Big buddies help to evaluate the process by listing any areas of difficulty and/or success the little buddy experienced during practice. Buddies practice without any time constraints until they are familiar with the conference format. In the final practice, the older student is asked to keep track of the time spent on each conference step in order to stay within the 30-minute time limit of the actual conference.

This practice process has become an important step in our conferencing process, both for older and younger learners. Each student has an opportunity to practice communication skills, which builds confidence in presenting his or her work. Observing another student presenting his or her work models other options and ideas to include in a presentation. When older students are given the opportunity to play the role of the parent, they gain insight into the parent's point of view.

The Student-Facilitated (SF) Conference

After many hours of preparation, the students are finally ready to share the results of their work with parents. The classroom atmosphere becomes tinged with excitement and some anxiety. As teachers, we look forward to being part of a conference in which our students take charge and have an opportunity to discuss their accomplishments with parents.

On the day of the conference, child and parent arrive together and make themselves comfortable in the classroom. The child's portfolio, teacher narrative, and checklist are ready and waiting. The degree of teacher participation in the student presentation portion of the conference decreases as the student progresses through the grades. In the child's very first experience with the conference in the K–1 class, the teacher follows the same format that the children have practiced with their buddies, encouraging or helping each student through the sharing process as necessary. The conference takes place at a round table where the student sits close to his or her parents and the teacher sits on the opposite side.

In the fifth–sixth grade classroom, each student decides where he or she wishes to conduct the conference. Students have the option of sitting at a table or on a couch in the library area. They can either position themselves between the adults or in close proximity to their parent.

After a brief introduction of the conference process by the teacher, the student begins sharing the portfolio. The teacher sits on the periphery and intervenes when he or she feels that reinforcement or clarification is necessary. As practiced with their classmates, the students describe the evidence of growth and share their goals for the future. Parents ask questions, and typically offer support and give praise. Time is allotted for the teacher to share her own records, and to make any comments or suggestions to help the child reach for academic excellence.

Parent Involvement

Parents are actively involved in the self-assessment model at Orion School, and their ideas are highly valued in the Orion portfolio process. When the portfolio binder is sent home, it includes a cover letter requesting parent comments. Based on parent feedback, for instance, we extended the confer-ence time from 20 to 30 minutes in order to provide the students ample time to present their work and answer questions. This extension also ensured that the teacher had time to present his or her report and to confer with the parents.

The Orion School staff also conducts a parent education night when the staff explains the portfolio process and the student-facilitated conference. Information and examples of previous portfolios are presented, and veteran Orion parents discuss their experiences with the process. Teachers talk about how important it is for adults to shift their attention to the child during this type of conference. They role play the conference process, offering sugges-tions about where to sit, whom to look at, and whom to address when asking questions. Sample questions are presented and discussed during the role playing. Parents are encouraged to be clear in their expectations, but also to be supportive, not only in the questions they ask, but also in their attention to what the child is saying and in the body language they exhibit.

EVALUATION OF THE ORION PROJECT
AND NEXT STEPS

We have observed a variety of positive changes in Orion students since the initial implementation of our portfolio program and the conference. Students recognize that they have assumed much greater responsibility for their own learning. They can thoughtfully correct their own mistakes, but often express amazement when discovering how much they have grown. They can identify their accomplishments and take pride in them. The students have also become much more organized in keeping track of their work. They have learned to choose more realistic goals and accomplishments that are achievable in a reasonable time frame. Additionally, the students appear more confident and in control when facilitating the parent–teacher–student conference as they progress through the grades.

The parents have begun to show a greater trust in developmentally based learning. They are more confident that their child is achieving and gaining skills at a natural rate of development. Some parents have even taken the self-assessment process further, asking their children to choose goals for the home environment as well!

Even those children who are less than completely successful with the self-assessment and conference process are showing growth and development because of it. In fact, the conference has proven to be an invaluable tool for both teacher and parents for learning more about how to help children with special school needs. Some children are not successful because they have not been putting forth sincere effort. This lack of motivation becomes quite obvious at the conference; students cannot show evidence of growth. In an immediate and concrete way, parents, teacher, and student see the problem. Conference time is spent in these cases defining the problems the child is facing, and together taking the next steps to help the child create more focused goals.

Some children have difficulties not with their schoolwork, but with the self-evaluation process, especially when it comes to admitting shortcomings in their own work. During the conference, these students cannot avoid this issue. With parent and teacher present and supportive, the child must take a more honest look at his or her work. The adults then have an opportunity to establish a more direct monitoring and support system for the student.

A few children encounter social barriers to success in the conference. Despite preparation and practice, they may have stage fright during the actual event. When we have run into such cases, we return to the goal-setting process to help students improve their public speaking skills and develop a public voice. We have seen several students become more open and confident as they practice year after year.

Of course, any instructional innovation naturally involves obstacles and snags that need to be worked out. We encountered challenges in managing time and materials in the classroom, lack of parent "buy-in," and a decline in portfolio use after the mid-year conference.

Especially in the beginning, we found that there was not enough time for students to work on their goals, nor for teachers to check students' goals and help them select new goals. The only answer to this problem was to prioritize. We have made an effort to ensure that goals time is a regular part of the week's program, and to better use parent volunteers to help us manage this important process.

As the program got underway, we discovered several organizational challenges. Where do we store the binders, showcase portfolios, and tapes (audio or video) to ensure that children and parents have easy access to them? Each teacher eventually found the space in his or her room, and we openly invite parents to visit at any time. How often should the binders go home? In response to parent requests, the work has gone home more and more frequently. The current guideline is every 2–6 weeks. Other questions we have tackled include how to keep up with the filing, and what to do when the binder does not come back to school after a home visit. We have tried to involve both parents and students in the resolution of these problems, and although some issues remain to be resolved, we have a sense of clear-cut progress.

The unresolved issues are predictable ones. Although most parents are openly supportive of developmental learning, some remain skeptical, and therefore, unhappy with the student-centered conference and the goal-setting process. It is difficult for the child to fully benefit if his or her efforts are not valued at home. The staff puts forth a great deal of effort to communicate to parents how crucial their role is in helping their child's education progress. As noted earlier, we conduct parent education nights, distribute educational literature, and communicate to parents how crucial their role is in helping their child's educational progress. Nonetheless, a small group has remained reluctant to support this assessment strategy.

A second problem is the "poop-out" effect. Portfolio activity tends to decline after the mid-year conference. In an effort to sustain the level of activity throughout the entire year, some teachers have extended the process with a spring follow-up conference or with an at-home conference. A few staff members have conducted mini-conferences in which several students meet with their parents at the same time and place. This "portfolio preview" occurs before the last set of parent–teacher conferences in May. Other teachers have attempted to bring closure to the whole process after the final parent–teacher conference by asking students to take home the binder portfolio, choose new "showcase" pieces, and fill out "I am Proud" papers with their parents. Then student and parents together review the child's goals for summer and prepare a letter for the next year's teacher. Upper-grade students write a letter to their next year's teacher, outlining the contents of their showcase portfolios and listing new goals for the upcoming school year.

Orion School will continue to change and expand with new staff members, new families, and the changing needs of our student population. As we do, our portfolios and conferences will continue to be refined. For the coming year, we have planned professional inservice meetings in which the aim is to establish more common ground for efficient and effective portfolio implementation. The meetings will also allow us to enhance our techniques for teaching children to assess themselves. We intend to develop a more consistent schoolwide program, in which a child's "showcase" portfolio advances with him or her each year, and in which children who leave the school have something to carry with them.

Orion is a small school in a district of 14 schools and approximately 8,400 students. We are currently the only district school using portfolios and the student-facilitated conference as our primary assessment tool. There are pockets of interest throughout the district in portfolio use, and many teachers are using portfolios for other purposes.

Given the smallness of our school, and our previous commitment to a narrative reporting system, the conference was a natural outgrowth and now has become a vital component of our program. The self-analysis and self-direction that the conference develops could, in principle, be a valuable addition to any school's assessment program. For example, a program that uses a grade-based system of evaluation could lend deeper meaning to letter or number grades through the use of rubrics and the conference. But the process is likely to be workable only as it operates developmentally; the student who shifts from one assessment procedure to another with changing grades is unlikely to benefit, and may well become confused and frustrated—likewise for the parents.

Nonetheless, our experience leads us to encourage others to adapt, adopt, and reap the benefits of our experience. Our advice is to proceed slowly, involve parents and students, determine and maintain a purpose for the portfolio process, include child reflection and response, be open to new ideas, and remain flexible. It is difficult to put into words the excitement we share with our students as they recognize their own growth, as they choose their own learning goals and reach them, and as they communicate their strengths (and weaknesses). Our cross-age interaction program significantly enhances the educational experience for all involved—for teachers, for parents, and for students, who will ultimately use these skills throughout their lives.

CHAPTER ELEVEN

Portfolios: Bridging Cultural and Linguistic Worlds

Nanette Koelsch
Elise Trumbull
Far West Laboratory for Educational Research and Development

This chapter examines the potential of portfolio assessment to create a bridge between the cultural and linguistic worlds of ethnolinguistically nondominant students and the dominant culture and language of schooling. In particular, it focuses on a cross-cultural portfolio project under development that links the culture and community of Navajo students in an Arizona public school with district and state educational requirements for accountability. This project provides a center point from which to consider how portfolio assessment can promote meaningful teaching and learning opportunities for both Native students and Native and non-Native teachers. Portfolio assessment for ethnolinguistically nondominant students is considered in light of theoretical perspectives on language, learning, and assessment. The balance and tension between the assessment practices that potentially inform teaching and those that serve the requirements of statewide accountability are also examined.

PORTFOLIO ASSESSMENT AND THE ARIZONA
STUDENT ASSESSMENT PROGRAM

The Chinle Portfolio Project attempts to link district and community goals for education with state requirements for learning. Chinle Unified School District, an Arizona public school district located in the heart of the Navajo Reservation, began portfolio assessment within the context of changes in testing and accountability requirements at the state level.

In 1990, assessment in Arizona changed dramatically. The Arizona legislature, the state Board of Education, and the Department of Education implemented the Arizona Student Assessment Program (ASAP). This comprehensive accountability program aims at improving teaching, learning, and assessment throughout the state, and requires, as part of the reform effort, that all districts assess students for mastery of the Arizona Essential Skills in mathematics, reading, and writing. In addition, Grades 3, 8, and 12 are audited by the state for student achievement through performance assessments directly linked to the Arizona Essential Skills. These assessments include short answer, essay, and other direct demonstrations of students' achievement in mathematics, reading, and writing.

All 210 school districts are struggling with the demands of assessment reform. Districts are required to develop a District Assessment Plan (DAP), which describes how and when they will assess students for mastery of the essential skills throughout the grades. Districts may use portfolios, criterion-referenced tests, and nonstate forms of the ASAP that have been designed for several grade levels. Some districts have opted to retain computerized criterion-referenced tests. Others, like Chinle, have fashioned an assessment plan that includes portfolios as well as the nonstate ASAP assessments.

The Chinle Context

The decision of the Chinle Unified School District to develop a portfolio system that yields information for external reporting of student achievement *and* for teaching and learning was based on several factors. First, Native American students historically underachieve on state tests. District student performance on the first administration of the state level ASAP followed this trend; Native American student scores were the lowest in the state on the first statewide administrations of assessments in 1992. Second, state forms available to districts were too difficult for fourth-, fifth-, and sixth-grade students at Chinle. During the first year of district assessment, the proportion of students attaining mastery at the fifth and sixth grades was 1% and 2%, respectively. Teachers reported that the assessment provided by the state for district use was inadequate for the district's context. The topics of the performance assessments were so far removed from the reality of life on the Navajo Reservation that students were unable to demonstrate what they knew. Teachers and students did not have access to appropriate performance-based assessments for several years between benchmark testing. Third, the district developed Navajo curriculum and thematic-integrated curriculum in response to the needs of Chinle students. Chinle educators wanted to begin development of a district portfolio that would fill in gaps, link culturally responsive curriculum with state level accountability requirements, and show others what their students can do.

Why Portfolio Assessment: Theory to Practice

Portfolio assessment is especially appealing for use with ethnolinguistically nondominant students because of its ability to contextualize student performance and because of its flexibility to include a range of types of student performance. For example, a teacher or student can clarify the conditions surrounding a performance (e.g., kind and degree of assistance, preceding instruction/experience, student conative and cognitive response) by annotating entries that are included in the portfolio. That is, the teacher or student may write brief comments that describe exactly what took place between teacher and student or between/among students to result in the performance. A student may simply write a sentence about what helped him or her to complete a task.

Important cultural context can be reflected in the use of flexible content focus within a task, as when students write about topics meaningful to them or link literature or subject-matter reading to their own experiences. A portfolio may contain not only written performances but spoken (audiotaped) or videotaped performances in any language, as well as many other kinds of entries. In short, the portfolio assessment process allows standards and criteria for judging student performance to be held constant, while activities (and their form and content) can vary to reflect local meanings.

Contextualization of student performance is especially important for students whose first language is not English (and who are being taught and assessed in English). In fact, some experts have argued that to fail to document the context of performance makes judgments about it invalid (Anastasi, 1990). We must not forget that part of the context is the curriculum and instruction to which students have had access.

In addition, when portfolios include multiple samples of different types of student work over a period of time, they can provide a more complex and meaningful portrayal of students as learners. This feature of portfolio assessment is particularly important for ethnolinguistically nondominant students because of the susceptibility of measures to bias—and the resulting misdiagnosis of such students' educational needs.

The previous description of portfolios presents the positive use of this assessment methodology to reflect individual context and to inform teaching and learning at a local level. If equity in assessment can be conceived of, in part, as allowing students opportunities to show what they have learned and how they understand it, portfolios (through their processes) may constitute one of the more equitable assessment tools available. At present, many educators using portfolios argue that the best use of portfolios may be between teachers and students, rather than for widescale accountability (Tierney, 1994; Yancey, 1992).

However, a portfolio that is comprehensible to only a few cannot be used to report student performance to others. For this reason the purpose and audience for portfolio assessment determine its development and use. If portfolios are meant to be assessed by those outside of the classroom, questions of validity, reliability, and generalizability become critical. Lack of attention to psychometric principles may result in the dismissal of portfolio assessment by outside readers. If portfolios can be understood only at the local level, they cannot be used to report achievement between levels—whether the articulation occurs within the K–12 system, or between secondary and post-secondary schooling or employment. Other measures, many of which are inequitable, become the only tools available to judge student performance. Thus, tension between the use of portfolios at a local level and their use outside of their place of origin represents a challenge to the field.

Chinle Portfolio Assessment: High Standards and Negotiated Meanings

The Chinle portfolio project is testing the belief that portfolios can be used simultaneously for the purposes of assessing student work against standards and criteria and for negotiating meaning in a culturally congruent way, without compromising either purpose. These purposes are both distinct and incompatible with a traditional measurement model.

The measurement model assumes that a student's achievement in a given subject area can been treated as a trait that can be measured and compared to that trait in other students; excellence is equivalent to outranking other students (Taylor, 1994). Taylor (1994) suggested that by choosing the measurement model we have in effect reinforced what we already know—"that test performance is highly correlated with social and economic conditions. We need not face the difficulties of structuring schools in ways that help students achieve standards. We need not face the social and economic changes that are necessary for success . . . The measurement model will not provide standards of quality toward which we want our students to strive" (p. 248).

In contrast, the standards model (Taylor, 1994) eliminates the whole concept of comparing students to each other as well as the notion of a "normal curve" of performance. Instead, student performances are assessed against sets of standards, using agreed-on criteria. At this time, national groups are in the process of developing broad standards that may or may not be acceptable to local communities. If it turns out to be possible to subscribe to broad standards that allow latitude for local interpretation (incorporating cultural contexts), and if ways of assessing students can be kept flexible enough to reflect community contexts, then the standards model may prove more equitable and valid than the measurement model. In any case, moving away from ranking students against each other toward assessing them in light of standards reflects a more current and defensible view of student learning: All students have the potential to achieve at a high level, given adequate opportunities to learn.

Within the project discussed in this chapter, the question of which standards and whose standards has been resolved from the bottom up. During the first year of the project, attention was focused on developing a system that worked for teachers and students and for the district context. Standards, tasks, and rubrics that reflect the shared values of the school and the community are now in place. An essential aspect of this connection is the incorporation of the Navajo philosophy of learning into the portfolio through the inclusion of a cultural standard (the Life Skills standard) and through integrated standards and tasks. The notion of integration and interconnection is key to Navajo philosophy. Learning, whether it takes place in school or within the community, is holistic. That is, within the community, realms of knowledge are not necessarily analyzed or taught as disciplines, nor are thinking processes taught independent of application to the contexts in which ideas are meaningful.

The Navajo philosophy of life is expressed in the phrase *to walk in beauty.* To walk in beauty refers to the ongoing process of recognizing the interconnectedness of all life and of engaging in ways of knowing and being that promote harmony among all living things. For the Navajo, this philosophy is grounded in directionality—north, south, east, and west; and the sacred mountains located in each of these points play an important role in all aspects of life. The traditional Navajo home, the hogan, a six- or eight-sided structure, opens to the east or the sun. Other directional points are specifically located within the hogan. All activities taking place within the hogan occur within these points of reference. The multiple sides of the hogan encompass these points but also suggest the circularity or organic whole of life through the creation of spherical, interior space. The child first learns to walk in beauty within the home and within the clan he or she is "born to" (Kinship relationships provide a structure for interaction within Navajo life. Very young children learn to reference their mother's clan as the clan they are born to and their father's clan as the clan they are born for. Marriage must occur outside of one's clans.). This learning is extended to the larger community of the tribe and the world outside of the Navajo nation. Walking in beauty entails a complex awareness of points of reference, multiple layers of relationship, and the interconnectedness of all life.

The district's long term goal for schooling is that Navajo culture and the Navajo way of being walk side by side with non-Native culture (referred to as "Anglo" in the community) and ways of being throughout students' K–12 education. In keeping with this goal, the district has developed extensive curriculum that integrates language arts, science, and social studies at the elementary level and is committed to developing integrated curriculum at the secondary level. School curriculum is delivered through oral, written, and visual texts. Navajo culture is taught via both English and Navajo languages. Although all students study Navajo each day—and some teachers speak Navajo in the classroom—students, for the most part, learn and display their school and cultural learning through reading, writing, listening, and speaking in English and through visual arts projects.

Chinle Portfolio Standards

Teachers developing the portfolio model felt strongly that portfolio standards should address the district's goal of bi-cultural education. They wanted to develop integrated standards, tasks, and rubrics that embodied the values of the community and the schools. The decision to include only four standards reflected an awareness of the importance of the the four directions and four sacred mountains within the Navajo philosophy of learning. The standards are:

- *Environmental or Cultural Awareness and Responsibility.* Students will develop an awareness of their local and global environment through exploration of the cultures and ecosystems within them. They will be able to identify systems of organization and cause and effect relationships which exist in the world now and historically in order to effect change.
- *Communication.* Students will communicate their academic, social, and affective knowledge and understanding to a variety of audiences and for a variety of purposes.
- *Life Skills. Shá Bik'eh Hozhóón* (a phrase that refers to the principle of walking in beauty throughout one's life): Students will be able to analyze, synthesize, apply, evaluate, and produce knowledge for basic life skills.
- *Mathematical Understanding and Power.* Students will be able to communicate mathematical concepts as they demonstrate their understanding through modeling, identifying, and extending concepts as they learn.

Navajo teachers working on the Life Skills standard drew a figure (Fig. 11.1) to symbolize the connection of school learning to the Navajo Way. For them, the portfolio model paralleled the model of learning embodied by the hogan. Their graphic has become an important tool for communicating the goals of the portfolio to the parents and to the community.

The fourth standard, Mathematical Understanding and Power, is the only domain-specific standard. This standard emerged from two contradictory sources: one, the National Council of Teachers of Mathematics (NCTM) standards and two, the textbound mathematics curriculum in the elementary schools. The NCTM standards are important to the district. Curriculum guides that emphasize the teaching, learning, and assessment of mathematical strands at every grade level have just been developed. However, in the absence of new textbooks and teaching methodologies, teachers tend to teach mathematics in a sequential, skills-based way. The teachers involved in the portfolio project felt that the subject-specific math standard reflected both their need to develop their teaching of mathematics and the reality of how they teach currently. As time goes by, and teachers become more accomplished at

Shá Bik'eh Hózhóón

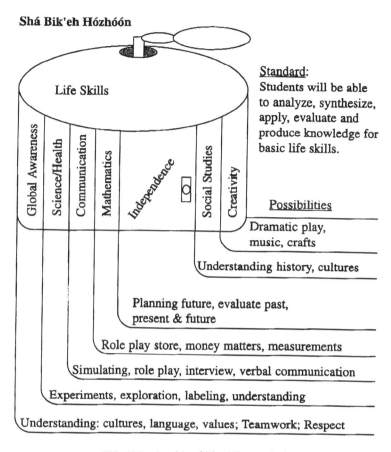

FIG. 11.1. Graphic of life skills standard.

performance-based mathematical teaching and learning, it may well be that the mathematics standards will change to reflect a more integrated approach.

Student performance is assessed through the use of rubrics tied to the standards and through state generic rubrics. The incorporation of two sets of rubrics into the portfolio occurred for several reasons. First, the state requires that all districts report the number of students achieving a mastery level using the generic rubrics. However, the generic rubrics in reading, writing, and mathematics are not in line with the district's goal of integrated, bi-cultural education and are inadequate for that purpose. Because teachers wanted a way to assess environmental, historical, cultural, and symbolic ways of knowing, they developed rubrics tied to the district's portfolio standards. Second, although the four-point generic rubrics are easy to utilize, they do not provide meaningful teaching and learning information. They are too general to be of use in the classroom. The more specific and detailed portfolio rubrics provide assessment information that teachers wanted to have to inform instruction.

At present, teachers have the choice of which rubrics to use. If mastery in reading, writing, or mathematics based on the portfolio task is to be reported to the state, the generic rubrics are used. If student achievement of district and community expectations for learning is the focus of assessment, the district's rubrics are used. With these components in place, the focus of the second year of the project will be on implementing a system that remains contextualized and meaningful as well as reportable.

Addressing validity and reliability in the context of a cross-cultural portfolio raises complex and intriguing questions. Native teachers have developed the tasks specifically referencing Navajo culture and language. Questions of content and construct validity for these tasks will need to be negotiated cross-culturally. At present, teachers feel that Native educators, tribal members, and non-Native educators should all participate in this process.

The participation of educators who are knowledgeable about Navajo ways is important to the success of the Chinle cross-cultural portfolio. If a teacher is not knowledgeable about the culture and what is valued for student performance, the expertise of others, including the students, becomes crucial for valid and reliable assessment. For this reason, a hermeneutic model of assessment concerned with constructing the meaning of a performance guides the portfolio project. A hermeneutic approach values validity over reliability—that is, what is traditionally viewed as reliability. The job of a teacher as an assessor is to document in negotiation with the student how student performance is understood. Reliability then consists in a second reader's being able to confirm the judgment of the first reader/assessor through examining the same evidence and the assessor's documentation (Delandshere & Petrosky, 1994; Moss, 1994).

A hermeneutic approach assumes that contextual and negotiated meanings are available, that there is access to opportunites for authenic teacher–student interaction. The development of the Chinle portfolio proved to be a valuable learning tool for non-Native teachers. The standards, tasks, and rubrics elucidate connections between school and community contexts, and the negotiation processes that occur focus on constructing the meaning of a student's performance from Native and non-Native points of view—a necessary step toward establishing grounds for bicultural meaning.

Negotiating Authorship and Authority: Portfolio Texts and Contexts

The portfolio model developed by Chinle teachers represents an intersection of the perspectives schools within the district and of Native American and non-Native teachers. The demographics of Chinle Unified School District shape interactions among schools and teachers involved in the portfolio project. There are three elementary schools in the district. Chinle Elementary School is located in the town of Chinle, and 11 of the 16 teachers participating in the project teach fifth grade at this site. Many Farms Elementary School is approximately 13 miles away from Chinle, and three participating fifth-grade teachers teach there. Tsaile Elementary School, where the other two fifth-grade teachers teach, is located in the northeastern corner of the district, about 40 miles from Chinle.

Chinle Elementary, the largest and most centrally located school, attracts a yearly crop of non-Native teachers who learn of the school at job fairs around the country. During the portfolio development year, 5 of the 11 fifth-grade teachers at Chinle Elementary were new in the district; and three were new to teaching. Other teachers at this school are Navajo or are married to Navajos and have been in the district for years. Teachers at the other sites are veterans. With the exception of one non-Native, all four teachers at the other sites are Native American; three are Navajo. Thus, the majority of non-Native teachers are new to the district; and they teach at Chinle Elementary, the school with the largest population of fifth-grade students.

New teachers do receive some support for learning about Navajo culture. They attend two days of inservice at the curriculum center in which they learn the importance of integrated teaching, cooperative structures within the classroom, and some techniques for teaching students who are learning English. New teachers receive information about Navajo curriculum developed by the district. In the past, one district staff person took the new non-Native teachers to her hogan, a traditional Navajo home, for a 1-week introduction to traditional Navajo life. The week of sheep herding and living without water or toilets that flush culminated in the butchering of a sheep and the eating of mutton stew, a staple of the traditional Navajo diet. Because of work commitments, this staff person has not been able to take the new teachers to her home in recent years. New teachers regret this lack of real-life introduction and believe that if the practice were still occurring they would understand more about the lives of their students, many of whom travel 1½ hours by bus to reach school.

Teachers developing the Chinle portfolio project believed that encouraging student authority and student ownership of the portfolio developed additional connections between the norms of school and community. Navajo children are given responsibility for livestock at a very young age. They herd sheep and tend to animals year-round. Elders teach new responsibilities through an apprenticeship model. Children assist and help their elders until the elders feel the children are ready to assume the tasks themselves. Teachers want students to assume similar responsibility for their learning. However, if school ways of knowing and displaying knowledge clash with home and community norms, students feel they must choose one over the other or split school from the rest of their lives. Because the portfolio model embeds assessment in instruction and across time and allows for multiple measures of achievement, the portfolio model is more congruent with the Navajo philosophy of learning than the other measures available to school districts in Arizona. On a very concrete level, the portfolio can function as an apprentice model of teaching and learning.

To provide an apprentice-like structure, Chinle teachers organized the portfolio so that teachers and students work together to author the portfolio. At times, teachers author the portfolio by virtue of deciding that an assessment activity or task will be included in the portfolio, a decision that students are informed of before they begin the performance assessment. Standards and rubrics are also shared with students. At other times, students author the portfolio by deciding on "free choice" selections or writing letters of introduction, reflections on their work, self-assessments, and their own conference comments. Students, however, have authority over their portfolios in that they can say who, other than their teacher, has access to the work.

Questions of authority and authorship extend beyond the ways in which teachers and students within classrooms negotiate power to larger cross-cultural questions of what constitutes knowledge and how student performance is judged. The portfolio model developed by teachers represents a synthesis of school and community ways of knowing and doing, a cross-cultural negotiation of authority and authorship. Teachers convey portfolio standards through teaching and learning events that reflect their own teaching style and classroom and school contexts. Far West Laboratory (FWL) "task shells" frame the cognitive and structural components of tasks across disciplines and leave content flexible. The task shells are, in effect, templates for task development. Each of the four shells, as seen in Table 11.1, outlines cognitive descriptions of types of tasks. The structural descriptions remain stable across task shells to promote reliability of tasks across settings.

Teachers may develop their own tasks using these shells, use each other's tasks, or use tasks adapted from outside sources. The model balances structure with flexibility and allows teachers and students to negotiate cultural and school worlds in varying ways. Any one portfolio or portfolio entry substantiates how a teacher and student traverse cross-cultural teaching and learning.

The Importance of Cultural Context and Schooling

Both Native and non-Native teachers involved in the portfolio development process voiced the need to make explicit the multiple ways in which the portfolio model connects the contexts of schooling with the contexts of the community. Non-Native teachers, especially those new to the district, need and want knowledge about Navajo culture and how they might integrate it into their teaching. On the reservation, non-Navajo teachers live in compounds far removed from the life of the community. Although Navajo district

TABLE 11.1
Domains of Performance for Chinle Portfolio Tasks

Overview	Task Shell 1	Task Shell 2	Task Shell 3	Task Shell 4
Task shells describe domains of performance across the curriculum	Collecting and representing real data	Investigating the world	Examining, representing, and evaluating information	Creating new models and symbols
Content requirements of shells	• Make predictions of, generate or collect data to verify • Describe methods and organize data • Interpret data • Evaluate results	• Make connections between academic learning and world • Apply communication techniques or academic concepts to represent current situations • Evaluate application of academic tools and techniques	• Demonstrate knowledge of a subject • Describe significant aspects of a subject • Provide concrete representation of understanding • Evaluate learning	• Generate original models and symbolic forms • Create symbolic representations using aural, written, visual, or other modes • Evaluate models and forms based on tools and goals • Set further goals
Subject matter	Science and mathematics	Writing, mathematics, social studies, health, and science	Reading, science, social studies	Art, writing, social studies, mathematics, and science
Structural requirements	• Tasks are introduced and discussed in class but completed on a group or individual basis independently • Tasks include time for revision • Final products may include support materials • Tasks include individual evaluation of final product			
Examples of specific tasks	• Job task • Science fair task • Household survey task	• Position paper task • Hero task • Scale model task • Environmental task	• Voyage of the Mimi • Plant book tasks • Biome tasks • Generic social studies task • Generic reading task	• Fine arts task • Poetry task • Invention task

staff do live in the compounds, for the most part non-Natives are segregated from the Navajo way of life. Yet, they teach in a community in which the Navajo way, walking in beauty, is a vital and nourishing way of life. The new teachers' lack of knowledge about the customs and practices of the Navajo results in a kind of cautious distance from talking about culture in the classroom. The violation of a cultural precept can result in a family's holding a costly ceremony to undo the damage done by an unsuspecting outsider. New teachers are aware of this and are anxious about placing such a burden on families.

The demographics of the district and the need for consensus building had been discussed prior to FWL's first workshop in September of 1993. The desire and need for cultural training on the part of the non-Navajo teachers surfaced during the second workshop in October, as teachers engaged in activities designed to identify and describe key content standards.

During the presentation of the Life Skills standard, Navajo teachers discussed the graphic they had developed to communicate the connection between school learning and the Navajo philosophy of learning (Fig. 11.1). One teacher, a non-Navajo Native American teacher married to a Navajo, asked about the inclusion of planning for the future in the graphic, a practice she thought against the Navajo way. Several Navajo teachers began discussing the ways in which planning occurs in the culture: feeding and caring for livestock, holding ceremonies, caring for family and clan members, and planting were mentioned. In Navajo terms, the health and viability of the community rest on these planned activities. A key difference between the Navajo and Western notions of planning, they explained, was the negative value Navajos attach to planning for personal or individual gain. Such a practice runs counter to the collective good and leaves a person vulnerable to personal disaster.

Teachers continued the discussion by talking about how traditional and less traditional Navajos differed on what constituted personal gain. One teacher offered the information that her mother had difficulty with the fact that she was saving money for her child's education when family members needed help. This teacher told the group that she felt she was "walking in two worlds," because she was helping her family and clan by saving for her son's future. Another teacher discussed how she incorporates the notion of future planning within her classroom. She explained that she keeps a timeline of historical events in her classroom and that each year she notes the year that her current fifth-grade class will graduate from high school. However, when she refers to the timeline and the future, she is careful to talk about graduation as one possible narrative of how a person's life might unfold—not as a linear certainty.

After this discussion, one teacher voiced how much she had learned and how vital the information was to her as a new teacher in the district, a sentiment echoed by other teachers. Non-Native teachers had heard that "Navajos don't plan for the future" and that to stress the future in the classroom violated the culture. The opportunity for in-depth discussion afforded by the portfolio development, particularly through the inclusion of the Life Skills standard, partly satisfies the desire and need for cultural knowledge and negotiation.

As teachers began to develop tasks, they often integrated the Life Skills or cultural standard with the Communication standard. These tasks were assessed through the dual lens of school based and culturally based standards for performance.

One instance of such integration is seen in a literacy task, the "Hero Task," shown in Fig. 11.2. When mapped to both the Life Skills and the

Hero Task

Standards: Communication and Life Skills

Performance Task Domain: Investigating the World

Task Overview: For the task the student will use the writing process to publish a fictional or nonfictional narrative about a "hero," whether personal or well-known. The book will incorporate the visual symbolism of a mandala, or circular symbolic design depicting the character traits of the chosen "hero." The student will also design an end-of-the-book activity. A student may list key vocabulary words in a glossary and hide them within a linear drawing. Or, after assigning each letter of the alphabet a numerical value, a student may use these values to write vocabulary words in a secret code, and then into a message.

Time: 3-4 weeks

Prompt to Students: In this task you will write a narrative story as fiction or nonfiction about a person you see as a hero. You will examine the values, strengths, achievements, and struggles of this person, as we did when we brainstormed the personality traits of the main character in the novel *Island of the Blue Dolphins.*

Re-explanation for Students: You will complete this book individually or with a partner and present or share the final copy with the class.

To accomplish this task you will need to:

- Complete the class study of the novel in cooperative groups.
- Discuss the thoughts and reactions one of the characters has to an event in the story. (How does this help determine personality traits? What are some of their personality traits?)
- Recall why people were introduced as heroes in art class, music class, and in the thematic unit on heroes presented by the librarian.
- Brainstorm various types of heroes. (Ask yourself why they are considered to be independent, responsible, creative, or courageous, including people in your family or community.)
- Write in your journal about the reasons you consider this person to be a hero.
- Design a mandala of symbols which reflects traits of your hero, and then write a simile.
- Write and illustrate your narrative fiction or nonfiction piece.
- Design a cover, using the mandala if you wish.
- Design end-of-book activity.
- Share your work with others and the teacher as you develop it. Ask for feedback. Go public with it, and present the final copy.

FIG. 11.2. Hero writing task.

Communication content and performance standards, it illuminates how one non-Native teacher and her students negotiated school and community values. The task asked students to write a fiction or nonfiction narrative about a hero. Students had read the novel *Island of the Blue Dolphins* and engaged in a series of literacy-based activities to connect their understanding of the story of a young girl becoming a hero to talking and writing about heroes in their own lives.

As a preliminary writing activity, students wrote a short piece on a hero in their own lives. One student wrote about her grandfather's taking her to a medicine man who performed a ceremony. The teacher talked about her response to the piece during a classroom visit. She said that she treated the piece very differently from how she would have in the past. Once, she would have placed the student's work in the hallway in keeping with writing process pedagogy of "publishing" student work and creating an audience for student writers. However, she reported that she now questioned that act on the basis of two factors: one, the sensitive nature of the material (elicited by the nature of the task); and two, she questioned whether she had the authority to display a description of a ceremony that non-Navajos are excluded from. She sought the advice of her Navajo aide who told her that she should not display the piece, that to do so violated cultural precepts.

At the next group meeting the teacher shared the incident and sought the advice of Navajo teachers about the appropriate way to handle publishing and assessing sensitive work. They suggested that non-Navajos seek the advice of any Navajo in the school if they had doubts about the sensitivity of cultural practices. The group discussed the need to see others as cultural guides and important knowledge sources in the classrooms. Later, one of the new teachers said that the role of Navajo school staff took on added meaning with the project and that she did not see herself as so alone and so without the resources to gain knowledge about the culture as she had prior to the portfolio project.

Later in the year, several student samples of the "Hero Task" were informally assessed with the Life Skills and Communication rubrics. These rubrics are shown in Fig. 11.3. As Navajo teachers read the student work through these two lenses, each rubric revealed different literacy strengths of the writers. For instance, the use of personification in one student's fictional narrative of a young girl herding sheep was cited as evidence of the writer's ability to integrate cultural meanings with works of imagination (a dimension falling within level four of the Life Skills rubric). The use of personification was seen as an instance of imagination. However, the fictional narrative itself was not viewed as a work of imagination, rather as an instance of cultural narration. That is, the writer's creation of a fictional narrative that described important cultural practices of very young children's assuming responsibility for their own livestock and doing what is needed to care for

Standards & Rubrics

Communication

Students will communicate their academic, social and affective knowledge and understanding to a variety of audiences for a variety of purposes.

Beginning Level → **Higher Level**

I	II	III	IV	Higher Level
Conveys some type of communication.	Conveys meaningful communication.	Uses methods of communication which encourage audience interest.	Uses methods of communication which maintain interest and anticipate audience response.	Transcends the basic elements and methods of communication to inspire.
Begins the process of a given type of communication.	Follows some parts of a particular form of communication.	Follows a given process for effective communication.	Independently applies a given process of communication.	Selects and applies an appropriate process for any given type of communication.
Creates a form of communication that is rarely relevant to the assigned task.	Is sometimes able to stay within the dimensions of the assigned task.	Stays within the dimensions of an assigned task.	Extends the dimensions of an assigned task.	Extends the task to encompass a more extensive understanding.
Locates specific information from a given source.	Selects or locates one or more sources of information.	Uses a variety of sources of information.	Compares, selects and applies a variety of sources of information.	Evaluates, compares, and formulates a variety of sources of information.
	Communicates personal understanding of information in a given source.	Communicates personal understanding and interpretation of information.	Interprets and compares information.	Uses prior knowledge to interpret, compare, judge, or assign personal value to information.
		Identifies a particular sense of purpose in communication.	Uses methods which demonstrate a particular purpose in communication.	Analyzes the purpose of a given piece of communication.

FIG. 11.3. (Continued)

Life Skills: Shá Bik'eh Hózhóón

Student will be able to analyze, synthesize, apply, evaluate and produce knowledge for basic life skills.

Beginning Level — I	II	III	IV	Higher Level — V
States an opinion.	Expresses personal opinions.	Identifies and relates with others of the same opinion.	Presents and defends personal beliefs and values.	Reflects on past experience and apply knowledge to the future.
Identifies components of a community.	Identifies the role of services available within the community.	Communicates understanding of his/her role in a family to the community.	Portrays personal and community relationships through communication.	Relates personal perspective and the perspective of others in the community.
Lists facts but does not make strong connections.	Relates a process of sequencing.	Demonstrates role of cultural narratives and their cultural meaning.	Uses past events to reflect on current issues.	Analyzes a social and economic organization in a community.
Illustrates meaning by creating a story.	Has conceptual knowledge of cultural narratives and their cultural meanings.	Shows a sense of leadership.	Integrates cultural meanings with works of imagination through projects.	Demonstrates a complete understanding of cultural narratives and cultural meanings in past and future.
Identifies personal goals with guidance.	Identifies personal goals and is aware of personal needs.		Forecasts knowledge of personal goals.	Expresses personal vision goal beyond self and community.
				Show independence and self-direction.

FIG. 11.3. Communication and life skills rubrics.

them as the family moves from their winter to summer homes was seen as an instance of narrative skill describing culturally significant practices. The development of narrative skill and the inclusion of cultural narratives in the present is a dimension of the Life Skills rubric but not the Communication rubric. Under the Communication rubric, the writer's story was judged to have gone beyond the task to create larger implications of understanding on the basis of the drawings that extended the text of the narrative.

The use of both rubrics allowed for a discussion of the writer's strengths that went far beyond what generic writing rubrics or analytical rubrics could generate. The student's work was evaluated in terms of her proficiency with literacy in both Navajo and "school" terms. Her strength as a Navajo storyteller was exemplified in her creation of a story that stressed responsibility and awareness of the environment. From the point of view of school-based literacy, she was assessed as having a strong voice, a beginning, middle, and end to her story, developed action, and descriptive language. The structure of the task allowed her and others to bring their own worlds into school. The cross-cultural content and performance standards allowed teachers to value the content of her work in multiple ways.

Portfolio Reflections

The ways in which students and teachers negotiated the "Hero Task" suggest that cross-cultural work is not without its difficulties. Teachers need to be sensitive to cultural practices, and they may need to reconceive authority roles in the classroom as well as within their professional community. What is perhaps significant here is that Native teachers and students are more familiar with the demands of cross-cultural negotiations than are non-Native teachers. They have no choice but to be so. Another difficulty is that non-Native teachers also need to be trained to judge work cross-culturally—an endeavor that will begin next year in Chinle.

Student response to the portfolio project has been positive. One student described her portfolio as a "treasure chest." Others spoke of the portfolio as being much more meaningful than grades or regular tests. Students differed on whether they wanted their portfolios to go home or go on to their next teachers. Some said that they could use the portfolio to show younger family members "techniques for school"; others said that the portfolio would be a good way for their next teachers to see their "strengths and weaknesses."

In one classroom, students were asked to evaluate their own portfolios and to select the pieces they felt best showed their learning and achievement in core subject areas. Students were then interviewed during portfolio conferences about their work. One student selected two books she had written, one on *Talking Boy and the Changing Woman* (a Navajo narrative) and the other a story about an English princess living in a castle. Along with these, she selected several grammar worksheets. Her teacher blanched when the student presented the worksheets, because she felt the sheets did not reflect the important goals of her writing curriculum. When asked her rationale for including them, the student offered that they showed next year's teacher that she was good at "stuff like that" and besides, they must be important if the teacher had students do them. Leaving the value of grammar sheets aside, it is perhaps most notable that this fifth-grade student had the opportunity to display such a range of skills in her portfolio and that others have more than one way of talking about her literacy development.

In Chinle, the interconnection between cultural worlds has produced a wealth of knowledge for teachers and students. It is evident that the opportunity for cross-cultural standards allows for the coexistence of multiple worlds in the classroom, and the conversations occurring through and around the portfolio allow educators to engage in a multilevel discussion rich with meaning.

However, the work in Chinle is in constant development. During the 1994–1995 school year, fifth-grade teachers will implement the model, ensuring that parents are included in the portfolio process. Two sites are expanding to Grades 4 and 6; Chinle Elementary, with the largest population of upper elementary students, will expand to Grade 6. Junior high teachers and staff from the Navajo Curriculum Center will begin attending portfolio workshops. Closer connections will be made between the portfolio project and accountability requirements. The task at hand is to nurture the richness that is present and to include others in making meaning of cross-cultural teaching, learning, and assessment.

DISCUSSION

Culture and Language in the Classroom

Despite widely varying local community cultures, the culture of schooling tends to be remarkably uniform. The belief that "good teaching is good teaching" is tenacious, in the face of considerable evidence that teaching is better when it incorporates some elements of students' home cultures (Au & Kawakami, 1994; Delpit, 1988; Nelson-Barber, 1991). Students' home cultures often differ considerably from that of the school in the ways language is used; in approaches to problem solving; and in what is valued as important knowledge, ways of acquiring knowledge, uses for knowledge, or occasions for and means of displaying knowledge (Cole & Scribner, 1974; Delpit, 1986; Heath, 1986; Hymes, 1972). For example, in subsistence cultures, such as those in Alaska that rely on fishing to survive, children are taught essential life skills and the scientific principles associated with them in the natural setting—where consequences to behaviors are immediate and important (Nelson-Barber &

Estrin, 1994). Such children may find book-based school learning unmotivating and remote. Likewise, assessment itself takes on different forms and meanings in different cultures. School-style testing practices are particularly alien to many Native American students, for example (Deyhle, 1987). Some have suggested that for Native American students, tests have historically been viewed as "something to endure" or "something which holds students back and 'proves' that they are not worthy" (Chavers & Locke, 1989, pp. 15–16).

Language use has been identified as something that is highly variable from community to community and the source of numerous difficulties for teachers and students in the classroom. For example, use of language by an adult to explain how to do something rather than modeling it directly in an everyday situation is by no means universal across cultural groups, but it is common in the classroom. Children who are unaccustomed to this particular language use may require time and support to engage in it successfully. We must not assume that they are incapable of doing so simply because they have not learned to do so before entering school. As Hymes (1972) has observed, "if we are to understand what children from a community are saying, and how they hear what we say to them, we must come to be able to recognize more than the language of what is being said. We must recognize how the community norms of interpretation are embodied in speech" (p. xxx). It is "not that a child cannot express himself or that a thought cannot be required of him, but that he expresses in one style of expression rather than another. Not that a child cannot answer questions, but that questions and answers are defined for him in terms of one set of community norms rather than another, as to what count as questions and answers, and as to what it means to be asked or to answer" (p. xxxi).

A cross-cultural approach to language in the classroom involves discovering new ways—students' ways—of using language as well, rather than exclusively enculturating the child to the ways of communicating in school. Ideally, instruction and assessment should be designed to provide students with opportunities to use the capabilities acquired in their home communities and to expand their repertoires to include others; and ideally, teachers should develop fluency with students' cultural ways of knowing and communicating as well. Without understanding students' kinds of competence, teachers are unlikely to discover ways to help students develop new, school-associated competence.

The Language Demands of Reformed Curriculum and Assessment

The standards movement is associated with an increased call for higher-order thinking and for students to learn to use language to explain and justify their thinking. As previously noted, some students may not be accustomed to using language on demand in this way. The framework of standards to aim for, and criteria for judging performances relative to those standards, provide an external scaffold that can be referred to strategically. Knowledge and understanding can be understood at deeper levels over time in transaction with reviewing actual work and setting learning goals.

The portfolio process itself is language-laden and thus offers both opportunities and hazards. Student–teacher conferences need to allow for differences in norms of communication. For example, Native American students may not be comfortable with demands to display knowledge directly or to do so when the teacher judges they should (Philips, 1983); they may need to determine for themselves when they are ready (cf. Taylor, 1994). Or, if talking between adults and children is not common in a community, students may respond with extreme brevity to conference questions (Chamberlain & Medinos-Landurand, 1991). So, even this process, which may appear benign to teachers, needs to be adapted to the needs of individuals. Moreover, it may matter whether the student's cultural group is represented in the teaching staff, not only because the student has access to known cultural norms of communication, but because of what the teacher represents vis-à-vis the power relations within the larger society (cf. Labov, 1969).

Portfolios as an Emancipatory Tool

Power relations must always be considered as part of the context of students' performances. In classrooms that are mixed in terms of socioeconomic, racial, and/or ethnolinguistic status, students typically have unequal access to opportunities to participate or perform. Teachers need to be aware of the ways power relations in the larger society are almost inevitably reproduced in the classroom (cf. Cohen, 1994) and be willing and able to intervene to equalize access for students. Even in a classroom where all students come from the same culture, if that culture does not have equal status to others in the society, students may feel disenfranchised or believe that their accomplishments in the classroom will never translate into equal access to opportunities in the wider world.

Beyond meeting the criteria for equitable assessment just mentioned, portfolios can also be vehicles for cross-cultural communication and for "unsilencing" historically silenced voices (cf. Aronowitz, 1993; Freire & Macedo, 1987). If portfolios are used not only for assessing student achievement but for promoting student choice, reflection, and autonomy, truly negotiating meanings between teacher, student, and community, they have the potential to accomplish this goal. If any community has felt invisible or silenced, it is certainly the collective community of Native American groups throughout the U.S. The challenge that Chinle teachers want to face is to ensure that students' voices—arising from both Navajo and dominant culture experiences and values—are heard through portfolios. We find it more constructive and perhaps realistic to characterize the challenge not as an op-position between dominant and nondominant forces but as a negotiation of meaning across these forces—recognizing that "aspects of people's practice . . . that may look to be the result of external oppression . . . may not in fact be inhibitive of the human potential of the individual or of her community" (Erickson, 1992).

The question of how authentically a particular context can be interpreted by outsiders is raised when non-Native researchers interpret the experiences of Native communities. The authors recognize the need for Native people to conduct their own research and speak for themselves, and we hope that this chapter can alert others to some important issues and spur colleagues to pay greater attention to the needs of Native communities. In a strong sense, voices of Native teachers are present in the Chinle standards, rubrics, and assessment tasks cited.

We believe that the cross-cultural portfolio holds great potential for bringing together what on the surface are discrepant values, different ways of knowing across school contexts and community contexts.

The cross-cultural portfolio development process itself is worth exploring as a professional development tool. Based on the experience in Chinle, we see strong possibilities for using this process to generate a multifaceted discussion about the nature of teaching and learning in a particular context. In Chinle, teachers were dedicated to developing content and performance standards and performance tasks that would be constructed from multiple cultural viewpoints. This shared goal, addressed collaboratively, allowed for a depth of cultural exchange that could not be achieved (we believe) through routine multicultural professional development. Moving beyond the connections among teachers involved in development, the cross-cultural portfolio holds promise as a tool to enculturate new teachers. As such, the portfolio process under development in Chinle is, in effect, a hermeneutic tool for consensus about bi-cultural student achievement.

As the project moves into its second year, questions of authorship and ownership for new faculty are expected to arise. The teacher mobility, not independent of the sociocultural context, means that nearly 30% of the faculty in one school are new. In the best case, the portfolio process may be an effective introduction to a brand new teaching situation. In a less sanguine scenario, it may simply be daunting—particularly because new teachers enter the process well along the way and are not privy to the thinking and processes that went into the portfolio's development.

Chinle's teachers have already judged that portfolios are useful for communicating to the community. Beyond linking one school district to one community effectively, the Chinle portfolio project may serve as a model for other communities trying to bridge worlds. Other communities need to decide how to design portfolios and related tasks to meet the needs of their own students, parents, and teachers. We believe that one issue every district must confront is the need for representation, from the development phase (of any assessment system) on, of people who are knowledgeable about the cultures of the students. In Chinle, the commitment to have cultures walk side by side resulted in the building of a bicultural assessment project from the ground up. A second cultural viewpoint was not "infused" after the fact. Nor was culture reflected only in the content of student work. Support for the voice of Navajo culture is present in all aspects of design.

There is no way that an outsider can carry off this kind of project successfully. Members of the local cultures must participate. Unfortunately, such cross-cultural representation is not the norm, which is why the literature speaks of oppositional forces. Generic portfolios cannot be cross-cultural. A major problem with both district-level and large-scale assessment reform efforts that are underway is that they are not representing ethnolinguistically nondominant communities adequately. It does not make sense to put portfolios (or other forms of assessment) in place and then adapt them to meet the needs of students.

Teachers have very real questions about how portfolios will fit with grading practices. At present, they are required to keep dual sets of records, one based on standards and one based on a percentage system (90–100% = A, etc.). The scores of the new assessments cannot legitimately be converted to a percentage score. However, parents are used to receiving report cards with grades, and many are concerned that the new system is not based on strict enough standards and that students are receiving a "dumbed down" curriculum.

The state is grappling with how to report student scores to the public in a way that is comprehensible. Districts are required to determine what a mastery score would be (some point on the noninterval 0–4 scale) and then report what percentage of their students reach this mastery level. Many parents and even educators themselves are not clear on the difference between a "3" score on a rubric scale and a 75% score (reasoning that 3 out of 4 = 75% and 75% = C). In fact, a "3" represents a rather strong performance. It is clear that for some time, educators at every level, from the classroom on up, may be caught in a muddle of paradigms and politics.

In the meantime, the fifth-grade teachers in the Chinle School District have made great strides toward sorting out some of these issues and toward designing an equitable, informative, and authentic assessment system for Navajo children who will walk in both worlds.

ACKNOWLEDGMENTS

The authors are on the staff of the Rural Schools Assistance Program at Far West Laboratory for Educational Research and Development in San Francisco. Elise Trumbull, who is an applied psycholinguist, has worked with education agencies and rural districts to support improvements in assessment practices. Her focus has been ensuring equity for ethnolinguistic minority students. Trumbull's work with the Native Education Initiative, a national task force of the regional laboratories, has sensitized her in particular to issues with assessment of Native students. Nanette Koelsch is conducting her doctoral research in the Chinle Public Schools on the Navajo Reservation in Arizona. Her dissertation work focuses on negotiations and connections among language, literacy, culture, and assessment in the development and implementation of portfolios within a bicultural context. The portfolio project reported here has been fully developed by 16 teachers from the Chinle schools in collaboration with Ms. Koelsch through her work at Far West Laboratory.

REFERENCES

Anastasi, A. (1990). What is a test misuse? Perspectives of a measurement expert. In *The uses of individualized tests in American education.* Proceedings of the 1989 ETS Invitational Conference. Educational Testing Service.

Aronowitz, S. (1993). Paulo Freire's radical humanism. In P. McLaren & R. Leonard (Eds.), *Paulo Freire: A critical encounter.* New York: Routledge.

Au, K., & Kawakami, A. (1994). Cultural congruence in instruction. In E. Hollins, J. King, & W. Hayman (Eds.), *Teaching diverse populations: Formulating a knowledge base.* Albany: State University of New York Press.

Chavers, D., & Locke, P. (1989). *The effects of testing on Native Americans.* Albuquerque, NM: Native American Scholarship Fund.

Chamberlain, P., & Medinos-Landurand, P. (1991). Practical considerations for the assessment of LEP students with special needs. In E. V. Hamayan & J. S. Damico (Eds.), *Limiting bias in the assessment of bilingual students* (pp. 112–156). Austin, TX: Pro-Ed.

Cohen, E. G. (1994). Restructuring the classroom: Conditions for productive small groups. *Review of Educational Research, 64*(1), 1–35.

Cole, M., & Scribner, S. (1974). *Culture and thought.* New York: Wiley.

Delandshere, G., & Petrosky, A. (1994). Capturing teachers' knowledge: Performance assessment. *Educational Researcher, 23*(5), 11–18.

Delpit, L. D. (1986). Skills and other dilemmas of a progressive Black educator. *Harvard Educational Review, 56*(4), 111–119.

Delpit, L. (1988). The silenced dialogue: Power and pedagogy in educating other people's children. *Harvard Educational Review, 58*(3), 280–298.

Deyhle, D. (1987). Learning failure: Tests as gatekeepers and the culturally different child. In H. Trueba (Ed.), *Success or failure* (pp. 85–106). Rowley, MA: Newbury House.

Erickson, F. (1992). *Post-everything: The word of the moment and how we got here.* Paper delivered in "Qualitative Methods in Education: The Long View" at the annual meeting of the American Educational Research Association, San Francisco, April 24.

Freire, P., & Macedo, D. (1987). *Literacy: Reading the word and the world.* South Hadley, MA: Bergin and Garvey.

Heath, S. B. (1986). Social and cultural factors in schooling language minority students. In *Schooling and language minority students: A theoretical framework* (pp. 143–186). Los Angeles, CA: Evaluation, Dissemination and Assessment Center, California State University.

Hymes, D. (1972). Introduction. In C. B. Cazden, V. P. John, & D. Hymes (Eds.), *Functions of language in the classroom* (pp. xi–xvii). New York: Teachers College Press.

Labov, W. (1969). The logic of non-standard English. In J. E. Alatis (Ed.), *Linguistics and the teaching of standard English*. Monograph Series on Languages and Linguistics, No. 22. Washington, DC: Georgetown University Press.

Lucas, C. (1992). Writing portfolios—changes and challenges. In K. B. Yancey (Ed.), *Portfolios in the writing classroom*. Urbana, IL: National Council of Teachers of English.

Moss, P. A. (1994). Can there be validity without reliability? *Educational Researcher, 23*(2), 4–12.

Nelson-Barber, S. (1991). Considerations for the inclusion of multicultural competencies in teacher assessment. *Teacher Education Quarterly*, Summer, 49–58.

Nelson-Barber, S., & Meier, T. (1990). *Multicultural context: A key factor in teaching*. Washington, DC: The College Board.

Nelson-Barber, S., & Estrin, E. T. (1995). Bringing cross-cultural competencies to the teaching of mathematics and science to Native American students. *Theory into Practice, 4*(3), 174–185.

Philips, S. U. (1983). *The invisible culture: Communication in classroom and community on the Warm Springs Indian Reservation*. New York: Longman.

Taylor, C. (1994). Assessment for measurement or standards: The peril and promise of large-scale assessment reform. *American Educational Research Journal, 31*(2), 231–259.

Tierney, R. (1994). *Roundtable discussion*. Portfolio conference, sponsored by the National Center for the Study of Writing and Literacy, Stanford University, April.

Yancey, K. B. (1992). Portfolios in the writing classroom: A final reflection. In K. B. Yancey (Ed.), *Portfolios in the writing classroom: An introduction*. Urbana, IL: National Council of Teachers of English.

CHAPTER TWELVE

Teacher Parity in Assessment With the California Learning Record

Mary A. Barr
Center for Language in Learning, El Cajon, California

Phyllis J. Hallam
Martinez, California

As the year began in his third grade classroom, Brad confided to his teacher, Dana Anderson, that he didn't like to read except for the times he read with Mrs. Clarke, the classroom aide. He added, "Chapter books are hard." Math and art were his best subjects, Brad said, and he really liked to write. Brad's mother had already told Dana that her son had a "wonderful imagination," that he drew a lot at home and had even made Christmas cards the previous year. But she was concerned that he seemed to get side-tracked when he read with her. The fact that he had been identified to receive Chapter 1 services for another year squared with his mother's appraisal that Brad had a tough year in second grade. This information, collected early in the year as part of the California Learning Record (CLR), supplied Dana with some of the clues she needed to help Brad become a reader. Together with some preliminary observations of her own, she used it as baseline data from which to gauge Brad's progress in becoming an independent reader.

During the year, she provided opportunities for Brad, as well as for all her students, to hear text read aloud, to draw and write about his experiences, to have his writing read by others, and to talk to others about what they and he were learning. Using the CLR's Data Collection form, Dana kept dated notes on what she saw Brad doing. These indicated that he was progressing in five dimensions of learning: (a) his confidence and independence as a reader; (b) his ability to connect his prior experience, both in and outside of school, to what he was reading in school; (c) his ability to apply a range of skills and strategies to his reading; (d) his ability to use the knowledge and information from his reading to fulfill his own intentions; and (e) his ability to reflect on himself as a reader.

In April, for example, Dana assessed Brad's reading strategies on an unknown text, *Gregory, the Terrible Eater* (Sharmat, 1980). She observed signs of developing confidence, for example, he sat up tall and read in a clear voice. He tracked the printed lines visually, using phonics to unlock unfamiliar words. He skipped some words without any problem in meaning. He made consistent miscues, for example, fancy for fussy. Brad thought the story was "kinda good," said the main character "wants to eat the wrong things," and was able to retell events in the story that had happened over five pages of text. In June, Dana listened again, this time as Brad read aloud from a story written by Danielle, a classmate. She observed that he chose this book quickly and, although he struggled at times with medial vowels, his grasp of initial consonants enabled him to work through unfamiliar vocabulary. He read to construct meaning from the text, persisting in the face of difficulty. Although his voice changed on difficult words, he was usually right or he self-corrected. He looked up at times to comment on Danielle's style, stepping back and forth from attentive reading of content to an awareness of the writer's choices. In addition, Brad's portfolio of selected pieces of work—a reading log, writing samples, drawings—showed that he was doing quite a bit of silent reading and was annotating his art work.

Dana's observations documented what Brad showed he could do as he concentrated on becoming a reader. By the end of the year, she had gathered convincing evidence that he had developed stamina as a reader, could use appropriate cueing strategies, habitually focused on constructing meaning from text, and seemed to have surmounted a debilitating lack of confidence. He had, that is, reached the point in his literacy development where he was ready to read enough to develop the automaticity for pleasurable, efficient reading. Although he could not yet read as confidently nor with as much ease as most of his peers, Dana provided evidence that he was not only closing the gap but she was able to describe the nature and extent of his development since the beginning of the year. His record of accomplishment bears testimony to the proposition that knowledge of the particulars of his progress (in this case, his progress in becoming a reader) can influence Brad's continuing achievement.

Oddly enough, such close attention to student progress by teachers has not yet been considered an important part of the national standards school reform talk, nor is it contained in the talk about portfolio assessment. Some of those involved in assessment research, however, have begun to speak of the need for richer pictures of student learning than that afforded by externally designed and scored examinations of uninterpreted student products. They have advocated the testing of new models, ones which can, perhaps, link classroom assessment to that conducted for public accountability of schooling outcomes (Ball, 1993; Barrs, 1990; Calfee, 1992; Freedman, 1994; Johnston, 1994; Moss, 1994; Sadler, 1987; Syverson, 1994).

Conventional modes of large scale assessment, even those that are performance-based, however, privilege external judgments rather than promoting and validating internal ones. In this chapter, we devote our attention to describing the California Learning Record (CLR) as one way to redress the imbalance in what and who count in the assessment of student achievement, our response to an unasked but nevertheless fundamental question: How can assessments made by those who witness student learning, that is, teachers, be made equal in importance to assessments constructed by those outside the classroom?

Mounting pressures on schools to demonstrate to a concerned public that students enter the workforce and/or the university with the necessary literacies make evaluation of student performance a high priority in educational reform. However, as Brad's story makes clear, only parents and classroom teachers have the daily proximity to learners to know just what and how they are learning. As a consequence of this special connection to the very heart of student progress, what is needed, we believe, is an assessment system, such as the CLR, which acknowledges the parental role in education and which legitimizes teacher judgment.

Although we recognize the parent's role as being of equal importance, we limit our argument in this chapter to the inclusion of teachers in assessment practices. Mary first describes what the CLR offers in this regard, including the part that portfolios play in its use. Phyllis then provides concrete example of the effects of using the CLR in her teaching in a middle school. Following this account, we describe how the CLR approach to a fair and accurate assessment system can produce results for policy and programmatic purposes—without losing or compromising teachers' voices. Mary then specifies the theory and research influencing the design for such a system followed by Phyllis' description of its practical effects. We conclude with a brief look at future developments.

THE CLR AS A CLASSROOM ASSESSMENT: DESCRIBED BY MARY

The California Learning Record is a system of student assessment that flows from the classroom outward to meet school and district needs for public accountability. For the past 5 years, teachers in elementary, middle, and high schools in California, and I, as project director, have been working to adapt the British Primary Language Record (PLR) to K–12 schools in the U.S. The Centre for Language in Primary Education in London, England, which holds the PLR copyright, granted us adaptation privileges in 1988, and Centre Director Myra Barrs, along with staff members Hilary Hester, Anne Thomas, and Sue Ellis, continue to work with us in CLR development. The result is that, as of June 1994, the CLR has been introduced into approximately 1,000 K–12 classrooms across the state. As mentioned earlier, work is currently in progress on schoolwide use by 20 lead schools in nine regions. It is one of the models for California's entry into large scale portfolio assessment.

Dana's chronicle of Brad's literacy development, which introduces this chapter, was constructed with the help of the CLR. She used its standardized format for collecting, organizing, and summarizing student information for a comprehensive report at the end of the year. Evidence of the nature and quality of his work accumulated throughout the year on the eight pages of the CLR forms, first as provisional conclusions of her observations, then as summative ones. As Brad worked on classroom tasks and projects—individually, in groups, with a classmate—Dana noted what he demonstrated he knew and could do. His mother contributed her impressions of his literacy early in the year and noted his progress at its close. The completed CLR included samples of Brad's work, drawn from his portfolio, as well as descriptions of his overall achievement summed up both in verbal and in numerical placement on the reading and writing scales for Grades K–3. (Other scales trace literacy development over grade spans 4 through 8 and 9 through 12.)

The CLR belies its appearance as a mere record keeping device or a portfolio, for that matter. It promotes a constructivist view of learning, that is, one in which learners bring their prior experiences, their world views, their linguistic capabilities as well as their skills to bear on making sense of experiences offered in school. With the CLR as a framework for observing and documenting learning as it happens, teachers provide authentic occasions for students to use language, both oral and written, to generate solutions to given and discovered problems and to evaluate their consequences, to question experience, and to demonstrate their abilities to find answers.

This kind of classroom practice requires that assessment move away from post hoc review and judgment of student work products only in favor of including ongoing teacher appraisal of student work in progress. Such a practice acknowledges, among other things, that those learning English (or French or Spanish, for that matter) as a second language possess valuable capabilities. Therefore, teachers may document evidence of growth in language and/or subject matter, whether these demonstrations are in English or other languages. Judgments are made at scheduled times throughout the year, for example, at the ends of quarters, in terms of criteria and standards used jointly and openly by teacher, student, and (especially with elementary-aged students) parent.

At the end of the year, students assess their accomplishments and determine, along with their teachers and their parents, what goals to set for the next year. Writing and reading samples from their portfolios complement teacher placement on CLR performance scales in reading and writing. When the CLR is used for public reporting, copies of a few representative work samples are attached to each student's record to illustrate and substantiate the teacher summaries of progress.

Completed CLRs and complementary student portfolios contain unique descriptions and samples of student work, reflecting accomplishment on nonstandarized tasks performed by individual students in particular classrooms. Each collection, however, provides evidence of how well students can read, write, and discuss with others in ways and on topics appropriate for a specific grade level. For example, teachers note signs of development in the work as students collect their writing in progress and at completion, their reading responses and their oral presentations, their drawings with complementary text. Student reflections about the quality of their work as it changes over time and situation are also an official part of the record. Student work generated as practice for externally prepared standardized tasks administered under test conditions can be included at the teacher's discretion. Many teachers value this additional perspective on student growth, balancing such information with demonstrations of student learning completed in more natural settings. For example, the results of practicing for on-demand tests in reading and writing can be compared to what can be learned when the teacher sees and hears students actually read and write text of various kinds over the course of the year. For the most part, however, both the teacher-compiled CLR and the portfolios of their students contain evidence that students are meeting standards in non-standardized ways.

A TEACHER REFLECTS ON HER USE
OF THE CLR: PHYLLIS' VIEW

I joined the CLR Core Development Group of teachers in 1990, after experimenting with it in my middle school classroom since 1988. I had become interested in extending its use among secondary school teachers. With several classes a day and with more mature students, secondary teachers face different hurdles in implementing the CLR but I contend they can garner equally beneficial returns. As I describe my experience—from introduction to adoption into my practice—I realize again how I first adapted the CLR to fit my own, mostly tacit, knowledge about learners and learning and then how this knowledge led to questions that led to more knowledge.

I first heard about the CLR at the California Literature Project's Summer Institute. Its approach to assessment aligned closely with the Institute's theme of using student-centered, constructivist approaches to learning, so we were treated to a workshop on the CLR's organization and attributes. Initially, my reaction was a typical one, "Documentation and anecdotal observation for my large class load? No way!" But then, as I thought about implementing my goals for the next school year, the methodology and philosophy of the CLR began to make more and more sense. I was teaching sixth grade language arts at that time, in a low-income neighborhood with students from diverse cultures. Utilization of cooperative groups with literature-based activities would, I knew, bring out talents and best efforts, but how could I assess the learning that was going on? The evaluation of end products of group efforts and peer conferencing was one way, but I knew that the dynamics of student discussions were also key to an understanding of how and what students were learning. I wanted to be able to assess listening and speaking in these contexts, and the CLR not only addressed important issues of oral language, but also offered specific methods of analysis. I was hooked. The next year, I tried it.

In my first year of using the CLR, I also started an ambitious portfolio project for which students selected and gathered samples of their work from literacy events along with their corresponding reflections throughout the year. I tried to concentrate on collecting observations of students' oral discourse as they talked about literature, grappled with ideas in cooperative groups, and made oral presentations. I took notes on mailing labels and students affixed them to the "Listening and Speaking Sample Observations" page I had them place in the front of their portfolios. My aspirations were high and my intentions good, but my first year of trying authentic assessment was not very successful. Stacks of papers and projects ringed the walls of my classroom because I was not sure what students would want to put in their portfolios. The cryptic observational notes that I had taken were not understandable nor useful by the end of the year. The students' portfolios were nice collections of writing to pass on to the seventh grade teachers, but I had never used them for analyzing student progress at grading time. I went back to the drawing board.

Once again, I spent a summer reflecting on how I could incorporate active learning techniques with a dynamic form of assessment. I perused the materials given to me at that first workshop, especially the *Primary Language Record Handbook for Teachers* (Barrs, Ellis, Hester, & Thomas, 1987). Little lightbulbs started flashing in my head as I made two important discoveries about the nature of authentic assessment:

1. The CLR, as a system of collecting student samples, is integral to portfolio assessment. I had been mistaken in thinking about the two as separate entities. Portfolio assessment did not have to be just writing samples. It could also include reading logs, metacognition journals, and records of peer collaborations during writer's workshops. The CLR did not have to contain just my observations. Student self-reflections on a wide variety of literacy events could also be included. The CLR, with its philosophical and theoretical grounding in constructivist learning is an excellent guide to what

goes into a portfolio and how to use this information for evaluating students' strengths and goals, theirs and mine.

2. My uninformative anecdotal notes were that way because I was used to recording evaluative data into gradebooks. End of the unit tests assessed student growth by producing numbers or letters that could easily fit into little squares, for example, "95%" or "B+." My early observations reflected this rush to judgment with such notes as, "Almost all correct on *Gilgamesh* test. Good comprehension," or "Read poetry to class with confidence." After being influenced by the CLR's approach to assessment, this type of information was not valuable to me. I was more concerned with what *level* of comprehension the student had trouble with—literal, critical, inferential? Is this a pattern? Did the student have a chance to discuss *Gilgamesh* as part of the test? Did the student read with a peer? Did the student lose the book? Test? What kind of test? How can a test be constructed to take into account the various kinds of prior knowledge that my students from such diverse backgrounds bring in? Did the subject matter influence the students' motivation? The answers to questions like these uncovered information that both the students and I needed to know. The way to address this issue became clear—toss the gradebook.

The next year I used the *PLR Handbook* to guide the portfolio collections of my students, and the pieces of the puzzle began to fall into place. Without the tedious task of recording grades, I found that I had more time for observations and for writing comments on students' work. I began to use paper-and-pencil tests less and less often, which freed up class time for instructional approaches such as reader's and writer's workshops. The students and I together developed rubrics to judge the effectiveness of our reading, writing, listening, and speaking instead of my bestowing grades, a practice that gave the students ownership of evaluative tools. The students began to be more astute in judging their progress and that of others, a result that allowed me to spend more time with individual and small group conferences. By the end of the year, we had developed new methods and terminologies for recording relevant data and summarizing it for parents and administrators on the newly available CLR form. Parents loved the changes I had made and administrators were satisfied with the careful documentation of student progress.

The summer between my second and third year, my reflections were quite different from the previous 2 years. Because the integration of the CLR as a portfolio assessment system had brought about many successes, my epiphanies were of a different nature. I became aware that I had made many changes in my approach to teaching. I was surprised, for instance, to realize that I had not given any tests the last half of the year. Rigorous instruction and challenging assignments stemmed from informed decisions that the students and I made together based on their performance on previous tasks. I no longer thought of planning curriculum by myself; including my students' needs and interests became a natural part of the process. Assessment was informing instruction as an integral part of the learning environment, not an intrusive activity that caused stress in students and me.

All of this led me to consider the questions that now seemed relevant about the intrusive, time consuming, nonproductive assessments that took away from learning, yet were required by those outside the classroom. Were report cards and norm-referenced tests really necessary? What if every teacher were trained in the CLR portfolio assessment system? I fantasized about idealistic answers to these questions: Think of the time that would be freed for teaching and learning! Traditional report cards would not be necessary because parents would know a whole lot more about their child's progress than what a letter grade could say any day! No progress reports! Team teachers in science and math could collect data for language arts, and visa versa! We would not need norm referenced tests! From this little exercise of the imagination, it dawned on me that my judgments as a teacher were more valid than the standardized, bubblized forms of assessment, and that a whole lot of good could come from a movement away from them toward one that honored the information that teachers carry around in their heads all the time. The empowering aspect of the CLR, to me, was that it gave me a way to get it out of my head and onto paper in a way that is efficient and productive.

TOWARD A FAIR AND ACCURATE SYSTEM
OF LARGE-SCALE ASSESSMENT

When teacher judgment of student progress is cited as an essential factor in improving teaching and learning, the question of how to prevent teacher bias receives little attention. When the arena for such judgment expands into the light of public accountability, however, the potential for bias is often viewed as an insurmountable obstacle to fair testing. Traditional externally designed assessments have been developed, after all, for the express purpose of bypassing teacher judgment in favor of standardized tasks administered according to standardized procedures with the levels of student achievement determined by people who do not know the student. The lack of context in tasks and procedures and the anonymity of the test taker provide a sense of objectivity and, as a consequence, of fairness. Linda Darling-Hammond (1995) agreed that "the presumed 'objectivity' of current tests derives both from the lack of reliance upon individual teacher judgment in scoring and from the fact that test-takers are anonymous to test-scorers" (p. 98). Such distrust of teacher judgment and a disregard for the differences (which, it seems necessary to say, are not the same as deficits) in student experience does not encourage teachers to use evaluation results to improve student achievement. Questions of bias in these tests, however, are now being asked: What about their damaging effect on teaching and learning (Helgeson, 1992), the lack of context for constructed responses (Moss, 1994), their disregard for divergent response (Johnston, 1994), and the lack of opportunity for the reflection and engagement necessary to conceptual understanding (LeTendre, 1991)?

The time is at hand, it would seem, to stop the either-or nature of the debate over testing and instead to acknowledge the vital role teachers must play in assessing student achievement. With acknowledgment comes a shift in focus to schoolwide attention to evidence of what and how students are learning. Individual teachers can and should lead this effort but they cannot by themselves create the infrastructure needed at each school to examine and support the academic progress of each student.

Phyllis describes her experience with the CLR, supported by schoolwide restructuring, as one that enhanced her teaching because it helped her make her tacit knowledge explicit and, therefore, open to change. But Phyllis has now left her school to start work in a doctoral program at the University of California at Berkeley. Her growth and development will continue but students at her school will not have the benefit of her CLR experience because assessment reform did not go beyond her classroom. Dana, too, provided a clear picture of Brad's increasing ability to read independently in third grade after earlier experiences had put him at risk of academic failure. In a full school use of the CLR, his fourth-grade teacher would have helped him build on his learning in third grade. Using the CLR reading performance scale for Grades 4–8, she would have helped him focus on widening and deepening his reading experience, building on the confidence, knowledge, and skills gained the year before. The curriculum and instruction in Grades 4 and 5 at Brad's school, however, was tied to classwide reading of basal texts, unit tests, and formal preparation for the on-demand state assessment. Without a schoolwide, sustained program of staff development, his teachers could not evaluate student progress along developmental continua. Without support for his fragile control over the reading strategies gained in third grade, Brad's progress was stymied, his confidence as a learner undermined.

Classroom use of the CLR, as both Phyllis's and Brad's experiences over 3 years illustrate, is potentially powerful in helping teachers improve their practices and students boost their achievement. Sustaining the growth of individual teachers and students, however, is the work of the whole school. This is not a new concept, of course. In fact, such whole school and district programs as mastery learning and clinical teaching have been instituted on such a premise. But these earlier efforts have sought to standardize curriculum and instructional practices, relying on standardized tasks, scripted behaviors for both teachers and students, and externally controlled assessments.

The CLR, on the other hand, supports a move away from such constraints as these practices impose on teachers. It is they, after all, who should be models of the literate thinkers and problem solvers we want students to become. They, therefore, need what Darling-Hammond (1995) called "top-down support for bottom-up reform" (p. 103), to prepare themselves to focus the purposes of assessment on improving student achievement school-wide, using classroom evidences of what student can do to justify their judgments. We believe that when teachers are permitted the time and opportunity to establish the necessary knowledge base to interpret how and what their students are learning, then and only then will they be able to use assessment to improve the learning of their students and engender trust from parents and school boards. We also believe that students, when given increasing responsibility for providing the evidence of their own achievement, will invest more of themselves in its pursuit.

THEORETICAL FOUNDATION FOR THE USE
OF VALIDATED TEACHER JUDGMENT
IN ASSESSMENT: MARY'S PERCEPTION

Documentation about how these benefits—trust in teacher judgment and student engagement in their own learning—take shape are emerging from CLR research and development. Articles have recently been published (Miserlis, 1993; Thomas, 1993), which detail how teachers use the CLR to become researchers in their own classrooms, confident about their growing abilities to help their students to new heights of achievement. One doctoral dissertation (Syverson, 1994) provided a theoretical foundation for the use of the CLR in classrooms, where complexities have all too often been undervalued. A second dissertation (Thomas, 1994) used the CLR as a research instrument to study teacher change. A master's thesis (Arnston, 1994) described a study of how primary age students learned to assess their own work, using CLR performance scales adapted for their understanding. Use of the Primary Language Record (PLR) in New York City schools has also generated studies from the National Center for Restructuring Education, Schools and Testing (NCREST) that have found similar effects on teaching and learning (Falk & Darling-Hammond, 1993; Falk, MacMurdy, & Darling-Hammond, 1995).

An internal evaluation study in 1992–1993, conducted among teachers from California schools with Chapter 1 programs, helped pinpoint just what happens as teachers begin to implement the CLR among academically disadvantaged students. Of the 93 teachers involved, 78 were using the CLR for the first time. The rest were teachers who had tried out the PLR when we first started adapting it to California classrooms.

Much of what the study documented attests to the positive effect of the CLR on teaching practices. For example, 40 teachers in the pilot responded to a survey conducted as part of the study and most of them saw the CLR as valuable in obtaining information about students and their literacy development. They reported knowing substantially more about the literacy and oral language abilities of the student for whom they completed a CLR than for the rest of their students. In interviews, many of the teachers reported making changes in their teaching as a direct result of using the CLR with just one student. They frequently described seeking out or adapting materials to appeal to the special interests and needs of a CLR student; altering assignments or offering choices designed to fit that student's developing skills. Some said they had made broad-scale changes in their pedagogy, in response to both the practical demand of the CLR that they observe and document students at work and to its educational principles embodied in five dimensions of learning—confidence and independence, experience, skills and strategies, knowledge and understanding, and reflectiveness.

Teachers reported that they adopted or had validated the specific practices listed below as a result of their experience with the CLR:

- granting of more responsibility to students for their learning,
- creating more opportunities for student directed group activities,
- assigning reading logs or journals,
- increasing or developing the use of portfolios,
- establishing goals for the year and explaining them to students,
- creating more opportunities for student self-reflection, and
- interacting more frequently with student groups or individual students, especially at the secondary level.

Teachers in the study cited the increased interaction and observation required by the CLR as responsible for stronger relationships with the targeted students, that is, the one or two Chapter 1 students for whom they were keeping a record, and their parents. They noted the value for students of the CLR's focus on academic strengths, allowing them to see progress in their own performance over the year. Approximately 40% of the teachers reported that the CLR students gained confidence and enthusiasm for learning. Most found the kind of teacher–student conferences that are part of the CLR had increased student attention in class, stimulating self-reflection so that students began, as one teacher put it, "to notice for themselves how they've progressed."

Although this early response from teachers, most of whom had not yet finished their first CLR, was overwhelmingly positive, they were generally concerned about expanding its use to more students because of the time it took them to conduct and document their observations. Many seemed to value the results of conducting the observations and writing the anecdotal records so much, however, that they changed their practice in ways that have been recommended by educational reformers for a long time. For instance, approximately 40% reported that using the CLR became easier once they had developed their own routines (and, probably, their own reasons) for observing and recording. Many also found that innovations they made in classroom structure or pedagogy—particularly changes geared to creating a more student-centered environment—helped them adapt the CLR into their own practice. In addition, 40% reported that if the CLR could replace, or be integrated with, other forms of assessment (e.g., report cards and Chapter 1 requirements), the time and management concerns would be greatly eased or, in some cases, eliminated. In general, these changes in teaching practices over such a short span of time (7 months) confirmed our belief in the soundness of the CLR and its support for teachers in taking on their professional role in assessment.

The findings from this study and the others mentioned have been incorporated into the design of a CLR system of assessment. To provide support for teachers as they first take on the CLR in their own practice, a three-year program of professional development has been developed; to communicate commonly agreed-on interpretations of performance standards, a school-by-school use of CLR exemplars and on-site coaching by certified teacher-leaders is being implemented; and to ensure equity and consistency of CLR results when they are to be used as summative reports of student achievement across schools and districts, regional moderations of student records are planned as an annual event.

Sadler's (1987) description of "standards-referenced assessment" as an alternative to norm- and criterion-referenced assessment has also influenced our design. He described four components of a standards-referenced system of classroom-based assessment: numerical cut-offs, shared tacit knowledge of teachers, exemplars, and verbal descriptions. The CLR system of assessment has incorporated all four in its statewide pilot now underway.

Numerical Cut-Offs

The system uses numerical as well as narrative descriptions of five levels of student performance in reading (writing and mathematics are still in development) for use in Grades K–3, 4–8, 9–12. The five numbers on the scales at each grade span correspond to progress along a continua of development. In primary grades, the continua are built (or are being built) to describe stages of becoming a reader, a writer, a mathematician. Beginning in fourth grade, the continua describe stages in becoming an experienced reader, writer, and mathematician. In high school, the scale points 1–5 describe a reflective/strategic reader, writer, and mathematician. Cut-offs have been established for the end of each grade span at scale points (4), proficient level, and (5), advanced status. Scores can be aggregated to provide the percentages of students at the various stages of development to meet the needs for program evaluation and public accountability by schools and districts. The implication is that students can move ahead as they demonstrate that they can meet the standards set for their grade span. At the same time, students who need support can be identified by the CLR, with its record of what they can do and its recommendations for what is next to be learned. Students, parents, and all teachers of the student must, of course, become familiar with the verbal descriptors. The more they all can focus on what is known and what is needed, the better chance the student will have to succeed.

Shared Knowledge of Teachers

Sadler (1987) said that, despite the dismal research picture that shows how unreliable teacher judgment has so far been found to be, he believes that teacher judgments can be made dependable if commonly agreed-on standards are used in conjunction with the appropriate professional development. He also explains that the tacit knowledge which characterizes the expert, the connoisseur, is often tapped to appraise complex phenomena, such as the evaluation of a painting, of wine, of an ice skating contest. The standards reside inside the heads of the experts, who agree with each other but whose criteria for judgment often remain inaccessible to the layperson. The evaluation of student learning also qualifies as a complex phenomenon and the teacher as the expert who meets with peers to develop common interpretations of the standards as they apply to the work of their students. In the CLR system, these moderation meetings took place for the first time in 1994 at four sites around the state. Teachers submitted their own student records to be validated. Their placement of students on the appropriate reading performance scale were masked and other teachers in the region read the work described and sampled in the CLR and scored the record. If the second score matched the first, the first teacher's placement was considered to be validated.

Exemplars

Sadler (1987) pointed out that the fact that the standards for judgment are unarticulated is detrimental to learners, who must learn to judge their own work; it causes mistrust among the public; and it is too expensive to underwrite the costs of bringing teacher-experts together for days at a time to arrive at consensus. For these reasons and more, he advocated developing ways to "give tacit standards some external formulation" (pp. 199–200) through the further provision of exemplars and verbal descriptions.

We began last year to specify standards of achievement by distributing copies of four actual completed (or almost completed) CLRs, one each from kindergarten, as well as from Grades 2, 3, and 6. Each describes a particular student's academic progress for a given school year. A complete CLR includes the following: the four page teacher-written summary record and the four page data collection form with selected student work samples attached.

The summary record contains Part A (intake information, including language(s) spoken, read, and understood, and summaries of initial parent and student conferences), Part B (summaries of student progress as revealed in talking and listening, reading and writing; record of how the student learns best and recommendations for what is next to be offered as learning activities/contexts), and Part C (comments by parent and student about the year's work and final quarter updates by the teacher about student progress and recommendations to next year's teacher).

The data collection form contains dated observation notes of student performance revealed in oral and written language and analyses of student work samples from student portfolios with the selected work samples attached.

Exemplars were distributed in professional development seminars as examples of representative completed records, rather than idealized models. The process of gathering and sharing exemplars is ongoing; twelve new exemplars have emerged from the moderation readings held in May and June, 1994.

Verbal Descriptions

The disadvantages of numerical cut-offs, the shared but tacit knowledge of teachers, and the use of exemplars can be off-set, Sadler (1987) said, when they are combined with written criteria for judging student work (p. 201). The problem is that language requires context for its meaning so verbal definitions rely on concrete referents (p. 207). In the CLR, teachers are seen as experts who can select and describe salient features of student achievement and widely distributed exemplars model such selections and descriptions. Both teachers and the exemplars use the verbal descriptions of the performance scales to interpret student work and to reach judgments of student achievement.

THE EARLY EFFECTS OF THE APPLICATION
OF THEORY: EXPLAINED BY PHYLLIS

As the time for my region's moderation meeting approached, I was apprehensive. The exemplars that had been sent to us were so impressive, they were intimidating. My records from the classroom were not as polished nor as complete. I worried that the methods of data collection I had used had not provided rich enough information to persuade another teacher I had made the appropriate judgments about a student's progress. What if teachers found instances of cultural insensitivity in my records? What if I found instances in theirs?

But I knew from my graduate studies that the moderation readings were extremely important. The term *reliability* pounded my cherished notion of the need to value the knowledge of other teachers. If the paradigm shift I had experienced within my classroom was ever to be realized in the larger educational and political arenas, then these issues would have to be addressed. I put my minor insecurities aside and approached the moderations with an adventurous attitude.

My apprehensions about being wrong or making mistakes in front of my peers illustrate how difficult it is to get beyond the deficit approach to evaluation. The moderation experience turned out not to be a time of embarrassment over perceived failures, but of learning, support, and celebration about students and teaching. Just as the CLR entails scaffolding by experienced learners in the classroom, the moderation process provides scaffolding for teachers, building from strengths as we helped each other apply commonly interpreted standards to evidence of student learning.

The moderations started with the dozen or so participants reviewing and discussing the verbal descriptors, that is, the performance scales. Then we split up into small groups and looked at new exemplars of completed CLRs, so that we could calibrate our understandings of what kinds of evidence are necessary for teachers to place students at the different levels on the scales. (We conducted this moderation on reading performance only so we used the CLR's reading scales.) By the time the subsequent debriefing session with the rest of the groups was completed, I felt a new sense of confidence. As a community of teachers, we found that we had discovered common bases for our judgments as we articulated our previously tacit knowledge. This process provided us with the recognition of our worth and our identities as experts in assessing student growth.

When we split up into grade-alike pairs after the general moderation session to read CLRs, to discuss them in terms of the appropriate grade span scale, and to arrive at consensus about the scale placement of the student work provided, we found the exercise almost enjoyable, not one that was pressure-filled. Working in pairs allowed us to offer different perspectives and often we could see different and important aspects of the student work. Indeed, the most common response shared at the end of the moderation was that of enthusiasm for the process. We all felt that we benefited from the interactions with other teachers as we interpreted the pictures of how students learn provided by the CLRs. Despite the rigor of the assessment, the high standards set for students seemed less daunting than before. The whole experience made clear how my assessments of student achievement are connected to my instructional goals and stances. I consider this to be another major step forward in my journey as a teacher.

CONCLUSION

In this chapter, we have argued for the elevation of teacher judgment to a par with external judgments in the assessment of student achievement. To do this, we hope to link what individual teachers see and document as far as student progress is concerned to school and regional assessments. The piloting of the CLR as a classroom-based assessment model will now expand from single classrooms to whole schools or to target groups of students within whole schools, for example, primary grade span, ninth grade, all bilingual students. Twenty schools, from Ukiah to San Diego, have become lead schools in this pilot of a statewide classroom-based assessment system with the possibility that faculties will be able to substitute the CLR for the present norm referenced testing requirement for their Chapter 1 students as a major incentive.

Each school will be registered as a part of the CLR Assessment System to ensure that appropriate support and understanding of the system as a whole are in place as site teachers voluntarily incorporate it into their ongoing programs. Over a 3-year period, faculty will phase in the use of the CLR within their classrooms. A teacher from the core group of statewide teacher leadership will serve as a coach at each of these schools and will lead site and regional moderation of student records near the end of the year. As coaches, they will use their CLR experience to help other teachers begin the process. As ongoing core group members, they will continue to share resources and develop others. The Center for Language Learning will coordinate their efforts and assemble the results of the moderations—individual scores for reading and for writing given by the classroom teacher and validated by others at the school and across the region. The moderations hold the key to answering the question we posed at the outset: How can assessments made by those who witness student learning, that is, teachers, be made equal in importance to assessments constructed by those outside the classroom? The answer is a crucial one because, although valid and reliable classroom-based assessments are essential to improving student achievement, they will be possible only when a teacher's judgment, informed and validated by other professionals, is respected.

REFERENCES

Arnston, D. (1994). *Reflective reading: Self-regulating strategies for emergent readers.* Unpublished master's thesis, University of California San Diego.

Ball, A. F. (1993). Incorporating ethnographic-based techniques to enhance assessments of culturally diverse students' written exposition. *Educational Assessment, 1*(3), 256–281.

Barrs, M. (1990). *Words not numbers: Assessment in English.* Exeter, UK: Short Run Press, Ltd.

Barrs, M., Ellis, S., Hester, H., & Thomas, A. (1987). *The Primary Language Record Handbook for Teachers*. Portsmouth, NH: Heinemann.

Calfee, R. (1992). Authentic assessment of reading and writing in the elementary classroom. In M. Dreher & W. H. Slater (Eds.), *Elementary school literacy: Critical issues* (pp. 211–226). Norwood, MA: Christopher-Gordon.

Darling-Hammond, L. (1995). Equity issues in performance-based assessment. In M. T. Nettles & Arie L. Nettles (Eds.), *Equity and excellence in educational teasting and assessment* (pp. 89–114). Boston: Kluwer Academic Publishers.

Falk, B., & Darling-Hammond, L. (1993). *The primary language record at P.S. 261: How assessment transforms teaching and learning*. New York: Columbia University, Teachers College, National Center for Restructuring Education, Schools, and Teaching.

Falk, B., MacMurdy, S., & Darling-Hammond, L. (1995). *Taking a different look: How the Primary Language Record supports teaching for diverse learners*. New York: Columbia University Teachers College, National Center for Restructuring Education, Schools, and Testing.

Freedman, S. W. (1994). *Linking large-scale testing and classroom portfolio assessments of student writing*. Berkeley, CA: University of California, Berkeley, National Center for the Study of Writing and Literacy.

Helgeson, S. L. (1992). *Assessment of science teaching and learning outcomes* (monograph No. 6). Washington D.C.: National Center for Science Teaching and Learning.

Johnston, P. (1994). Assessment as social practice. In C. Kinzer & D. Lea (Eds.), *Examining central issues in literacy research, theory, and practice* (pp. 11–22). Chicago: National Reading Conference.

LeTendre, M. J. (1991). The continuing evolution of a Federal role in compensatory education. *Educational Evaluation and Policy Analysis, 13*(4), 328–334.

Miserlis, S. (1993). The classroom as an anthropological dig: Using the California Learning Record (CLR) as a framework for assessment and instruction. In *Learning from Learners*, 57th Yearbook of the Claremont Reading Conference (pp. 103–118). Claremont, CA: Claremont Graduate School.

Moss, P. A. (1994). Can there be validity without reliability? *Educational Researcher, 23*(2), 5–12.

Sadler, D. R. (1987). Specifying and promulgating achievement standards. *Oxford Review of Education, 13*(No. 2), 191–209.

Sharmat, M. (1980). *Gregory, the terrible eater*. New York: Scholastic Book Services.

Syverson, M. (1994). *The wealth of reality: An ecology of composition*. Unpublished doctoral dissertation, University of California at San Diego.

Thomas, S. O. (1993). Rethinking assessment: Teachers and students helping each other through the "sharp curves of life." *Learning Disability Quarterly, 16*(Fall), 257–279.

Thomas, S. O. (1994). *Knowing Learners—Knowing Ourselves: Teachers' Perceptions of Change in Theory and Practice Resulting from Inquiry into Authentic Assessment*. Claremont Graduate School.

CHAPTER THIRTEEN

Profiles and Portfolios: Helping Primary-Level Teachers See the Big Picture

Susan Carey Biggam
Nancy Teitelbaum
Vermont Department of Education

In Vermont, one might think portfolio nearly a household word. Assessment holds a key place in Vermont's aggressive approach to systemic school reform, and portfolios are a cornerstone of its assessment initiative. Since 1990, Vermont students have been encouraged to develop portfolios for their work, and teachers have increasingly used portfolios and other means of authentic assessment to document student progress and guide instructional decision making. So far, it is only at the fourth, fifth, and eighth grade levels, however, that portfolios have been sampled for accountability purposes. Portfolios are clearly not universal in Vermont, but their use is certainly widespread.

In this chapter, we describe the Primary Literacy Assessment Project, a pilot project that is aligned with the statewide Vermont portfolio initiative, but is not part of statewide assessment. Focused instead on internal, classroom-based assessment, the Primary Literacy Assessment Project extends the breadth of the writing portfolio to include additional areas of literacy (reading strategies, concepts of print), and, through the use of a multidimensional profile, provides one method of organizing and evaluating a literacy portfolio during the primary years. We describe a pilot study, guided by the authors of this chapter and a district curriculum coordinator, that involved 20 teachers who volunteered to help us revise and then try out the use of the profile in their classrooms. We embarked on the pilot project with three "hunches" about the use of a profile:

- It might help teachers and students build confidence in developing reading/writing (literacy) portfolios that could follow the child from year to year.
- It might help teachers pay attention to areas of literacy assessment as well as instruction that had not previously been a focus, and help them focus on what students can do, as opposed to what they can not do.
- It might help teachers organize and communicate assessment information and provide standards for classroom-level assessment of primary-level literacy portfolios.

To explain the context of this project, we briefly describe portfolio use (focusing on writing) in Vermont, then note some challenges that are present and additional influences on the development of the project. We then describe the profile itself and what the teachers who participated in piloting it have said about its uses and effects. Some of what we learned confirmed our hunches at the beginning of the project, but we also emerged with some intriguing questions and plans for continuing with this model.

PORTFOLIOS IN VERMONT

Portfolios are used both for instruction and assessment in Vermont. During instruction, students and teachers talk about what constitutes good writing, and use the state's agreed-on scoring criteria—purpose, organization, details, voice/tone, and grammar, usage, and mechanics (fondly nicknamed GUM)—as they develop, critique, and revise writing. As part of Vermont's statewide assessment program, teachers score portfolios, which have some uniformity because of guidelines for minimum contents, for accountability purposes, using the same standard scoring criteria. This scoring takes place, for writing, at the end of students' fifth and eighth grade years, and for mathematics at the fourth and eighth grade levels. The intent of this statewide assessment of portfolios is twofold: to find out how well students perform and to improve writing and mathematics performance (Mills & Brewer, 1988). The instructional impact of portfolios in Vermont is just beginning to be researched; the RAND Corporation (Koretz, Stecher, Klein, & McCaffrey, 1994) reported that educators "found the program to be a powerful and positive influence on instruction" (p. 6). Much of this effect seems to come from a shift in instructional emphasis. One Vermont administrator, who was also a member of ASCD's Assessment Consortium, reported, "I've seen some real changes in teacher behavior—probably as dramatic as anything I've seen in 22 years" (O'Neil, 1993, p. 5).

Challenges and Influences

Promising as this sounds, it would be misleading to suggest that in every school and classroom teachers and students are currently using portfolios to guide instruction, celebrate progress, and communicate student achievement. Several challenges are present.

Issues With the Implementation of Portfolio Assessment. One issue is continuity. Although in many schools portfolios are now being used at all grade levels, a number of fourth-, fifth-, and eighth-grade teachers still report that students come to them without portfolios and without an understanding of the criteria used to evaluate performance.

Consistency in scoring is another issue. Particularly in writing, the program has had continued difficulty in meeting established standards of reliability for scoring (Koretz et al., 1994). This has hampered the reporting and use of results, and prompted additional staff development to help teachers score more consistently.

Concern about the use of the portfolio for accountability purposes has been an issue for some Vermont teachers (Tavalin, 1993), although others have seen the portfolio as a much needed complement or alternative to standardized tests (Biggam, 1992). On a practical level, finding time for conferencing with students and scoring portfolios has been a frequent concern as well. Nevertheless, Koretz et al. (1994) reported that most teachers felt portfolios to be a "worthwhile burden" (p. 14).

Curriculum Guidelines. Other influences have to do with emerging curriculum guidelines in the state and current literacy practice. Vermont has never had a statewide curriculum or prescribed textbooks, but has had a strong tradition of local control and a high degree of teacher autonomy. Recently, as part of its approach to systemic school reform, and in response to growing pressures for accountability, Vermont (like several other states) has developed a *Common Core of Learning* (Vermont Department of Education, 1994a). This set of 20 vital results for all learners is organized into four key areas: communication, reasoning/problem-solving, personal development, and social responsibility. Building on the basis of the Common Core, a statewide commission is currently drafting the *Common Core Framework for Curriculum and Assessment* to provide a bridge for local curriculum development and assessment as well as further development of statewide assessment.

The framework, when completed, will be composed of content standards, essential learning experiences, and student performance standards. Content standards will describe the "what" of curriculum: the knowledge and processes that all students should learn. Essential learning experiences will outline the key instructional practices (in classrooms as well as extended classrooms) that enhance the likelihood that students will be successful. Student performance standards will answer the question "how well?", and will describe the degree of proficiency that students should demonstrate, through local and state assessment, during the grade spans of K–4, 5–8, and 9–12.

Vermont's Framework is designed to be multidisciplinary; many of the draft content standards (e.g., those having to do with asking questions, reading, writing, or applying problem-solving methods) apply across all disciplines (Vermont Department of Education, 1994b). Other content standards are organized by "field of knowledge": arts and humanities, history and social science, and science, math, and technology. Although not a state mandate, the framework is expected to drive further development of state-wide assessment as well as local curriculum and assessment.

Needless to say, such a major policy initiative, particularly within the context of a state that has formerly left curriculum and assessment development to local educators, will need a good deal of support for implementation. Building local capacity in using the framework to guide local curriculum development and assessment is critical. For the framework to have a real impact, teachers will need to see actual models of assessment and curriculum that are aligned with the draft standards, seem "doable," and can make a difference for their students.

Literacy Practice. The status of primary-level literacy practice in Vermont has influenced the development of the Primary Literacy Profile project as well. Like other primary-level teachers, many Vermont teachers have been strongly influenced by the whole language movement as well as multiage approaches, and have shifted their philosophy and practice to a more holistic and integrated model (emphasizing elements such as process writing, teaching of strategies vs. isolated subskills, response to reading, reflection on reading/writing, and ownership of literacy).

At the same time as—and perhaps because of—these instructional shifts, the need for enhanced assessment skills and accountability is increasingly evident. Many Vermont teachers have expressed interest in assessment that matches the instruction currently occurring in classrooms. In addition, in a recent policy study (University of Vermont, 1994a) concern was expressed about the limited reading skills of many Vermont primary-level students and limited accountability on the part of teachers and schools. Increased professional development in literacy assessment was recommended to help ensure that all Vermont children have strong literacy skills by the time they leave the primary grades.

Literacy portfolios are still relatively new in Vermont classrooms. A few schools are piloting New Standards Language Arts portfolios, and several others are trying out the Work Sampling System from the University of

Michigan. Mostly, however, where literacy portfolios do exist in primary classrooms, they seem to be collections of student work, and do not yet include reflection or evaluation.

Our Involvement; Initial Profiles

Influences such as these led us, as consultants with the State Department of Education, to an early stage of this project. Recognizing the need for enhanced literacy assessment at the primary level, and for portfolios that extend beyond writing and connect with the Common Core vital results for Communication, we responded to one district's request for help in developing an alternative approach to literacy assessment. We worked with 34 teachers over the course of a year, and adapted the model used by Paris et al. (1992), to produce six draft profiles, one each for kindergarten, Grades 1, 2, 3–4, 5–6, and 7–8. Each profile contained several dimensions of literacy development (e.g., concepts of print, response to reading, writing conventions, ownership and engagement), descriptions of student behavior or development across four levels of proficiency, and a list of sample strategies for classroom assessment (e.g., running records, book logs, analysis of spelling stages).

The profiles reflected a holistic, literature-based orientation to literacy, and emphasized strategy development and the use of Vermont's writing criteria. We were also strongly influenced by Marie Clay's (1985, 1993) focus on observing what the child *can do* (as opposed to what he/she cannot do), Au, Scheu, Kawakami, and Herman's (1990) emphasis on the importance of ownership and engagement in literacy development, and the neo-Vygotskian concept of teaching as assisted performance (Gallimore & Tharp, 1990).

After receiving feedback on the initial profiles from participating teachers and others, we decided to focus our next step at the primary level because of interest and apparent need. In addition, we decided to combine the kindergarten, first grade, and second grade profiles into one. Doing so, we reasoned, would recognize the idiosyncratic nature of early literacy development (each youngster developing differently), and would better accommodate the wide range of literacy abilities in most classrooms. In addition, a multi-level arrangement would be responsive to the increasing number of multiage classrooms in Vermont, and might help to reduce narrow conceptions of "grade-level reading," while still delineating shared standards, with increasing expectations, for students.

We hypothesized that the revised, multiage profile would help primary-level teachers gauge the development of literacy, and would prompt development of well-rounded literacy portfolios at the same time. We knew that the multilevel profile still needed to be tested out and refined, however, so we spent the next year conducting an informal pilot project using the profile.

THE PRIMARY LITERACY ASSESSMENT PILOT PROJECT

Profile

The revised profile (Table 13.1), instead of a collection of grade-specific documents, included descriptors for kindergarten through Grade 2, and was printed on one large sheet of paper. For each of the ten dimensions of literacy, a corresponding question was listed (to make clear why one might be interested in the area), as well as a "menu" of possible assessment strategies. Six levels of proficiency, from early emergent to fluency, were described for each dimension.

The profile, by guiding the teacher's observations of student progress in each dimension, yet displaying a composite view of achievement and progress across dimensions, was intended to represent an individual student's "big picture" of literacy development. It was expected that students would have different profiles (as indicated by teachers' highlighting the extent of their achievement or proficiency at regular, perhaps marking-period, intervals), and that students' rates of progress would vary as well.

The purpose of the profile was twofold: to guide teachers' instructional decision making (for next steps) by using shared language for observations of student literacy behaviors, and to facilitate communication with parents, teachers, and others. It was not intended for scoring or beyond-the-classroom accountability purposes, so no efforts were made to standardize teachers' judgments made through use of the profile. Rather, it was developed to depict students' development as evident in literacy portfolios and thereby assist the teacher in communicating the results of assessment and in his/her classroom decision making.

Nature of the Pilot

A pilot was needed to refine the profile and to provide an opportunity to test out the use of the profile in classroom settings. We were primarily interested in three things. First of all, its usefulness: How would the profile work for teachers—as a tool for communication, for organizing assessment? What helped, and what was difficult? Were there additional changes that needed to be made in the profile?

Second, what kind of impact might it have on teaching? Might the profile function as a form of cognitive structuring (Gallimore & Tharp, 1990), as one means of assisted performance to help teachers focus and attend to various aspects of literacy development in students?

Finally, we wondered about the potential influence of the profile on assessment itself and its uses. Would it expand the kinds of assessment methods teachers use? Would it influence how they looked at the contents

TABLE 13.1

Primary Literacy Assessment Profile Showing Developmental Levels for Major Dimensions of Reading and Writing

Dimension Tools, Methods	Key Question	Early Emergent (K)	Transition to Early	Early	Transitional	Early Fluency	Fluency (2)
CONCEPTS OF PRINT *concepts of print assessments *observations recorded in monitoring notebook *conferences	How familiar are students with print, and with the world of books?	Students may have a few concepts about print, recognize their own name, but are not yet paying much attention to print around them.	Students have basic control over L-R directionality and return sweep; may not have voice-print matching. Can distinguish letters from words.	Students have control over directionality, voice-print matching.	Students have most concepts of print, including the function of periods, question marks, commas, and quotation marks.	Students demonstrate consistent control over concepts of print in reading.	Students demonstrate consistent control over concepts of print in reading
READING STRATEGIES *running records *monitoring notebook *partner reading sheets *conferences	To what extent are students learning the strategies/processes of reading?	Students can read silently with comprehension and are beginning to self-monitor for comprehension difficulties. With prompting, students use strategies such as visualizing and reading ahead.	Students frequently self-monitor for comprehension difficulties, using fix-up strategies such as rereading, visualizing, and reading ahead.	Students are beginning to cross-check, use multiple cues, reread, and self-correct. They need a good deal of support.	Students predict and confirm independently, use multiple cues, and frequently self-correct. They are developing the ability to read silently for meaning.	Students can read silently with comprehension and are beginning to self-monitor for comprehension difficulties. With prompting, students use strategies such as visualizing and reading ahead.	Students frequently self-monitor for comprehension difficulties, using fix-up strategies such as rereading, visualizing, and reading ahead.

309

TABLE 13.1
(Continued)

Dimension Tools, Methods	Key Question	Early Emergent (K)	Transition to Early	Early	Transitional	Early Fluency	Fluency (2)
TEXT LEVELS *running records, miscue analysis *retellings *logs of books read *conferences	Are students able to read and understand books at increasing levels of complexity?	Students recognize their own names and familiar environmental print (signs, labels).	Students can read simple, predictable books such as *Brown Bear, Brown Bear* or *Monster Sandwich* with adult voice support. (see Appendix for sample books)	After a suitable introduction, students can independently read books such as *All by Myself* or *Rosie's Walk* (see Appendix) and demonstrate understanding	Students can read books such as *Caps for Sale* or *A Kiss for Little Bear* (see Appendix) and demonstrate understanding.	Students independently read books such as *Henry and Mudge, Nate the Great, Owl at Home* (see Appendix) and demonstrate understanding.	Students independently read short "transitional" books such as *Freckle Juice* or *Ramona Quimby* (see Appendix) and demonstrate understanding.
WRITING STRATEGIES/ PROCESSES *portfolios *conferences *observations recorded in monitoring logs	Are students developing writing process skills?	With prompting, students come up with ideas for drawing/ writing.	Students generate their own ideas and respond to others' prompts for writing and drawing. They often add to what they've done.	Students are gaining confidence in writing independently, and with prompting, will reread what they have written.	Students are learning to listen to others' feed-back to their writing, and are beginning to self-edit their own writing-- checking if it makes sense or looks right.	Students are developing skills in brainstorming and planning their writing. They often self-edit their own writing --based on what conventions they have control over.	Students have a range of strategies for prewriting, drafting, and self-editing. They are developing skills in giving/ receiving feedback in conferences, and revising independently.

310

TABLE 13.1
(Continued)

Dimension Tools, Methods	Key Question	Early Emergent (K)	Transition to Early	Early	Transitional	Early Fluency	Fluency (2)
ORAL LANGUAGE *observations recorded in monitoring log *discussions *conferences	Does students' language development show increasing development in flexibility, vocabulary, and syntax?	Students express thoughts and ideas with phrases or a few simple sentences. A good deal of support is needed in following simple directions.	Students usually speak in complete sentences and use expanded vocabulary. They participate in two-waycommunications, usually staying on the topic, and can follow simple directions.	Students usually speak in complete sentences, and engage in dialogue to exchange information. Students ask questions when they don't understand, and, with support, can follow two-step directions.	Students speak in complete sentences, and use conversation for a variety of purposes. Vocabulary and sentence structures expand, and most two-step directions can be followed.	Students use increasingly clear language and expanded vocabulary and sentence struc-ture. They are beginning to show an aware-ness of audience by varying tone, rate, word choice, etc.	Students express ideas with clarity and use compound and complex sentences when relevant. They begin to show an awareness of audience by varying tone, rate, word choice, etc.
READING/ WRITING OWNERSHIP/ ENGAGEMENT *reading logs *student /parent interviews, questionnaires *Reading Atti-Inventory *Writers' Chair, Readers' Chair *portfolios	How engaged are students with reading and writing?	Students show interest in books when read to. Students discuss what's been read and draw/label/write when encouraged.	Students seek out books to explore independently & demonstrate involvement with the story/-content. Students show interest in draw-ing/labeling/writing to respond to stories, etc.	Students self-select books for reading. They show interest in authors, books, reading, and writing. They often select their own topics for writing.	Students show interest in reading and writing and are beginning to show confidence in sharing their reading/writing choices with others.	Students often initiate their own reading and writing, demonstrate confidence in pieces they have written, and can tell a variety of audiences about books they have read.	Students actively seek out books, read voluntarily on most days, and write with confidence. They can con-centrate for ext-ended periods of time, & can explain their reading/writing choices to others.

311

TABLE 13.1
(Continued)

Dimension Tools, Methods	Key Question	Early Emergent (K)	Transition to Early	Early	Transitional	Early Fluency	Fluency (2)
RESPONSE TO READING *discussions *retellings *rewrites, response journals, story maps, other written responses *visual arts, performing arts *monitoring log	How well do students respond to what is read?	Students can identify the topic of what is read (to them) and offer a basic emotional response.	Students can connect what is read (to them) with their own background knowledge, and draw/talk about main characters of key ideas.	Students' responses to what they read show some connection to background knowledge and a basic "gist" of characters, storyline, or key ideas.	Students' responses show their background knowledge and understanding of basic story elements (character, setting, problem) or key ideas and details.	Students' responses show their background knowledge, understanding of text/story structure and some evidence of imagination, application, or extension.	Students' responses show understanding of text/story structure (using supportive evidence from text) and evidence of imagination, application, or extension.
WRITING: CONTENT AND STYLE *drawing or writing samples *monitoring log *journals	Can students write clear/ purposeful messages/ stories?	Students draw pictures to express ideas.	Students label or construct written messages-- either alone or with pictures.	Students can write a coherent message of a sentence or two and retell what they have written	Students can write and reread short pieces that make sense and stick to a topic.	Students' writing is often longer, increasingly clear in its purpose and details, and has a beginning, middle, and end.	Students' writing shows increasingly clear purpose and details, has a beginning, middle, and end, and beginning voice/tone. Pieces increase in length and reflect a range of genre.

312

TABLE 13.1
(Continued)

Dimension Tools, Methods	Key Question	Early Emergent (K)	Transition to Early	Early	Transitional	Early Fluency	Fluency (2)
WRITING CONVENTIONS *students' writing samples *portfolio *spelling stages sheet Spellwrite sheet, Spellmaster, Hearing Sounds in Words	Does students' independent writing show development of grammar, usage, & spelling/ mechanics?	Students may be using scribble writing or random symbols/letters to accompany pictures. Students can write at least part of their first names.	Students write from left to right, top to bottom. Some letters are used for beginning/ ending sounds	Students' messages show that they use letters for most beginning and ending sounds. Students leave spaces between words and are developing use of punctuation and upper/ lowercase letters. **	Students' writing shows a mixture of spelling patterns: some phonetic, some conventional, and use of acceptable sentence structure. Capitals and periods are usually used appropriately. **	Students' writing shows increasingly standards spelling, with attention to endings, some vowel combinations and spelling patterns. Use of punctuation includes question marks and exclamation points.	Students' writing shows standard spelling of most commonly used words, with attention to vowel patterns and common prefixes and suffixes. Ending punctuation is usually appropriate.
REFLECTION/ METACOGNITION *interviews, surveys *conferences *partner reading sheets *Think-alouds *monitoring logs *"I am learning to / I can" sheets	Do students reflect on their writing/ reading and monitor/ revise accordingly?			With strong adult support, students notice reading and writing strategies (what's working and what isn't) and work.	With some adult support, students begin to express what they notice about their reading and writing strategies and work	Students sometimes reread, reflect, and express what they notice about their reading and writing strategies and work.	Students frequently reread, reflect, and can clearly express what they notice about their reading/writing strategies and work.

Note. *Students who do not seem to be making progress (after instruction) in the use of reading strategies (difficulty in using visual cues or confusing the sequence of graphic/phonic information); might need additional assessment and instruction in phonological abilities. **Students who do not seem to be making progress (after instruction) in attending to the sequence of sounds in words or in recording sounds in words; might need additional assessment and instruction in phonological abilities. Table developed by Sue Biggam, Nancy Teitelbaum, and Shayne Trubisz, with original assistance from teachers at Orleans-Essex North SU, VT.

of students' portfolios (noticing strengths instead of deficits) or how they made decisions using assessment information?

Participating Teachers

Twenty primary-level teachers were invited to join the project, and agreed to try out the profile as they used literacy portfolios with three sample students in their classes. Participants also agreed to try out the profile as a communication tool with parents, and to respond to three questionnaires over the course of the pilot project.

All were female: 4 kindergarten teachers, 5 first-grade, 1 multiage K–1; 2 second-grade, 6 multiage 1–2; 1 multiage 1–2–3; and 1 Chapter 1 teacher. Most participants were from small, rural schools (although a few taught in urban or suburban schools) and had at least 8–10 years of teaching experience. All were eager, committed teachers whom we knew to be highly regarded in the area of literacy instruction.

Pilot Group Activities

All pilot group members met together in January for an all-day session where participants reviewed the intent of the project, recommended some additional changes to the K–2 profile, and were introduced to a few new assessment strategies. This was not a training session, but rather a time for questions, exploration, and sharing assessment practices. In order to be a pilot project member, participants simply needed to agree to try out the profile with three students, address at least three dimensions, and use at least one assessment strategy for each dimension.

We agreed to use a highlighter on each student's profile, to indicate students' development or achievement. (Teachers would color the boxes to indicate each student's proficiency or development for each dimension.) It is important to note that the use of the profile was intended to be both formative and summative. The formative aspect involved using both the assessment methods and the language of the profile to assist teacher decision making during instruction. The summative function involved reviewing the student's portfolio and indicating (by use of the highlighter) each student's levels of development.

At the first session, several participants had expressed strong interest in learning more about leveling books (so as to better understand the "Text Levels" dimension), so we scheduled an optional half-day session with a Reading Recovery Teacher-Leader, who helped us develop an appendix of books listed by cluster for the "text levels" dimension. We used Peterson's (1991) work to help us in this task of selecting representative trade books to act as benchmarks for different clustered levels of difficulty.

Data Collection: Self-Reports
From the Pilot Group Teachers

The purpose of the pilot was not to formally evaluate or validate the profile and its applications, but rather to enlist the support of some progressive teachers in revising the profile as needed and giving us feedback as to its possible uses, effects, applications, and adaptations. We collected two kinds of data: written responses to a questionnaire, and responses to an extent of use scale. The questionnaire, shown in Table 13.2, was administered for baseline information at the start of the project, and then again after 6 weeks and 3 months. It was designed to help us learn about the potential impact of the project on teachers. We did not attempt to validate teachers' judgments using the profile or to collect student data; those were clearly important questions, but not our immediate concern.

Our questions were shaped by our initial hunches and by our need for information: we wanted to know about the potential impact of the profile on teaching as well as on the uses teachers made of assessment information. We also wanted to know if the profile influenced what teachers noticed, and how feasible the use of the profile was in communication with parents.

After 8 weeks, at the project's mid-point (and then again at the close of the project), participants noted extent of use by indicating if they had used the profile: (1) *not at all*, hardly at all; (2) *a little bit*, paying attention to 2–4 of the dimensions of the profile, using at least one assessment "tool" for each dimension; (3) *a fair amount*, attending to over half of the dimensions, using at least one assessment tool for each; (4) *quite a bit*, attending to most of the dimensions listed, using at least one assessment tool for each; or (5) *extensively*, attending to all of the dimensions of the profile, using at least one assessment tool for each.

TABLE 13.2
Survey Questions for Participating Teachers

Questionnaire

1. What do you currently do to assess reading and writing development and progress for the three students? (What kinds of information do you collect; how do you collect it?)
2. How do you currently use that information?
3. What's difficult for you about early literacy assessment?
4. What seems to be coming along? What's helped?
5. What are you noticing about your teaching?
6. What are you noticing about your students?
7. Were you able to use the profile in discussion students' literacy development/progress with parents? How did that work?
8. Are there any changes to the profile itself that you would recommend?
9. Interest in further involvement?

In the final questionnaire, after an additional 6–8 weeks, participants were also asked about their use of the profile in communicating with parents, their recommendations for changes in the profile, and their possible interest in future involvement.

What We Learned

With a high rate of return (17 out of 20 teachers returning questionnaires at the mid-point, then 19 final questionnaires returned), we reviewed and coded the responses. For some questions (e.g., kinds of assessments strategies used or extent of use of the profile), data analysis involved tallying the incidence of responses. For most others, qualitative analysis, which involved sorting and categorizing responses according to similar patterns, trends, or unique responses, was used.

In reporting the responses made by participants at the middle and end of the pilot project, we note common patterns of responses made by the teachers. Overall, we found that most of the major shifts were made between the baseline questionnaires and the mid-point of the project; responses to the final questionnaire seemed to show refinement and reinforcement for the most part, rather than new reactions or insights from teachers. (It is important to remember that the entire pilot project only lasted 3–4 months). In addition, we indicate some responses that were unique and did not follow a pattern, and we also include some quotes from the teachers to illustrate findings.

Degree of Implementation. Before describing teachers' responses to the questionnaire and comparing responses to our initial hunches, it is important to note their degree of participation as indicated by their self-reports halfway through and at the close of the (voluntary and purposefully flexible) pilot project. We had expected that teachers would "ease in" to the use of the profile, but, as soon as 6 weeks after beginning the project, most of the participants, 70%, indicated that they had used the profile "a fair amount" or "quite a bit," attending to more than half of the dimensions or to most of the dimensions. This, along with other responses, seemed to indicate that the profile did present, at least for this sample of teachers, a feasible strategy for organizing and guiding early literacy assessment, particularly if done so with flexible expectations for implementation. The absence of gradual implementation may be due to a number of factors, and we did not probe that question in the current study.

By June, only 2 of the 19 responding teachers reported that they were attending to fewer than half of the dimensions; 7 attended to more than half of the dimensions; 6 to most of the dimensions, and 4 attended to all of the dimensions of the profile. We did not ask the teachers how many students they used the profile with, but three volunteered the information that they were using it with all of the students in their classrooms.

Extending and Refining the Focus of Literacy Assessment and Instruction. Most of the pilot teachers indicated that they expanded their methods of literacy assessment in some way over the course of the project. Most seemed to add a few strategies to their repertoire, despite the fact that the project offered no formal training in specific tools for assessment. One of the most notable trends was an increase in the number of teachers who used running records to help them assess students' developing strategies in reading (from 50% at the beginning of the project to 88% at the close). In addition, an increase was reported in the use of anecdotal records/monitoring logs, writing samples, and spelling "stages" assessments. Perhaps the conversations around assessment methods influenced group members to expand their repertoire of methods?

Teachers also said that the specificity of the profile helped sharpen the focus of their observations so that they noticed more of students' emerging literacy behaviors. With one exception, all teachers who responded commented that specific aspects of their teaching had changed since using the profile. One teacher explained, "My teaching is centered more around the needs of individual children, less around grade-level objectives." Another said, "I'm now noticing more children's reading behaviors which—in the past—I may have overlooked in favor of looking for skills." Some found that their teaching showed an increased focus in a particular dimension, such as strategies or reflection: "I'm asking 'why?' or 'what made you decide that?' more often; I'm realizing the value of knowing the learner's strategies!"

Most teachers noted the influence of the profile on their planning and decision making. One reported, "My planning focuses more now on authentic reading/writing activities and less on 'theme' activities." Another found that the specific focus of the dimensions helped her become more focused. "I'm crisper and clearer, more concise . . . what time I have with students I'm using better." After the group session on analyzing and clustering books, several teachers remarked that the knowledge they gained was particularly helpful to them in selecting appropriate books for assessment and guided reading with students.

Teachers also reported that the project led them to reflect on and evaluate their own teaching effectiveness. One teacher commented, "I use it (the profile) to monitor my own growth as a teacher." Another noted that by comparing her areas of focus in teaching and assessing with the dimensions listed, she noticed imbalances. "It's helped me to see that I stress reading more than writing, and I am trying to balance/integrate them within my limited time with kids each day."

Focus on What Students Can Do. Our hunch in this area was supported as well. Teachers consistently reported an increased awareness of student progress. Kindergarten teachers, in particular, frequently expressed surprise at their students' developing literacy skills. One said, "I'm amazed at how much they know, even at age 5, about reading and writing." Another remarked, "They are excited about their progress because I am pointing it out all the time!"

Teachers also told us that student self-awareness seemed to increase. One teacher noted, "Students are beginning to use the language of strategies—they are better able to vocalize problems, etc." Another said, "Their images of themselves as 'real' readers and writers have improved and become more solid—and I can sense the excitement!" Several teachers noted the specificity of students' self-awareness: "They are now more tuned in to noticing which skills they are demonstrating in writing, and now they show me examples of that." "They are more aware of what they are doing; they're using more 'book language', and have a clearer sense of purpose for literacy activities."

Organizing Portfolios, Setting Standards, and Communicating With Parents. Most teachers' comments supported our hunch that the profile and literacy portfolio would help organize and focus literacy assessment. One teacher noted, "Portfolios are pulling it all together for me"; another commented that "the profile is great because it's easy to understand and to get an overall picture of a child . . . it helps me stay organized, and I can see where I need to do more assessment right away." Still another remarked "It (the profile) makes sense! And, it makes me more accountable in preparing students for the 'next step'." The questions (on the far left) of the profile particularly seemed to help some teachers. "They have given me a reason to assess, a purpose—specific things to look for—and I'm working now on using one assessment tool to answer more than one question!" One teacher noted, "Currently, I keep the profile at my side at all times to help assess reading/writing development and progress."

Although several teachers remarked on the benefits of common language, group problem-solving, and exchange that were part of the pilot project group meetings, only some of the teachers explicitly referred to the use of the profile in setting shared standards. This may be due to the fact that in the pilot project none of the pilot teachers came from the same school, or it may simply reflect that we did not use the term "standards" extensively with the teachers. One teacher did note the impact of the profile in heightening her own standards for students. "When writing, my students sometimes complain now because I am more consistent about my expectations." Another said, "I am constantly looking for and finding ways to adjust, to involve students in their own reflection processes and their own record keeping—even at ages 5 and 6: this is new!" Still another noted, "I'm talking to students more now about what they're doing, what I have seen."

Most of the teachers used the profile in some way in communication with parents, and were positive about its potential in visually displaying a composite picture of an individual student's literacy development. Several teachers remarked at how impressed parents were. One recalled an incident at a recent parent conference, where the parent, who happened to be an attorney, commented, "Wow! I never knew teaching was so much work!" The same teacher used the profile as a foundation for a presentation to parents on multiage teaching, and received a positive response.

However, a number of teachers said that they had found the profile difficult to use with parents because of the time needed to explain the dimensions, the language of the descriptors, and individual student progress—particularly during already tightly scheduled parent conferences. Several indicated that in the next school year they would use the profile at the beginning of the school year to outline the breadth of the reading-writing program as well as the developmental nature of literacy learning.

Changes Recommended and Interest in Further Involvement. Although about half of the teachers made no recommendations for change, others made suggestions: making format changes so that the profile can be more easily read, adjusting the oral language strand to better reflect authentic language use, and including reflection descriptors at the two earliest stages on the profile.

At the close of the project we asked participants whether, and how, they would like to be involved in the future. All but one (who would not be teaching the next year) indicated interest in continuing and expanding their use of the profile with students, either by focusing on more dimensions or more students. They also indicated interest in attending follow-up sessions and being kept abreast of further development. More than half said they would be interested in contributing to the development of a Resource Guide, and about the same number indicated possible interest in learning to coach other teachers to use the profile and key assessment methods.

Beyond Our Hunches: Surprises and Issues. One surprising finding was that only one teacher mentioned using assessment information to signal referrals to Chapter 1, special education, or other services. We had expected that, because the profile was intended for classroom-based assessment, teachers might use it as a guide for referrals, which often are shaped by teacher judgment as well as more formal assessments. Perhaps teachers did not mention this because many of them only used the profile with three students—a very small sample. Another factor may have been the time of year that the pilot project was initiated (January); most students who are a concern to teachers have already been referred by that time. Perhaps the use of the profile as a guide for referrals needs to be explicitly discussed?

Another surprise involved the consistently positive response from participating teachers. We had not expected that participants would be so enthusiastic in their reaction either to the profile itself or to the pilot project. Of course, inviting teachers who already had a reputation for being highly skilled and professional might have been a factor, along with the flexible, voluntary nature of the project.

Because we expected that managing and finding time for assessment would be an issue, it was not a surprise that almost all (82%) of the teachers said that finding time for assessment was an ongoing problem. This was true not only at the beginning of the project, but throughout the 4-month pilot. Many of the teachers expressed this as difficulty in management (of other youngsters in the classroom) while trying to undertake individual assessments. One teacher remarked about the difficulty of "getting to each child often enough—and recording and documenting all that I notice and carry around in my head." Another commented on the difficulty of "being a disciplined observer."

None of the teachers mentioned the profile itself as being a time-consuming or unwieldy add-on, yet we noted that two of the pilot teachers were only able to attend to a few of the dimensions listed, and several focused on about half of the dimensions. Were some dimensions easier to assess than others? Should some of the dimensions be combined? Or, is this more limited participation a result of the "relaxed" nature of the pilot, the evolutionary nature of teacher change, difficulty in managing time—or all of the above?!

Reflections and Questions

Admittedly, drawing too many conclusions about the use of literacy profiles with portfolios after a 4-month pilot project with 20 highly professional and committed teachers might be hasty. At the same time, the pilot project has provided us with an ideal opportunity to listen, observe, begin to form questions, refine the profile, and plan further professional development opportunities for teachers. First, we list some of our reflections and related questions.

1. *Teachers are managing to use literacy assessment not as an add-on, but as an essential part of instruction. At the same time, issues of management and concerns with time continue to be a problem.*

The extent to which instruction and assessment are interwoven continues to impress us. Teachers showed us that how they taught influenced what they would assess. How they assessed, in turn, influenced their teaching. Assessment took place during their teaching, and vice versa. What was often thought of an assessment dilemma, finding the time for careful observation, was frequently an issue of instructional management.

We have been continually reminded how central the issue of time—and the use of it—is to all of this. For some teachers, rethinking the use of time (e.g., replacing some activities with others) can make a big difference. For others, perhaps even the most efficient management of time may not be sufficient, and a more radical restructuring of how time is spent may be needed. Perhaps we cause more problems for ourselves by pretending that we can squeeze all that we expect highly professional teachers to do into the same 5½ hour, 180 day "boxes" as we have in the past?

2. *Literacy assessment cannot be fostered in isolation.*

We have recognized that there are many assumptions about literacy learning and teaching that underlie this entire effort. One teacher called them an "iceberg of assumptions"! As we continue, we need to be keenly aware that these assumptions are not yet shared; neither are the instructional opportunities and strategies broadly available. The implications for professional development—that is tailored to the individual needs of teachers, that includes demonstration, practice, and coaching, and that stresses collegial work—are clear but sobering in many cases. What kinds of conversations among teachers within a school must take place to build a common vision for a literate community?

3. *Teachers are beginning to agree on shared standards, common lenses, and language for looking at students' emerging literacy.*

We wish that we had asked participants, at the beginning and at the completion of the project, to list what they expected of students and what they value in literacy. (Hindsight seems to be particularly acute in pilot studies!) Nevertheless, we emerged from the first phase of this project with a strong sense that a common language and shared expectations were emerging. We *knew* what we meant when we talked about "strategies" or "ownership" in reading, or "content and style" in writing. Participating teachers said that they liked the explicit, descriptive language of the "developmental benchmark" statements: these were standards that reflected actual classroom practice, and provided realistic but increasingly sophisticated indicators of literacy development. We are anxious to see what happens when a profile is used by all of the primary-level teachers in a school. Does the use of a profile on a school-wide basis help to build common expectations across grades?

4. *Teachers value the availability of a "big picture" of literacy—for their own use and for communicating with others.*

We have been encouraged by the positive response of the pilot teachers and impressed with their involvement in this literacy assessment project. The 20 teachers appreciated the way that the profile gave both a structure and a set of lenses for literacy portfolios. They did seem to use the profile as a means of cognitive structuring, as a way of guiding their observations and giving names (dimensions or descriptors) to what they observed.

In exploring the potential of the profile and portfolios, the teachers showed persistence, insight, risk taking, and professionalism, which probably should not surprise us because we invited them because of those same qualities. Many of the teachers seem to fit Fullan's (1994) description of individuals who spur change, often because of their own commitments, moral imperatives, and perseverance. Yet they are clearly unique, each with their own strengths and needs. Perhaps some brief "snapshots" of three of our pilot teachers, Kit, Shelly, and Lisa might illustrate this.

Kit, Shelly, and Lisa

Kit had only been teaching for 3 years when she joined the project, but was recommended for participation because she had a high degree of interest in classroom-based assessment as well as a good deal of skill. A first-grade teacher, she attended all of the group meetings, and impressed us all with her calm, sensible approach to organizing her classroom for assessment. Kit's portfolios in January, at the beginning of the project, consisted of a "collection of samples" as well as varied checklists and notes, which she used to present to parents and to guide her instructional decisions. Yet she noted that the "range of developmental stages within a large classroom" made literacy assessment difficult. By March, Kit had added a number of assessment tools, and was using most of the dimensions of the profile with her sample students. Although she still said that the span of achievement levels was a challenge, Kit commented that the "scope" of the profile made it a "great guide," and helped her to pull her current portfolios together, and "round them out." By June, Kit was using the profile with most of her students, and said that it (the profile) had "put all of the pieces together—by child and by the class as a whole." Kit, a skilled teacher with strong potential for leadership, is now helping others to learn about the profile. Because she expresses hesitancy about her limited experience, however, she will need a good deal of support to gain the confidence to share her strategies with others.

Shelly, a Grade 1–2 multiage teacher with 15 years of experience, also began the project with many assessment skills, but with a strong need for help in "managing the whole thing." By March she was using most of the dimensions of the profile, but still found it difficult to keep up with "17 different reading levels." Shelly used the profile with her sample students, found the profile to be "a good tool," particularly useful in communicating with parents, and said that the "get-togethers helped." Shelly's commitment to addressing the needs of a diverse group of students in her classroom was her reason for joining the profile project. By June, she was focusing on "over half" of the dimensions with her sample students, and said that she would be expanding her use of the profile in the coming year. Shelly is still looking for help with classroom organization/management issues, which, to her, are the biggest roadblock to effective assessment.

Lisa, another multiage (1–2–3) teacher, with 18 years of experience, began the project with a good deal of skill in assessing and supporting emergent literacy, but with concerns about "too much paper." By March, the Primary Literacy Profile became an integral part of her students' portfolios. She stapled a copy of the profile inside each folder, and said that it helped her be "more accountable in preparing students for the 'next step.' " By June, Lisa found that she was able to attend to most of the dimensions on the profile, and said that the "visual" organization of the profile was particularly helpful to her in seeing the progress of her students. Also, she said that she found herself becoming more articulate to students about what they need to be doing. Lisa changed grade levels at the end of the pilot project, so will not be using it in her classroom, but is now helping other K–2 teachers learn about the profile.

THINKING AHEAD

In reflecting on teachers' involvement and the insights we have all gained during the pilot study, we have began to look ahead to further implementation and expansion of the project. With a yet-to-be-fully-charted path, several points strike us and some plans are already underway.

The profile itself is being revised, and will probably continue to be a "working" document as we learn more. We will be adding a dimension on researching/investigating to better link it with Vermont's Common Core Framework. We will also be making several changes in the reflection and oral language dimensions. In addition, the names of the writing dimensions ("Writing Content and Style" and "Writing Conventions") will be changed so that they match more explicitly Vermont's writing criteria: "Purpose, Organization, Details, Voice/Tone" and "Grammar, Usage, and Mechanics."

We need to think about the multiple uses of the profile. Should it be simplified for use with students? Is that an appropriate use at the primary level? How and when can the profile best be used with parents—at Open House time? Should it be simplified for that purpose, or is it important to maintain its complexity to avoid oversimplifying literacy, as may have been done in the past?

So far, we have focused almost entirely on the uses of the profile for internal, classroom-based assessment and for communication with parents. Although our intentions have been to use the profile only at this level, is it possible to consider its use as a *framework* for school-wide accountability as well? In other words, the profile would describe the agreed-on dimensions of literacy as well as descriptions of increasing student proficiency. All dimensions would be the concern of classroom teachers; a few dimensions would be of interest to school/district stakeholders. In order to provide the kind of uniform tools/administration that are usually seen as necessary for this purpose, benchmarks would probably be necessary for some of the dimensions. Or, might external assessments such as New Standards tasks be used to validate or "audit" teachers' observations in particular dimensions?

Perhaps one scenario would involve each grade level or grade-level cluster (e.g., grades 1–2) identifying two dimensions to be "tapped" for external (school or district) assessment purposes. For example, at the first-grade level, reading strategies and writing conventions might be particularly appropriate dimensions for schoolwide accountability, while at the second-grade level, text levels and writing content/style might be tapped. Then, at the fifth-grade level, where the statewide (Vermont) assessment program requires a sampling of portfolios with specific types of writing genre (e.g., reflective letter, imaginative piece) included, another sort of "tapping" might occur. Teachers and students would "pull from" the classroom literacy portfolio to submit the minimum content required by the state assessment program. This notion of external assessment being "embedded" in internal assessment (Wixson, Valencia, & Lipson, 1994) is powerful, intriguing and worth further exploration.

Plans are underway for expanded professional development to introduce interested teachers to the use of the profile and primary literacy portfolios. We are planning a series of Primary Literacy Assessment Seminars to be available around the state, with 11 teachers functioning as Literacy Assessment Coaches in school or district staff development projects. About half of the coaches are past members of the pilot group; the others implemented the profile and literacy portfolios in their classrooms after the pilot project. The seminars will be modeled after the pilot project, encouraging teachers to gradually implement the profile and portfolios with just a few students at first. In addition, work is beginning on a profile for Grades 2–4. We expect to convene a similar pilot group to further shape it and try it out.

We see potential in more explicitly linking the profile to the communication strand of the Common Core Framework, and have, in fact, renamed it the Primary Literacy/Communications Profile. It is this kind of linkage that seems to hold the potential of enabling systemic state reform to "seep" into and take hold in classrooms. The profile may well function as one model of local, classroom-based literacy assessment that uses Vermont's Common Core Framework as a template, but is flexible enough to be adapted by individual teachers and schools.

Returning to the challenge that began this exploration, we are definitely encouraged that efforts such as the Primary Literacy Assessment Project seem to have the potential to help teachers and others not only see a big picture of literacy development through profiles and portfolios, but to see with increased focus and clarity. Like learning to use eyeglasses that have a new prescription, or 3-D glasses (for those who can remember them), learning to use such a complex set of lenses will take time, patience, persistence, and a willingness to adjust.

The potential benefits are enticing, however: teachers who notice what students can do, not what they cannot, and adjust instruction accordingly; parents who can see the complexity of their youngsters' literacy learning, yet have a picture they can use to support further learning; and schools that have a common vision for literacy development and shared standards—connected to statewide curriculum and assessment efforts—but without rigid and unrealistic expectations that all students will develop the same capabilities at the same time and at the same rate. This kind of big picture is worth all of our efforts.

REFERENCES

Au, K. H., Scheu, J., Kawakami, A., & Herman, P. (1990). Assessment and accountability in a whole language curriculum. *The Reading Teacher, 43,* 574–578.

Biggam, S. (1992, December). *The meaning and use of portfolios in statewide assessment.* In K. Wixson (Chair), Symposium conducted at the National Reading Conference. San Antonio, TX.

Clay, M. (1985). *The early detection of reading difficulties.* Portsmouth, NH: Heinemann.

Clay, M. (1993). *An observation survey.* Portsmouth, NH: Heinemann.

Fullan, M. (1994, March). *Harnessing the forces of educational reform.* Presentation at the 49th Annual Conference of the Association for Supervision and Curriculum Development, Chicago, IL.

Gallimore, R., & Tharp, R. (1990). Teaching mind in society: Teaching, schooling and literate discourse. In L. C. Moll (Ed.), *Vygotsky and education: Instructional implications and applications of sociohistorical psychology* (pp. 102–125). New York: Cambridge University Press.

Koretz, D., Stecher, B., & Deibert, E. (1993). *The reliability of scores from the 1992 Vermont portfolio assessment program* (Tech. Rep. No. 355). Los Angeles: University of California, Center for Research on Evaluation, Standards, and Student Testing; Center for the Study of Evaluation.

Koretz, D., Stecher, B., Klein, S., & McCaffrey, D. (1994). The Vermont portfolio assessment program: Findings and implications. *Educational Measurement: Issues and Practice, 13*(3), 4–16.

Mills, R., & Brewer, R. (1988, November). *Working together to show results: An approach to school accountability for Vermont.* Paper prepared for the Vermont Department of Education.

O'Neil, J. (1993). The promise of portfolios: Vermont effort reveals benefits, shortcomings. *Update,* (Association for Supervision and Curriculum Development)*35*(7), pp. 1, 5.

Paris, S., Calfee, R., Filby, N., Hiebert, E., Pearson, P., Valencia, S. W., & Wolf, K. (1992). A framework for authentic literacy assessment. *The Reading Teacher, 46*(3), 88–98.

Peterson, B. (1991). Selecting books for beginning readers. In D. Deford, C. Lyons, & G. S. Pinnell (Eds.), *Bridges to literacy: Learning from reading recovery* (pp. 119–147). Portsmouth, NH: Heinemann.

Tavalin, F. (1993). Vermont writing portfolios. In M. A. Smith & M. Ylvisaker (Eds.), *Teachers' Voices: Portfolios in the classroom.* Berkeley, CA: National Writing Project.

University of Vermont. (1993). *Literacy for all Vermont children by age nine* (Policy study). Burlington, VT.

Vermont Department of Education. (1994a). *Common Core Framework for Curriculum and Assessment (Draft in Progress).* Montpelier, VT.

Vermont Department of Education. (1994b). *Vermont's Common Core of Learning.* Montpelier, VT.

Wixson, K., Valencia, S., & Lipson, M. Y. (1994). Issues in literacy assessment: Facing the realities of internal and external assessment. *Journal of Literacy, 26*(3), 313–315.

CHAPTER FOURTEEN

Restructuring Student Assessment and Living to Tell About It

Carol M. McCabe
Bay Village City Schools, Ohio

The Bay Village school district outside Cleveland, Ohio, enrolls 2,500 students from kindergarten through grade 12. Class sizes in our K–6 program range between 25 to 28 students. The language arts program is integrated across the disciplines. All curriculum materials are developed by teachers and shared at the same grade level. The experience of our staff ranges from new graduates to 30-year veterans. For the last 6 years, the district has involved the entire staff in extensive staff development related to effective teaching of the language arts: reading, speaking, listening, and writing process. Consultants from local universities work with the staff on a regular basis.

The district mission, developed by more than 200 staff, students, and community members in 1988, calls for young people to learn more than the basics. Instead, the goal is that Bay Village graduates learn to think critically and creatively, communicate effectively, make decisions independently, and solve problems. This mission requires substantively different curriculum design. This change in mission leads to movement away from the exclusive use of traditional testing practice; and provides an ideal springboard for a more balanced system of assessment.

A conflict exists in this country today about how to accurately assess student achievement. Educators know that a balanced assessment program incorporates many sources of data and a variety of assessment strategies that provide the most accurate picture of what students have learned. On the other side of the issue are increasing demands for accountability based primarily on standardized test scores. Bay Village was caught in the conflict and sought to overcome the problem.

New assessment practices evolved from a dramatic change in the district's language arts program. We moved from a basal reading, skill-oriented philosophy to an integrated literature-based language arts model in which students were thoroughly immersed in reading and writing. Although expectations for language arts outcomes had changed and different teaching strategies were being utilized, we continued to test students in traditional ways. None of us knew a better way. The district administration was concerned about teacher accountability and teachers were searching for ways to account for student learning. In a misguided effort to insure accountability and for lack of anything better, the district administration required teachers to continue to use old tests with the new curriculum. This policy resulted in major disparities between classroom instruction and classroom assessment.

Problems with the existing testing program were evident:

- test items did not match the content and processes we were teaching
- test items did not reflect actual student work
- teacher artistry and creativity were neither honored nor expected
- students were neither engaged nor motivated
- student self-assessment and reflection were not goals
- students were not expected to reflect: to set personal learning goals, to think about the progress they had made, or to think about how they had learned
- tests showed what students did not know rather than identifying and celebrating what they had learned.

Teachers were frustrated. Administrators were frustrated. Students and parents were frustrated. Faced with the prospect of abandoning a course of study we knew was best for students we began to look for a solution. The annual conference of the National Council of Teachers of English (NCTE) offered the perfect place to find answers to our assessment problems. Fate smiled on Bay Village in a cab in Saint Louis where Alan Purves introduced us to an assessment guru, Professor Robert Tierney of Ohio State University. Tierney had been researching assessment practices with several Ohio public school districts. We picked his brain and we agreed to work together to further his research and to meet the needs of our students and teachers. Through his work in the district, we discovered how portfolio assessment would improve the way we assessed and evaluated student work.

As we embarked on the portfolio journey, all teachers K–6 became involved. Although the research project required a control group and an experimental group, the district plan called for including all teachers during the second year. The K–6 teachers in the portfolio group, the experimental group, used portfolios in their classrooms. The other half served as a non-portfolio control group. Portfolio users were divided into three groups, based on the notion of a cascading implementation. Each group introduced the portfolio concept to students at different times during the year. Teachers in the first group coached each of the subsequent groups. Each teacher identified four students who were used as case studies for whom information was gathered throughout the school year.

Teachers interviewed the four students periodically during the year. Attitudes about reading and writing, beliefs about themselves as readers and writers and changes in attitudes and beliefs were documented through structured interviews. Changes in teacher beliefs about their students as readers and writers were also traced throughout the year. In addition to the interviews, Tierney visited classrooms, discussed issues of concern with teachers and students, and participated in staff and administrative meetings each time he visited the district.

Analysis of the data gathered in Bay Village and other districts led Tierney to the following conclusions:

- Students from kindergarten to college appear empowered, enthralled, and appreciative of the opportunity to develop, share, and reflect on their portfolios.
- Students take ownership of the portfolios and have a richer, more positive, and expanded sense of their progress and goals as readers and writers across time.
- Assessment becomes collaborative rather than competitive.
- Teachers obtain a richer, clearer view of their students across time.
- Teachers negotiate a view of the student that is more fully informed in terms of what each individual child has achieved.
- Teachers have available to them records or receipts of what students are actually doing.
- Teachers have a vehicle for pursuing assessment practices that are student centered and focus on helping the learners assess themselves.
- Administrators have a vehicle for pursuing audits of classrooms and individual performance that represent what their students and classes are doing. (Tierney, Carter, & Desai, 1991)

Although we were clear on the need for a different assessment system for our students, articulation of more clearly defined goals was an evolutionary process. Each time we met we reshaped our purposes for using portfolios. Our goals were ultimately stated as follows:

Student Goals
- Establish accountability for reading and writing

- Develop self-selection and self-assessment
- Give ownership to their own learning
- Develop self-esteem

Teacher Goals

- Recognize reading and writing as development processes
- Create an ongoing process
- Provide a long-term record of student growth
- Bridge the gap between instruction and assessment

Parent Goals

- Make assessment collaborative; involve teachers, students, and their parents
- Emphasize the positive
- Establish a closer bond between home and school

Like student use of portfolios, the goals for portfolio assessment have continued to evolve as teachers and students have more experience with implementing portfolios.

In addition to setting goals and expectations for portfolios, we considered the value of the portfolio process for students and teachers. Teachers believe that portfolios themselves are valuable because they contain varieties of classroom work that show products, processes, and strategies. Portfolios evidence a long-term view of the real work students do, making evaluations clearer to teachers, students, and parents. Evaluation is solid and direct, based on ongoing classroom performance. It is not limited to one day of testing.

Students create their own portfolios. We have found that designing the portfolio and selecting the pieces to be included is in itself a valuable learning experience. Students gain pride and ownership in their learning, they increase their ability to reflect on their own learning and they improve skills in working together and communicating what they learned and how they learned with peers, parents, and teachers. Students are involved and invest in the process as well as the products.

IMPLEMENTATION

Many questions and uncertainties plagued us each day. We had no idea how to engage the staff in what appeared to be an unplanned path. How can we model portfolio assessment in classrooms? What are our purposes? How can students develop the ability to self-assess? What impact can we expect on teachers, students, and parents? What definitions apply? Answers to these questions evolved as we embraced the process and explored new avenues.

The staff recognized the need for a balanced assessment system. Traditionally teachers maintained folders of students work, projects, and papers. We analyzed the contents and realized that grades resulted from end products and criterion referenced tests. We seldom utilized student application of processes and strategies. We realized that contextualized measures related to specific thematic units and reading and writing processes would complement the picture. To achieve this we adapted our assessment system from a data gathering profile developed by Anthony, Johnson, Mickelson, and Preece (1991; see Fig. 14.1). Although we did not require the teachers to keep specific items in the portfolios, we did require a balance among the four quadrants of the data gathering profile.

Definitions and Types

Most teachers have traditionally maintained folders of student work for use with parents and to provide data to support the report cards. The portfolio, however, is not a folder. It is more than a folder, richer than a folder. Our definition of portfolio evolved as we continued our exploration. It is a systematic collection of student work primarily selected by the student through which the pupil reflects on his or her own learning. The heart of the process is the expectation that students make the portfolio selections. Student selection and reflection are the key elements which distinguish portfolios from folders. Students are expected to manage their portfolios. Design of the management system is left to the teacher's and students' artistry and is unique to each classroom.

Materials and Supplies

Each teacher was given a plastic crate and a variety of file folders. Students personalized their folders by adding photographs, stickers, sayings, and drawings. We quickly learned that kindergartners and first graders had difficulty maintaining their folders. Tying was a problem for many 5- and 6-year old children, so we obtained brightly colored folders with Velcro closures for the primary grades. Some teachers preferred three ring notebooks for their showcase portfolios. The district supported whatever style the individual teacher chose.

As we were developing the process, we did not really have any models to use. We frequently talked about the different kinds of things that could be included in a portfolio. Examples included such things as journal selections, videotapes, audiotapes, summaries of discussions, dramatic interpretations, plays, oral readings, poetry, participation in group work, explanations,

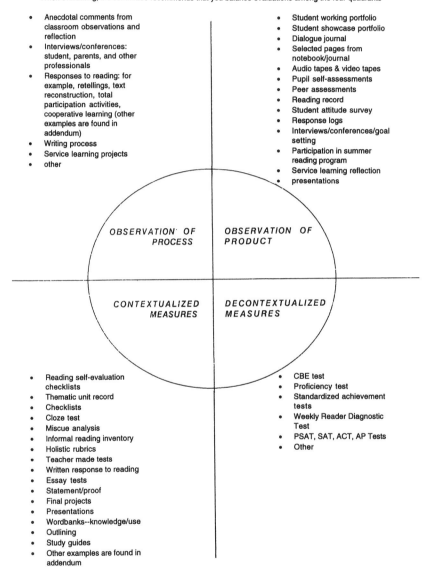

ASSESSMENT OPPORTUNITIES
DATA GATHERING PROFILE

When evaluating, the committee recommends that you balance evaluations among the four quadrants

- Anecdotal comments from classroom observations and reflection
- Interviews/conferences: student, parents, and other professionals
- Responses to reading: for example, retellings, text reconstruction, total participation activities, cooperative learning (other examples are found in addendum)
- Writing process
- Service learning projects
- other

- Student working portfolio
- Student showcase portfolio
- Dialogue journal
- Selected pages from notebook/journal
- Audio tapes & video tapes
- Pupil self-assessments
- Peer assessments
- Reading record
- Student attitude survey
- Response logs
- Interviews/conferences/goal setting
- Participation in summer reading program
- Service learning reflection presentations

OBSERVATION OF PROCESS

OBSERVATION OF PRODUCT

CONTEXTUALIZED MEASURES

DECONTEXTUALIZED MEASURES

- Reading self-evaluation checklists
- Thematic unit record
- Checklists
- Cloze test
- Miscue analysis
- Informal reading inventory
- Holistic rubrics
- Teacher made tests
- Written response to reading
- Essay tests
- Statement/proof
- Final projects
- Presentations
- Wordbanks--knowledge/use
- Outlining
- Study guides
- Other examples are found in addendum

- CBE test
- Proficiency test
- Standardized achievement tests
- Weekly Reader Diagnostic Test
- PSAT, SAT, ACT, AP Tests
- Other

FIG. 14.1. The assessment record. After Anthony et al. (1991).

brochures, research papers, projects, reports, art exhibits, computer print-outs, science demonstrations, lab reports, math processes and interpretations of mathematical concepts, interviews, newspaper articles, and analysis of particular reading selections. In addition to products, students also collected interpretations and reflections in the form of reading records, goal sheets, and cover sheets for individual assignments where the student is asked to explain why this particular piece is important and what was learned by doing it. Reflections about reading and writing are also included and check-lists analyzing group processes. Teacher and student autonomy are critical to the selection process.

We faced a dilemma in the conflict between teacher-assigned work that students select for their portfolio and student-selected responses and topics. If the student selects an assigned project for his or her portfolio, we question if this is truly a student selection. How much choice do students really have in the matter? The district course of study dictates the objectives for each grade level. We proceed cautiously with the types of questions we pose to students as they reflect on and make selections for their portfolios. We are trying to strike a balance between assigned work and student generated opinions. This topic continues to be analyzed.

We identified five types of portfolios. The *working portfolio* contains all the stuff on which the student is working—drafts, revisions, reading logs, response journals. The working portfolio is a treasure trove for anything the student chooses to continue working on. In addition to student choices, teachers may suggest that particular items be kept for future use. Student access to the working portfolio is critical. If the youngster is a kindergartner, you will find the box of portfolios on the floor. If they are sixth or seventh graders, you may find them on top of a bookcase or a file cabinet. In any case, they have to be in an area where the students have easy access to them. If they are locked in a file cabinet or a cupboard, they are not very accessible to the students.

The *showcase portfolio* is derived from the working portfolio. The student culls the working portfolio at least four times a year to select the work that best shows growth during that grading period. Teachers ask a variety of open-ended questions to involve their students in metacognitive thinking. Thinking about thinking and talking about thinking require careful ques-tioning techniques and substantial wait time for students to formulate their thoughts. Teacher questions are important for guiding students. Examples of typical questions include: What can you do now that you could not do last quarter? What was hard for you? What was easy for you? What will you work on next? What are your goals for next quarter? What makes this piece special? What did you learn? How did you decide that?

Students sort their working portfolios by dumping the contents on the floor and deciding which pieces they want to keep in the showcase. Once they have decided on selections, they share the selected pieces with a peer, asking for written comments. After the selection is finished, the student conferences with his or her teacher to discuss the specific selections and reflections. The questions just listed are a guide for the quarterly conference.

The *teacher portfolio* houses any information the teacher finds insightful in charting a student's progress. It is similar to a grade book, but is more fluid, complete, and elaborate. The teacher keeps a hanging folder for each child. Among the different items kept in the teacher portfolio are conference notes and summaries, goals sheets, teacher observations, anecdotal records, paper-and-pencil tasks, and significant student work. The teacher portfolio, the working portfolio, and the showcase portfolios are pulled together for the summative evaluation at the end of each grading period.

The *cumulative portfolio* is a repository for the annual selection of work to be passed to the next teacher to trace student growth throughout the student's career in the Bay Schools. Two pieces are selected each year from the showcase portfolio for the cumulative portfolio: one by the student, one by the teacher. The superintendent's vision is to present the graduate with his or her completed cumulative portfolio, along with a diploma. Storage of the cumulative portfolios is a practical problem as students continue through the portfolio process, and principals are concerned about the volume of materials needing storage. As yet, the district does not have a doable answer for this aspect of portfolio assessment. Perhaps one day technology will be an affordable and manageable vehicle for storage.

The *competency portfolio* served for the state-mandated competency assessment. However, we had developed many other ways to demonstrate accountability on competency assessments: locally developed competency tests, statewide proficiency tests, third grade "guarantee" (a state-developed checklist of skills expected of all students on entry to third grade), report cards, summaries of parent conferences, and cumulative record folders. Because the contents of the competency portfolio duplicated records and created extra work, we did what the military refers to as organized abandonment. We eliminated it.

Parent Involvement

A primary purpose of district assessment is to inform parents of their children's academic progress. Changes in instruction and assessment (even changing the name from testing to assessment) were confusing and troubling to many parents. In general, parents view assessment narrowly—as paper-and-pencil tests where the students' task is to give the right answers. We intended to broaden that conception to include all aspects of language arts growth. To be successful with the new assessment practices, we knew that we needed to help parents recognize their beliefs about instruction, as well as assessment, and to change those beliefs.

Initially, many parents felt disengaged from their children's education because they received fewer papers each day. Teachers explained that students were doing substantial work on projects lasting more than a class period. Work sent home is often in the form of journals, sloppy copies, or work still "under construction." Students are doing much more writing than they ever did before. As a result their errors are more evident. Even work that is edited and published can have mistakes. We are not after perfection, but continuous growth. We believe that our classrooms are places where it is safe to take risks. We want to expand the opportunity to learn beyond the issuing of a grade. We expect to see the developmental stages of reading and writing reflected in the portfolio, which means that the teachers cannot ask that everything be perfect. Most parents' experience is that children show them work only after it has been graded and corrected. The goal of schooling in the experience of many parents is "to get it right." Few parents see mistakes as essential steps in the learning process. Some parents were alarmed when they saw misspellings and grammatical errors. They were worried that their children might be missing the basics of the English language. They thought that mechanics, usage, grammar, and spelling (MUGS) were being ignored. Friday spelling tests and isolated grammar exercises were the only kinds of English instruction most parents knew. In their schooling experience, everyone got the same thing at the same time whether they needed it or not. The job of educating parents was enormous. In addition to changing beliefs about assessment, we had to demonstrate that teaching MUGS within the context of reading and writing could provide students with a solid education in the basics.

To overcome this hurdle and to address other changes, we conducted a series of parent information meetings. Teachers and administrators planned and presented the sessions intended to teach parents about the change and support them as they learned about new methods of teaching and grading. The parent information meetings were a start, but the new assessment system continued to evoke fears, uncertainty, and skepticism for some parents. We heard comments like "Just tell me if he has an A or an F; That's the way we did it when I was in school; How is she doing compared to the rest of the class?"

Teachers recognized the ongoing need to keep parents informed about student progress and the types of assessment strategies they were using, and we increased our communication efforts. Rather than limit our efforts to community-wide meetings, we decided to divide and conquer. Teachers and principals hosted small evening meetings and grade level and building meetings; informal question and answer sessions were held in homes; topical seminars were planned and presented once a month. The superintendent, the assistant superintendent, the curriculum director, and the public information officer came to "cottage" meetings in individual homes where small groups of parents discussed the assessment plan.

Parents were also informed through monthly classroom newsletters. Articles included suggestions for parents to help their children at home, lists of concepts learned during the month, language arts themes, and related skills. A few teachers arranged for weekly newsletters, written and published by students. The home-school journal was another strategy. Once a week the youngsters wrote a letter to their parents telling what they had learned in school. Parents were invited to respond to their children in the journal. That has proven to be very effective.

Spelling, a continuing parental concern, was exacerbated by the home-school journal, which often contained unedited rough drafts. We pointed out to the parents that the purpose of the journal was for students to communicate what they had learned and how they felt about the learning. Although they might feel tempted to grab a red pen and start circling all the errors, we asked them to hold that reaction in check. We asked that when they respond to their child's entry, they use correct mechanics, usage, grammar, and spelling.

In spite of frequent parent education sessions, some parents persisted in the call for traditional teaching practices for reading and English. They heard conflicting messages from many sources, and our community has not yet reached consensus on what constitutes satisfactory language skill when it comes to MUGS. Everyone agrees that students should be able to communicate effectively in writing and speaking. That much is clear. Confusion arises in how best to instruct students to achieve that goal. We continue to wrestle with this paradigm through dialogue with all those involved. Our experience suggests that to successfully change the assessment system requires constant communication with parents and other community members and enormous amounts of support for those experiencing the changes.

Staff Development and Professional Growth

The new language arts curriculum required considerable change on the part of teachers in how they approached what to teach, how to teach it, and how to assess student progress. All teachers were required to attend in-service sessions that focused on the developmental stages in reading, writing, speaking, and listening. The aim was for teachers to become more sensitive to variations in developmental levels of literacy among their students, allowing them to plan more appropriately for curriculum and instruction. Most teachers had been prepared to follow scripted lessons in basal manuals, which were suddenly no longer sufficient to meet the standards. They encountered a variety of new terms:

- invented spelling
- peer editing
- process writing
- holistic scoring of writing

- portfolio assessment
- proficiency tests
- writing across the curriculum
- curriculum integration

We collaborated with a group of professors from universities throughout Ohio on the identified topics. All of these in-service opportunities were offered during the school day on a released time basis with substitutes covering the classes. Many teachers seem hungry for more information. They crave opportunities to work together, to share common concerns, and to learn from one another. In-service sessions must be continually provided.

Embarking on the portfolio journey has not proved expensive in terms of materials and supplies. It is expensive in terms of staff development. This is a people enterprise and requires a sincere commitment on the part of the administration and teachers. Everyone must be willing to make changes in current practice, to take risks, and to try on "new ways of doing school" if the project is to have success and lifelong impact on children. Staff development is an essential ingredient for effective implementation of our plans.

Our teachers wanted to be a part of developing the alternative assessment practices. They had an intense desire to cooperate; they asked for guidance. They were accustomed to being given very specific directions and being told what to do. The teacher manuals they had used for years were teacher proof. They followed directions given in teacher manuals. They did not have to make too many judgments. The manuals listed questions and anticipated answers. The whole process required very little thinking for teachers or students. The tests were all written for them, and the recording system was well defined. They had become technicians. Students passed from one level to the next if they could do these tests that were written by someone else. Changing the language arts outcomes and assessment system created much conflict and insecurity for teachers.

Through staff meetings and in-service sessions, the teachers identified the many problems with traditional testing. A great deal of evidence supported the notion that change was necessary. They agreed to participate in the project. To begin, the staff met with Professor Robert Tierney, of Ohio State, discussed the project, and agreed on the materials they needed. Materials were purchased and distributed and alternative assessment was underway in Bay Village. Portfolio assessment created a great deal of disequilibrium. This was a brand new system in which teacher judgment and student ownership were key elements. Tierney and his staff provided support and encouragement. Principals also were encouraging. Frustration did arise, however, when Tierney's response to a specific, concrete question was another question. Tierney's strategy was designed to emphasize the ability of the teachers to make professional judgments. A few examples follow: Teachers would ask questions from the staff "Is this right?" "Am I doing the right thing?" "Is this OK?" Tierney's responses would be: "Is it working? What do you want it to do? What are your goals? Is it working for you? How do you feel about it?" He never answered their questions directly, but rather asked them to reflect on their own practice and to determine whether or not it was the right thing to do for their particular students. They were very frustrated because staff development for other new programs had been much like a cookbook. Classroom teachers were told exactly how to implement the new practices immediately. In the past, their own judgment was seldom valued, nor were they expected to make judgments about how students learned or developed. To successfully implement a new program (usually a new textbook series), teachers needed only to follow the directions. Student-centered learning was a very different matter.

Permitting students to have control was difficult for most of the staff. They were accustomed to managing every aspect of their classrooms. In fact it was expected and many employment evaluations were based on classroom management and control. Now we were saying, "Step aside, and let the students take some ownership. Let the students take care of themselves." That was a big struggle for almost all the teachers. The Bay Village teaching community was suffering culture shock.

As the year progressed, many teachers became comfortable letting go of some control. They invited students to participate in the portfolio process. They gained confidence in making decisions about instruction based on the developmental nature of learning. Growth in this arena is continuous. All staff members recognize the need to keep focused on student empowerment.

To reinforce the gains and to work with teachers new to the district, we initiated several support groups. The district reading consultants spearheaded this effort. Groups of teachers met at mutually agreed on times to discuss topics identified by each group. Teachers found that they needed much support and encouragement to continue to move toward more open-ended classroom environments. We hope to change the culture of the school by promoting a climate of sharing, collaboration, and coaching among teachers and students.

By the end of the year we knew we had made great strides in alternative instruction and assessment. Bay teachers believed they could help other teachers who wanted to implement portfolio assessment. But we were not sure how to replicate the process in other classrooms. We continue to investigate ways to share our experience. We knew we were on to something important.

BENEFITS

We see many advantages to using portfolios that emanate from the student, the teacher, parents, and the school district itself. Student portfolios offer rich evidence of growth and progress over time. Students are responsible for the portfolio process: collecting their samples, making the selections, reflecting on their work, and assessing their progress. The children have a constant point of reference to their base line work samples. This circular process provides the framework for students to set goals for future learning. Students present their learning to others (peers, parents, and teachers) by discussing their goals, their accomplishments, and their attempts. What a celebration when students meet with their parents to demonstrate what they have learned using the portfolio for evidence. At least once a year, on Portfolio Night, students invite their parents, grandparents, and any significant others to share their showcase portfolio. Each child has his own space in the classroom.

The teacher's function on this night is only to be sure that everyone has a space in the room and that the child has the floor. It is the most rewarding evening of the year, I think. The parents appreciate the program because their children tell what they have learned, and the portfolios show their accomplishments as readers and writers.

The following selections are taken from student portfolios to demonstrate their ability to discuss their reading and writing progress. The first set of selections are from "Laura's" third-grade portfolio. The first extract, from September, demonstrates her ability to set learning goals for the year, to evaluate her learning style, and to acknowledge what she can and cannot do in writing and in mathematics:

> What kind of learner I am. . . . .
> I learn best by reading. I can concentrate when I read. I love to read anything. I ecpshily like animal stories. I also learn by doing math it helps me to figure things out faster. My favorite subjects in school are readin and writing. I like writing creative storys. My favorite book series are the Little House on the Prarie books. I want to improve my math a little but I am getting better.
>
> Laura in September

In the second selection, written near the end of the school year, Laura's reflections cover several aspects of classroom instruction. She cogently assesses her improvements in reading and writing skills in a self-evaluation that demonstrates how her communication skills have blossomed. A goal of portfolio assessment in our program is the improvement of student self-esteem, and Laura's comments demonstrate the positive feelings that she has about herself as a learner:

> *How I Improved in Writing*
> I think I have improved in writing in alot of ways. I indent my paragraphs, use more details, write longer stories, use quotation marks, use better words, and have neater writing. I have fun thinking of charecteristics and quotes to make my stories better. I am proud of my improvment.

How I Improved in Reading

In reading I have improved in 2 ways. I can read longer books in shorter time and I can understand longer words. Even though those are few things they are improvments and I am proud of them.

Laura in May

Another benefit of portfolio assessment is the opportunity for teachers to provide focused feedback in a positive and nonthreatening way. Here is a sample from Laura's teacher. Laura had written that "I liked the pieces that I picked for the bulliten board. I like the Mad Scientist because it is full of adventure and exitement." The teacher responds:

Laura,

I liked the *Mad Scientist* too! I liked your word choices. It was exciting to read—I couldn't wait to find out what happened. Keep up the good work! Love,

Mrs. S.

The portfolio process also makes it possible for parents to become participants in the process. The following excerpts are from Laura's mother and father, whose support and encouragement become explicit and vivid:

I like your portfolio because . . .

You did all the writing that is inside! Wow, am I proud of you, Laura. It is obvious that you love to write because you do it so well and with such creativity. That is a gift that you will use for the rest of your life!

I think I like *The Table* the best. It has a very good message! Your story about the kitty in the tree is a favorite of mine too! I learned alot from the desert and rainforest stories also! See if you can bring your portfolio home to share with Grandpa and Ann! It is such fantastic work!

I love you and am proud of all you do!

Mom

Dear Laura,

As always, you should be very pleased with your portfolio and the wonderful stories you have written! The desert and the rainforest vacations were my favorites. Those climates are unusual ones for me and your descriptions helped me understand them more clearly.

Write often and continue to try various kinds of writing—poems, stories, plays, essays.

The three easiest words to write to you:

I love you! xxo

Dad

November

Here is one of Laura's final reflective pieces. Written in June just before the summer vacation, it evidences the growth that she has achieved since the September self-assessment:

I picked these pieces of work because I think I worked very hard on them. They took me alot of time and I am proud of them. I picked *The Plant that are Incredible Bulk* because it has lots of creataivity and I can relate to Bulloga's feeling because sometimes I'm really shy. I like my Literature Study because I like mystery storys and suspense. I also love dogs. Desmond sounds like a good and fiathful dog. I have spent a long time on those stories and I am proud that they turned out so well.

Laura in June

In the second set of selections, also from third grade, Kelli's quarterly reflections in November and January attest to her willingness to stretch academically and her ability to recognize her accomplishments:

Kelli

1st Quarter Reflection (November)

1. How have I Grown as a reader.
I can now talk loud when I am reading.
I used to be afraid to read aloud to people but now that I do it all the time I'am not afraid.
2. How have I grown as a Writer.
I can not write that Good but I have made lots of Books.
But I do know how to spell lot's of words.
3. How have I grown in Math.
I think I do well in math. But I can't realy do the take away with Zero's.
4. How have I Grown in Science Health and Social studies
That is hard for me. But I do like doing science and learning about health but when I do it there is alway's someone talking and I can't think.
5. My biggest achievement was in math. I havenever done the take away with zero is hard.
6. I have read 30 Books.
7. My goal for next quarter is to be able to take away with zero.

2nd Quarter (January)

1. I have grown pretty good because I like to read And I always practice.
2. I learned real good because we do lots of writing and I always write to myself to see if it is right.
3. I have grown o.k. I'am not the best at math but I do good in multiplcation
4. I have grown o.k. I do pretty good in health.
5. I have done really good In reading
6. My next goal is to do more social studies.
7. 39 books

I think my most favorite thing was opening stores. I am the vice president of our store. It is fun. It's cool to have our own checks. I liked when we went to Marcs and the candy sore. I also liked the folk tale fest. We made a few mistakes but I don't think anyone noticed. It was really fun. I think I worked really hard on my folk tale stuff. I also liked the volcanos and earth quakes.

It is fun to learn about active volcanos and the plates of the earth. I though Cinderela books were neat. I liked it when we wrote about them on note cards. I also think multiplucation is fun. I am learning the strategies to make it easier.

Kelli's added comments at the end of the January self-assessment, an extra effort that is unusual for a student who might easily be classified as "low-achieving," evoked the following written reaction from her teacher:

Your play for the Folk Tale Fest was super! You spoke clearly and with feeling. *Hansel and Gretel* is a great story to act out.

Mrs. S.

The preceding excerpts demonstrate several desirable features in the assessment of student achievement that are distinctive to portfolios. Students are actively engaged in their own work and are acquiring real sense of ownership and control. Within a meaningful context, they are learning to read and write. They monitor their growth over time. They are capable of reflective self-evaluation.

Teachers also benefit from observing students' growth over time. Portfolios provide concrete evidence of what students have learned. By analyzing portfolio contents, teachers streamline instruction to meet students' needs. Parent conferences are enhanced. Summative evaluations are accurately supported. Teachers are reassured that their observations, analysis, and judgments are grounded in context. Continuous learning is encouraged. Student progress is documented over time creating a holistic picture. Traditional testing and grading practices focus on decontextualized measures. Portfolio assessment promotes the notion that instruction and assessment are one and the same. We found portfolio assessment to be a credible way of approaching and solving the problems inherent in traditional testing programs.

Parents know what their children have learned. They experience their children's progress first hand. Report card grades and comments are supported by the portfolio pieces. When parents talk to their children about their portfolios they are amazed at the children's ability to engage in metacognition. Students articulate their goals to their parents. Discussions often include both the cognitive and affective domains. Key questions are: What did you learn? How do you feel?

A truly rewarding experience for a school principal, the superintendent, or curriculum director is to have a student share his or her portfolio with them. Students love to show their work, to discuss what they have learned, and reveal their goals.

Portfolios permit administrators to audit the curriculum. Review and analysis of portfolios at each grade level assist in identifying district strengths and weaknesses and staff development needs. Examination of portfolios provides district administrators with exemplary practices to recommend to their staffs. Portfolios promote a higher level of professional practice among teachers and administrators.

Challenges and Concerns

We have faced several challenges and are left with a number of concerns in implementing portfolio assessment. How does a district move from traditional testing to alternative assessment practices? Implementing portfolio assessment, like any other change in beliefs, requires extensive staff development. Bay Village supported the staff through the change process for two school years. We believe that much more staff development is necessary if we expect to maintain the changes teachers have made.

Some of the concerns we have about involving students are:

- Who has control over the selection?
- Who decides the standards for selecting pieces?
- How do students use their portfolios to gain information about themselves?
- What is the developmental nature of students' ability to reflect on their own work?
- How can peers provide informed encouragement and feedback?

Although we are aware of unanswered questions, we believe the advantages of this endeavor surpass the ongoing concerns. This whole process has created a welcome sense of unrest. We continue to research our theories and practices.

Standards. Standards for quality work are often not clearly established. Frequently students do not know what is expected of them. We did not clearly define our expectations in terms that students could understand. In fact, we were not very clear on our standards. Overcoming this obstacle meant many sessions with the staff hammering out consensus on grade level expectations. We realized that a range of performance is appropriate and desirable within a classroom. As we consider grade-level objectives, we discuss what we expect to see in student portfolios that demonstrates progress toward the objective. Collaboration among teachers is required to insure consistency across grade levels. We used samples and studied a good collection of works from students before we could determine what standards would be appropriate for each level of performance. We have much work to do in this area.

Administrative Support. Administrators can be a challenge and a concern, but also a benefit. While we were working with Dr. Tierney, the superintendent held regular review meetings. Principals reported the status of their buildings. Specific areas of concern were identified. The group of administrators brainstormed suggestions for dealing with specific problems. Principals were expected to discuss the portfolio process at staff meetings, to arrange substitutes so that teachers could have time to engage in peer coaching, to encourage risk taking, to accept their mistakes as steps in their learning, and to see that all materials and supplies were available to each teacher. Their support was key to the success of the program. Administrators were expected to be cheerleaders for teachers who were making enormous changes in their assessment practices. The principals were expected to assist their staffs in identifying their staff development needs. Not to be overlooked was the role the principal played in helping students talk about their portfolios. They were expected to conference with students on a regular basis and to report their success and problems with the other administrators.

CONCLUDING THOUGHTS

Portfolio assessment thrives in a community of learners. None of us operate in isolation. Collaboration among teachers and students is an important aspect of implementing alternative assessment. We are all learners and need time to grow and progress. The district must be committed to team planning. Teachers are decisionmakers, not merely technicians following a cookbook recipe. Parents and the community participate. Everyone in our school is successful. All children can learn. We value group learning and group work, and we assess it. We expect student work to be displayed and we expect the classroom environment to be inviting. We honor holistic learning. We want an integrated curriculum. We need principals to understand where the students are in the beginning of the year, and to support all the growth that the students experience. We need principals also to know where the teachers are at the beginning of the year, and to help them expand their repertoires. We communicate through reading and writing with a variety of literature and classroom conversation. We do not expect quiet classrooms. We expect noise and conversation. We value and celebrate alternative assessment that informs the learning process. It is used in all classrooms. We have not abandoned testing. We know that tests have a place to measure specific content in limited ways, but they are certainly a part of the whole process. We also need observational and anecdotal records that provide diagnostic information.

To replicate portfolio assessment we recommend a few guidelines. Focus primarily on writing and written responses to reading during that first year.

When teachers give feedback to the student writer, say what he or she liked about the selection. Help the student see things that are the same and different in this piece of writing as compared to another one. Ask the child what he or she has learned about himself or herself in this piece of writing. Ask the child what he or she plans to do the next time he or she writes. Let the students do most of the talking. Enjoy the fact that different people like different things. The teacher may not like a particular piece of writing, but a child may feel that it is just wonderful.

Be very careful about criticizing. Avoid being negative when giving constructive feedback. Avoid closed-ended questions that come off as an interrogation. Do no invalidate the child's ideas at the expense of mechanics. This list is much like walking a tightrope. Perhaps the best advice we can give is that we must use candor and integrity as we work with students.

We have so much to celebrate. We can celebrate student learning. We can celebrate the fact that students are able to take risks and that it is safe for them to do that. We can celebrate that we can trust our students. We can celebrate the collaboration, the professional decision making and the quest for the best instruction and learning that our teachers can give our students. We should applaud the efforts of our teachers and encourage them to forge ahead as pioneers, committed to professional growth.

I want to share with you some of the reasons to celebrate. Here are some goals left by a third grader who said that during the first grading period his goal in reading was to read seven picture books and four chapter books. At the end of that grading period, he said he had accomplished his goal and how he accomplished it was that he read at school and at home. He said he also wrote in his response log. When asked about his favorite book, he responded "*My Life as a Cartoonist* because I like cartooning." His goal in writing was to write 3 stories which he said he accomplished. When asked how he accomplished his goal he responded and I quote, "I just kept trying, not luck, me." When asked what he thinks he does best in writing, he says, "I use my mind and tell the stories." In the next grading period, he wants to read 20 chapter books and write 4 stories.

Here is a fifth grader's response, a reflection on his writing. "I like writing a story, thinking about it in my own mind and writing it down. I learn to spell by reading and writing. I have taken a lot of writing risks, just trying out words, thinking it out, spell it out, read and see if it makes sense."

This is a kindergartner's response to her portfolio at the end of her kindergarten year. A picture of her portfolio is drawn and she says, "In my portfolio, is all my work. It makes me feel special." Ryan, a third grader, responded at the end of the year regarding his portfolio: "My reading and writing has become spectacular. We do a lot of reading with partners and reading out loud. Spelling tests get me nervous. My spelling has gotten better because we do a lot of writing."

REFERENCES

Anthony, R. J., Johnson, T. D., Mickelson, N. I., & Preece, A. (1991). *Evaluating literacy: A perspective for change.* Portsmouth, NH: Heinemann.

Tierney, R. J., Carter, M. A., & Desai, L. E. (1991). *Portfolio assessment in the reading-writing classroom.* Norwood, MA: Christopher-Gordon Publishers.

PART FOUR

THE POTENTIAL OF WRITING PORTFOLIOS

CHAPTER FIFTEEN

Portfolios: The Good, The Bad, and the Beautiful

Patricia A. Belanoff
State University of New York at Stony Brook

The chapters in this volume and, indeed, the conference presentations that gave birth to the chapters, are a kind of portfolio: a coming together of widely divergent approaches to portfolio use in widely varied settings, as seen from widely disparate sites—but unified nonetheless by common threads and common visions. My role at the conference and now in this epilogue is to uncover and comment on these threads and visions and reflect on the context in which portfolios are flourishing. But just as one can never come to a conclusion about a portfolio that truly captures its richness, I can never quite capture the richness of the conference and of these chapters. Nonetheless, I drew some conclusions while listening to others, participating in discussions growing out of their work, and reflecting on what I heard and saw.

I am humbled by the power of the portfolio concept to stimulate innovative, exciting teaching. The sheer scope and variety of portfolio uses and kinds testify to their seemingly limitless adaptability. For years, I have claimed from my perspective as a college teacher involved with portfolios that portfolios are appropriate at all educational levels and for varied educational purposes: the conference and these chapters confirm theory—and practice does not always do that even when we desperately want it to. Those of us at post-secondary institutions have much to learn; my hope is that there will be more conferences that cross grade levels.

Portfolio use also testifies to the strength of the process movement in writing. We all know that the teaching of writing underwent a paradigm shift beginning in the 1960s and early 1970s, a shift that is now labeled the "process movement." I am not one of those who believe there has been a complete shift, a complete dismissal of all that went before. New paradigms always build from prior paradigms, the teaching of writing has retained much from the past, but the main thrust has moved from a focus on product to a focus on process—or at least to an equal concern for product and process.

The process movement may well be having a greater impact in the elementary schools than anywhere else—partly due to the growth of writing-project sites associated with the Bay Area Writing Project. A recent survey by Richard Larson of college and university writing programs suggests that the process approach to the teaching of writing is not as widespread as its adherents would like to believe.[1] Nonetheless, the process movement is well-established in the power centers of the discipline of composition and rhetoric: in the journals and in major organizations such as the Conference on College Composition and Communication and the National Council of Teachers of English. I am not suggesting here that the process movement is one thing: those who find fault with it attack it as such. By definition, the process movement is broad: it is an approach that focuses on the importance of getting students to reflect on *how* writing gets done.

When I arrived at Stony Brook 11 years ago, Peter Elbow had already established a teacher-training strategy that emphasized the process movement. The catch was that we had inherited a proficiency exam that all students had to take to certify writing proficiency before they graduated. This exam did not allow students to write in the way they were being taught to write in their classrooms. Students rightly criticized both the exam and the class on that basis. Peter and I successfully lobbied to eliminate the exam. The resulting legislation passed by our faculty senate said nothing about portfolios; all it mandated was that no one teacher could be the sole determiner of whether a particular student had satisfied the writing requirement. We devised the portfolio system as a way of introducing the collaborative decision making the legislation mandates.

The conference presentations that serve as the basis for this book demonstrated that portfolios have appeared in elementary and middle schools for much the same reason: they suit the new way teachers have learned to teach writing. But what is also apparent to me is that portfolio systems often grow in much richer soil in elementary and high schools (particularly in the former) because teachers at these levels are much more informed about and interested in how we learn. They make firmer theoretical and pedagogical connections between current learning theory and portfolios than most of us as the college level. Partially these connections grow out of the ubiquity of

---

[1]See Richard L. Larson (1994, July), *Curricula in College Writing Programs: Much Diversity, Little Assessment*. A Report to the Ford Foundation on the Project in College Curricula in Composition.

assessment these teachers face. Assessment is not something they can push aside as so many of us at the college level can. We can teach and disavow any connection to whatever assessment occurs outside our classrooms. For the most part, elementary and middle school teachers cannot be this cavalier. Assessment demands to be attended to when it enters their classrooms. Portfolios allow for a kind of assessment teachers can be more comfortable with. Portfolios also mesh well with the new emphasis on performance assessment and with the growing concern for critical thinking and metacognitive reflection, both of which have been developing parallel to the process movement. These chapters speak to unified pedagogy and practice in terms of learning theory far more effectively than most articles on portfolios. Pedagogy is suspect at the college level. Sad, but true.

PORTFOLIOS AND NATIONAL STANDARDS

It is sobering to recognize how often the authors of these chapters refer to the increased pressure for national standards and how that pressure interacts with their particular uses of portfolios. Currently the public appears to be much disenchanted about education in general. Elected officials are responding this disenchantment by advocating Goals 2000, a project designed to establish national standards in most discipline areas.[2] It is not at all surprising that establishing standards in English and language arts creates difficulties because language is, after all, the constituent material for the communication of knowledge in all fields. Portfolios can cope with these difficulties because they allow for a variety of tasks whereas standards suggest that all writers can be successful in much the same way.

Thus, we have on one hand a push for portfolios that grow out of the desire to recognize the variety of kinds of excellence and on the other hand a push for standards that suggest very limited forms of excellence—or, at the very least, a definite hierarchy of excellences. I sensed in the conference presentations and now in these chapters an awareness of the potential for increasing conflict between these two approaches in the years to come, though such conflict need not be inevitable. Compromise and negotiation are certainly possible.[3]

A CHANGING STUDENT BODY

We may once have been an almost homogeneous nation whose ancestors were predominantly northern Europeans; whether we were or not, we cer-

---

[2]Goals 2000: Educate America Act, HR 1804, Senate Amendment.
[3]Pamela A. Moss (1994b), Validity in high stakes writing assessment, *Assessing Writing, 1,* 109–128, suggests one way to resolve this impasse.

tainly no longer are. Within the past 30 years the country has become more and more culturally and linguistically diverse as a result of immigration from all over the globe. Nonetheless, there are many who value homogeneity and long for its return. Thus, they attempt to reestablish it through education. I often hear the following argument: "My grandparents came over here as immigrants and they didn't speak the language, but they went into the school system and they expected it to turn them into Americans. What's wrong with these kids who are coming here now? Why can't they go into the school system and have that same goal?" Cultural diversity is frightening to many because it threatens traditional, established values and goals.

Performance assessment of all kinds, including portfolios, values and even encourages difference. No performance assessment can ever be exactly like another because performance assessment is, by its nature, highly contextualized. Traditional testing, on the other hand, tries to strip the testing situation of all context. That is not possible; in the past what has happened is that most of those being tested came from similar backgrounds so we could depend on the contexts not being a significant variable. We can no longer depend on that; context matters, and it varies in ways we cannot always predict. Contextualization is one of the strengths of portfolios: it allows context to help students and allows us to be better coaches and judges of our students. Many of the chapters in this volume demonstrate quite well how portfolios successfully function in classrooms of linguistically and culturally different students.

The authors of these chapters value this diversification of our society and culture and believe that we are a healthier country because we have so many different kinds of cultures and value systems. Consequently, they want to nurture it rather than pressure students and themselves into rigid conformity to some set of standards imposed from the outside. However, the issue is not conformity versus diversity: life without some degree of conformity is inconceivable; the issue is whose conformity and to what end. Portfolios permit diversity within the requisite degree of conformity. The chapters demonstrate a variety of ways teachers have balanced diversity and uniformity.

The diversity of the students who now sit in our classrooms has led many of us to recognize that we too are not the unified, monologic beings we may once have considered ourselves. We uncover affinities with our students: we are like one in one way and like another in another way. What I am saying is that the growing diversity of our students allows us to recognize our own complexity. I came to this same conclusion as a result of listening to the conference presentations: I discovered that I had much in common with teachers and administrators from widely different settings and widely different cultural backgrounds. Their diversity allowed me to experience my own diversity—and, most important, recognize that diversity does not preclude similarity. Nor does diversity in a portfolio preclude my drawing conclusions.

The current wisdom on IQ tests mirrors similar concerns. We have come to realize that there is no such thing as a single IQ.[4] Human beings have complex patterns of abilities and skills; in terms of teaching writing, this complexity helps us understand why students do not perform equally well on all writing tasks. Portfolios make this unevenness a virtue to be analyzed.

Portfolios also allow us to display our multiple selves. We feel ourselves to be complex; perhaps it is that which makes all of us—students and teachers—resist standardized tests. We never believe they can measure us. In truth, standardized tests are always something we—teachers, systems, government bodies—do to others, never to ourselves. I am convinced all of us experience ourselves as a complex of varied abilities, none of which are of exactly similar quality. A portfolio gives us the space and the right to demonstrate our personal richness. We can show a part of ourselves that we might not otherwise display for fear an audience would judge us as limited to and by it. A portfolio also allows us and others to understand that we are not always exactly the same person all the time. We change and remain stable at one and the same time. The portfolio can be a frame for both our variegated and united selves.

Varied instances of writing thus present themselves to us simultaneously in a portfolio. It is often not easy to find some generalized statement that captures the nature of all of them. Nonetheless, our tendency as evaluators is to attempt such a generalization. In fact, we often must do just that, and despite the unarguable richness, we may despair when we have to. What we see often appears fragmented instead of rich. But our students may be less troubled by seeing separate fragments of some category of objects than we are. Their world may actually be conditioning them to accept fragmentation or division into nonequivalent parts as the norm. Our students can often watch three basketball games at once and keep track of what is going on in each. They have learned to tolerate commercial interruptions without our frustration at the resulting discontinuity in whatever we are watching.

I see this kind of fragmentation tolerated on e-mail networks also. (I use the word *fragmentation* with full acknowledgment that many read this word as negative. Perhaps "separateness of parts" might be a better choice of words.) I have difficulty making corrections in e-mail messages and consequently I tend to just write "Oops, that's not the word I meant, I meant X" and not correct the error. When we receive e-mail messages, they are often out of sequence (I sometimes read answers before questions); furthermore, we often sustain several conversations at once when using e-mail. Most of us navigate this fairly well. Do we do so because we have some inherent sense of coherence against which we read these messages? I suspect so, but

---

[4]Howard Gardner (1993), *Multiple intelligences: The theory in practice*. New York: Basic Books.

can we build coherence without that background? I suspect so. Can we be sure that the messages belonging to different threads do not somehow influence one another? I doubt it. But that is characteristic of modern life. Tomorrow's college students will be far less troubled than we are by sustaining several conversations at once. Thus, portfolios that contain three or more quite different pieces of writing are likely to seem quite natural to them. In the long run, they will be able to appreciate the simultaneous richness and the fragmentation much more easily than many of us can now.

My point in alluding to these issues—diversity in our student body, recognition of our own complexity, changes in the nature of various genres, the influence of media, the workings of computer mediated forms of communication—is to underscore much of what I read in these chapters: we are having great difficulty generalizing about our classrooms, including defining what good writing is. How then can we possibly measure it with one test? How can we assess it effectively piecemeal in the classroom?

DIVERSITY OF JUDGMENTS

During their presentations at the conference and in their resulting chapters in this volume, a number of participants expressed some discomfort about differences in evaluation. You and I look at the same piece of writing; you say it is terrific and I say it is weak. We do not agree. If we average our scores and give that average to the student, we have told him or her nothing because no one in fact gave the student that score. (This, of course, is the problem with all generalizations: they are a kind of lie.[5]) The student will benefit much more if you write something explaining what you think is terrific and I write something explaining what I think is weak. Or it will probably serve all of us—the student and us—much better if the two of us sit down and talk, if we negotiate the reasons why we have come to this different kind of conclusion. We then can agree on something that we can tell the student as a result of our negotiation. Or, better yet, we should include the student in the negotiation sessions too.

But, I hear someone say, that's the teacher's job (giving feedback to students). Let her do that in the classroom; the evaluator's job is different. Evaluation cannot be entangled with the student in the classroom: it must be objective. I would answer that evaluation is never objective; anthropologists long ago discredited the idea of the disinterested observer, but that lesson has not been disseminated widely enough. Furthermore, assessment is often undertaken, not to discover something about students, but to produce statistics

---

[5]Robert Reich noted recently that he and Michael Jordan were *on average* about the average height—but this misses the point that he's 4'10" whereas Jordan is almost 7 feet tall!

for the system. Consequently, assessment can treat students and teachers as ciphers. I do not want that. I want to assess—indeed I need to—in order to help my students and me get better at what we are currently doing. Evaluation and teaching must go hand in hand because then everyone learns—not just the student. These chapters demonstrate that in unequivocal ways.

In a recent issue of *Educational Research*, Pamela A. Moss examines two different kinds of approaches to assessment.[6] She calls one of them the *psychometric approach*. In this approach, it is the constructs of validity and reliability that determine how effective a particular evaluation is. But she questions whether this is the only approach and examines another that she labels *hermeneutic* or *interpretative*. To evaluate a piece of student writing is to interpret a text; none of us do that exactly like anyone else. Consequently, if we can negotiate our interpretations, as I just suggested, we will come to a conclusion. Moss advises that at least one of the negotiators be someone directly engaged in the context in which those being assessed are engaged. In the process of the negotiation, then, standards can be determined that relate directly to the situation to which they are applied. I am convinced that we will see more and more research such as this that provides theoretical support for what good teachers are discovering.

Many of us have participated in highly structured holistic scoring sessions in which we are given a set of range finders that represent each of the scores on whatever grid we are using. Others have already selected these range finders (that is, established the standards); our responsibility is to determine which of these range finders a paper is closest to and then give that paper that score. We have no responsibility for setting up the grid, for explaining it, for selecting range finders, for justifying our score to anyone, or for reporting that score to the writer. There is almost no discussion about teaching during these sessions: the only result is that a score is passed along to the student. In truth, regimented holistic scoring actually forbids what all of us should be doing more of: collaborative critical thinking. Almost every teacher I have talked to acknowledges peer talk as the single most effective path to better teaching. As a side benefit, teachers who share designing and reading portfolios also develop improved language to use when talking to their own students because they have done so much talking with their colleagues. Most of the talk during highly structured holistic scoring sessions is aimed at justifying previously established scores. Such an assessment process is of no value in promoting better teaching and learning.

It is easy to argue that portfolios take too much time: time to design, time to create, time to evaluate; the practices described in the chapters in this book demonstrate that quite clearly. Detractors point to the eating up of all this time

---

[6]Pamela A. Moss (1994a), Can there be validity without reliability? *Educational Research*, *23*(2), 5–12.

and criticize portfolios for not being cost-effective. When I hear this criticism, I want to say: "Yes, assessment is hard; you should be suspicious of any form of assessment that is not hard." Portfolios take time to design and prepare. One of the problems in the field is that too many people are looking for the quick, the easy, and the cheap. Good education is none of these. Neither is good assessment—either at the classroom or system level.

POWER AND OWNERSHIP

The final thing these chapters and the conference led me to reflect on is power. Many of the presenters talked about the issue of ownership. Who owns a portfolio? Does it matter? There is never any question about standardized tests: we do not want to own them and our students certainly do not want to own them. In truth, none of us wants to be judged on the basis of a standardized test. We will all make excuses about our performance, about what we do well that the test did not even touch on, about how our lack of sleep or some family crisis distracted us, and so forth. We would make exactly the same excuses students make.

Who then does own standardized tests? They are copyrighted by the organization that constructs them: that is one form of ownership. These organizations exert enormous influence—on schools, on publishers, on the consciousness of parents and students. The administrators or committees that select a particular test experience another form of ownership, the kind of ownership that results from having the power to decide what students ought to know and how best to discover how well they know it. Classroom teachers experience some of that power, but in terms of evaluation, they often feel powerless because the instruments for evaluation are out of their control and in the control of mysterious hands outside the classroom somewhere.

Who owns the portfolio? The standardized test goes to the designer to score and they keep it. Where does a portfolio go after it serves its purpose? Students often like to have them back. That itself says much about them, but ownership of portfolios can become as worrisome as ownership of standardized tests—especially if portfolio programs are imposed on teachers and students. What I see in these chapters are student-owned portfolios—but what I too often read about and hear about from teachers is that they are being asked to implement a portfolio system they have not been given any power to design or critique. Consequently they feel no more ownership for portfolios than for any other system of evaluation and assessment. Those of us who believe in the power of portfolios to alter teaching and learning environments need to recognize that they do not do that per se; they do that only when we reflect on the power structures involved and take them into consideration in our planning.

Portfolios have the potential to upset established power structures. Having many sites of decisionmaking can be disconcerting, but that is what portfolios can create. I design a portfolio for my situation; you design one for yours; others design them for their situations. None of these portfolios are exactly alike, as we see in these chapters, although they have similarities. Power has been dispersed. There is far more discussion and difference in democracies than in autocracies. But, alas, there are many ways in which educational systems are more like autocracies than democracies.

The issue of power, of who has the power to determine forms of assessment, is potentially explosive. Those who currently have it may be threatened by the seeming anarchy of portfolios. It is easy for those currently in charge to argue that portfolios do not allow for comparisons between and among students, schools, systems, and states, comparisons that are so dear to many government officials—and to many parents also. Of course we need to identify schools and classes in which effective teaching and learning are occurring—but those are not necessarily the schools whose scores are the highest. Do we need standardized tests to identify such schools? It is also easy to argue that portfolios are contaminated by too much teacher input, an argument based on the assumption that the best work is done by individuals in isolation or that validity in scoring is too low. As portfolio users, we feel we can answer those arguments—and, in fact, some of the pieces in this book take on those arguments. But we must not forget that there are educators, administrators, politicians, and parents who seek something very different from their schools. Coming together for mutual support is crucial if we are all to learn how to counter the arguments of others and if we are to maintain the energy and commitment to continue to make those counterarguments. We cannot wish away these criticisms—we need to acknowledge that they have some validity, but that our way has advantages that outweigh these defects.

Conferences such as the one that led to this volume are important; they must provide space for self-criticism as well as for self-praise. We cannot become so devoted to our portfolio systems that we fail to see their faults. All systems have flaws. It is healthy to see these chapters acknowledge that and challenge us to continue to seek ever better ways to learn, educate, teach, and assess.

In summary, the conference and these chapters made me realize more thoroughly than I ever had that portfolios have the ability to nurture what is most needed in our society today: some way of recognizing and rewarding diversity both within individuals and within society as a whole, some way of dispersing power more equally throughout this diversity, and some way of encouraging negotiation and collaboration within this diversity so that difference leads us to collaborate and negotiate rather than compete. Altered power structures of this sort will create a dispersion of power that will help us all.

We create knowledge through working together. Portfolios create knowledge about the writer who creates them because their contents interact with one another. This mirrors the knowledge creating we would all like to see in our classrooms. The conference out of which these chapters grew and the chapters themselves continue this knowledge-making process. Just as the very diversity of materials in a student's portfolio allows us to assess better, so the diversity of these chapters allows us to understand better the movement toward portfolios. As this movement grows, we will need to continue to assess ourselves through collaborative efforts such as this one. Together we learn.

REFERENCES

Larson, R. L. (1994). *Curricula in college writing programs: Much diversity, little assessment. Goals 2000: Educate America Act of 1994*, 103-227, *et seq.*, 108 Stat. 125. Washington, DC: U.S. Government Printing Office.

Gardner, H. (1993). *Multiple intelligences: Theory into practice.* New York: Basic Books.

Moss, P. A. (1994a). Can there be validity without reliability? *Educational Research, 23*, 5–12.

Moss, P. A. (1994b). Validity in high stakes writing assessment. *Assessing Writing, 1*, 109–128.

Author Index

Subject Index